THE WATCHERS

THE WATCHERS

THE RISE OF AMERICA'S SURVEILLANCE STATE

SHANE HARRIS

THE PENGUIN PRESS

New York | 2010

THE PENGUIN PRESS
Published by the Penguin Group
Penguin Group (USA) Inc., 375 Hudson Street, New York, New York 10014, U.S.A. ·
Penguin Group (Canada), 90 Eglinton Avenue East, Suite 700, Toronto, Ontario, Canada
M4P 2Y3 (a division of Pearson Penguin Canada Inc.) · Penguin Books Ltd, 80 Strand,
London WC2R 0RL, England · Penguin Ireland, 25 St Stephen's Green, Dublin 2, Ireland
(a division of Penguin Books Ltd) · Penguin Books Australia Ltd, 250 Camberwell Road,
Camberwell, Victoria 3124, Australia (a division of Pearson Australia Group Pty Ltd) ·
Penguin Books India Pvt Ltd, 11 Community Centre, Panchsheel Park, New Delhi – 110
017, India · Penguin Group (NZ), 67 Apollo Drive, Rosedale, North Shore 0632, New
Zealand (a division of Pearson New Zealand Ltd) · Penguin Books (South Africa) (Pty)
Ltd, 24 Sturdee Avenue, Rosebank, Johannesburg 2196, South Africa

Penguin Books Ltd, Registered Offices: 80 Strand, London WC2R 0RL, England

First published in 2010 by The Penguin Press, a member of Penguin Group (USA) Inc.

While the author has made every effort to provide accurate telephone numbers and
Internet addresses at the time of publication, neither the publisher nor the author assumes
any responsibility for errors, or for changes that occur after publication. Further, the
publisher does not have any control over and does not assume any responsibility for author
or third-party Web sites or their content.

Library of Congress Cataloging-in-Publication Data

Harris, Shane.
    The watchers : the rise of America's surveillance state / Shane Harris.
        p.   cm.
    Includes bibliographical references and index.
    ISBN 978-1-59420-245-2
    1. Terrorism—United States—Prevention—History.   2. National security—
United States.   3. Intelligence service—United States.   I. Title.
    HV6432.H378 2010
    363.325'1630973—dc22   2009037205

Printed in the United States of America
10 9 8 7 6 5 4 3 2 1

DESIGNED BY NICOLE LAROCHE

For my grandmother, Bettiann Kinney,
who taught me to tell stories

CONTENTS

Introduction   1

Prologue   9

ACT ONE

Chapter 1 **FIRST STRIKE**   15

Chapter 2 **KNOWLEDGE IS POWER**   27

Chapter 3 **AND HE SHALL PURIFY**   36

Chapter 4 **UNODIR**   50

ACT TWO

Chapter 5 **A CONSTANT TENSION**   71

Chapter 6 **THE GENOA PROJECT**   81

Chapter 7 **THE NEXT GENERATION**   95

Chapter 8 **THE CHINA EXPERIMENT**   104

Chapter 9 **ABLE DANGER**   115

Chapter 10 **"YOU GUYS WILL GO TO JAIL"**   129

ACT THREE

Chapter 11 **ECHO**   139

Chapter 12 **A NEW MANHATTAN PROJECT**   144

Chapter 13 **THE BAG**   155

Chapter 14 **ALL HANDS ON DECK**   172

Chapter 15 **CALL TO ARMS**   184

Chapter 16 **FEED THE BAG**   199

Chapter 17 **SHIPS PASSING IN THE NIGHT**   210

Chapter 18 **FULL STEAM AHEAD**   214

Chapter 19 **THE UNRAVELING**   230

Chapter 20 **GOING BLACK**   236

ACT FOUR

Chapter 21 **BASKETBALL**   251

Chapter 22 **RESURRECTION**   254

Chapter 23 **THE BREAKTHROUGH**   264

Chapter 24 **EXPOSED**   271

Chapter 25 **REASONABLE BELIEFS**   282

Chapter 26 **BETRAYAL**   290

Chapter 27 **BOJINKA II**   302

Chapter 28 **INHERIT THE WINDS**   315

Chapter 29 **ASCENSION**   322

Chapter 30 **RENEGADE**   344

Epilogue   357

Acknowledgments   367

Notes   369

Index   403

INTRODUCTION

To me, 9/11 never felt like the beginning of a story. Nor the ending. It always felt like the middle.

I woke up on September 11, 2001, far from the center of the action—in a quiet hotel room in Palm Springs. I'd been working at a magazine in Washington, D.C., for nine months, writing about the information technology business in the federal government. I'd planned my first real vacation for mid-September. On Day 2, I awoke to an urgent phone call from a friend back home, who insisted that I turn on the television.

It's the reporter's instinct to write and talk about what he can see, or about what he knows to be true. But as the television came into focus, the stunned silence from news broadcasters told me that no one could explain the enormity of what we all were watching. The South Tower of the World Trade Center had fallen. The North Tower was burning. The Pentagon had been hit. My friend was standing on the roof of a building in northwest Washington, watching the smoke rise over the Potomac River. The attack, I learned later, was almost finished. I had jumped into the story midstream.

I returned to Washington the day the federal government authorized commercial aircraft to fly again. Back at the magazine my editor instructed me to figure out how what I wrote about every day connected to this new, rapidly developing narrative. I spent the next six years figuring that out, and one more writing this book.

One of the first themes to emerge from the 9/11 attacks soon became a familiar refrain: The government had failed to "connect the dots" about terrorism, specifically the Al Qaeda network. It wasn't widely known that some of the 9/11 hijackers were already on terrorist watch lists when they entered the United States. Mysterious phone calls intercepted on September 10, which hinted at the next day's calamity, weren't translated in time to be of any use. No one—no *system*—had gathered all the pieces of the puzzle and put them together.

Because I'd been writing about how government agencies acquired and then used information technology, I understood the bureaucracy's language. Those elusive "dots" were actually data. They were discrete pieces of information that intelligence, law enforcement, and security agencies either hadn't shared with one another or had failed to collect in the first place. My technology beat quickly became an intelligence beat. And that's when I became acquainted with a group of people who had painfully understood what I had only suspected. This story didn't begin on 9/11. And it wouldn't end there.

I call them the Watchers. They are a little-known and little-understood band of mavericks who've spent most of their careers working in the intelligence and national security agencies of the government. They are united by a common conviction: They believe they could have stopped the 2001 attacks if they had only been allowed to try.

The Watchers know better than anyone that the signals of terrorism were out there, waiting to be detected in a sea of noise. They have spent the past quarter century working to perfect a system that can make sense of all that noise. For them the attacks of 9/11 resonated on a particularly haunting level. They'd been expecting this moment, had worked hard to prevent it, and when it happened, they felt emboldened, and entitled, to act.

The Watchers are not always who they seem to be. First and foremost, they consider themselves patriots, and they are convinced that the future of national security depends on detecting and preempting attacks before they occur. But they are also the architects of secretive surveillance programs, watch lists, and "data mining" regimes that operate largely unchecked, and sift through innocent people's everyday electronic transactions in search of telltale clues. The Watchers are both guardians and spies, protectors of security and renegades of the law. They make no apologies for their preferred path to security, which many leaders of American intelligence have long shunned as the gateway to a police state. That critique is nothing new to them. The Watchers have been fighting their own establishment for as long as they've been fighting terrorists, since the first salvo of a new era in war.

It was October 23, 1983, when a suicide truck bomber set off twelve thousand pounds of explosives in the lobby of the Marine barracks in Beirut, Lebanon. That's where this story begins. The attack on the Marines, who were deployed as part of an international peacekeeping mission, introduced Americans to the concept of "suicide bombing" by religious extremists. That term has woven itself into our popular lexicon, but a quarter century ago this style of attack was something new and—true to form—terrifying. It was preceded by a suicide attack on the American embassy in Beirut. Taken together they form the starting point in a war fought largely in shadow, one that saw its bloodiest turn in the events of September 11, 2001, and continues to play out toward an uncertain end.

Unlike any war in American history, this one has been driven almost entirely by the covert gathering and use of intelligence, represented in the form of those ever illusive dots. And unlike most of the nation's wars, the casualties are not always counted in those killed and wounded. The rule of law, as well as our decidedly modern notions of privacy, are confronted in this fight, because in order to detect the signs of the next assault, the Watchers believe that they must be prepared to watch everyone and the seemingly benign things they do every day. What they buy. Whom they call. Where they travel. The 9/11 attacks confirmed the Watchers' deeply held conviction that surveillance and aggressive analysis of information offer the best hope of preventing the next attack. The plot was executed by a small number of men who had assimilated into American life and slipped through the cracks of a cold war intelligence system that was designed to confront nation-states, not rogue actors. The attackers used the tools of modern communications and an open society to their advantage and pulled off their murderous rampage under the Watchers' noses.

The Watchers insist that they are defenders of civil liberties and a core of enshrined values and rights that distinguish the United States among great nations. But on that score, many people see an inherent contradiction. How can they propose to extend a net of largely unchecked government surveillance and proclaim themselves the guardians of constitutional virtues and personal privacy? It's a fair question. In seeking to answer it I discerned a much more complicated and compelling story than what has been told so far.

After years of reporting marked by hundreds of interviews with authorities on terrorism, technology, and the law, I came to know the Watchers. I covered some of them as a journalist when they held senior positions in government. A number of them I came to call friends, which posed a considerable challenge whenever I had to write unflattering things about their lives, their ideas, and their actions. It is never easy to disappoint people whom you've come to respect. But I chose to tell their stories, including the parts they'd rather forget, because these people are the faces behind the "war on terror." They are human, and far more complex and confusing than the caricatures some have painted of them. Until we understand the Watchers, and the goals they pursue, I don't think that we can confront the conflict between security and liberty that lies at the heart of this war.

The Watchers have had their debate already, and they've made their choices. I cannot say that I agree with all of their conclusions, any more than I condone the extraordinary breaches of public trust that some of them have committed in the pursuit of their goals. But I have sat with them. I have listened to them. And I have watched them. After all that, I have arrived at this alarming realization: We are witnessing the rise of an American surveillance state. I use that phrase with some trepidation, because it conjures up images of the Stasi in East Germany, and I think that overstates the situation. Our system of government is not imperiled. The Constitution is not on the verge of dissolution. In that respect, the most strident civil libertarians among us have either missed what's really happening or have chosen to ignore it. At the same time, many of our national leaders—the very same architects of this new apparatus—have understated the basic risks it poses to how we communicate, move about, and conduct commerce without fear that our ordinary behavior will attract extraordinary and unwanted attention from the government. The surveillance state is an amalgam of laws, technology, and culture in which the government's default position is to collect information about people on a massive scale for the broadly defined purpose of protecting national security. Saving the country from disaster is a laudable and necessary goal, but the means of achieving it are often ill-conceived and poorly controlled. Preventing the abuse, misuse, and misdirection of deeply revealing personal information has become a secondary concern to gathering and hoarding it.

I was surprised to find how well some of the Watchers understand this dangerous imbalance and how hard they've worked to correct it. But I was also disturbed to learn how few people in power have listened to them and heeded their warnings.

This book is the fullest, most honest, and ultimately most empathetic account I can give of the Watchers' stories, one that most people haven't heard. It's in large part the story of how a handful of men and women struggled to build a system that could detect the signals of an impending disaster. But I found that for all their toil, for all the money, time, and political will they have spent, the Watchers have become very good at collecting dots and not very good at *connecting* them. That should trouble them as much as it does the rest of us.

This book is the product of many years of reporting, reading, and research. But most important, it is directly informed by long interviews with most of the principal figures herein. With remarkably few exceptions, the people featured on these pages agreed to sit down with me for multiple sessions, often lasting several hours. They were all on the record—that is, everything that they said to me they were willing to see attributed to them on the page. I am indebted to them for their time and their patience. But most of all, I thank them for their candor. It is a terrible thing, I should think, to subject oneself to the probing, often impertinent questions of a stranger who offers you nothing in return but the potential for notoriety. Having not been acquainted with the sharp end of a journalist's interrogatory, I can imagine only that the experience was at times uncomfortable and unsatisfying.

But having done this kind of thing for many years now, I also understand that people long to be heard. They want to tell their stories. In the course of my interviews I was offering these people some measure of relief and affirmation. I have no doubt that some of them approached our sessions as a chance to shape history in a flattering light. But I can also assure the reader that I offered no assurances about how the story would finally turn out to anyone I interviewed. They are reading this for the first time too.

Many of the people in this book provided me with extraordinary access to their personal time, and to their professional records, notes, and memories. One deserves particular mention. I had written about John Poindexter during his tenure at the Defense Advanced Research Projects Agency, the Pentagon's high-tech research and development unit. Following the 9/11 attacks he established DARPA's Information Awareness Office (IAO), which managed an ambitious and extraordinarily controversial set of programs that aimed to detect the weak signals of a terrorist plot by mining ordinary electronic transactions, such as credit card purchases and airline reservations. Poindexter left his position in 2003 amid a storm of consternation about the nature of the program and the fact that he, of all people, had been put in charge of it. In a previous tour in government Poindexter was a leading figure in the Iran-Contra affair, which for a time threatened to topple Ronald Reagan's presidency. He'd been accused of lying to Congress and the American people about a covert intelligence operation in Nicaragua and a secret arms-for-hostages swap with Iran.

Poindexter and I met in 2004, a few months after he left the Defense Department. He walked up to me at a conference at Syracuse University, where we'd both been invited to speak, and introduced himself by apologizing; he'd been unable to grant my multiple interview requests because the Pentagon had forbidden him to talk to the press. I told Poindexter that there was still a lot to talk about, and that I'd like to write a profile of him now that he had returned to private life. He agreed, and we conducted a series of two-hour interviews that culminated in a brief portrait for *Government Executive* magazine, where I was employed at the time. In our first meeting Poindexter asked me if I entertained any ambitions to write a book. I said yes and, to his credit, he did not suspend the interview.

We stayed in touch over the years, and in 2008 we began the first of fourteen long interviews about his life and his central role in this story. It begins, as does this book, in the wake of the Beirut attacks in 1983. Poindexter was the deputy national security adviser to the president, and from his perch at the White House he launched a systematic reorganization of the national security bureaucracy for a new "war against terrorism," as the administration called it. Poindexter oversaw or directed operations that formed the foundation of a national counterterrorism strategy, something the United States had never had. His primary ambition was to harness information in order to predict crises, and this quest has animated him ever since. After leaving government, he continued the pursuit for several years as a government adviser. He had no plans to return to government until the attacks of 9/11. This book is in large measure the story of how Poindexter, the godfather of the Watchers, has shaped the war on terror and in the process helped to redefine our definitions of privacy and security. I know that he will not like everything he reads here. But I also know that he will find truth. Of all the people I interviewed, he gave the most. He asked for nothing in return.

I am also indebted to the other key figures in this story who consented to multiple long interviews. Rather than acknowledging them individually, I will note that this story would not be as complete and as accurate without their participation. None of the principal figures whom I interviewed agreed to anything less than an on-the-record discussion. The records of our interviews are noted at the end of the book.

Finally, there were some key sources of information and insight who would not—and in some cases, could not—agree to be cited directly. In those cases I have done my best to give the reader some sense of the importance of these participants, and of the particular information about which they have direct knowledge. I thank them too for their contributions and their time.

PROLOGUE

This is a mistake, Erik Kleinsmith told himself as he stared at the computer and placed his finger on the delete button. *We shouldn't do this.*

He'd been agonizing over his orders. He considered disobeying them. He could make copies of all the data, send them off in the mail before anyone knew what happened. He could still delete all the copies on his hard drive, but the backups would be safe. There would be a record. No one could say they hadn't tried, that they hadn't warned people.

Kleinsmith hadn't been sleeping much the past three months. He'd started his work in February 2000, when the officers from Special Operations Command showed up at his office. They'd heard about some of his exploits. The earnest thirty-five-year-old Army major had drawn attention to himself as the leader of an innovative, some said renegade, band of intelligence analysts. They worked in a secure facility at the Army's Information Dominance Center, a futuristic-looking office space in the headquarters of the Army Intelligence Command at Fort Belvoir, Virginia. Kleinsmith had his own office next to the IDC's main floor, which had been designed by a Hollywood visual effects artist to mimic the bridge of the starship *Enterprise.* With wall-mounted computer panels and a captain's chair in the center of the room, the IDC was meant to inspire the kind of futuristic confidence conveyed by the *Star Trek* franchise.

Kleinsmith was a geek, no doubt about it. He'd been working miracles of a sort, using untested data-mining technologies to reveal connections between the Chinese government and American defense contractors. Kleinsmith and his team had uncovered a potential spy network in the United States.

Word had gotten around the military brass, and now Special Forces had a job for him. They wanted Kleinsmith to map the global network of a shadowy and largely unknown terrorist group called Al Qaeda.

Its assassins literally had burst onto the international scene less than two years earlier, simultaneously destroying the U.S. embassies in Kenya and Tanzania. The suicide bombers had killed more than 220 people, the most brazen assault on U.S. interests since the attack on the Marine barracks in Lebanon in 1983.

Working under the code name Able Danger, Kleinsmith compiled an enormous digital dossier on the terrorist outfit. The volume was extraordinary for its size—2.5 terabytes, equal to about one-tenth of all printed pages held by the Library of Congress—but more so for its intelligence significance: Kleinsmith had mapped Al Qaeda's global footprint. He had diagrammed how its members were related, how they moved money, and where they had placed operatives. Kleinsmith showed military commanders and intelligence chiefs where to hit the network, how to dismantle it, how to annihilate it. This was priceless information but also an alarm bell—the intelligence showed that Al Qaeda had established a presence inside the United States, and signs pointed to an imminent attack.

With his neat brown hair and wide eyes, Kleinsmith exuded a boyish honesty bordering on gullibility. He could pass for a simple functionary. But, in truth, Kleinsmith was a nonconformist spy. He had used technological expertise combined with a detective's penchant for hunches to produce meaningful insights, while the graybeards of intelligence at the CIA and in the Pentagon had come up empty-handed. The Army wanted to find Al Qaeda's leaders, to capture or kill them. Kleinsmith believed he could show them how.

That's when he ran into his present troubles. Rather than relying on classified intelligence databases, which were often scant on details and hopelessly fragmentary, Kleinsmith had created his Al Qaeda map with data drawn from the Internet, home to a bounty of chatter and observations about terrorists and holy war. He cast a digital net over thousands of Web sites, chat rooms, and bulletin boards. Then he used graphing and modeling programs to turn the raw data into three-dimensional, topographic maps. These tools displayed seemingly random data as a series of peaks and valleys that showed how people, places, and events were connected. Peaks near each other signaled a connection in the data underlying them. A series of peaks signaled that Kleinsmith should take a closer look. He liked to call this visual approach to information "intelligence on steroids." Kleinsmith's methods were years ahead of those favored by most intelligence analysts and spymasters, who were inherently suspicious of the promise of technology and jealously guarded their prized human sources in the field.

Few outside Kleinsmith's chain of command knew what he had discovered about terrorists in America or what secrets he and his analysts had stored in their data banks. They also didn't know that the team had collected information on thousands of American citizens—including prominent government officials and politicians—during their massive data sweeps. On the Internet, intelligence about enemies mingled with the names of innocents. Good guys and bad were all in the same mix, and there was as yet no effective way to sort it all out.

Army lawyers had put him on notice: Under military regulations Kleinsmith could only store his intelligence for ninety days if it contained references to U.S. persons. At the end of that brief period, everything had to go. Even the inadvertent capture of such information amounted to domestic spying. Kleinsmith could go to jail.

As he stared at his computer terminal, Kleinsmith ached at the thought of what he was about to do. *This is terrible.*

He pulled up some relevant files on his hard drive, hovered over them with his cursor, and selected the whole lot. Then he pushed the delete key. Kleinsmith did this for all the files on his computer, until he'd eradicated everything related to Able Danger. It took less than half an hour to destroy what he'd spent three months building. The blueprint of global terrorism vanished into the electronic ether.

ACT ONE

A small group of senior officials believed that they alone knew what was right. They viewed knowledge of their actions by others in the Government as a threat to their objectives.

—"*Report of the Congressional Committees*
Investigating the Iran-Contra Affair," *November 1987*

Those who question us now owe the country an explanation of how they would have acted differently given the stakes, the opportunities, and the dangers.

—*National Security Adviser John Poindexter, in a 1986*
Wall Street Journal *editorial defending the Reagan*
administration's decision to trade arms for hostages
in Iran, published one day before he resigned

ACT ONE

FIRST STRIKE

OCTOBER 23, 1983

The sun dawned about a quarter after six on Sunday. Most of the Marines were still asleep. A few who were up and moving about the compound noticed a yellow truck outside the concertina wire that guarded the perimeter. It was a Mercedes-Benz stake-bed, a workhorse used to carry heavy cargo. Before anyone could figure out why it was there, the truck picked up speed and crashed through the fence.

A sentry in one of the two guard posts nearby turned in time to see the truck heading straight for the Marines' barracks. He grabbed his unloaded M16 and reached for a magazine of ammunition. The truck sped through an open gate, swerved around a sewer pipe, and aimed for the small sergeant-of-the-guard post stationed at the entrance to the hulking concrete building.

That guard was facing the lobby and heard the roaring truck behind him. He turned, and he thought for a moment, "What's that truck doing inside the perimeter?" An instant later he was sprinting through the building to another entrance on the far side.

"Hit the deck!" he yelled. "Hit the deck!" He glanced back over his shoulder and watched the truck flatten his post before crashing into the lobby. It halted there. One or two seconds passed, and then the guard saw a bright orange and yellow flash. Then he realized he was flying through the air.

First Lieutenant Glenn Dolphin awoke to the barks of an early-rising Arkansas captain. He exhorted the roomful of exhausted men to join him at the barracks gym for a workout before reveille. They were splayed out on cots set up in the parking bay of an old fire department building. Dolphin looked over. The guy worked out constantly, and he thought he looked like a million bucks. But it was Sunday, the one day Dolphin could sleep in. The only Marines up now were jogging the perimeter, enjoying the rare morning quiet. The rest would stroll down later to the chow tent, where the cooks set up an omelet station on Sundays. Dolphin had been on duty in the Combat Operations Center until midnight and had been looking forward to the extra rest. *Fuck it,* he thought, eyeing the energetic captain. Dolphin rolled over in his cot to steal a few more minutes' sleep.

Dolphin had been encamped with the Twenty-fourth Marine Amphibious Unit at the Beirut International Airport for seven months now, ostensibly as part of an international peacekeeping force. Only two days earlier, the Marines had held another memorial service, the fifth in two months. Alan Soiffert, a twenty-five-year-old staff sergeant from Nashua, New Hampshire, had taken a sniper round in the chest as he patrolled the airport perimeter in his Jeep. The vehicle flipped over, and Soiffert bled onto the hard, dry ground. He was the first Jewish Marine to die in Lebanon. A rabbi had come in especially for the memorial.

Beirut, a religiously diverse cradle of antiquity and once the glittering cultural and economic heart of the Levant, seemed on an irreversible descent into hell since the Marines arrived. They'd taken persistent rocket and artillery attacks in recent weeks from Muslim Druze militia redoubts in the Shuf Mountains, which overlooked the city. The Americans had first come ashore the previous June, evacuating U.S. citizens in the wake of an Israeli invasion. The Israeli Defense Force had launched a massive campaign against Palestinian militants, who had long since turned a politically disorganized and factional Lebanon into their lawless launchpad for attacks into Israel. It took only three days for the Israelis to reach the outskirts of Beirut. There, they hooked up with Christian Lebanese militia opposed to the Palestinians. Two weeks later the forces rolled into the town of Alayh, killing a dozen Druze soldiers. The next day the Christian militia first entered the Shuf, sparking long and terrible artillery battles with their Muslim enemies. Lebanon, which had teetered for so many years on the brink of civil war, careered over the edge.

To halt the outbreak of regional war, the United States joined a multinational force with France and Italy and managed to get fifteen thousand armed Palestinian and Syrian forces out of the capital. The Syrians dominated Lebanese politics and had hobbled the country and its government during six years of occupation. But the American-led peace was fitful. Syrian operatives assassinated the young, Christian president-elect. The Israelis then seized West Beirut and for two days stood by as the Christian militia exacted revenge, slaughtering untold hundreds of Palestinian and Lebanese civilians in a pair of refugee camps.

Dolphin's unit descended into the bedlam on November 3, 1982. They staked their ground at the airport, wedging themselves between Israeli positions and the heavily populated areas of Beirut. The relative calm fractured five months later, when someone slammed a bomb-laden truck into the lobby of the U.S. embassy. The suicide attacker killed sixty-three people, including most of the CIA station in Beirut. After that, the notion that the Americans were in Beirut on a peacekeeping mission struck the twelve hundred Marines as absurd.

Rather than pushing out into the craggy Shuf, which hid the snipers and artillery batteries, the Marines sheltered in place on the south side of the airport. They built makeshift bunkers out of sandbags, which cast long shadows on the vast, open expanse of dirt and asphalt, providing easy marks for gunmen. The Marines' rules of engagement, handed down from the Pentagon, said they must maintain a noncombat presence—that meant no heavily fortified bunkers, nothing more than concertina wire to mark their compound, and, in what struck so many of the men as sheer madness, no loaded weapons. Beirut was teeming with agitated, gun-toting boys enamored of the radical Iranian leader, Ayatollah Khomeini, whose dark eyes peered from posters plastered around the city. The few men who'd gone on limited patrols in town came back with stories of ominous black hands painted on buildings, the sign that its residents had been marked for death. They watched young boys stare menacingly at the Stars and Stripes patches sewn on the peacekeepers' sleeves. The Marines were trapped in what *Time* magazine, in a story about Soiffert's death, had called "the fratricidal quagmire that is Lebanon."

Dolphin was twenty-five, but he felt old. The wind and sand had beaten the shine off his skin and dulled his red hair. He'd been wondering if his unit's reinforcements might arrive by Thanksgiving or Christmas. The sun still low in the sky, he started to fall back to sleep on his cot.

Dolphin felt a wave of pressure before he actually heard the explosion. He and the other Marines were lying next to six huge metal doors. They flew off their frames and away from the building as daylight flooded into the parking bay.

Dolphin saw the doors slow down in midair, and then careen back toward him, sucked in by a vacuum created in the blast. One door clipped him on the back. Then he heard the boom, so loud he couldn't have imagined it before that moment. Everything in the bay that wasn't nailed down flew up in a maelstrom of shrapnel. A skylight at the top edge of the building shattered, and glass rained on the Marines.

The open-air lobby of the barracks, known to the Marines as the battalion landing team headquarters, or BLT, was surrounded by food storage areas, weight machines, and an armory cache. The first, second, and third floors held the Marines' quarters. Its central location on the airport grounds made it the perfect distribution hub for water, rations, and supplies, and its roof offered 360-degree panoramic views and a platform for radio antennae. But more than that, this former-office-building-turned-fortress had obviously withstood the punishment of war. It had played host to a line of foreign invaders—first the Palestinians, then the Syrians, and later the Israelis, who had turned it into a field hospital during the invasion. When the Marines took over, the BLT was a bombed-out, battle-scarred shell of a building. The second, third, and fourth floors, once encased in plate-glass windows, looked now like rows of broken teeth. The holes were patched with plywood and scrap cloth from sandbags, and makeshift screens of plastic sheets flapped in the wind. The elevator shafts had been burned out. But for all that, the decrepit, Brutalist monstrosity was still standing. The damned thing had not been moved, and so the Marines naturally gravitated to it.

The racket of a Mercedes truck crashing into the building surely woke some of the men. But for a few seconds before the driver detonated his cargo, the truck sat still and quiet in the lobby. The blast severed the base of the building, a set of upright concrete columns measuring fifteen feet in circumference and reinforced with iron rods nearly two inches thick. The BLT's most prominent design feature, an open courtyard that extended from the lobby up to the roof, captured the blast like gas in a bottle, and intensified its force.

The entire structure rose into the air. The top of the building exploded upward in a V shape, like two great arms stretched up to the sky. The BLT hung for a moment in midair, then fell back in on itself, crushed downward, and poured into a crater nine feet deep.

Blood dripped off Dolphin's back. He walked over the glass-covered floor and made his way outside. He saw pieces of concrete falling from the sky. At least half a minute had passed since he'd heard the blast.

He ran to the Combat Operations Center located next to his sleeping quarters. This was his default duty station during Condition One, a basewide emergency. Another communications officer was pulling himself up off the floor; the blast had thrown him from his chair and separated his shoulder. Long cracks ran up the wall of the COC. Dolphin could see daylight through them.

The Marines on duty scurried to reassemble the radios littering the floor. Something must have landed on us, Dolphin thought to himself. Something huge. Rumors had circulated that the Soviets were supplying the Syrian military with intercontinental ballistic missiles. Could someone have nuked the base? Was that what this was?

"I can't raise the BLT," a young corporal called out. "I can't get them to pick up the phone."

A staff sergeant flew into the room. "The BLT is gone!" he yelled. "It's gone!"

Dolphin was confused. *Did they deploy? Maybe they're going out after whatever hit us,* he thought. Then a third man came in, a major, reporting that the building itself was gone.

Dolphin went outside. First he saw the smoke. And then Marines, walking around in circles, some of them with almost all their clothes blown off. On a few men Dolphin could make out only the standard-issue red exercise shorts the Marines wore during workouts. Everyone was covered from head to toe in a gray powder, as if he'd rolled in it. Facial features, hair color, race—everything was obscured under the ghostly cover of pulverized concrete.

Dolphin spotted a staff sergeant named Lawson speeding in his Jeep toward a medical post across the street. Lawson tried to steady a wounded Marine in the passenger seat with his free hand; the man's head rolled and bobbed like it might come off. One of his eyes had blown out of its socket and flopped down on his cheek. Dolphin turned and looked down the road. Where the BLT should have stood, he noticed a new view—the ocean.

Shit! Oh, shit! I've got to get on task here.

A catatonic Marine was standing in front of him, wearing nothing but the waistband of his red shorts. His body hair had been burned off. His arm hung limp. Dolphin tried to lift him, but the pain from his back swelled.

"Listen!" he said. "Help isn't going to come to you. You've got to help yourself." The Marine started walking. "I don't want to lose my arm," he said. "I don't want to lose my arm." He kept uttering the refrain as Dolphin walked with him up the road. He spotted Lawson driving back to the blast site. Dolphin loaded the man into the Jeep. "Just take him," he said, and then went looking for more.

The whole day went like that.

The ring of the secure phone at his home in suburban Maryland summoned Admiral John Poindexter from slumber. He reached over to his bedside table and lifted the receiver. It was nearly 1:00 A.M.

A watch officer in the White House Situation Room relayed what he knew. A bombing at the Marine compound. Minutes later the French regiment also had been hit at their base, not far away. Near simultaneous attacks. Perhaps copycats of the embassy bombing.

Poindexter absorbed the information. Someone had to tell the president. "Call Bud," he said.

Ronald Reagan had selected Robert "Bud" McFarlane as his national security adviser only a week earlier. He'd moved up from the deputy slot, and Poindexter had become the new number two. McFarlane was traveling with the president on a weekend outing at the Augusta National Golf Club in Georgia. The Situation Room would raise McFarlane on a secure phone, and then he'd have to trot across the dark links to Reagan's cottage, wake him, and impart the dreadful news. Meanwhile, Poindexter would hold down the fort in Washington until McFarlane could return.

The two had come up through the Naval Academy together, Poindexter graduating in 1958 and McFarlane a year later. At the White House they'd been working for some time now at a step above their official titles. The previous national security adviser, Bill Clark, an old friend and aide of Reagan's, enjoyed uncommonly intimate access to the president and preferred to play the role of chief confidant instead of security adviser. That left McFarlane and Poindexter to actually run the National Security Council staff, the president's gateway to the vast, unwieldy, and often competing bureaucracies of the Defense and State departments, as well as those of the CIA and several other agencies that comprised the intelligence community.

They made a handy pair. McFarlane assumed the political aspects of the job, advising the president and working with Congress, a task that Poindexter was happy to avoid, since he held American lawmakers in about as high esteem as he did pirates. Poindexter handled the back office, managing the NSC staff with precision and, everyone seemed to agree, genuine affability. He liked the staff, and they respected him. He expected no more or less than their loyalty and devotion. But not just to him—to the system that served the president. At this moment, it was revving up for crisis mode.

Poindexter got out of bed and descended the staircase of his modest two-story Colonial, careful not to wake his wife, Linda, and their sleeping sons. He opened a small door just off the kitchen. Another set of stairs took him to the basement, where he kept a private set of rooms—an electronics shop and a home office. He bent down, spun the combination lock on a government-issued two-drawer safe, and pulled out a new "laptop" computer, called the GRiD Compass, which he'd rigged up with an encrypted data connection to the White House.

At about ten thousand dollars apiece, the Compass's only significant customer was the U.S. government. It had purchased the machines for space-shuttle astronauts and Special Forces troops, who appreciated that the rugged apparatus wouldn't break when they jumped out of a plane with it. Poindexter, an engineer by training, was impressed with the machine; its designers included a British engineer who went on to design the first computer mouse for Apple and a Cornell electrical engineering graduate who later invented two handheld computers, the Palm Pilot and the Treo.

Poindexter set the heavy device on a table he'd built into the wall and opened its clamshell case. The orange monochrome screen glowed, and the forty-seven-year-old sailor donned his large Navy-issued trifocals, which had gold aviator frames. He'd requested the midrange lenses especially for looking at computer screens, which he found himself doing a lot lately. Poindexter had designed his office like a secure facility. He augmented the usual phone line with encrypted voice and data connections. An intricate panel of wires hung on the wall of the electronics shop, just behind the office. Telephone repairmen stared at the setup in slack-jawed amazement on the rare occasions Poindexter summoned them to the house.

At the White House the staff was likely in a frenzy. But here, in darkened serenity, Poindexter went to work. He checked message traffic on a new electronic mail system called PROFS Notes, which he'd talked IBM into letting the NSC staff try out. Poindexter had grown tired of playing telephone tag and chasing people down at the office. The e-mail system was quite a timesaver and such a hit that eventually all White House staffers got access.

Poindexter had been brought to the White House to bring the place into the technology age. In June 1981, Dick Allen, Reagan's first national security adviser, gave Poindexter the intimidating task of upgrading the Situation Room, which was, despite popular notions, a technological backwater that lacked many of the basic necessities for keeping the president in touch with the world. Poindexter, then a military assistant, eagerly assumed the position and made great strides in little time. The Situation Room was outfitted with modern communications equipment. And now he was putting the finishing touches on the new $14 million Crisis Management Center, a technological outpost in the Old Executive Office Building, the imposing Second Empire–style building next to the White House where the NSC staff kept their offices. Poindexter had installed videoconferencing systems, large screens on the walls, and links to the systems that ran diplomatic, military, and intelligence cable traffic.

This new nerve center—combining the Situation Room and the Crisis Management Center—represented a generational leap for the White House, and it was the kind of work for which Poindexter had shown an early inclination. Just prior to graduating first in his class from the academy, he was tapped by the Navy for an elite new technology and engineering program, launched as a reaction to Sputnik. Poindexter, with four other midshipmen, was offered a free ride to any doctoral program that would admit him, and in keeping with his track record he aimed for the top—the nuclear physics program at Cal Tech. He had no particular background in the subject, but he was fascinated by the inner workings of complicated things. And when the civilian leading the scholars program concluded Poindexter would never meet the admissions requirements, much less keep up with the other students, he was convinced it was the right program for him.

He sailed through, despite one hiccup with a particularly challenging course in classical mechanics, a basic requirement for the program but a field for which Poindexter had received no training at the academy. After discovering early on that he was in danger of failing the course, he piled up all the books he'd have to read on the floor next to his desk. He put what he knew on top and worked his way down to the unknown, through three feet of texts. He finished the course with a B. A year later he was studying gamma rays alongside a German scientist who won the 1961 Nobel Prize in physics.

In 1966, Poindexter joined yet another cadre of elites that set him on his trajectory to the White House—Defense Secretary Robert McNamara's "Whiz Kids." McNamara hand-selected geniuses from the nation's top universities, corporations, and think tanks and deployed them throughout the Pentagon bureaucracy. The Whiz Kids had a mandate to infuse the system with new thinking. Technology, economics, metrics-driven management. These were the tools and saviors of a new military, and the keys, so McNamara thought, to winning the war in Vietnam—the generals and admirals be damned. Poindexter landed in the aptly named Systems Analysis division where, under the guidance of another prize-winning scholar, he and his new colleagues set to work trying to understand problems whose complexity was surpassed only by their grimness: the causes and consequence of a nuclear war, or the survivability of a land battle with the Soviets. Its disciples called it "the science of war." And Poindexter approached it with the same systematic determination and faith as he did a three-foot stack of physics books.

Poindexter hadn't anticipated that the rest of the White House staff wouldn't share his discipline. When he arrived the entire crisis management apparatus was in shambles. He often remarked to friends that the White House was like a ship at sea without a map. Across the government, crisis management fared no better. The president and his cabinet, the decision makers in government, were ill served by the intelligence agencies and the military, he felt. Reagan had not run as a foreign policy president, and yet the most significant challenges of his first term came from abroad. Beyond the horizon, an array of threats lined up—the Soviets, socialists in Latin America, and now suicidal fanatics.

Poindexter wanted the system to predict those surprises. And when crisis bloomed, to control it. He thought he was getting a handle on things. But sitting there in the early-morning dark, reading the first reports on the mayhem and devastation in Beirut, he knew the system had failed.

Poindexter was not angry. He was not morose. He was annoyed. *We should have seen this coming,* he told himself.

The signals of a major terrorist attack on the Marines in Beirut had gone unnoticed by almost everyone in a position to stop them. Since May, U.S. intelligence agencies had received more than one hundred warnings of car bombs in Lebanon. Each one was regarded as part of the background noise in war-torn Beirut. The military chain of command was regularly briefed about the widening threat to the Marines. But then, in Beirut, people were always making threats. The Pentagon never allowed the Marines to take more defensive positions and had essentially turned them into sitting ducks.

Underneath the constant warnings lay a discernible sequence of events that led to the assault at the airport. After the embassy attack in the spring, FBI forensic investigators discovered that the bombers had laden their explosives with ordinary pressurized gas bottles, which magnified the force of the blast. Oxygen, propane, and similar gas canisters were simple to obtain almost anywhere in the world, the FBI noted in its final report. The fact that terrorists had not only set their sights on U.S. targets but were enhancing conventional explosives with everyday materials was never made known to the military commanders in Beirut. That's because the FBI never disseminated its report; it stayed locked within the CIA and the State Department.

The most fateful signal came in late September. The National Security

Agency, which intercepted radio and satellite communications around the globe, snatched a message from the Iranian Ministry of Information and Security to the Iranian ambassador in Syria. The ministry ordered the ambassador to get in touch with a man named Hussein Musawi, the head of an Islamic terrorist group called Amal. Musawi was to turn his sights on the multinational forces in Lebanon and was ordered to mount a "spectacular action against the United States Marines."

The Beirut airport was the only place to launch such a spectacular attack. The NSA intercept was the clearest indication yet that the Marines sat in the crosshairs. But owing to the cumbersome military chain of command and an inexplicable failure to grasp the "spectacular" urgency, the message wasn't delivered to senior military officials until two days after the bombing. Only then did the chief of naval intelligence notify his superiors in the Pentagon that the NSA was sitting on what one official later called a "twenty-four-karat gold document." A bona fide warning, unnoticed. The missed signal foreshadowed another overlooked phone call placed on September 10, 2001. It warned, in Arabic, that "tomorrow is zero hour," and it wasn't translated by the NSA until September 12.

If there was a national security system at work in Beirut or in Washington, it hadn't shown itself. The government had no way of capturing information and making it available to those who could discern its importance. The NSC staff was the closest thing to an information traffic cop, and Poindexter and his colleagues struggled to control and understand the data swirling around them. But time and again a recalcitrant bureaucracy foiled their best efforts. The Pentagon refused to let the NSC staff have direct access to generals and field commanders. The State Department jealously guarded access to ambassadors and embassies. And the intelligence community was caught up in its own internecine battles.

Someone had to wrest control, Poindexter thought.

As dawn approached, he reached McFarlane on a secure phone kept in the president's golf cart. He'd briefed Reagan, who absorbed the news quietly, sitting in his pajamas and silk bathrobe. Most of the Marines had been asleep in the BLT when it was hit. Reagan understood that the loss of life would reach catastrophic levels, and that identifying the dead would be difficult if any of them had removed their dog tags before bunking down for the night.

"What does he want to do?" Poindexter asked.

"Hit them back," McFarlane replied.

Reagan and his traveling team prepared to head back to the White House, where the press would soon be gathering. Poindexter got up from his desk; it was time to go in. There would be an all-hands meeting in the Situation Room. The defense secretary, the secretary of state, the CIA director. They'd gather around a long oak table in a surprisingly cramped room and try to figure out what the hell had happened.

As sure as he was that this disaster could have been prevented, Poindexter was certain of something else. This was just the beginning.

CHAPTER 2

KNOWLEDGE IS POWER

When he was a young man, John Poindexter hunted goblins.

It was the winter of 1958. The newly commissioned ensign had received his first billet out of Annapolis with a new antisubmarine warfare unit named Task Force Alpha. Aboard an aging, cramped, and leaky World War II destroyer he prowled the icy North Atlantic, perfecting techniques to hunt Russian subs. It was Poindexter's inaugural cruise, the first step in the Navy's long grooming ritual for its future leaders.

Sub hunters called their Russian quarry "goblins" because they seemed to creep out of nowhere, ugly and terrifying, and then slip back into the cold darkness. Missile-loaded Russian boats were said to pop up off the East Coast at least once a week. As quickly as they surfaced, they disappeared. The Navy estimated that the Russians had amassed a fleet of five hundred subs, ten times as many as the Nazi U-boats that had roamed the open oceans at the dawn of World War II.

Task Force Alpha comprised a new line of continental defense—detecting the unique sound waves emitted by a submarine in the vast and cacophonous expanse of the deep. Submarines were designed to approach by stealth, and antisubmarine warfare tactics were among the most complex and danger-ous in the Navy, demanding a finely tuned mix of engineering, cunning, and intuition.

Poindexter was assigned to the Operations Department of USS *Holder,* a rickety 220-ton World War II destroyer that leaked in the rain, which seemed to fall incessantly during the unforgiving Atlantic winter. Poindexter spent much of his time on the bridge or in the combat information center, concocting new sub-tracking devices and methods. Task Force Alpha was under the command of Admiral John Thach, a revered combat innovator who'd spent thirty-five years at sea and logged six thousand flying hours. In the Pacific Theater he patented a two-plane dog-fighting technique, dubbed the Thach Weave, which helped the Navy's bulky fighters overcome their more maneuverable Japanese adversaries. Thach's new cold war command had earned him a cover profile in *Time* in which he elegantly described the daunting and exquisite craft of detecting a signal in a sea of noise:

> You've got all sorts of noises down there in that jungle. They are decoys protecting the enemy. Fish talk to one another and smack their lips. Porpoises whistle and amorous whales sound like a fleet moving at full steam. Shrimps chew on things and make an ungodly racket. But those whales! They even foul up our magnetic detectors. They nibble at old wrecks and get nuts and bolts in their bellies. Reading the sound and the clues in that jungle is an art.

The *Holder*, like all the older destroyers, had a cramped, enclosed bridge with tiny round portholes. As the junior officer of the deck Poindexter had to stand the watch outside, on a metal catwalk. The watch lasted four hours. He swaddled himself with multiple layers of warm, waterproof clothes. Men told stories of horrible sounds in the night. How a ship's hull cried as she pressed against the wall of a mounting wave and climbed high into the air, so far it seemed that the vessel might slide back down and flip over. When a boat finally crested the wave and came down the other side, the propellers lifted clear out of the water, screaming as they spun free in the black night air.

Poindexter stood the watch, feeling the *Holder* heave and yaw beneath him. White foam whipped across the water, sheared by an invisible blade. Great swells of water rose up and broke against the boat, drenching him in salty cold. He could see the direction of the wind. Feel the pull of the wave. Hear the symphony of distinct sounds. A banker's son from landlocked Indiana, he had never set foot on a boat until he arrived in Annapolis. What he knew of the sea he had read in romantic novels. But he took to the ocean as if he and it had been separated in a previous life. Finally they were reunited, and a penchant for adventure, and for risk, came up from some unfathomable place within him. It seemed to have always been there, like the sea where the goblins hid.

They were out there somewhere, leaving a trace, a tell. He could close his eyes as the sea roiled, befuddling the human senses, and imagine a blackness many feet below the cresting surface. The noise of wind and wave subsided as he sank down, deep. The sound of the waves and the whales faded. The chattering fish fell silent. And now, in the expanding silence, a new sound. A pulsing. A rush of water, followed by an unmistakably man-made, mechanical whirl. Propeller and steel hull, coming out of the black, emerging in this place. He could open his eyes now and see it there in front of him, just where he knew it would be.

One crisp September morning in 1984, Lieutenant Colonel Oliver North, a 1968 Annapolis graduate and a rising young star on the NSC staff, walked into Poindexter's tiny West Wing office carrying a stack of photographs snapped by orbiting satellites. He had something he thought Poindexter urgently needed to see.

The admiral was at his desk, poring over intelligence reports and damage assessments from the latest assault in Beirut. A few days earlier a truck bomber had struck the new U.S. embassy, which had moved to the suburbs to avoid the dangers of the capital. Poindexter examined the set of photos North had brought. Right away, he recognized a familiar scene.

It was the Sheikh Abdullah barracks, an old military post in the Bekaa Valley now inhabited by fighters of the Amal terror group. He had suspected they were behind this. Not long after the airport bombing the NSC staff and the intelligence agencies had confirmed Amal as the culprit. Under orders from Reagan, plans were put in motion for a joint U.S.-French air strike on the camp. The president wanted to eliminate Amal and send a message to other would-be attackers, especially those who might be operating as Soviet proxy forces intent on driving the United States out of the Middle East.

But the reprisal never came. Despite Reagan's unmistakable instructions at an NSC staff meeting the day after the bombing, Defense Secretary Caspar Weinberger scuttled the U.S. raid moments before the planes were set to launch. A staunch opponent of the Marines' mission from the beginning, Weinberger thought that an air strike would only inflame hostilities and potentially rupture ties with friendly Arab governments. But in light of the latest embassy bombing, the failure to act had sent an unmistakable message to Amal and their fanatical brethren: They could strike the United States with impunity. As if to confirm that fact, the Marines pulled out of Lebanon altogether in February 1984.

Poindexter had tried to put the meddlesome secretary behind him. It was harder to forget the 241 men who perished in the attack. The last time the Marines had seen so many fall so fast, they were storming the beach at Iwo Jima.

Poindexter examined the latest photos of the Abdullah barracks. He had always thought the compound looked more like a medieval castle. Hulking and impressive, it stood out amid the bleak desert expanse. An easy target, for sure. But there was something different about these new images. He looked closer, focusing on a row of gray cylindrical dots.

Barrels, he thought to himself. *No. Oil drums.*

Several of them, arranged in parallel lines, like cones on a driving course. They ran along the perimeter of the barracks, then turned a corner and stopped in front. Within the path, Poindexter could see smudged impressions in the ground. *Tire tracks.* Then, where the path curved, the tires left skid marks. *High-speed turns.*

Poindexter knew that the embassy bomber had driven along the perimeter of the compound, then turned suddenly, careening into the front entrance. All at once the goblin emerged from the darkness, and as Poindexter pulled back from the photograph the realization hit him with the clarity of a single, sustained note. He was looking at a practice course.

"How long have we had these photos?" he asked North.

North replied that his CIA contact on terrorism, Charlie Allen, had just brought them to his attention. But they had been taken days before the embassy bombing. None of the photo analysts had realized their significance, and the images were never shared. If the CIA had notified the State Department, the embassy could have installed concrete barriers, or perhaps moved the staff temporarily. The Navy could have dispatched reconnaissance planes, and—hope of all hopes—bombed the damn fortress to the ground once and for all. Poindexter's mind ticked off the options, each of which was predicated on seeing these photographs *before* it was too late.

He had seen a new enemy. But now he recognized, more clearly than ever, that this was a new war. So he went looking for new weapons.

Scientia est potentia. Knowledge is power. It was an old maxim, and one that Poindexter had lived and prospered by. And in their way, so had the many intelligence agencies—knowledge is power; therefore, do not share your knowledge.

When he saw the photographs of the Sheikh Abdullah barracks, Poindexter called up his friend CIA director Bill Casey. The two had developed an honest rapport, and Casey was one of the few senior officials Poindexter felt he could speak to frankly.

"We have got to do a better job sharing this kind of information," Poindexter said. Casey agreed. It was inexcusable. He turned to Charlie Allen, North's agency contact, who then set up a secure hotline connecting the State Department, the NSA, the Defense Intelligence Agency, and the NSC staff with the CIA's photographic intelligence center. This was the government's primary resource for imagery analysis, and yet there had never been any data links into or out of it. That was about to change.

As Poindexter took stock of other imbalances in the system, he found a bureaucracy bowing under its own weight. A slumgullion of nearly three dozen agencies claimed some role in counterterrorism, and collectively they were spending almost $2 billion a year on those activities. From the FBI to the State Department to the IRS, it seemed everyone had a finger in the pot. Each agency possessed an essential skill for preempting terrorism. But not one of them, acting alone, had achieved notable success. The agencies would have to work in concert now, like a well-tuned orchestra. Poindexter wanted to be their conductor.

He did not assume the position. Indeed, following the disastrous defeats of 1983, the administration became highly motivated to go on the offensive. Reagan, in particular, was deeply moved by the plights of U.S. journalists and academics who'd been killed or kidnapped in Beirut by another Islamic fundamentalist group. The president of American University there had been shot, and in April 1984 the CIA station chief in Beirut, William Buckley, was kidnapped at gunpoint outside his apartment. The attack on Buckley, a decorated soldier and career CIA officer, pulled an emotional trigger in Reagan, who tended to see the world through personal stories of triumph and tragedy. He began writing about Buckley and the other hostages in his diary at night, calling them by their first names and displaying an almost familial fondness and concern.

In April, just weeks after Buckley's kidnapping, the White House sent four new antiterrorism laws to Congress, an early effort to shore up holes in national defenses and to take a more offensive posture. In a public statement accompanying the bills, the president's aides coined a new phrase: "war against terrorism." The White House threw down the rhetorical gauntlet, declaring it was "essential that we act immediately to cope with this menace" and address "this growing threat to our way of life." The existential frame for a new war was set.

The intelligence agencies and military Special Forces would have to walk point in this fight, in which preemption was prized above retaliation. Poindexter preferred to make the war a secret campaign, fought mostly out of the public eye and through actions taken without Congress's approval. Presidential directives and executive orders became the preferred catalyst for jolting the recalcitrant system. And he turned the NSC staff into his base of operations.

Two senior-level policy groups had been established early in the administration to advise the president during a crisis. But they'd never fulfilled their mandates. Now, Poindexter would reengineer that structure to deal more directly with terrorism. He found a willing ally in Vice President George H. W. Bush, who chaired the NSC's Special Situation Group set up in December of 1981. Bush had stood amid the smoldering stones of the Marine barracks only days after the bombing, and in a prelude to a similar scene two decades later, declared the nation "would not be cowed by terrorists."

Bush led a top-to-bottom review of the government's haphazard counterterrorism and intelligence efforts, culminating in the most comprehensive examination to date. Poindexter headed a policy review group and proposed a slew of recommendations, including a new intelligence clearinghouse that would bring together all the terrorism reporting from across the government. The panel also called for stricter border control, enhanced aviation security, more intelligence sharing with foreign governments, and closer cooperation with the media, both to obtain more favorable coverage and to undercut terrorists' use of the press as a megaphone.

While the most senior levels of government tackled terrorism policy, Poindexter dove deeper into the bureaucracy to forge an operational response. Another NSC subcommittee, one without the glitter of a cabinet-level roster, gave him his most influential perch.

The Crisis Pre-Planning Group had been established in the spring of 1982 to support the higher-level committees offering policy advice to the president. The CPPG focused on the nuts and bolts, the details that decision makers had neither time nor inclination to master. According to the group's charter, the head was the deputy national security adviser. Poindexter turned the CPPG into the engine of the government's antiterror campaign.

The staff consisted of deputies from key national security departments—Defense, State, and Treasury—as well as the CIA and the Joint Chiefs of Staff. The members had the power to recommend freezing individual and state assets, to develop covert intelligence programs, to communicate with ambassadors at all U.S. embassies, and to send proposals to the military chain of command. They met in the increasingly well-outfitted Situation Room or the Crisis Management Center, tapping into new data sources, holding teleconferences, and crafting a playbook for managing crises—whether caused by bands of terrorists or whole armies. The essential discipline was the same.

Poindexter's personal access to the president, a privilege he'd long enjoyed, gave the CPPG a rare bureaucratic muscle that the group flexed in one extraordinary way. By law, the president had to issue an intelligence "finding" whenever he planned to deploy CIA or other clandestine forces abroad. Drawn up at the agency level and eventually passed along to senior members of Congress, findings were customarily reviewed by the national security adviser or his deputy. He ensured they comported with the president's policies and then passed them along to the commander in chief.

Poindexter turned the CPPG into the clearinghouse for *all* intelligence findings. Poindexter and his crisis management team reviewed, vetted, and shaped every plan for covert action. Before anything moved forward for the president's signature, Poindexter saw it first.

The intimate group of deputies devised new ways to use covert forces in the field. They challenged themselves to think ahead of time about how to strike, especially with elite Special Forces and small commando teams that moved with stealth and agility. The CPPG had a singular focus: prevent crises before they happened. "Horizon scanning," Poindexter liked to call it.

Poindexter oversaw the creation of emergency teams at the State Department, the CIA, the Pentagon, and the FBI, all of which reported to command centers set up at their own agencies to stand watch during an emergency. The staff forged personal contacts with working-level intelligence officers, the career spy class that knew how to navigate institutional roadblocks. This was new territory for the White House. Before Poindexter's arrival, it was not in the business of central control.

In addition to the CPPG, Poindexter chaired yet another subgroup that focused solely on terrorism preplanning. But he left most of its management details to North, his favorite and, he thought, most capable staff officer. North, ten years Poindexter's junior, had captivated the admiral, who had a history of taking bright, ambitious young officers into his charge and then occasionally giving them the con.

North had felt overwhelmed when he arrived at the White House, shortly after Poindexter. Other military officers on the NSC staff held advanced degrees in international relations and political science. They were wonks. North was a Marine; his expertise lay in combat training and field operations.

But he worked like a dog; he was loath to decline an assignment and often the first to volunteer. He became invaluable. A go-to man whom Poindexter gave responsibilities without questioning his capacity to handle them. While his colleagues struggled to keep up, North sailed ahead, and he never missed the chance to remind them of it. Poindexter knew that North exaggerated his own influence on the NSC staff. That he took credit for creating many of the new rules of which Poindexter was the principal author. He was, as Poindexter often conceded to Ollie's detractors, flamboyant. But he was also indispensable. A man of seemingly infinite capacity who, Poindexter thought, would protect both their interests. If he pissed people off as he passed them by or stepped over them, then that was their problem, Poindexter figured, not Ollie's.

As the months rolled on, Poindexter could sense the system coming into alignment. Order and discipline were taking hold. The once ill-tuned layers of committees understood their roles better now. They had focused. Poindexter and his NSC terror fighters were making sense of information, corralling disparate data sources, and coming up with richer and more informative reports for the president than at any time in recent memory. They were, at last, starting to look like a respectable orchestra. All they needed now was a chance to play.

CHAPTER 3

AND HE SHALL PURIFY

Poindexter arrived to a buzzing West Wing on the morning of Monday, October 7, 1985. The CIA's operations center had received word less than an hour before that an Italian cruise ship had been taken over by Palestinian gunmen. A radio station in Sweden had picked up the distress call. Apart from those bare facts, the White House knew only that the vessel was somewhere in the Mediterranean.

Hijack a ship? This was a new tactic. Poindexter was actually grateful that whoever these latest characters were they had chosen a slow-moving, contained vessel to mount their operation. Four months earlier Poindexter and his crisis team had scrambled to keep up with the hijackers of TWA Flight 847, which was en route from Athens to Rome. The terrorists had demanded the release of more than 700 Palestinian prisoners from Israeli jails. For three days they and their 161 prisoners hopscotched around the Middle East, landing to refuel and negotiate as they brandished handguns before throngs of journalists assembled at each airport pit stop. Their demands unmet, the hijackers singled out a twenty-three-year-old Navy diver, Robert Stethem, beat him with the broken arm of a passenger seat, shot him through the head, and then dumped his limp body onto the tarmac at the Beirut airport before rolling cameras. Other passengers were stashed in hiding places in and around Beirut. The ordeal stretched on for two weeks and caused a global media spectacle that the NSC crisis team wished not to repeat.

TWA 847's captors had bought invaluable time as they hustled from country to country, involving ever more governments in their escapade. The U.S. military had no time to react. But a ship—that offered some distinct advantages. Presumably the vessel was still in international waters, where the military was freer to act without diplomatic incident.

But there were other problems. Finding a cruise liner in the vastness of the Mediterranean would be like finding a fly on the wall while looking through a straw. And if the hijackers stayed off the radio, they'd make the search even harder. But if the crisis team could locate the ship and keep it from docking, then a commando team could storm the vessel and take it back. The hijackers also would have no means of escape in the open water. A battle at sea didn't sound half bad to Poindexter.

He called a meeting of the Crisis Pre-Planning Group and the Terrorist Incident Working Group, which had been formed in April of 1982 to provide tactical advice and support during an emergency. Ollie North was in charge, leading a team drawn from the State Department, CIA, Pentagon, and FBI. By now the members had their roles down. They knew one another well, and they understood what their agencies could accomplish on short notice.

More details trickled in over the next few hours. The ship, the Italian passenger liner *Achille Lauro*, had been hijacked by gunmen after leaving port in Alexandria, Egypt, on the sixth day of a twelve-day cruise. Americans were on board, though it wasn't yet clear how many. A number of the passengers had disembarked in Alexandria to tour the pyramids, and they had planned to meet up with the ship again in another port.

The intelligence agencies hadn't identified the hijackers, who had yet to signal their intentions. Experience had taught the crisis team not to wait for demands and dead bodies. They must get ahead of the hijackers now, anticipate their next move.

The team members sent word back to their home agencies. First, isolate the ship. The State Department contacted U.S. ambassadors in countries along the Mediterranean littoral; they should ask their host governments to refuse any docking request from *Achille Lauro*.

Next, track the ship. The eavesdroppers at the National Security Agency trained their electronic ears for any radio transmissions from the terrorists or others trying to contact them. Meanwhile, the NSC staff fielded intelligence reports from friendly governments in the region, principally Israel. The Navy launched a search for *Achille Lauro* using radar and aerial reconnaissance.

Poindexter advised to not let any aircraft hover over the ship if they did manage to find it. He didn't want to give the hijackers a reason to start shooting.

Finally, take the ship. That tricky task fell to an elite military unit, handpicked from the best of the Army's Delta Force commandos and the Navy's counterterrorism squad, SEAL Team Six. Known as the Joint Special Operations Command, the group had been formed in response to the blundered rescue of U.S. hostages in Iran years earlier. The JSOC was called in for unique jobs that posed unanticipated challenges. They improvised. Hostage rescue was their specialty. The commandos had practiced raids using empty airliners, and they had been trained to distinguish hostage from hijacker in a cramped, confusing space.

Poindexter wanted the JSOC to get aboard *Achille Lauro*, kill or capture the terrorists, and return the ship safely to port. The commanding officer, a twenty-year veteran of the Special Forces from Tennessee coal country named Carl Stiner, happily accepted the mission.

While the Navy and the White House searched for a fix on *Achille Lauro* the JSOC prepared to deploy. Poindexter's team had asked them to come up with a rescue plan literally on the fly—Stiner and his men left their home base in North Carolina and worked on the details on a plane ride to the Mediterranean.

The JSOC needed a jump-off point that offered easy access to wherever the ship might try to go. Ideally, somewhere in the eastern Mediterranean. Poindexter called up his counterpart in British prime minister Margaret Thatcher's office. "We want to send our unit to Akrotiri," he said.

It was a British sovereign base nestled on the tiny southern peninsula of the island of Crete, a holdover from colonial rule. Akrotiri seemed an ideal staging area, and the British readily agreed, since some of their own citizens were aboard the ill-fated cruise liner.

The JSOC wasn't the only team speeding toward the region. The Italian defense minister deployed a special military unit to meet up with Stiner at Akrotiri. It included experts on *Achille Lauro*'s design and layout. The Italians were eager to be publicly helpful—the ship was under their flag—but Bettino Craxi, the prime minister, found himself in a bind. The Americans were allies, but Craxi was anxious to maintain good relations with Arab governments. Italy too had been a target of terrorism, and the prime minister knew that a bloody battle aboard an Italian cruise ship could inspire retribution. Craxi publicly asked Yasser Arafat, the chairman of the Palestine Liberation Organization, if he was responsible for the hijacking. Arafat insisted that he had played no role, condemned the terrorists, and offered to send two top advisers to Egypt to negotiate a surrender.

The Americans were no longer the only ones with skin in the game. The rescue operation was getting ever more complex, and the NSC team hadn't even found the ship.

Early Tuesday morning the Situation Room picked up a radio transmission from one of the hijackers to port officials in Tartus, Syria, requesting permission to dock. More than thirty-six hours after the gunmen had stormed *Achille Lauro*, Poindexter's team finally could put a finger on them. The choice of staging area had been flawless—Tartus was due east of Akrotiri. Now, nothing stood between *Achille Lauro* and Stiner's men but open water.

The hijacker on the radio identified himself as a member of the Palestinian Liberation Front, which, though it bore a nominal resemblance to the PLO, was not controlled by Arafat. The PLF wanted fifty Palestinian prisoners released from Israel, and the hijackers said that if their demands weren't met by three o'clock Damascus time, they'd start killing passengers. It was 11:00 A.M. in Syria, seven hours ahead of Washington. Port officials didn't immediately respond to the ship's request to dock. *Achille Lauro* waited as the hours ticked off.

Poindexter's team wasn't aiming for a negotiation. Neither Washington nor Tel Aviv responded to the terrorists' demands. Shortly after 3:00 P.M., the hijacker again took to the airwaves. He told a Syrian port official that one hostage was dead, and he would soon kill another. The Syrian was unshaken. "Go back where you came from."

Achille Lauro went back out to sea, heading for Port Said, Egypt, about three hundred miles away. Stiner and his men followed aboard USS *Iwo Jima*, an amphibious assault ship that a few years earlier had supported the Marines in Beirut. Their window of opportunity to board the ship would close as soon as *Achille Lauro* entered Egypt's territorial waters. Poindexter conferred with the staff of the Joint Chiefs; they agreed that Stiner's JSOC team should hold for the moment. *Achille Lauro* dropped anchor fifteen miles off Egypt early Wednesday morning as the ordeal entered its third day.

An Egyptian gunboat carrying a handful of men sidled up next to the massive blue-hulled cruise liner. One of the hijackers peered over the side and recognized a familiar face among them: Abu Abbas, the founder of the PLF. Arafat had sent Abbas, along with a PLO official, as his emissaries, which raised the obvious question of just how limited Arafat's involvement actually was. The White House had never trusted him, and Poindexter regarded Arafat as a demagogue who was more inclined to keep the Palestinian people poor and outraged than to help them make peace with Israel.

Abbas was joined by a team of Egyptian and Italian officials and for a few hours engaged in what passed, at least onshore, for negotiations with the *Achille Lauro* hijackers. Arafat had suggested that if the Egyptians and Italians agreed to hand the hijackers over to the PLO, he would see that they stood trial.

After the shipside meeting, the delegation sent back word: The hijackers would let the hostages go in exchange for free passage off the ship and direct negotiations with the U.S. ambassador in Egypt, as well as his Italian, West German, and British counterparts. The hijackers were eager for guarantees that none of these countries would try to take them into custody on dry land.

The Egyptian foreign minister hurriedly called the emissaries to his office in Cairo and urged them to take the deal. Nicholas Veliotes, the American, and his British counterpart were nonplussed. The hijackers had threatened to kill their captives, and, as far as anyone knew, they had kept their word. Neither government was prepared to negotiate with these people, now or under any circumstances.

The Italian and West German weren't so sure. Getting the passengers off the ship safely trumped matters of prosecutorial strategy. They wanted to end the ordeal.

As the ambassadors haggled over whether to take the hijackers' offer, a confusing radio transmission arrived from *Achille Lauro*.

It was a man's voice, calm sounding, assured. "I am the captain," he said. "I am speaking from my office, and my officers and everybody is in good health."

No one had heard from *Achille Lauro*'s skipper, Gerardo de Rosa, since the terrorists' first deadline had passed. Had the hijackers been bluffing when they claimed to have killed a passenger? The PLF issued an apologetic statement, claiming that their soldiers were merely aboard *Achille Lauro* trying to get to Israel, where they planned to strike a military target. The men had been surprised by a ship steward while cleaning their guns and, in a panic, they took control of the vessel.

The story had changed. What began as a hijacking now sounded like an unfortunate mishap. The captain attested that everyone, passengers and crew, were fine.

It sounded good to Cairo. The Egyptian foreign minister publicly conveyed de Rosa's statement, and shortly after five o'clock Wednesday evening an Egyptian military boat ferried the hijackers safely to shore. A small crowd of well-wishers greeted them, shouting jubilantly, "Allahu Akbar! Allahu Akbar!"

With the hijackers off the ship, Italian prime minister Craxi called de Rosa on the bridge. Italian authorities hadn't had a chance to come aboard and interview the passengers, and Craxi wanted to confirm the captain's prior assurances before he declared an end to the crisis.

De Rosa, who had seemed so at ease in his radio transmission, broke down. One of the hijackers had held a gun to his head, he said. He'd forced him to say no one had been hurt. But actually, the terrorists shuffled the Americans' passports and picked one out at random—it belonged to Leon Klinghoffer, a sixty-nine-year-old wheelchair-bound passenger from New York. One of the hijackers took Klinghoffer to the aft deck, shot him twice, and then forced *Achille Lauro*'s crew to toss his body overboard off Tartus.

Craxi relayed the grim news to the press. An American had died, and the hijackers were now at large.

Ambassador Veliotes headed to the ship. He found de Rosa on the bridge, his body shaking, tears welling in his eyes. The captain silently handed him Klinghoffer's passport. The hijackers had chosen Klinghoffer, he said, from among the passengers they suspected were Jewish. Enraged, Veliotes grabbed the ship's radio and called the embassy. The deal with the Egyptians was off. The U.S. embassy staff was to call the foreign minister immediately and tell him that the Americans had had no idea a man was dead.

"In my name," Veliotes boomed, "tell them that we insist they prosecute those sons of bitches."

And one more thing. "I want you to pick up the phone and call Washington and tell them what we've done. And if they want to follow it up, that's fine."

News of Klinghoffer's death reached Poindexter and the crisis team. The sheer villainy of the act made them shudder with rage. To shoot an old, unarmed man in his wheelchair and toss his body into the sea. So far terrorists mostly had targeted soldiers and Marines, or other representatives of American influence, such as university professors and journalists. Klinghoffer was a vacationer. A civilian. He was as purely innocent as anyone could be.

A few hours after the hijackers set foot in Port Said the State Department conveyed an urgent message to the White House. Hosni Mubarak, the Egyptian president, said the hijackers' whereabouts were unknown. "They have left Egypt. I do not know exactly where they have gone."

"He's lying," Poindexter told his colleagues flatly. "They're still there."

The hijackers hadn't enough time to mount a getaway. Surely they were planning to leave, but the crisis team still had time to stop them. They couldn't be hiding far from where they'd come ashore.

Mubarak wanted to wash his hands of the affair. If he let the hijackers go, he'd enrage the Americans. If he handed them over for trial, he'd face outrage at home. He would try to get rid of them quietly and quickly. Poindexter knew there was only one easy way to do that.

Poindexter walked over to his office and called Art Moreau, the assistant to the chairman of the Joint Chiefs. Moreau was an Annapolis man, five years Poindexter's senior, and slated to become the new commander of naval forces in Europe. Poindexter clicked with Moreau, a fellow admiral. And now, he needed another Navy man's mind to test the idea he had in his.

Poindexter predicted that the hijackers would try to fly out of Egypt. It was their best chance to move undetected and swiftly. He wasn't sure when it would happen. But he asked Moreau to start thinking about how the Navy might intercept their plane in midair.

Moreau told Poindexter to stand by as he ran it up the flagpole. In the meantime, Poindexter went looking for information.

The National Security Agency had been slurping up Egyptian communications already, and new intercepts indicated that Mubarak knew the hijackers' whereabouts. Poindexter needed more specifics, something to act on.

North shot into his office. He and Jim Stark, a Navy captain on the NSC staff, had been picking up the intelligence traffic on Mubarak, and they agreed that signs pointed to an airborne escape. North told Poindexter that if he could obtain the plane's flight number, or some other identifier, then the Navy could grab them. Not shoot them down, but force them to land at a friendly airfield.

Poindexter was pleased, since he'd had the same thought. Now it was time to turn North loose.

At Poindexter's instruction, North had cultivated a relationship with the military attaché at the Israeli embassy in Washington, General Uri Simhoni. Poindexter wanted the crisis team to have its own access to intelligence, and especially to timely sources, as they delved deeper into covert operations planning.

Poindexter and North guarded this private channel assiduously, which was both useful and highly unusual. If the State Department or the CIA had discovered NSC staffers exchanging intelligence directly with a foreign military officer—in the United States—there'd be hell to pay. Not only were Poindexter and North treading on their turf, but the connection to the embassy was dangerous. North had let the Israelis get close to sensitive U.S. operations. No one could be sure what kinds of information he was trading, or what promises he had made. How could he be sure that the Israelis weren't playing him? When intelligence flowed between governments it had to be filtered through layers and back channels, held up to the light and stripped of biases, and then perhaps reinjected with a few. The dance was done at arm's length, with elbow-high gloves. Healthy relations between national intelligence agencies were built on the dependable pillars of shared interests and mutual distrust. North was throwing it all off.

But he was getting results, and the delicate steps suited Poindexter's new tempo. North called Simhoni at the Israeli embassy and explained that the NSC was thinking about an aerial intercept. The Israelis had dependable human sources in Egypt. Could they obtain the flight information?

Simhoni didn't say no, but he also knew that North's fleet feet could get him in trouble. "Just confirm to me that you are not acting on your own," he said. North assured him that this wasn't a solo project. The boss was in.

Simhoni agreed. He phoned the Israeli chief of military intelligence and within an hour delivered to North the name of the air carrier, the plane's tail number, the departure time, and the runway the hijackers planned to use for their escape from an airfield near Cairo.

Poindexter had spent two years painstakingly building a system that could obtain this kind of golden intelligence. At last he could feel the gears clicking into place.

The crisis team had only a few hours to coordinate a clandestine and danger-ous mission that under the most forgiving circumstances would take days to plan. All the players—Defense, State, the Joint Chiefs' staff—would have to play all the right notes, and with precise timing. Poindexter conducted, and the marvel to the men surrounding him wasn't that he embraced the chal-lenge, but that he did so unflappably. He moved with an effortlessness that to the uninitiated might have suggested Poindexter didn't fully grasp the sever-ity of the moment. But he was utterly and completely in control, for the first time in a long time.

Moreau, the number two man to the Joint Chiefs' chair, called back from the Pentagon. His boss was on board. Now it was time to get the president's blessing.

Reagan was in Deerfield, Illinois, speaking to workers at a Sara Lee bakery about his new tax plan. Poindexter rang up McFarlane, who was standing in the warm kitchen, and gave him the details.

"Mubarak has reported that the hijackers have left Egypt. He's lying to us,"

Poindexter said. He explained the intelligence, that the hijackers planned to fly out, and that the team could identify the aircraft precisely. The Navy could send up reconnaissance planes and fighters to identify the airliner and then persuade the pilot to land. It was risky, but would the president authorize the plan?

"Let me ask him," McFarlane replied.

After the president finished his speech, McFarlane quickly delivered the brief, emphasizing the technical difficulty of the mission. The Navy would have to find the plane in the dark. Beyond that, there were no guarantees of success. The U.S. Navy would force down an Egyptian civilian airliner. The diplomatic stakes were perilous.

Reagan replied that the hijackers had murdered an American. He told McFarlane to go ahead, an order that staff would soon start calling "the Sara Lee decision."

Poindexter phoned Moreau. "I'm calling on behalf of the president."

The NSC crisis team would manage the takedown from Washington. They would provide detailed intelligence for the commander of the Sixth Fleet, who would plot the intercept using the aircraft under his command. Poindexter didn't advertise his Israeli source, but he let Moreau know that the intelligence was solid. The Navy wasn't going to fly in blind.

Stiner and his JSOC team, who had been preparing to head home after the hijackers abandoned ship, received new orders. They would follow the aircraft in their own plane and then apprehend the hijackers at whatever airport they ultimately landed.

North received nuggets from Simhoni, then passed them to Moreau, who in turn handed off the details to the Sixth Fleet. Ordinarily, the defense secretary, Cap Weinberger, would have weighed in at every step and likely put the brakes on the entire operation. Poindexter had never truly forgiven Weinberger for calling off the raid in Beirut two years earlier. But fortunately for Poindexter, Weinberger was out of town this day. And when he got word of the pending mission and tried to reach the president, he couldn't seem to work his secure phone. The device required the caller to press levers and speak only when he had a coded channel. Weinberger had never gotten the hang of it, and Poindexter made no special effort now to help the defense secretary overcome his technical difficulties. The operation moved forward.

Eventually, Weinberger reached Reagan aboard Air Force One using a public radio frequency. He implored him to call off the plan, insisting that the United States would be castigated the world over for a rogue attack. Reagan blew Weinberger off with uncommon tenacity. An American was dead. End of discussion.

While the defense secretary objected, the Navy devised a clever plan. The commander of the Sixth Fleet ordered a squadron of F-14 Tomcats and E-2C Hawkeyes to take up positions off Egypt. The Hawkeye was a flying command-and-control station equipped with an early-warning radar system that could sweep the skies in any weather conditions. Its crew would monitor commercial aircraft coming out of the target area, and once the plane was positively identified, the Tomcats would approach.

The president had not authorized them to fire, but he was willing to let the fighters scare the hell out of the airline pilot. They could blast their cannons across his path if he didn't yield. Once they secured his cooperation, the Navy planes would escort the pilot to the NATO base of Sigonella, near the coast of Sicily, where they'd force him to land. The base was on Italian soil, but the United States had long maintained a military presence there, which was under the command of a Navy captain.

The Hawkeyes and Tomcats took their positions, and the description of their target came in over the radio. EgyptAir flight 2843. A Boeing 737, tail number SU-AYK. The Hawkeyes' commanding officer scanned the dark skies for aircraft traveling west, possibly toward Tunis, the PLO's headquarters and a logical safe zone for the hijackers.

The skies were busy. Planes taking off from Egypt diverged along a number of standard travel routes over the Mediterranean. The Hawkeye got a hit and sent a pair of fighters in for a closer look.

As the pilots approached they could make out the shape of a 737 against the starry sky. One Tomcat moved in for a closer look. The radar operator, seated in the rear of the cockpit, peered through the dark at the plane's logo. EgyptAir.

"Get the flashlight," the pilot said. The fighter closed within feet of the two-engine jet. The radar operator shined a beam on its tail. SU-AYK. The pilot radioed back—contact confirmed.

Flight 2843 was already on a westbound course, taking it in the direction of Sigonella. The Tomcats fell in behind it, running without any lights and keeping enough distance to disappear into the black sky. The Hawkeye commander tuned his radio to intercept the airliner's communications. The pilot was looking for a place to land, radioing airports at Tunis and Athens. Each turned him down—Poindexter and the crisis team already had sent word to each country to deny the plane landing rights.

His choice of escape routes diminishing, the pilot took up a holding pattern south of Crete. He radioed Cairo, where controllers told him to change course and come back to Egypt. Now was the time to pounce.

The Tomcats pushed forward, fell in behind the tail, and blasted their lights onto the 737, illuminating it as if under a spotlight. The Hawkeye commander broke through on the radio: "EgyptAir 2843, you are being escorted by U.S. Navy fighters and are instructed to proceed to Sigonella."

Alarmed passengers, the *Achille Lauro* hijackers among them, looked out their windows and saw the F-14s zip alongside the aircraft. The fighters pulled up to the cockpit, locking eyes with the airline pilot, and dipped their wings— the international signal for forced landing.

"I am following your orders," the pilot declared, with remarkable calm. "Don't be too close. Please." He set the plane on a new heading and sped across the Mediterranean to his landing spot.

Stiner and his JSOC team caught up with the improbable band of fighters and a civilian jet in the air. A few of his men were already on the ground in Sigonella, allegedly for a refueling stop. The ground team would surround the EgyptAir plane on the ground, whisk the hijackers onto their military transport, and then take off before anyone could stop them.

The plane touched down at 1:30 in the morning, as if forced from the sky by some invisible hand. As the pilot taxied off the runway, a team of Navy SEALs surrounded him. Stiner's transport planes, running with their lights off, landed on the main runway, blocking any escape. More JSOC troops poured out, and snipers took aim at the airliner's doors. Stiner picked up the radio and informed the pilot he was about to be boarded.

The passenger side door opened, and a ladder slowly lowered. Stiner, accompanied by one of the SEALs, climbed up and entered the cabin. As they stared down the aisle, the four hijackers stood out—they were the ones surrounded by a clutch of armed Egyptian guards.

The White House was humming. Word of the audacious mission had filtered out, and staff was eagerly roaming the halls for any tidbits about how it all went down. The drama wasn't quite finished. A band of Italian carabinieri had surrounded the JSOC team, and for several tense hours it was unclear whether there'd be a shoot-out. But the White House agreed to hand the hijackers over to the Italian authorities and immediately got to work on extradition orders. One way or another, they thought, Leon Klinghoffer's killers would stand trial. The NSC even had managed to get Craxi and Reagan on the phone together, after North called a friend who knew the prime minister's mistress and tracked them down at his residence in Rome.

As the Navy fighters closed in on the airliner, around dinnertime in Washington, one face was conspicuously absent in the Situation Room and its surrounding offices: Poindexter's. Keeping to his normal schedule, the admiral went back to his office and enjoyed his evening meal, a grilled ham and cheese sandwich and a glass of white wine.

Poindexter sat in his cubbyhole of a work space, located on the first floor of the West Wing, next to McFarlane's spacious quarters. He enjoyed the view of Pennsylvania Avenue out the window. Savoring the sandwich and sipping his wine, he felt no sense of urgency to oversee the final act. There were no calls to make. No lists to check. The Navy had improvised a beautiful plan. The system had worked. The only things that bothered Poindexter were those he could not understand. And right now, there weren't any.

Three White House aides came into the office. They'd been living vicariously through Poindexter's adventures. Didn't he know the planes were in the air? Didn't he want to be there for the landing?

Poindexter looked up from his dinner. His placid face gave the answer.

The next morning, 9:30 sharp, the door to the Oval Office swung open and Poindexter strode in for the president's daily security briefing. Reagan jumped up from his desk, clicked his heels together, and put hand to brow. "Admiral, I salute you!"

Poindexter allowed the well of pride to bubble up, but just a bit. He smiled. "Thank you, Mr. President. But you should really salute the Navy."

"Well, then, I salute the Navy!"

Poindexter, the president, and a few attending White House staff took their seats and got on to business. But no one could deny that something had been altered irreversibly. The air seemed different. Poindexter had purified it. Purged it of doubt. Like a smelter, he had rearranged the pieces of the system and forged something new. From now on, when the time came to act no one would question who was in charge.

CHAPTER 4

UNODIR

One wintry morning in 1986, Ollie North strode into the spacious West Wing office of the national security adviser, where John Poindexter had set up shop. A few months earlier, Bud McFarlane had resigned his post, and Reagan chose Poindexter to replace him. Poindexter and North were still riding a wave of success after the *Achille Lauro* operation. They'd had to give up the hijackers, at least for now, but the system had worked. Poindexter had never had more credibility and political capital in the administration, and he intended to use it.

North arrived this morning, like so many others, in search of his boss's approval. For some time now the NSC staff's ultimate can-do man had been running a clandestine operation to aid the Nicaraguan Contra rebels, providing weapons and paramilitary training through an extensive network of private benefactors and a cohort of CIA officers. The Contras' struggle to overthrow the socialist government resonated deeply with Reagan, aligning both with his geopolitical view of good and evil and his personal affinity for the underdog.

Reagan had admonished his NSC staff to "keep the Contras alive, body and soul." But the fighters were in trouble. Congress had pulled the plug on U.S. funding the previous spring. The intelligence community was expressly forbidden to provide aid and assistance. And while the administration remained hopeful that lawmakers might lift the restrictions and approve a new financial injection, the NSC staff had been improvising ways to bridge the gap until then.

North had an idea how to do just that. And it involved a predictably tricky maneuver for a staff that had mastered the management of covert policies to serve the president's agenda and draw as little public attention as possible.

As he explained to Poindexter, North wanted to siphon money from a preexisting operation, this one involving weapons sales to Iran, which had run up an unexpected profit. He would divert some of the money into a funding scheme he had set up outside official channels. And he would run the transfer through the NSC staff, which, since it wasn't technically a member of the intelligence community, wasn't covered by Congress's prohibition on funding.

Poindexter liked what he heard, for a couple of reasons. First, he'd been looking for a way to get the troublesome Iran operation under control. For several months now the NSC staff had been managing a complex transaction to sell missiles and weapons parts to Iran in exchange for the release of seven Americans held hostage in Lebanon. The scheme had evolved from a rather straightforward quid pro quo into one of the most delicate and convoluted counterterrorism actions in the NSC staff's ever-widening portfolio. Several foreign governments were involved, as were a troubling number of shady intermediaries and brokers whose loyalty and discretion Poindexter questioned.

It wasn't even Poindexter's idea, which also bothered him. McFarlane had kicked things off months earlier, after Iranian officials claiming to represent a rising moderate contingent in the Islamic republic reached out to the White House through go-betweens in Israel. They were willing to intercede on the hostages' behalf, they said, if the U.S. administration would sell them antitank and cruise missiles. The moderates wanted to increase their credibility in Iran by proving that they could defend the country against their neighboring nemesis, Iraq, and against Soviet meddling. You sell us arms so that we can beat our chests, they proposed, and we'll make contact with the people holding your citizens.

Poindexter had disliked the idea. Not because it violated Reagan's public declaration that the United States never negotiated with terrorists. He thought that leaders said one thing publicly and did another privately with remarkable consistency. As long as their principles remained pure, he thought, the policy was intact; and the president's policy of doing all things possible to bring the Americans home had never been unclear.

No, it was the *arrangement* of the scheme that perturbed the order-minded admiral. It was sloppy. And it involved too many parties who couldn't be trusted, specifically the Israelis, who were selling the weapons to Iran with the White House's commitment that they would be replenished from military stockpiles.

The transactions ran up against a law governing weapons transfers to third countries and violated a U.S. embargo against arms sales to Iran. The White House had never informed Congress, and so the NSC staff walked a perilously thin line separating the executive and the legislature. Tip over to one side and the future promised indictments and possibly impeachment proceedings.

Poindexter had spent the past five years of his life making sure the NSC staff didn't have to rely on outsiders to carry out the president's policies. And the White House had paid a political price for his zealous service. In the corridors of the State Department and the Pentagon there were agitated complaints and whispers about a rogue NSC staff that had "gone operational," putting the president too close to controversial actions that by their very nature he should remain distanced from publicly. Poindexter, North, and the others didn't recognize Reagan's political vulnerabilities, people said.

Poindexter also had raised eyebrows by extending the administration's reach beyond government. As he added more sophisticated computer systems and networks to the counterterrorism mission, he grew fearful that hackers could penetrate those systems, stealing vital secrets or paralyzing the government's communications apparatus. A band of teenage computer whizzes had recently compromised the Lawrence Livermore National Laboratory, a real-life version of the techno nightmare popularized in the hit movie *War Games*, in which a precocious high school student cracks the codes of the U.S. nuclear arsenal. Poindexter wrote a lengthy national security directive, which Reagan signed in September 1984, that established a high-level committee to set security policies for sensitive government computer networks. Most of the members hailed from the intelligence agencies and the military, and the entire panel was overseen by the NSC. Technology-savvy libertarians and privacy activists howled at the audacious power grab, accusing the White House of anointing a shadowy "computer czar" to control a burgeoning new information system. Poindexter's critics called him Big Brother incarnate.

He brushed off any suggestions that he'd overplayed his hand, as he had with the critics who accused him of jeopardizing the president and of taking unreasonable risks. As Poindexter saw it, too many outside forces had stuck their noses where they didn't belong. Congress was the worst offender. In 1978, lawmakers had passed a sweeping new intelligence law that restricted the executive branch's ability to monitor foreign spies inside the United States. The Foreign Intelligence Surveillance Act was passed in the wake of explosive revelations about the FBI and intelligence agencies' illegally tapping the phones of civil rights activists, political dissidents, even justices on the Supreme Court. FISA was meant to rein in the intelligence community, and it set up a special court to review intelligence wiretapping requests and issue warrants in secret. The requirements for obtaining a warrant were much lower than in law enforcement cases, and in that sense FISA was an act of compromise, a way to give the spies the latitude they felt they needed to follow leads and expose foreign agents. But Poindexter still resented the incursion and saw it as a prominent example of Congress chiseling away at the executive's national security authorities. Ever since the Watergate scandal lawmakers had marched steadily into the executive's domain, asserting the prerogatives to micromanage foreign policy, national security, and intelligence. Poindexter believed that a significant part of his job was blocking any further advances by a group of men whom he derided as dilettantes.

It was against that backdrop of suspicion, mistrust, and disdain that Poindexter listened to North's proposal for merging the Iran and Contra operations. It was an economical plan, an opportunity to serve Reagan two ways at once.

It's a neat idea, Poindexter thought.

But he had no time to study the matter. There was no time to consider much of anything these days. Henry Kissinger, a previous occupant of his office, had been regrettably spot-on when he offered Poindexter a piece of professional advice not long after his promotion: Rely upon your staff, and upon everything you have learned up to this point, because you will have no time to learn anything new. Your only resources will be the hard work you've done, your intellectual capital. You can only hope that it will save you.

Poindexter pondered for a moment.

"Okay," he told North. "Let's do it."

———

In the days before satellites kept sea captains under the constant, watchful eye of a central command, sailors followed a dictum. The captain is the master and commander of the ship, and his orders are the only orders—unless otherwise directed.

UNODIR. Management by exception. Asking forgiveness instead of permission. The captain transmitted his intentions to his superiors, marked them UNODIR, and before anyone could protest he was already under way.

UNODIR (pronounced "yoo-no-dear") was the understanding of authority that led Poindexter to fuse the Iran and Contra operations without asking for the president's permission—and without telling him what he'd done. Unless otherwise directed, keep the Contras alive, body and soul. Unless otherwise directed, bring the hostages home.

Not only had Reagan not directed otherwise, he had left no doubt about his intentions. Only three days after he'd promoted Poindexter, Reagan called a meeting in the White House residence with his top aides: the newly minted national security adviser, the secretaries of defense and state, and the deputy director of the CIA, who was standing in for Bill Casey. It was a Saturday, the day of the Army-Navy game. They debated the merits of the Iran initiative and whether to move ahead or dial it down. Was it worth the risk of international scandal? Was there some other way to rescue the hostages?

Reagan's secretaries quarreled. But the president sat silently, his arms folded, perched on an ottoman made out of a camel saddle, rocking back and forth on the heels of his cowboy boots. Poindexter watched him closely and read his body language and the quiet resolve in his face.

"I think we ought to keep trying," Reagan said, after the others had stopped talking. "I just couldn't live with myself if we didn't take all possible action to get them back."

Reagan was haunted by things left undone. The hostages' families had scolded his administration publicly for not doing more to obtain their release. They said he'd devoted more energy to higher-profile incidents—the hijackings of TWA 847 and *Achille Lauro*. The sister of a Roman Catholic priest, kidnapped almost a year earlier, said Reagan wanted to keep her brother and the others "out of sight, out of mind." Perhaps he was guilty of the former, but in the pages of his diary Reagan kept a tortured, deeply personal vigil. He felt that he'd come to know these people. And Poindexter knew that as well as anyone in the residence that day.

Reagan was not ignorant of the risks of moving ahead with the weapons sales. "If it ever becomes public," he said, "it'll be very difficult to explain. It will be like trying to define the number of angels that can dance on the head of a pin." He paused. "But I think I can do it."

And that was the end of it. The ship had sailed, and on a banner day—Navy beat Army 17–7.

Poindexter set about reengineering the Iran operation. The first order of business was to get the president's rationale on paper. Remarkably, McFarlane had never asked the CIA to draw up an intelligence finding on the arms sales. Poindexter had no intention of notifying Congress; indeed, he took an expansive reading of the law's requirement that Congress be apprised of all findings in a "timely manner." Who could say what timely really meant? he reasoned. Adjectives were subjective.

Poindexter wanted the finding to keep discipline in the system. Structure. Process. So if the unthinkable happened, if the operation did become public, the president could turn to the American people and proclaim, Here are my reasons. Here are my principles. And they are good principles. Poindexter never believed that arms for hostages alone would win the public's approval, even though that crude exchange was precisely how Reagan saw the deal.

Poindexter refused to be rushed on the finding. Bill Casey's number two at the CIA insisted that Reagan sign something to cover the agency's own hide; he sent over a terse document describing the covert action as essentially a quid pro quo. Annoyed, Poindexter took it to the president and obtained his signature. But then he locked the only copy of the finding in his safe and called Casey's deputy back. "I'm keeping one copy. If you or anyone else wants to verify it, you can come over here and look at it."

He wrote a longer, more nuanced finding. It articulated strategic policy goals and principles, ideas that he felt reflected the grander, loftier order he'd constructed at the White House. Poindexter knew the president saw things much more simply, as a straight exchange of missiles for influence. But, UNODIR. The president would approve of the broader objectives, he told himself. And eventually, he did.

In January, weeks before Poindexter lit the fuse of Iran-Contra, he presented Reagan with the new finding. It enumerated three purposes: establish a more moderate government in Iran; obtain intelligence that could help prevent acts of terrorism; and—lastly—"furthering the release of the American hostages held in Beirut and preventing additional terrorist acts by these groups." What had started as Reagan's primary concern now was one of several.

At the end of the document, under the options "OK" and "NO," Reagan initialed the former.

The president now had a script. But whether he could learn the lines, Poindexter wasn't sure.

For some time now, Poindexter had watched Reagan slip beneath the cover of a fog. He forgot things. He got confused in meetings and in public appearances. At times, the head and shoulders of the man who seemed born to play the president rose above the mist, clear and distinguishable. But then the cloud wrapped up around him again, and he was lost.

Poindexter never had felt more responsible for the president's protection, because of both the precarious covert actions he'd undertaken and Reagan's frail mental state. It was his job, by law, to be the president's honest broker. He had warned Reagan of all the risks and taken steps to shield him. Poindexter advised the president in writing, "Because of the extreme sensitivity of this project, it is recommended that you exercise your statutory prerogative to withhold notification of the Finding to the Congressional oversight committees until such time that you deem it to be appropriate."

Poindexter worried that the potential exposure of the Iran initiative threatened the broader war against terrorism. But the mission itself seemed to have no effect on that conflict. The missiles were flowing, yet the hoped-for reciprocal release of the hostages was limited to two, not seven. The NSC staff quibbled with their Iranian sources over missile parts and prices as if they were haggling over rugs in a bazaar. Since the dialogue had begun the previous September there had been no attacks against the United States or Israel by

Iranian fundamentalists. But in late December Palestinian terrorists stormed the Rome and Vienna airports with machine guns and hand grenades, killing 18 civilians. The administration fingered Libya as the state sponsor, touching off military skirmishes that led, in April, to the bombing of a disco in West Berlin that killed two American servicemen. Nine days later Reagan ordered an air strike on Tripoli. The war had spread, and in ways no one could appreciate immediately. (Reagan's successor reaped the whirlwind two years later, when Libyan-sponsored bombers blew a Pan Am jet and 259 people out of the sky over a Scottish village; 11 residents died under falling debris.)

Yet Poindexter and his team never relented. The families of the American hostages had visited personally with him at the White House, presenting a nine-hundred-foot-long yellow ribbon covered with signatures and messages of support. The gesture moved him deeply, and he felt himself becoming committed to the cause in ways that transcended policy pronouncements.

"You can meet with anyone in our government at any time," Poindexter promised the relatives. In confidence, he hinted at initiatives under way, specifics that his predecessor McFarlane had never given them. Poindexter built up their hopes. The families left the White House convinced that he was working on the problem harder than ever. "He's a classy guy," the daughter of one hostage told a reporter.

But the system was coming apart. Not because of the terrorists but because of the complexity of the schemes to defeat them. The man who wanted to control and understand events found himself increasingly befuddled by them. That's when he started to make mistakes.

In July, six months after Reagan signed the broader finding on Iran, rumors surfaced about the NSC staff's other operations in Nicaragua. Lawmakers once again were debating aid to the Contras, but Poindexter was still operating within the confines of the funding prohibition. America's campaign against socialism in Latin America had become an on-again, off-again war.

Democrats were particularly outraged by newspaper and television reports that said North was personally involved in efforts to resupply the rebels, in defiance of Congress. Just what the hell was going on? several lawmakers wanted to know.

The powerful chairmen of the House Intelligence and Foreign Affairs committees asked Reagan for answers. Was the NSC involved in military aid, with foreign governments helping the Contras or any collection of private citizens on the outside? This wasn't the first time they'd asked—McFarlane had received Congress's questions, and answered them, when he was still at the White House.

Now the same questions fell to Poindexter, in the form of a paper folder containing a congressional correspondence and an accompanying document for his response. The folder was tucked into a pile of briefs, memos, and communiqués that resided on Poindexter's desk. He opened the folder, read the precise questions that the committees wanted answered, and then realized that McFarlane had provided them already. Poindexter reaffirmed that declaration, essentially telling the committee to see McFarlane's prior statement on the matter. But Poindexter didn't read what McFarlane had actually written.

They were lies. Or, in the most charitable light, deliberately misleading partial truths. In a written response to Lee Hamilton, the Democratic chair of the intelligence committee, McFarlane had averred, "I can state with deep personal conviction that at no time did I or any member of the National Security Council staff violate the letter or spirit" of the ban on aid to the Contras.

How could Poindexter have failed to examine carefully what he was signing on to? Looking back years later, he would find himself at a loss. He was just so busy. There was just so much information. He trusted that under his watch the Contra operation was being run more tightly. The NSC staff was not part of the intelligence community and therefore could be a legal conduit for funds. It was a narrow loophole, but he threaded it, never touching the line, apparently coming out clean on the other side.

But McFarlane had done something altogether different. He'd been reckless by broadly asserting, with unequivocal and practically indignant tones, that there had never been a covert Contra policy of any kind. He insisted that the letter *and* the spirit of the law were intact. He gave Poindexter no wiggle room. Had *he* written the responses to Hamilton this time, Poindexter would have been evasive, answering only what was asked. He would have phrased his responses jesuitically: technically true, though not entirely truthful.

As it happened, the House chairmen weren't buying Poindexter's assurances, at least not on paper. They asked for a meeting with North, the administration's alleged man in Nicaragua. In August, nearly a dozen members came down and met with North in the Situation Room. Poindexter didn't attend, but when he received a debrief from another staff member after the event, he concluded that North had handled it just right. He hadn't lied, but he hadn't told the members everything.

The committee seemed satisfied; they dropped their inquiries about the Contras. Poindexter expressed his satisfaction to North in an electronic mail message: "Bravo Zulu," the naval signal for "well done."

They walked a thin line. But thick enough to hang them.

When the climax of this comedy of errors played out, on a frantic stage crowded now with the king, his princes, and their enemies, there was cause for celebration. It was November 3, 1986. An American hostage in Lebanon had just been released. Congressional and gubernatorial elections were to be held the next day. And Reagan was preparing to sign a landmark immigration law, something he'd worked hard for since taking office. Then, on November 3, an independent Lebanese publication, *Al Shiraa*, published an exposé on McFarlane having made a secret visit to the Iranian capital. The details were sketchy but sharp enough for Iranian officials to confirm that the ex–national security adviser had come to Tehran at the behest of the U.S. government.

Two days after the article ran, a reporter covering the signing ceremony for the immigration bill asked Reagan pointedly, "Do we have a deal going with Iran of some sort?"

The president, who seconds earlier had jokingly congratulated himself for remembering the names of all the attending luminaries, replied simply, "No comment." But then a request. "Could I suggest an appeal to all of you with regard to this? That the speculation, the commenting and all, on a story that came out of the Middle East, that to us has no foundation—that all of that is making it more difficult for us in our effort to get the other hostages free."

Reagan had just let the cat out of the bag. The rest of his secrets unraveled quickly. Soon the press picked up on a seemingly unconnected item: the downing of a U.S. cargo plane a month earlier in Nicaragua. The sole survivor, an American named Eugene Hasenfus, told his Sandinista captors that he worked for the CIA. They scoured the wreckage, recovering documents that named a slew of Americans and a State Department humanitarian assistance office that North had subverted for the Contra aid program.

Administration officials told Congress that Hasenfus did not work for the CIA, which was true. He worked for North. Only twelve days after the shoot-down, Congress, once again placated by White House assurances, approved the administration's $100 million Contra aid package. The era of prohibition had ended. Poindexter and North had bridged the gap in tough times.

Less than six weeks later, they'd both be out of the White House.

McFarlane's secret visit to Tehran had been no less comic, and no less complicated, than every other step in this once pure-intentioned adventure. It was May 1986, only five months after McFarlane had left the White House and its unremitting demands, and the arms-for-hostages swap was not paying off. The NSC staff had become bogged down with a shady Iranian arms merchant named Manucher Ghorbanifar, who passed himself off as a conduit to the men holding the Americans. Release was at hand, he promised. And if the administration just would send a high-level delegation to Tehran, all parties could iron out the wrinkles.

Poindexter tapped McFarlane for the job. This was his mess; he could fix it.

McFarlane, accompanied by two CIA officers and an NSC staffer, touched down in Tehran bearing good tidings from the president of the United States. They waited for more than an hour for Ghorbanifar, and when he finally arrived, the U.S. delegation was whisked off to the top floor of a hotel, formerly the Tehran Hilton.

They cooled their heels for nearly four days, and in due course discovered that their Iranian contacts were utter charlatans. At most, the Iranians said, they now could promise to intervene on behalf of one American hostage. No more than two. But they hadn't made the proper arrangements. That would take time, contacts . . . more missiles.

The Americans packed for home. They turned back a plane full of spare missile parts en route to Tehran. No deal. McFarlane was defeated.

North sensed his old boss's desolation. They'd been in contact about the operation since McFarlane had resigned, exchanging messages over a secure communications channel the ex–security adviser kept at home. North could see now how humiliated McFarlane was.

Look on the bright side, North encouraged, as the group stood on a tarmac in Tel Aviv waiting to change planes. We've been funneling some of the profits to the Contras.

Oh shit, McFarlane thought.

Eventually the Iranians obtained an official price list from the Defense Department for the missiles they'd bought. Wise to North's deceptions, they confronted officials at the CIA, who said they had no clue what he'd been up to.

North told Poindexter that the Americans had to keep up their end of the bargain, now more than ever. He drew up a detailed sequence of transactions— one hostage goes free, the United States would ship some weapons parts. Another hostage released, more missiles. A third hostage, and so on.

The dangerous saraband was to culminate in freedom for all the Americans. But before the transactions were complete, two more Americans were snatched in Lebanon. Accounting for the two who'd already been released, the NSC staff was right back where it had started.

Poindexter tried to seize control of the sinking ship. He ordered North to open up a new channel with a source who'd come onto the radar recently, the nephew of a senior Iranian parliamentarian. But by November, after the *Al Shiraa* article, their cover was blown. Reporters started grilling the president openly. How, they wanted to know, did this exchange not violate all his policies on terrorism, as well as the arms embargo and the rules on third-party weapons transfers? The reporters also said that the Iranians were offering to intercede for the hostages if Reagan would release more missiles. Did he plan to do that? they asked.

On November 10, Reagan gathered his national security principals for a meeting in the Situation Room. He was adamant that the United States had not cut a deal directly with terrorists; the White House was selling arms to Iranian moderates who would intercede on its behalf. A big difference.

George Shultz, the secretary of state, was apoplectic. He hadn't known until now that Reagan had signed a finding on the Iran initiative. He had warned Poindexter against the scheme. He knew that Congress hadn't been informed of the arms sales. But worse than all that, the president had debased a basic precept of his war against terrorism, which rested, in Shultz's estimation, as strongly upon a single commitment as it did upon the show of force: We don't deal.

Reagan insisted that he had not bargained away his principles. He told Shultz that the terrorists themselves had not profited from the arms sales, only the interlocutors. Shultz said he wasn't sure the public would recognize the difference. Nor did he.

Poindexter, who was ever mindful of the commander in chief's increasing fragility, cut into the debate. "How else would we get these hostages out?" he demanded. In the finding Poindexter had written that approaching the government of Iran "may well be our only way." If Shultz had a better idea, Poindexter thought, he should have spoken up a long time ago. Instead, he had bowed out, telling Poindexter point-blank that he didn't want to be in the loop on this operation.

Shultz could see now that he'd closed himself off too soon. Poindexter, the rogue "honest broker," had exposed Reagan to ruin. The president didn't even know it.

"We don't deal," Shultz said, seething.

It was time to return to the script. The players had lost their place. "Line!" the president seemed to shout, the hot, bright lights of the stage shielding the upturned eyebrows and crooked mouths of a skeptical audience.

As Thanksgiving approached, Poindexter and Reagan's press secretary, Larry Speakes, prepped Reagan for a news conference in which he planned to field questions on the Iranian initiative. During the "murder board," a kind of grueling dress rehearsal for the main performance, various staffers played the roles of bloodthirsty reporters doing their best to trip the president into an admission of guilt, to poke holes in the logic of his policy.

Poindexter coached Reagan on the talking points, pulled directly from the finding: We wanted to further a more moderate government in Iran, obtain vital intelligence, and secure the release of American hostages.

But as the mock journalists volleyed questions at the president, he forgot his lines.

The Israelis hadn't been involved, he responded to one question.

"No, that's not right, Mr. President," Poindexter intoned from the audience.

The amount of weapons only amounted to what we could fit in a single plane.

"No, Mr. President, that's still not right."

Reagan seemed to commit the mistakes to memory. He stumbled again and again. As the rehearsal drew on, Poindexter looked across the room at Speakes. They locked eyes and exchanged a knowing shake of the head. They were losing him.

Later, when Poindexter had a label to affix to Reagan's condition, he would console himself that he could do only so much to save his commander in chief. He would recognize the familiar fog of Alzheimer's disease when it claimed his mother less than a year after it did the former president. Though the public and Reagan himself liked to joke about his forgetfulness—some even thought it a ruse—Poindexter knew the truth. His boss was sick.

Maybe, in the back of his mind, that's why UNODIR always had been the safest option. Tell the president nothing. Had he known, he would have said yes. But still best not to ask.

On November 21, just eleven days after the tense meeting with the national security principals in the Situation Room, Ed Meese, Reagan's attorney general, told the president it was time to close the book. He had to figure out which way was up in this Iran mayhem. Reagan's staff weren't protecting him, Meese felt. Would the president let him interview all the players and gather the facts?

It was Friday. Reagan gave Meese the weekend and asked for his report on Monday.

The same day, Reagan's White House counsel discovered that one of the missile shipments was large enough that it must be reported to Congress or be declared a violation of the weapons shipment law. Neither had occurred. The White House was officially over the line. And it was only Friday.

Meese didn't have to look long for more incriminating evidence. On

Saturday he spoke to Shultz, who blasted Poindexter and the NSC staff for selling the president a bill of goods. Meese said the president didn't remember the missile shipment that tripped the reporting requirement, but neither man thought it much mattered. The Democrats would zero in on the slightest infraction and bring down the White House. Something else bothered Shultz. He'd suspected that the Iran initiative might be connected somehow to funding the Contras. Meese should be on the lookout.

Meese took a break from poring over paperwork. He and two aides stole away for a quiet lunch at the Old Ebbit Grille, a local favorite not far from the White House. One of the aides said he'd been going over files from Oliver North's office, and he'd found a real whopper—the NSC staff was giving $12 million from the Iran missile sales to the Contras.

"Oh, shit," Meese said.

Poindexter liked to arrive at the White House early, at least by 7:00. Though as deputy he had to drive himself to work, the post of national security adviser came with a chauffeur. Poindexter passed the half-hour commute working or thinking in the backseat of a town car, paying no mind to the rush-hour traffic that he abhorred. He took his breakfast in his office, where he reviewed overnight message traffic. He ate heartily—usually two poached eggs on an English muffin, a bowl of cereal with fruit, and bacon. He met with the NSC staff in the Situation Room at 7:30, attended a meeting of the White House staff, and at 9:30 delivered the president's daily security briefing. At times he let his mind wander, only for a moment, to soak up the rarified air of the Oval Office.

On Friday, November 21, Poindexter added an extraordinary task to his regular routine. Ed Meese had called to say he wanted all relevant NSC staff documents related to the Iran initiative. Poindexter hung up the phone, opened his safe, and pulled out the sole copy of the first finding that Reagan had signed, which described the Iran operation as just an arms-for-hostages deal. He tore the finding into pieces and deposited them in a burn bag, which was collected each day and tossed into an incinerator. Then he turned to his computer and called up more than five thousand messages he had exchanged with North and others about the staff's covert activities. With the click of a button, he deleted them.

On Monday, Meese made his report to Reagan. He told him that the NSC staff had diverted money from the missile sales to the Contras. Then Meese questioned Poindexter about it directly, and Poindexter did not lie.

Later that day the president sat down with the file of memos and news clippings that his national security adviser prepared for him every day. Tucked into the stack was an op-ed Poindexter had penned for the *Wall Street Journal*, defending the administration's Iran policy. It had run in that morning's paper.

Under the headline "The Prudent Option in Iran," Poindexter defied the administration's detractors to come up with a preferable, more sophisticated policy. Some other way to fight terrorism, balance regional strategy, and get all the hostages back. "Those who question us now owe the country an explanation of how they would have acted differently given the stakes, the opportunities, and the dangers." *If you've got a better idea, let's hear it.*

Reagan took his pen and across the top of the article scrawled a note of praise: "Great—RR"

The next morning Poindexter met with Reagan in the Oval Office and told him the whole story. He had instructed North to give the Iran profits to the Contras. It was his decision, and he'd never told the president.

"I'm prepared to resign," he said. It always had been his plan if the operation became public.

Reagan took Poindexter up on his offer. He would return to another assignment in the Navy. North, however, was fired from the NSC staff. He retained his military commission.

Later that morning Meese laid out the entire affair to a meeting of the full cabinet and congressional officials. At noon he joined the president at a hastily arranged press conference and introduced Iran-Contra to the world. Reagan did no better explaining the latest twist in the debacle than he had a few days earlier, at another press conference just about the arms sales. In that performance the president forgot most of the lines Poindexter had taught him.

Now, Reagan said that he had no idea his staff had diverted money to Nicaragua, a "seriously flawed" move that was nevertheless part of a well-founded and important policy in Iran. He didn't even attempt to entertain questions. Amid howls from the press corps, Reagan turned the meeting over to Meese. They traded places at the podium like confused dance partners, not sure who was leading.

On April 7, 1990, Poindexter stood before a twelve-person jury culled from the citizenry of the District of Columbia. He'd been accused of five felony counts: one of conspiracy to obstruct official inquiries and proceedings, and two each of obstructing Congress and false statements to Congress. His earlier deference to McFarlane's false statements to the intelligence committee, as well as his destruction of e-mail messages, composed parts of the indictment. Poindexter considered the latter issue particularly preposterous. There were no rules on the retention of e-mail records. He should know, he said. He *brought* e-mail to the White House.

Poindexter fixed his eyes on the twenty-five-year-old jury foreman, a paralegal student at a local community college. To each of the five counts the judge read, the young man replied, "Guilty."

Poindexter rocked gently, but his blank expression never changed. He gave nothing away. The judge ordered him to return in two months for sentencing, when he could receive a maximum of twenty-five years' imprisonment. Poindexter turned to his wife, Linda, and kissed her. They walked out of the courthouse into the spring air.

Amid a throng of reporters, they kept silent as they exited the building. Three and a half years had passed since the day he came home from the White House for the last time. He had been so tired, and glad that at least one part of the saga had ended.

The trial had consumed much of his time since then. He had decided not to testify in his own defense lest he give the prosecution ammunition for its case, which portrayed Poindexter and North as bandits in a conspiracy run amok. He opted, instead, to rely on videotaped testimony by Reagan, hoping to demonstrate that Poindexter had operated under the broad umbrella of White House policy that was endorsed by the president. But many of the essential details of Iran-Contra, and Poindexter's precise role in it, seemed to escape the former president's memory. He failed to persuade the jury.

Did Poindexter wish he had testified? one of the reporters in the crowd shouted. He didn't answer. But Linda turned, looked the questioner in the eye, and replied, "No second thoughts."

They got into their car and drove home.

The jury foreman later said that "an overwhelming set of facts in support of the prosecution's allegations" left the jury no choice. But Poindexter was unapologetic and defiant. "That was not a jury of my peers," he would say years later, his tightened voice betraying the bitterness that simmered beneath his placid exterior. "Not one of those people understood the information presented to them."

It wasn't just innate brilliance that Poindexter thought gave him an edge. It was information. Information was power. It could work for you. It often turned against you. But there was always so much of it, more than most minds could handle.

The Iran-Contra affair had been a jumble of bad information, and it was John Poindexter's undoing. But it was also the catalyst for his rebirth. Rather than retreating into quiet solitude, he would redouble his efforts to change and master the complex interplay of intelligence, power, and technology that he generally summed up as "the system." He had no idea then just how radically it was about to change.

ACT TWO

Clandestine, foreign government, and media reports indicate Bin Ladin since 1997 has wanted to conduct terrorist attacks in the US. . . . Al-Qa'ida members—including some who are US citizens—have resided in or traveled to the US for years, and the group apparently maintains a support structure that could aid attacks.

—*Item from the* President's Daily Brief, *August 6, 2001*

"Data mining" would potentially access both foreign intelligence information and domestic information regarding U.S. citizens. . . . We need to think carefully how we want to deal with a capability which can gather such information into one cross-referenced super-data base.

—*Legal counsel to the chairman of the Joint Chiefs of Staff, in an*
April 14, 2000, memo on the Able Danger program

CHAPTER 5

A CONSTANT TENSION

There was a time when everyone was linked to a lug nut, and the agents of the FBI liked it that way.

It was 1985, and federal agents in New York were running cases against drug dealers, mobsters, and money launderers. They'd managed to take down gangs and expose criminal networks thanks to the bounty of evidence provided by one simple, reliable tool: the wiretap.

Agents had insinuated themselves into the inner workings of their targets by surreptitiously snatching their own words off copper phone lines. Crime fighting had a certain, comforting order owing to the simple engineering of the phone system: Everyone who used it was tied to the ground by a wire. On any given day an agent could stand on a street corner in Manhattan, gaze up at an apartment building, with its neat rows and columns of units stacked atop one another, and know that inside each one there was a telephone tethered by thin copper wire to a single point, sometimes several miles away. In his mind's eye he could have imagined shrinking himself to the size of an electron and traveling over the phone line, down to the bottom of the building, then shooting beneath the streets, until he ended up in the basement of the telephone company's switching station. There the wire emerged, pegged to a rack by a single copper lug nut. Acres of racks lined the walls, each holding rows and columns of lug nuts and their wires, neatly stacked atop one another—the city of New York in analog miniature.

With a warrant in hand an agent could tell the technicians at the phone office, with whom he had become friendly over the years, "Go up on RR326."

The tech would walk to the rack, find the wire, and clamp on a listening device. Instantly, the agent became an invisible interloper.

But there were rules to this eavesdropping. Under federal law the FBI needed to be absolutely certain that the line they were on belonged to the suspected dealer, or launderer, or capo named in the court-approved warrant. Not the guy in the apartment next door. Not someone down the block. This guy. This phone. RR326. Unless an agent wanted to risk a judge tossing his evidence, or perhaps tossing him in a jail cell, then he had to be sure. The phone number must belong to the very same line that snaked back through the subterranean maze of Manhattan, through all those blocks of concrete caverns, back to that apartment building, up through the walls and out of the jack and into the phone that was in the hand and next to the mouth of the FBI's target. It was, by design and necessity, a neat, specific system. And then it all went sideways.

The FBI's friends in the phone company put the bureau on notice: Over the next few years those racks and stacks of wires and lug nuts would be swept into the technological dustbin. The telephone network was going digital. Technicians would no longer stand at a rack; they would sit at a keyboard. In some parts of the country that had already made the change, phone calls were traveling as a stream of 1s and 0s. Thousands of lines commingled in a single computer. When New York went digital the phone techs would no longer be able to tap directly into RR326. In fact, they couldn't even tell for sure where RR326 resided in this new matrix.

Things got worse for the government. People started using cellphones. These wireless devices were inherently harder to tap because they used phone lines differently than their analog counterparts. In 1985, a mere 203,000 Americans were using cellphones. Within a year, the number doubled. Two years later, it climbed to 1.6 million. By the end of the decade, a staggering four million Americans counted themselves as cellphone subscribers. Organized criminals, the FBI's favorite targets, were among them.

Members of the Colombian Cali drug cartel operating in New York figured out how to throw agents off their trail by briefly using a cellphone and then tossing it and switching to a new one. To tap a mobile device the phone company technicians had to install listening equipment on an "electronic port," the modern version of the copper lug nut. But in most switching stations there were only half a dozen ports available at any one time. The crooks were chucking phones faster than the cops could tap them. Prosecutors and FBI agents found themselves standing in line at the phone company, fighting with one another over whose case should take priority, and threatening to haul phone company employees into court so they could explain to the judge why they hadn't executed a wiretap order promptly.

Electronic surveillance had been such a dependable craft. Now rapidly evolving technology was threatening investigations. The phone companies had no interest in making the government's life easier. By the end of the eighties their annual revenues from cellphone subscriptions were more than $2 billion. The new decade held the promise of more digitization, more mobility. The agents in the New York field office put their bosses in Washington on notice: "If we don't do something, we'll be out of the wiretapping business."

The digital revolution had crept up on the FBI and the intelligence community. Though law enforcement agents and spies were governed by different surveillance rules, they were all tapping the same network. And both sides shared the same basic philosophy about surveillance: The best evidence in a court of law or in an intelligence operation is a person's own words. No surveillance meant no intelligence. No intelligence meant the nation could be taken by surprise.

The National Security Agency, the intelligence community's primary eavesdropper, had perfected the art of clandestine wiretapping, but it had also built a global network of electronic surveillance equipment to snatch signals out of the air. As phone calls and transmissions shot out of radio transponders and bounced off satellites, the NSA could grab them in transit. Much of the NSA's foreign intelligence haul came through aerial capture. But when the world went digital, all those signals went underground. The new telecommunications system was a fiber-optic network of glass tubes, moving information through beams of light. It was out of the NSA's grasp.

The agency had another problem. Encryption technology—the computer algorithms that the NSA's code makers used to protect the nation's secrets—

was now available on the open market. Drug kingpins and mob bosses could purchase secure phones, which had long been a luxury reserved for defense secretaries and national security advisers. The technology was getting cheaper and easier to use, and it was becoming ubiquitous. Mike McConnell, who took over as director of the NSA in 1992, could imagine a day when criminals and spies around the world encrypted all of their communications using technology that his agency had helped invent. In this new global telecom enterprise, the NSA risked going deaf.

The cops and the spies had a choice to make. They could control this new revolution, or they could become its victims. They launched a two-front campaign to ensure that whatever the future of communications looked like, it would bend to their needs.

In the summer of 1994 the FBI and the Justice Department put forth a legislative proposal that would require phone companies to build their networks so that they could be tapped immediately with a judge's order. No more waiting in line for scarce digital ports. No computer-induced uncertainty about which phone number was targeted. The government demanded assurances that it could listen in at any time. The companies must not build an untappable system.

Louis Freeh, the FBI director, personally pushed for the new law. A former special agent and federal prosecutor, Freeh had used wiretaps to secure convictions in some of the most complicated organized-crime investigations in history. He showed up unannounced in the offices of reluctant lawmakers, who'd been hearing horror stories from the phone companies about stifled innovation and excessive regulation. Congress also had been pressed by an emerging movement of technolibertarians, whose ranks included some of the very same lawyers who had helped write the Foreign Intelligence Surveillance Act in 1978, passed in the wake of illegal spying on war protesters and political activists. They warned Congress: We have been here before. The government always will try to take more than it needs. (Only a few years earlier, Justice officials had gotten as far as placing language in an anticrime bill that would have allowed the attorney general to set standards for telecommunications equipment, effectively making him the new network's architect in chief. The bill did not pass.)

Freeh was undeterred. He started sitting in on congressional committee markup sessions—an unprecedented move for an FBI director—just so he could stare down recalcitrant members. At the same time, McConnell made his play at the National Security Agency. Acting under a presidential directive from Bill Clinton issued in 1993, the NSA began development of a cutting-edge microcircuit called the "Clipper" chip, which would be used to scramble telephone conversations. The agency wanted to install the chip in U.S. telephones, so that every phone call in America would be converted into a jumble of digital data that only the government could decipher. The "key" necessary to unlock the encryption codes would be in safekeeping with government authorities. McConnell and his colleagues reasoned that if the world was moving toward encrypted communication, then the NSA better try to set the standard, and protect its turf. With the Clipper chip the NSA would be the ultimate code maker and code breaker of the telecom system.

Libertarians and privacy activists reacted to these ideas with a mix of outrage and apoplexy. The government was coming at them from two sides—setting standards for the architecture of the network and becoming the traffic cop for everything that moved on it. An atmosphere of hostile skepticism permeated all conversations about the new telecom law and the Clipper chip.

Beginning in August 1994, senior law enforcement officials sat down for meetings in Washington with a coalition of more than four dozen activist groups and technology companies, including the biggest telecom provider of all, AT&T, as well as IBM, Microsoft, and the U.S. Telephone Association, which represented more than 1,200 local phone companies and the so-called Baby Bells, which were created after the government breakup of AT&T in the early eighties. None of these companies wanted to see draconian measures suffocate the spirit of invention. But they also couldn't object to the government's legal and security imperatives. Officials had to be able to monitor communications legally in order to protect the country against all kinds of threats, known and unknown. Somehow the two sides had to compromise.

The meetings featured intense, nitty-gritty debates over the technical aspects of the proposed law. The government wanted guarantees that the telecom system would never mature beyond the reach of its wiretaps. Some companies saw this as heavy-handed regulation, and a number of telecom officials shared the activists' belief that the government was after a permanent backdoor into the phone system. The negotiations helped to dampen the suspicions somewhat, however, and the talks went forward, because no one in the room disagreed with the fundamental premise that the government had the right to wiretap.

The activists had a bottom line. They only would agree to solutions for known problems. The new law mustn't be written to address future gaps. If the FBI had difficulty accessing the public telephone network, then the law would address only that public telephone network. The activists wanted to set a philosophical guideline, but they also had another strategic goal, one they felt must be defended at all costs: They wanted to keep the government's hands off the Internet.

In 1994, the net was so new that its future was still notional. Only a handful of subscribers were surfing online through providers such as America Online and Prodigy. The first Web browser had just been released, in a beta test version. But the activists knew that the Internet was a free space, an environment fueled entirely by innovation, and that it held as yet unimaginable promise. The government never would agree willingly to stay out of that space. If that's where the world was moving, that's where the cops and spies wanted to be. *Needed* to be.

During one of the meetings, David Johnson, a lawyer who had helped to craft a landmark electronic privacy act in 1986, demonstrated why the Internet was destined to be such a valuable intelligence resource. He held up a glass jar full of rocks and asked the room, "How many of you would say this jar is full?" Most everyone agreed that it was. Then Johnson took a fistful of pebbles and dropped them into the jar. They tinkled down through the rocks, finding resting places in the empty spaces. Then he poured in some sand. As it cascaded into the empty spaces, he told the onlookers that the sand was like the unseen, seemingly insignificant "transactional data" that traveled on the network. It held routing information for a text-based message like an e-mail—where the message came from, where it was going, what path it followed through the light-filled pipes. The transactional data also contained a series of digits that composed an Internet address, a unique location in cyberspace. It was starting to sound like RR326. A beacon in the electronic storm. This information someday would be of enormous value to the government, Johnson said, just as phone call records already were. The transactional data were small but meaningful, just like the tiny grains of sand that filled up the jar.

Two influential Democrats had attended the meetings, and they came out convinced that the government had to be restrained. Senator Patrick Leahy, from Vermont, and Congressman Don Edwards, whose district included Silicon Valley, formally introduced new telecom legislation and declared that it would apply solely to the public telephone network. The law specifically exempted "information services," which all the parties agreed included Internet companies and electronic-messaging technologies.

The Communications Assistance for Law Enforcement Act passed in the closing days of the 103rd Congress, two weeks before Republicans won control of both chambers in November 1994. CALEA (pronounced kuhLEEuh) would let the industry set its own standards to meet the Justice Department's needs. The department could list its surveillance requirements, but the act let companies decide how to build their own equipment. Officials could petition the Federal Communications Commission if they felt that the companies weren't fulfilling their obligations under the law.

The government could have stopped there. It could have settled for secure access to the phone networks and kept electronic surveillance intact. But the government had never intended to cede cyberspace to technicians and activists, any more than to coke dealers and hitmen. The law was merely a new starting point. Just weeks after Clinton signed CALEA into law, in January 1995, the raft of compromise sprung its first leak.

Law enforcement officials had made a calculated decision to leave the negotiations and then quickly regroup when it came time to set the standards for implementing CALEA. That's when the government would be able to present its list of technical requirements for the phone system. They'd lay out in precise detail what kinds of surveillance powers they needed, and what the telecoms were expected to provide. The privacy advocates were dragging their feet in the negotiations, FBI officials concluded. Delay would invite more debate, probably hearings, and possibly a less favorable outcome. Freeh made the political call: Let's take what we can get here.

In early 1995, the Justice Department issued its list of requirements for wiretapping, known as the "punch list." Telecom executives and their lawyers were dumbfounded. They thought the requirements exceeded reasonable needs for the government and violated the spirit of negotiation from the previous summer. Al Gidari, a lawyer who represented the wireless industry, was among the first to see the FBI's punch list during a standards-setting meeting in Vancouver, British Columbia. He thought it looked like the Cadillac of wiretaps.

Everything that the bureau could think of was on that list. It would be exponentially more difficult for the companies to comply with these demands, Gidari thought. This went beyond simple wiretapping. There were highly technical processes involved in the kinds of sophisticated surveillance that the government now imagined doing. Their list eventually grew to include real-time geographical tracking of mobile phones; the ability to monitor all parties in a conference call regardless of whether they were on hold or participating; and "dialed digit extraction," a record of any numbers that a subject under surveillance punched in during a call, such as a credit card or bank account number.

The FBI wouldn't be the only user of this data, of course. If the system were engineered to provide this fine level of data legally, the intelligence agencies would want it too. Again, the premise of wiretapping wasn't in question. But now serious doubts were rising about whether the government's consumption of information would stop with a simple phone call.

The standards meetings were tense and awkward, and the sides were unevenly matched. On one side of a conference table sat a dozen FBI agents, humorless, wearing neat blue suits—buttoned down and ready to roll over their opponents. On the other side, a disheveled, laid-back, quirky bunch of network engineers representing the telecom carriers and the equipment makers. It fell to them to tell the FBI, No, you can't have this. These are precisely the kinds of terms that the law says you cannot dictate.

The meetings bore no resemblance to negotiation. Some of what the government wanted looked illegally broad. Much of it just seemed excessive. The level of government surveillance was so low at that time that some questioned why the FBI wanted multifaceted access. In 1994, federal and state authorities were running only 1,154 wiretaps nationwide, mostly for drug investigations, at an average cost of fifty thousand dollars each. Intelligence wiretaps under FISA were rarer. As Gidari saw it, the government was asking carriers to design a nuclear rocket ship for a flight from Chicago to D.C. It seemed to him that officials thought there was no limit to the expense the companies should bear in order to save a life.

When the companies protested that the surveillance specifications were too complex, and that they'd add extra cost and force the equipment makers to adopt rigid technical standards, the government questioned the companies' loyalties. In one meeting Gidari watched as FBI and Justice officials slammed their hands on a table and screamed, "You're unpatriotic! What do you want to do, help the criminals?"

Unable to get everything it wanted from the punch list, the government petitioned the Federal Communications Commission, as the law allowed. Industry lawyers joined up with activists and told the commission that the negotiations had deadlocked because of the government's intransigence. Officials had made "unreasonable demands . . . for more surveillance features than either CALEA or the [analog] wiretap laws allow," they argued in legal papers. But the panel members were inclined to side with the government. The tussle dragged on for two more years, ending up in a court of appeals, where the FCC finally was overruled. The commission took up the matter again, and this time struck more of a balance between what officials wanted and the companies were prepared to give.

It was a temporary peace. Intelligence and law enforcement officials continued to eye changes to the law and made plans to go after the biggest prize of all—the Internet. Half a decade later the moment would arrive when a national crisis proved that the system had gotten out of their hands. Then, there would be no stopping them.

The FBI and the NSA had managed to survive the digital wave. The Clipper chip was ultimately junked, after privacy activists and a number of apolitical technology experts questioned its usefulness. But by the midnineties, the NSA, along with the rest of the government, could be sure that the networks would never be built beyond their eavesdropping capacity. That set a baseline for the information age. And it was the catalyst for a new, constant tension between the government and the governed that would last well into the next decade. The balance of power in a new world had been reset. And into those strange, uncharted waters, an aging sailor pointed his bow.

CHAPTER 6

THE GENOA PROJECT

Now nearly sixty, John Poindexter had assumed the curious existence of a Washington pariah: not really gone but officially not still around.

It was 1995, a decade since the Iran-Contra affair. And it wasn't that people were afraid to be seen with him. In a closet the size of Washington, skeletons never stayed put for long. Poindexter's friends and associates even could make light of the "scandal," a word he hated hearing people use, that sullied Reagan's twilight years and ensured Poindexter's status as an ignominious footnote. At a luncheon hosted by the Naval Academy, some time after the controversy had dissipated, Poindexter was seated at the same table as Tom Clancy, the bestselling master of the cold war sea story. His most recent book, *Clear and Present Danger*, centered on a renegade national security adviser and his deputy who wage a secret war in Central America and, in a climactic scene, try to delete the e-mails detailing their exploits. "Admiral," Clancy said across the table, "I just want you to know that I did not base the character in my book on *you*!" Poindexter smiled and nodded.

He had appealed his five felony convictions. His lawyers, paid for by friends and political supporters, argued that the testimony Poindexter had given to Congress under a grant of immunity was improperly used against him at trial. In November 1991, a panel of three federal judges agreed and overturned the jury's verdict. It was a quiet vindication. He had occasion to thank George H. W. Bush personally for not pardoning him: "I'm glad I did it on my own," he told him a few months later, at a White House ceremony honoring former president Reagan with the Medal of Freedom. Reagan, now in his early eighties, had testified for Poindexter in his criminal trial. But when he reached a now frailer man in the receiving line, he could see the disease was in bloom. "Mr. President, I'm John Poindexter," he said, reintroducing himself.

Plenty of people remembered Poindexter fondly, enough to erase any regret that his prodigious confidence and sense of righteousness couldn't. About a year after his conviction was overturned, Poindexter was stopped in his driveway by a man walking with his two daughters. "Aren't you Admiral Poindexter?" he asked. "Yes," he replied.

"Well, I just wanted to thank you and to tell you what a great man I think you are."

One of the daughters was confused. "Daddy, who is this?" she inquired.

"Well, this is Admiral Poindexter." It didn't register. "What does he do?" she asked.

The man thought a moment. "He helped the country. He used to work for the president."

People often remarked to Poindexter that the tumult of the past years didn't seem to have taken a toll on him. This was why. Moments like this sustained him.

Poindexter's contempt for Congress was not diminished by the spectacle of televised testimony before the joint committee investigating Iran-Contra. The lawmakers who had hauled him before the cameras hoping he'd hand them a smoking gun were incensed to watch him fall on his sword. Reagan had known nothing of the diversion of funds to the Contras, Poindexter said. He had authorized the operation himself and deliberately kept the president in the dark, a gift of plausible deniability.

"The buck stops here with me," he intoned.

Years later the image of the admiral sitting placidly before the lawmakers, seemingly disinterested as he stared through his trifocals, still burned on their minds with the slow intensity of the tobacco embers that coughed smoke into the hearing room from Poindexter's pipe. He smoked throughout the proceedings, lighting the bowl with a silver Zippo that was mailed to him by the owner of the company, an ardent political supporter.

The buck really had stopped with him. An independent investigator, a wave of journalists, and the president's attorneys spent years scrubbing every inch of documentary evidence on Iran-Contra. They conducted hundreds of hours of interviews and found no evidence that Poindexter had lied abut the president's role. That hardly exonerated either man; indeed, for many it reaffirmed just how unforgivably out of touch Reagan had been all along, and that Poindexter really was the rogue people had long described. But Poindexter's fall had saved Reagan's presidency. It was, in his eyes, a final act of service. Had Congress determined that Reagan knew of the diversion, and authorized it, they would have pursued impeachment.

The turmoil of that bitter period failed to diminish Poindexter's politics, his pride, or his passion. But it did take away his status. He had staked his career on trying to change a system from the inside, and he had failed.

But then a window opened. In late 1995, one of Poindexter's old academy classmates surfaced with a tempting invitation. He was working for a technology firm in Northern Virginia called Syntek. The business was started by another legendary Navy man, Reuven Leopold, who for most of the 1970s was the Navy's technical director for ship design. Leopold had spent much of his career fighting wars from the drawing board; he led the construction of twenty-one classes of vessels, including the famed Spruance destroyers. But now, with the Navy cutting back its shipbuilding budgets, Leopold wanted in on the next big thing: information technology. And he was eyeing a promising new program in the Pentagon's research and development office about which he thought Poindexter might have some special insight.

It was called Spinnaker, and it caught Poindexter's attention for more reasons than its nautical nomenclature. For starters, he was a great fan of the agency running the program—the Defense Advanced Research Projects Agency. Housed in an unassuming office building across the Potomac River in Northern Virginia, DARPA was the Pentagon's futurist brain trust. Its researchers had built the first "Internet." They developed stealth technology that turned aircraft invisible. DARPA tackled what researchers called the "hard problems," challenges for which a solution was years, perhaps decades, away. It was Poindexter's kind of place, reminiscent in some ways of the Whiz Kids' shop under McNamara but on a grander, far more ambitious and systematic scale. DARPA's province was one of risky ventures with revolutionary potential. The agency embraced failure as a necessary part of an idea's evolution.

Spinnaker fell under the aegis of DARPA's Information Systems Office, a unit whose mandate was as broad as its title. Information technology, particularly computer software, was altering the course of human society in ways that most people couldn't quite articulate but still understood were fundamentally important. But the fervor hadn't seized the ranks of the U.S. government, which remained locked in a technological dark age. The wave emanating from Silicon Valley hadn't yet swept over Washington.

A lot had changed in the decade since Poindexter left government. Now the technology existed to start building more sophisticated versions of the intelligence fusion centers and sharing systems that he had envisioned at the White House. Most of it was manufactured by companies, not by federal agencies. New products and concepts portended an information revolution, and DARPA wanted to harness it.

The military and intelligence agencies had built the world's most complex computer systems, and yet they hadn't exploited new, off-the-shelf technology that was putting once unimaginable computing power on desktop machines. Average Americans reaped the benefits. And yet spies and soldiers still worked on proprietary and clunky systems that were plodding a path toward obsolescence. There were smarter, faster ways to do business. And there was an imperative to change. America's cold war foes were vanquished, but a new breed of "transnational" threats was rising—terrorist groups, so-called rogue nations, and other adversaries that didn't play by the traditional rules of war. The United States had to outsmart its enemies by predicting their next moves. The Information Systems Office was designing information technologies to do just that.

Leopold wanted to win a support contract under Spinnaker. Typically, DARPA programs relied heavily on outside experts for development, and their own staff of managers turned over at regular intervals to keep the agency infused with fresh thinking. Leopold needed someone to spearhead his Spinnaker team. Would Poindexter be willing to attend a meeting with the DARPA program manager?

He hardly needed to ask. One afternoon, Poindexter headed over to the DARPA offices to meet with Brian Sharkey, a taciturn ex–submarine hunter. As Poindexter listened to Sharkey talk about his ideas, and what he wanted to accomplish, he realized he could have been listening to himself ten years earlier. Sharkey envisioned a collaborative system that would reach across disparate databases and help foresee the next disaster. Senior decision makers were the ultimate customer. The ones overwhelmed by a deluge of information. By noise. Sharkey was proposing much the same technological system that Poindexter had always wanted to build. Sharkey had the notion, and the funding. Poindexter had the vision and the will. And he brought two other invaluable qualities to the table: technological prowess and an intimate understanding of how the national security community worked. And how it often didn't.

The meeting broke up, and Leopold asked Poindexter if he'd come aboard at Syntek, under contract to Sharkey. As with so many of his most fateful decisions, Poindexter didn't think for very long. He'd been running a small software consultancy with a friend. But his sole client, an ambitious California-based company, was in danger of being vanquished by Microsoft. Recently, Poindexter had taught himself several complex computer programming languages, and he'd perfected his skills by designing a system to spot minute errors in software code, a task not that dissimilar to finding hidden signals in noisy data. He was more technologically fluent than at any point in his life. He was equipped. And since he had retained his full Navy pension after retiring in 1987, he wasn't worried about financial survival.

Poindexter agreed to Leopold's offer. He was back on a path he'd stumbled off years ago.

In January 1996, he joined the staff as a senior vice president. He had a new office. A new team. And Sharkey was gearing up for a new phase of Spinnaker, building on the first phase of research. He was looking for a new name, but the best he'd come up with didn't exactly inspire: Collaborative Crisis Understanding and Management. Poindexter didn't like it. Mindful that bureaucracies refer to programs almost entirely by their acronyms, he suggested that Sharkey's choice was . . . unfortunate. A number of his female colleagues apparently had raised the same point already.

"We need to change the name," Poindexter advised. Why not continue with the sail family? Something easy to remember but also symbolic. Thus, Spinnaker became Genoa, named for the headsail that's used when moving against the wind.

Sharkey had tried to make some headway on his own, by drumming up interest among the National Security Council staff, which was arguably where Spinnaker would be needed most. But Sharkey was a technician, not a pitchman. Some who'd heard his early descriptions of the idea thought it sounded rather fanciful—some kind of crystal ball to predict the future. Sharkey hadn't been able to translate for the staffers in language they could understand.

Poindexter wanted another shot. He called a former secretary, Wilma Hall, a career employee still working on the NSC staff. She was glad to hear from her old boss. It had been a while. Poindexter brought her up to speed on his new project. "Who's the right person on the staff now to talk to about this?" he asked.

"Oh, it's Dick Clarke," Hall said without hesitation. "He's the Ollie North of this administration."

Poindexter smiled. The go-to guy. He dialed Clarke's office and arranged a meeting; Clarke's assistant was more than happy to make room in the schedule for a former national security adviser, and an admiral.

Like North, Clarke ran the counterterrorism portfolio for the NSC staff. He'd forged a close working relationship with the national security adviser, Tony Lake. Clarke stood out as an innovative, hard-charging, and passionate operator who could navigate treacherous bureaucratic channels without attracting the wrong kind of attention. He'd risen steadily at the State Department, taking over a senior intelligence post in 1985, when North was in his prime at the White House. But when Clarke took over the political and military affairs brief, he ran afoul of investigators over, of all things, improper missile sales through Israel.

In 1992, State's inspector general chided Clarke for not acting on intelligence reports that Israel had improperly given or sold air-to-air and antitank missiles to third parties, including China, South Africa, Ethiopia, and Chile. The defense secretary, Dick Cheney, also accused Israel of illegally sharing Patriot Missile technology with China. It was the job of Clarke's department at State to investigate such allegations. But at the time, factions at State, in the Pentagon, and at the CIA were warring internally and with one another over the United States' Israel policy and what role America's key Middle Eastern ally should play after the cold war. The furor, or lack thereof, over the weapons deals were emblematic of each camp's appraisal of the others—one was too indulgent with the Israelis, the other was making life too hard on them. Clarke, the inspector general's investigation implied, was rooted in the former camp, and he had failed to do his job. He was transferred out of State and landed on the NSC staff, where he was asked to stay when Bill Clinton took the oath of office.

Clarke's first test on terrorism came quickly. On February 26, 1993, only thirty-eight days into the new administration, Islamic extremists set off a truck bomb in the parking garage of One World Trade Center. They'd hoped to topple one of the Twin Towers into the other, killing tens of thousands, but the massive buildings withstood the blast. Six died.

When the bomb went off, the intricate system of crisis management that Poindexter and North had built was nowhere to be found. In fact, it had been completely dismantled. In the late 1980s, when George H. W. Bush inherited the ghost of Iran-Contra, he directed his NSC staff to get out of the operations business. No longer would the White House direct the terrorist wars. The administration had paid too high a price for Poindexter and North's zealous pursuits. The crisis management center and its intelligence feeds were shut down. Officials threw out a manual on crisis indicators, meant to carry lessons forward into subsequent administrations. By the time Clarke came to the White House the nexus of the entire government's counterterrorism mission had disintegrated. And it had never been fully recaptured by another agency.

Clarke could see that firsthand when the bomb went off. No one in the Situation Room alerted him. Indeed, it took a call from his boss, Tony Lake, asking what in the hell just happened in New York to prompt Clarke to contact the Sit Room himself. A young Navy officer on duty answered the phone and hesitantly told Clarke that he wasn't sure whether he was supposed to call him about these kinds of things. Terrorism was just one of a number of generic "global" issues Clarke had been assigned. No one in the White House was on point for a domestic terrorist attack.

Clarke had managed to cobble together an anemic version of the Crisis Pre-Planning Group from the Reagan years. His Counterterrorism Security Group (CSG) included representatives from around government, principally the FBI and the CIA. But the members had limited influence with their home agencies, which regarded terrorism as a low priority. Indeed, the CIA's counterterrorist center was perceived as a dumping ground for career dead-enders, a kind of Land of Misfit Toys that offered little hope for promotion. The FBI, for its part, thought of terrorism as a foreign intelligence concern and therefore out of its lane both legally and professionally. The bureau stuck mostly to bank robbers, mobsters, and drug runners. The CIA and State could handle mad mullahs.

After the World Trade Center bombing, Clarke convened the CSG in the Situation Room, but the group came up empty on leads. The FBI had managed to identify the perpetrators through a painstaking forensic process at the bomb site, but none of the names got hits in the CIA's database. The bombers didn't belong to Hezbollah, Islamic Jihad, or any of the other known outfits. The FBI had learned that two of the men appeared at Kennedy airport the previous year without any immigration papers; one was detained when officials saw him carrying a manual titled "How to Make a Bomb." But he claimed political asylum, and so immigration officers let the man go with an admonishment to show up later at a status hearing.

Clarke was aghast. These guys had appeared out of nowhere, catching the entire national security community by surprise. What cracks had they slipped through? How many signals had been missed in the buildup to their attack? And what else did they have in store?

The 1993 bombing showed Clarke just how weak the government's early-warning capability had become. He spent the next few years pushing terrorism steadily up the list of threats. Clarke couldn't give orders to anyone outside the White House, so he had to finagle and fight for his authorities. But still, he managed to find the levers and trigger points, as well as the pools of money, in what passed for the government's counterterrorism enterprise.

By the time Poindexter called asking for a meeting, Clarke was very interested in the potential of information technology to uncover useful pieces of intelligence and to better connect the far-flung agencies nominally managing the terrorism problem.

"He's interested in widgets," Wilma Hall told Poindexter over the phone.

Clarke was also focusing lately on a shadowy Saudi expatriate named Osama bin Laden, whom the CIA had identified as a mere terrorist money-man, but who was clearly emerging as the commander of a troubling new terrorist network.

Poindexter approached the Old Executive Office Building, next door to the White House. It had been a while; aside from a few official visits, the last time he'd walked the floors of the palacelike building that had housed the Crisis Management Center, he was in uniform.

Poindexter walked the halls of the house he'd help build and, though he'd never wished for it, take apart. Old friends and staff who had stayed aboard in career billets stopped to greet him. When he let them know why he'd come calling, it all seemed so obvious. Of course he should be talking to Dick Clarke.

Poindexter knew just where to find Clarke's office—it was the one that Ollie North used to occupy. Clarke spotted the admiral coming through the door, and he rose to greet him.

"Hello, Admiral! It's been a long time." Clarke grasped Poindexter's hand, and his searching expression gave Clarke his cue. "Remember?" he asked. "I was with you on the trip to Oman."

The memory quickly filtered back to him. Yes, it was 1984, when Poindexter was talking to Oman and Saudi Arabia about basing a U.S. air squadron. The State Department had sent Clarke as its representative. Poindexter still didn't remember Clarke clearly, but apparently they had a history. They sat down, and as the conversation turned to Genoa, Poindexter could see they shared a common language as well.

Clarke was no technologist, but he intuitively grasped the concepts Poindexter articulated, now in a much more cogent and realistic form than Sharkey had been able to do. This wasn't magic. It was science. A systematic, decision-support tool, as the researchers liked to call it. Genoa was meant to help stop a World Trade Center bombing, or to more quickly pick up the pieces after the event. Already, Poindexter explained, the researchers were focusing on terrorism as an obvious application, and they'd studied one attack in detail.

In March 1995, members of a Japanese religious cult called Aum Shinrikyo released plastic bags full of sarin nerve gas in five Tokyo subway trains. A dozen commuters died, and hundreds were sickened by the toxic agent. The Genoa team researched the buildup to that attack, looking for signals that might have alerted observant analysts. They found quite a few.

For starters, the subway attack wasn't Aum's first use of chemical weapons. Only nine months earlier seven people had died from a sarin release in the mountain city of Matsumoto. Police blamed a local man who stored pesticides in his home; both he and his wife were sickened. Although investigators found no immediate linkage to Aum, other suspicious indicators preceding the Matsumoto attack went unchecked. In June 1993, the cult purchased a half-million-acre sheep farm in Western Australia. Locals reported seeing dead animals about the property—tests later confirmed they'd been poisoned with sarin. The cult sold the ranch less than a year later, at a loss.

Also in June 1993, noxious fumes emanating from a Tokyo building connected to Aum caused area neighbors to complain to authorities. Residents living near another facility complained almost a year later of peculiar smells. Then, in September 1994, more than two hundred people in seven towns in western Japan came down with rashes and eye irritations from unknown fumes. Less than three months later, an Aum member killed a man with VX nerve gas. And finally, within two weeks of the subway attack, eleven people were hospitalized after inhaling fumes on a train in Yokohama, less than twenty miles from Tokyo. Officials also found three attaché cases containing liquid, fans, vents, and batteries in a Tokyo subway station.

The Genoa researchers determined that all these signals were either known, or knowable, to government investigators and law enforcement officials. Much of the data appeared in news reports. No one had put the pieces together. The researchers concluded that if someone—or some system—had done so, Japanese officials could have stopped Aum from attacking the subway.

In sizing up the cult, the Genoa team focused on its ability to carry out an attack, not the attack itself. What materials would the cult members have to buy? Where would they practice? When would they conduct surveillance on potential targets? These were the questions with which terrorism analysts would fan out into the information space, looking for evidence, discarding false leads, building a hypothesis. Genoa aimed to understand not only the most likely path terrorists would take but other less obvious avenues they might pursue. For instance, if Aum could release sarin in a train, why not in the ventilation system of an office building? Indeed, the cult had tried to release anthrax spores and botulinum toxin, dabbled with cholera and Q fever, and tried to retrieve a strain of the Ebola virus in Zaire.

Genoa could handle queries from the top down: A policy maker comes up with a hypothesis about how a terrorist might attack and then uses the system to look for supporting evidence. But it also worked from the bottom up: An analyst starts by collecting disparate pieces to see what kind of story they tell. The system then constructed a transparent argument, like a sentence diagram, about what was most likely to happen. Analysts and decision makers could look at the diagram on their own computers and then edit it, adding new documents or reports, tweaking theories. They could debate not just each other's conclusions but the intelligence that led to them. In that sense, Genoa was revolutionary: It promised to flush out the parochial vagaries and biases that infused most intelligence and inevitably helped politicize it.

Clarke would have understood as well as anyone how intelligence often was abused and misused by human analysts. Could machines remedy that? He seemed hopeful.

Poindexter made it clear that Genoa would never replace human analysts. It was an aid, a way to take the heavy lifting, and the drudgery, out of the process, and to give everyone in the system more time to think.

Clarke nodded, affirming that he understood, and that he liked the idea. Poindexter wanted the NSC staff to use Genoa, to put the system through its paces and help work out the bugs. Now he had Clarke in his corner, at least.

"Keep me advised," he told Poindexter as they wrapped up their discussion. Clarke walked him to the door. "I'm glad to see you're back."

There was someone Poindexter needed to meet. After his meeting with Clarke another NSC staffer steered the admiral to the neighboring suite, the Office of Intelligence Programs.

"Mary, meet John Poindexter," the staffer said, making the introduction to Mary McCarthy, a career CIA officer who had joined the staff in 1996 as the office's number two. McCarthy had last served as the national intelligence officer for warning, whose job was, broadly speaking, to make sure the intelligence community wasn't taken by surprise. That she should know Poindexter seemed eminently logical.

McCarthy had never met him. She knew he was an admiral. Of course she knew Iran-Contra. But upon first glance, she thought he could have been an English professor as easily as a former national security adviser. McCarthy also knew he was a Republican, but in her experience so far, partisanship rarely came between professionals. McCarthy, who didn't hide the fact that she was a Democrat, had worked for plenty of Republicans, including the man who'd helped Poindexter and North build the first pieces of a government-wide counterterrorism operation, Charlie Allen. McCarthy was his deputy when Allen was in charge of warning at the CIA, and she took over his job in 1994. She revered Allen and told people that everything she knew about the business, she'd learned from him.

Poindexter briefly gave McCarthy the rundown on the Genoa program. What it was about. What problems he was hoping to tackle. As she listened, McCarthy had to pinch herself. This was her soapbox.

McCarthy disdained the analytic capability of her home agency, the CIA. She'd been trying to point out where the analysts were falling down. To her mind they were more concerned about writing pretty prose than collecting and weighing facts. McCarthy had published articles connecting this systemic problem to high-profile intelligence failures. And she was concerned about the implications for counterterrorism. Her old boss, Charlie Allen, had been the last national intelligence officer for terrorism—the position, as with so many others, had been a casualty of the Iran-Contra scandal. The only unit left doing warning for terrorism was the CIA's counterterrorist center, which McCarthy thought was an amateur operation.

Of course, McCarthy evinced none of this to Poindexter who, though retired, was so many years and ranks her senior. But as she listened she realized that she didn't have to say a word. They were already in sync.

"One of these days I'd like to come back and talk to you about my project," Poindexter said. She was surprised that he'd phrased it as a request. If a man of Poindexter's stature could make an issue of these problems, and improve the quality of not only the product but the intellectual process of analysis, she wanted to help. "Fine," McCarthy replied. "I'll be anxious to hear."

Poindexter kept Clarke updated, as he'd requested, but McCarthy became his primary contact in the White House. She was so different from most CIA officers; open to new ideas, to technology, but also not afraid to be wrong. And she held a position of influence among those Poindexter most wanted to impress.

McCarthy became Genoa's best advocate on the NSC staff. She helped to introduce Poindexter to the people who might actually use the tool or who'd be willing to experiment with it in their own agencies. She helped Poindexter attract a wide audience.

When it came time for the Genoa researchers to explain their ideas to the curious, they put on a show. In a black box–style performance space at DARPA headquarters, the team constructed a mock-up of a crisis command center. A team of actors sat at computer screens and deftly responded as an imaginary nightmare unfolded before the audience's eyes. Poindexter called it "A Day in the Life of an Analyst." Sometimes the performance was augmented by an animated video segment; McCarthy even showed up as an avatar.

The team built another staging center near the DARPA building, hiring a Hollywood set designer and former head of Disney Imagineering to give the place a futuristic quality. There was a little magic in Genoa after all. But what Poindexter wanted most was for his audience to appreciate what Genoa could be. The system was still in its infancy. There was no equipment behind the bright, flashing screens. But the scene was compelling enough to leave visitors with the distinct impression that maybe Poindexter and his wizards were onto something.

All the right people were coming to the shows. Clarke attended. So did a recently retired rear admiral named Mike McConnell, who'd stepped down as the director of the National Security Agency and taken a lucrative position as head of the intelligence business for Booz Allen Hamilton, a top-shelf consulting firm. Another former intelligence luminary also made an appearance— James Clapper, whose most recent position among a series of high offices was director of the Defense Intelligence Agency. He was also a senior member of the Downing Assessment Task Force, convened to investigate the June 1996 bombing of Khobar Towers, a U.S. military housing complex in Saudi Arabia.

Nineteen service members died there in the second attack on U.S. forces in Saudi Arabia in less than a year.

Poindexter had invited these wise men of the spy world not so much to find customers but to ask them if he was heading in the right direction. To a person, it seemed, everyone supported his ambition. They thought the problems he had tackled needed to be solved. The Genoa team was on the right track, exploring a new frontier. Poindexter was starting to build a power that they needed.

But he wasn't the only one.

CHAPTER 7

THE NEXT GENERATION

When Curt Weldon picked up the phone to call George Tenet, the director of the CIA, he wasn't expecting much. The agency had let the congressman down plenty of times; why should this one be any different?

Through an improbable series of adventures, Weldon had risen from the rough streets of Marcus Hook, Pennsylvania, where he grew up and served two terms as mayor, to Republican member of Congress and intelligence gadfly. An obstreperous debater, Weldon delighted in pointing out the many shortcomings of a bloated, disconnected, and at times politically defiant bureaucracy. The agency's so-called intelligence failures were legion—missing the collapse of the Soviet Union, failing to predict entrants into the nuclear club. More often than not America's spies seemed out of touch with a world quickly evolving beyond them. And so, when Weldon called Tenet in April 1999 to report that he knew of a foreign source who might help end the vicious ethnic war raging in the Balkans, he had reason to believe the CIA couldn't tell him much about the man.

That a seventh-term congressman from hardscrabble Pennsylvania was even in a position to have such contacts was perhaps the most improbable part of Weldon's career journey, and one of constant annoyance for the Clinton administration. For reasons that must have escaped many people who knew him, Weldon majored in Russian studies. He learned to speak the language fluently and, with little effort, became Congress's foremost Kremlinologist. He collected friends and sources in the former Soviet Union and its satellite states. By the mid-1990s, much to the State Department's chagrin,

Weldon had fashioned himself into a diplomat without portfolio. He trotted the globe, visiting with world leaders—and a few outcasts—on unofficial, and unendorsed, visits. As with the intelligence community, Weldon liked to publicly enumerate the ways the Clinton administration was spoiling its relations with potential allies. And, of course, he happily volunteered his services toward their repair.

Weldon called Tenet after receiving urgent calls to his office from contacts in the Russian Duma. NATO bombs and missiles had started falling on Yugoslavia two weeks earlier. The world had been waiting for Western intervention while thousands of ethnic Albanians in Kosovo were being murdered or displaced by the marauding Yugoslav army. Now the Clinton administration wanted those soldiers out of Kosovo, and they were prepared to topple Yugoslav president Slobodan Milošević to do it.

That put the Russians on edge. "We've got a real problem," Weldon's contacts fretted. Moscow was suspicious of Clinton's real intent in bombing Yugoslav civilian and military targets. Did he want to oust Milošević or to extend America's sphere of influence? It was hard to tell.

"What do you want me to do?" Weldon asked.

He should convince President Clinton that Russia could help end the war and get Milošević out, the Russians said. They intended to go to Belgrade to meet with the besieged leader. Weldon should come as the United States' representative.

This wasn't a public relations stunt, they promised. They would take Weldon, and any other congressmen who wanted to join him, to a refugee camp, so they could see for themselves the human suffering Milošević had caused. They also would intercede with the government to get it to release three American soldiers captured near the border with Macedonia. And the Russians assured Weldon they would set up a meeting with Milošević himself at a future date, to persuade him to step down.

Weldon was surprised that the Russians could offer so much. How would they deliver? The Russians replied that they had a man in Belgrade. A close personal friend of Milošević who could convince the president to end the war, with certain commitments.

"Who is he?" Weldon asked. His name was Dragomir Karic.

Weldon had never heard of him. Where had the Russians found this guy?

And how did he know Milošević? If anyone *should* know, it was the CIA. "I don't know who this guy Karic is," Weldon told Tenet over the phone. "The Russians are convinced he can give us information that will allow us to get Milošević to agree to our terms. Can you tell me something about him?" Tenet said he'd look into it.

Weldon liked to kick the CIA in the ass, but he told himself it was tough love. He wanted the agency to succeed, thought they had to. But he had to keep them honest. A dogged proponent of missile defense, like many of his fellow Republicans, Weldon once walked out on a closed-door briefing by CIA officials who had told him there was little risk that China or North Korea would fire off a ballistic missile at a U.S. city. Weldon claimed to have his own intelligence sources and firmly believed such an attack was not only plausible but imminent.

The CIA's assessment, contained in a National Intelligence Estimate, infuriated the congressman, and he publicly vented his appraisal of the secret document: "The NIE is the most outrageous politicization of an intelligence document that I've seen in the 10 years I've been in Washington," he told a reporter. Weldon was a master of rhetoric, and hyperbole was a favorite device. Tenet, himself a former Capitol Hill staffer, was used to handling men like Weldon, but he could test one's patience.

Tenet called Weldon back the next day, with little to report. His analysts had dug up a few sentences of information. "We think he's tied in with corruption in Russia," Tenet concluded. The same could be said for thousands of others, none of whom wanted to sit down with a congressional delegation. Useless, Weldon thought.

Weldon ran Karic's name up the flagpole with State Department officials, who were likewise at a loss. Strobe Talbott, the deputy secretary, warned Weldon not to meet with him in Belgrade. "We don't know who this person is," he cautioned. "He'll just use you."

But Weldon had set his mind to the task. He gathered a delegation of ten members, evenly divided between the two parties, and arranged for a flight. Weldon granted Talbott's request not to go to Belgrade by selecting an alternate meeting spot in Vienna.

Weldon still hadn't vetted Karic, a man who, for all the Russians' vouchsafing, had appeared with alarming suddenness. The CIA predictably had failed him. But Weldon had a plan B. He picked up the phone again, but this time he called his own sources.

When Erik Kleinsmith got the request from Weldon's office to draw up a profile on the enigmatic Karic, he didn't expect it to be an onerous task. The electronic sleuth with the Boy Scout demeanor had cracked much harder cases.

Kleinsmith recently had been assigned to the Information Dominance Center at Fort Belvoir, Virginia, just outside Washington. Weldon had become acquainted with the futuristic outfit during his relentless oversight of the intelligence community. He was enamored of the IDC's unconventional methods, and its people.

The IDC was a haven for computer-geeks-turned-soldiers like Kleinsmith. He and his civilian colleagues had wanted to ride on the bleeding edge of technology, and the IDC didn't disappoint; with its flat-panel screens, sleek surfaces, and mission commander chair in the center of the room, they could imagine they worked on the set of a science-fiction movie.

Kleinsmith and his fellow analysts were engaged in a dizzying array of secretive military operations. Much of their work involved tracking cyber attackers who relentlessly tried to penetrate military systems and steal secrets. The analysts had developed methods of tracking and tracing these bandits across cyberspace and, if need be, sending some digital fire their way in the form of a computer virus or an assault on their network. The IDC also practiced the dark art of information operations—the spread of lies, misinformation, and other forms of propaganda to make an adversary act contrary to his own best interests.

Kleinsmith was the chief of intelligence for the Land Information Warfare Activity, a subgroup of the larger Intelligence and Security Command. The IDC operated under LIWA's umbrella. Nestled deep within layers of acronyms, Kleinsmith suffered little outside interference. In the military bureaucracy, the lower one flew beneath the radar, the freer he could operate. Kleinsmith managed two dozen officers, soldiers, and civilian intelligence analysts. The IDC was their home base.

The analysts had a square-peg mind-set that the Army intelligence bureaucracy often rejected. Kleinsmith and his colleagues didn't always fit in, and they liked that. Their analytic methods relied heavily on information technology "tools," specially designed computer programs that processed vast amounts of electronic data and revealed connections among people, places, and activities that the human eye and mind often missed. The tools took the heavy lifting out of analysis, a tradecraft that had never kept up with the technological revolution. The IDC was a laboratory, and it attracted not just analysts but engineers looking to test the limits of the state of the art. Chief among them was a technologist named James Heath, who'd spent his career in the dark corners of the intelligence community crafting new surveillance and mining tools. He had visions of a master intelligence database, a collection of all the information known to all the agencies, held in one place that could be mined, sifted, and prodded. The IDC gave him a home base, and a testing facility. Kleinsmith and his peers saw Heath as a kind of "mad scientist," and they were often thrilled to work with him. People like this were so rare in the intelligence community.

The IDC relished testing new tools, putting them through their paces on real missions. Some broke under the strain. Some proved indispensable assets in the IDC's arsenal. The place was infused with a passion for the unconventional. And a hefty dose of competitiveness.

Kleinsmith enjoyed taking on tasks that befuddled the big agencies like the CIA and the Defense Intelligence Agency. They had an army of analysts and infinitely larger budgets than his scrappy outfit. But they didn't have his willingness to use new tools and methods, to take risks. Instead, other analysts adhered to an outdated tradecraft: read everything you can on a subject, become the expert, file everything you know away, and when someone comes looking for an answer, lecture them and intimidate them with all you seem to know. At least that's how Kleinsmith saw it.

Kleinsmith's immediate bosses had evangelized for the IDC's impressive capabilities. Some of the marketing was based in reality; a good bit of it was exaggerated. Still, the center was earning a reputation as a place to go when you needed to get things done quickly. Kleinsmith and his cohort of high-speed visionaries were cut from the same cloth as Poindexter and McCarthy.

Although they'd never met each other, their mutual ambition linked them. Even their physical environs shared a pedigree—the former Hollywood designer from Disney Imagineering who designed one of Poindexter's demonstration spaces for the Genoa project also designed the IDC. It mimicked one of his recent projects—the set for the fifth film in the *Star Trek* franchise.

Kleinsmith knew the Karic job would be pretty easy. Some quick research, mostly of "open sources" on the Internet like news articles. Then he'd package up a report and send it back to Weldon. It didn't require any detailed analysis; just organizing whatever information was available. And Kleinsmith could provide it faster; since the IDC was not classified in military parlance as a "producer" of intelligence, he could cut through layers of bureaucracy that slowed down other agencies. People could come to Kleinsmith directly to get answers. That also meant that whatever he sent back wasn't vetted according to community standards. But most of Kleinsmith's customers, including Weldon, could have cared less.

A day after he placed the call to the IDC, Weldon received its take on Karic. While the CIA had come up with a paragraph, Kleinsmith and his team produced an eight-page dossier.

The unofficial document claimed that not only was Karic tied to Milošević, but the men's wives and their siblings all were good friends. It said that Karic had four brothers, who owned one of the largest banking systems in Yugoslavia, employing some sixty thousand people. The bank had tried to finance the sale of an SA-10 missile system to Russia, the IDC discovered.

And that wasn't the half of it. The dossier also alleged that one of the Karic brothers had financed Milošević's election, that the house Milošević lived in belonged to the Karic boys, and that their wives were best friends with Milošević's wife. The IDC analysts said that they found all of this in the open source—information available to anyone with an Internet connection.

After reading the document, Weldon was convinced that Dragomir Karic and his siblings were the closest people in Yugoslavia to the embattled president. He was the genuine article, just as the Russians had promised. Armed with what he judged a thorough profile, Weldon and his fellow Congress members boarded a military plane for Vienna.

The delegation met for two days in a hotel with Karic and Weldon's Russian friends. Karic called Milošević several times on a portable phone. As the Americans and Russians negotiated a framework for compromise—which called for the release of prisoners and an international peacekeeping force— Karic relayed the details to Milošević. He agreed to the terms, on the condition that the delegation travel to Belgrade and meet with him in person. Karic said he'd provide the bus.

The American congressmen delighted over the possible end to the war— and the accompanying headlines in newspapers back home. Weldon called the State Department's Operations Center, raising the number three man at the department, Thomas Pickering, the former ambassador to Russia. He was unenthused.

Pickering still couldn't believe that Karic had the credibility to make these promises. The presence of the Russian delegation must have fueled speculation in the department that Moscow wanted to embarrass the Clinton administration. They would broker a deal with Congress instead. Force the White House to concede by releasing POWs as a sign of good faith. Pickering admonished Weldon that Karic was not to be trusted and that the delegation must not go to Belgrade.

Weldon relayed Pickering's misgivings, and Karic was incensed. "You just blew it!" he fumed to Weldon. They could have ended the war, he said. Some of the congressmen insisted they would still go to Milošević on their own, but Weldon forbid it.

Dejected, Weldon and his bipartisan gang got back on their plane. They would never know if Karic was the man the Russians claimed, the man that the IDC averred he was. The answer remained hidden as the plane lifted off from Vienna.

A few weeks after his return to Washington, Weldon's office got a phone call from the FBI. A couple of agents wanted to debrief him about Karic and his brothers.

"Fine," Weldon told his staff. "Set it up for next Monday." The congressman headed back to his home district for a scheduled visit. A few days later he received an emergency page from his staff, asking him to call the CIA's congressional liaison office immediately.

The agency wanted to fly two agents to Philadelphia right away. The State Department wanted to know more about Karic and had asked the CIA to find out. The agents would come to Weldon's home, a hotel, the airport, whatever he wanted.

They could wait. "The FBI already asked for that information," Weldon replied. "We can do it together on Monday afternoon."

Once again, Weldon found himself in an improbable spot: sitting in his Washington office with two G men and a pair of spooks who were begging *him* for information on an elusive Serbian banker. At the time, Weldon and his colleagues on the House's International Relations Committee were preparing for a hearing on diplomatic relations with Yugoslavia, at which Pickering was slated to testify. Apparently State had realized this Karic guy was interesting after all.

Weldon laid it all out for the agents. Karic. The brothers. The missile sales, the house, the wives. Weldon had been a schoolteacher before coming to Washington. When he'd finished the lecture, he asked, "Now, do you know where I got this information?"

The answer seemed obvious to the agents. From the Russians, and from Karic himself.

The congressman was delighted. "No," he said. "I got this from the Information Dominance Center."

The agents looked at him and at each other quizzically. "What's the Information Dominance Center?" one of them ventured to ask.

"They're the people who gave me eight pages," Weldon said. "The CIA gave me a paragraph."

He told the agents that both their organizations had come up short. And now, here they were asking a congressman to brief them, so they could report to the State Department.

"This is ridiculous," Weldon said.

NATO planes bombed Milošević's forces for seventy-seven days. The campaign convinced him of the alliance's resolve, and that Russia wasn't coming to his rescue. By mid-June he had withdrawn from Kosovo, under an agreement hammered out by the United States, the Russians, and the G8. Weldon had briefed the administration on the aborted Vienna agreement, and he told himself that it had provided a framework for the ultimate pact. He'd done his job.

But the encounter with the agents had left Weldon peeved. The Miloševićs of the world, and all the other big problems, were only going to get bigger. Human analysts slogged through swamps of data about an array of threats—warring ethnic factions in Albania, ascendant capitalists in China, dissident Saudi expatriates in Sudan. No one could keep it all straight, much less reach deeper conclusions about how the United States should act in this volatile world. Technology was the answer. Computers could do what humans couldn't—ingest heaps of data, then digest sensible, instructive information. The IDC was the next generation of intelligence, Weldon thought. He became its biggest congressional patron, singing the analysts' praises at the highest echelons of the Defense Department. And despite Weldon's outsized reputation, people listened.

Over at the Pentagon, word was getting around about the IDC's exploits. The armed services committee had been talking them up. And the military services, as well. Rumor was, the IDC could do amazing things. New things.

The men who ran the Defense Department decided it was time to put the tiny band of analysts through their paces, but this time on a bigger problem than Balkan businessmen.

CHAPTER 8

THE CHINA EXPERIMENT

John Hamre, the number two man at the Pentagon, had a big problem: Somehow, U.S. military secrets were ending up in Chinese hands. And he wasn't certain how.

The Defense Department had been aware for some time that hostile intelligence services were running agents against U.S. government facilities and military contractors, and Hamre, as the deputy secretary of defense, was actively trying to stop one aimed at the U.S. industrial base. But the scale and scope of clandestine operations were broader and more frightening than almost anyone outside the government knew.

In January 1999, a special congressional committee revealed that since at least the late 1970s, Chinese spies had stolen design information about advanced thermonuclear warheads from the U.S. national laboratories, a rich repository of military hardware secrets. The pilfered cache covered seven warheads, including all those currently deployed on U.S. ballistic missiles, as well as plans for the apocalyptic neutron bomb, which was designed to wipe out whole population centers with a massive dose of radiation. Chinese agents also had obtained other vital missile and satellite technology from U.S. companies allegedly doing unauthorized business with the Chinese government. The espionage was ongoing and heading toward a crucial point: The commission predicted that China had enough information to base the next generation of its nuclear arsenal on U.S. designs.

Hamre didn't really need a congressional investigation to tell him that the country's most sensitive secrets were up for grabs, and that the countermeasures in place to stop such a massive step were faltering. With the demise of the Soviet Union Congress and the administration had cut back intelligence budgets dramatically, a multibillion-dollar savings known as the "peace dividend." The agencies, along with the national labs and defense contractors, were becoming blind to the security threats arrayed against them, and in some cases appeared to unwittingly assist their adversaries. The very fiber of secrecy was disintegrating. So, Hamre decided to do something dramatic.

The government needed a new *counter*intelligence center for the post–cold war and national threats, he decided. And their first order of business should be to understand precisely how spies were "exfiltrating," in the parlance of the trade, so many technology assets. Hamre wanted to create a "threat mapping model" of the military technology supply chain. It should show all the security weak points, the conduits through which an individual could move secrets out of the country, physically or electronically. It wasn't enough to know that the labs or contractors writ large were vulnerable. How did the spies obtain access to those labs in the first place? Did they have contacts on the inside? Did they pose as legitimate researchers? And which technologies were most at risk of theft? In a losing game of Spy vs. Spy, Hamre wanted to know the bad guys' avenues of approach.

The question was, how? The intelligence agencies with their traditional craft had come up relatively empty. Hamre wondered whether this new counterintelligence unit needed to get ahead of the curve. A few months after the China report was released, Curt Weldon, who sat on the congressional committee that authorized it, recommended to Hamre that he pay a visit to the Information Dominance Center. He needed to see how these high-tech detectives were outrunning the CIA and others.

Hamre went down to Fort Belvoir. Not long after, he reported his impressions back to Weldon: "It's amazing what they're doing down there."

August was Washington's slow season, but Erik Kleinsmith was barely catching his breath from the Karic episode and the crush of a normal workday at the IDC. Requests were coming in from a range of customers now at the military command level. But when the call came down from Hamre's office, Kleinsmith snapped to attention.

The Pentagon had a challenge: Use advanced data-mining techniques to determine paths and avenues for hostile intelligence services. Hamre wanted to know whether he should invest in these cutting-edge tools for the new Joint Counterintelligence Assessment Group, or JCAG. Officially, what Hamre asked the IDC to do was just an experiment. But Kleinsmith saw a perfect opportunity to impress the Pentagon brass. *Let's show them what we've got.*

The rules of the game were simple. The IDC should pick a sensitive military technology, and then map out how individuals, working together or collectively, could gain access to U.S. facilities, obtain sensitive information, and then take it back to China. They should nail down, in as much detail as possible, which labs or companies had been compromised, which organizations were behind the theft, and—perhaps most important—which facilities were most at risk. This wasn't an investigation of past abuses. Congress had taken care of that. This was now about preemption. Kleinsmith and his team would have access to a limited number of classified databases, but they could also mine the Internet.

The IDC had a range of technologies to choose from for their experiment, but it was really an arbitrary point. The tools and techniques would work just the same. Kleinsmith and his team decided to focus on component technologies in the Joint Strike Fighter, a stealth aircraft then in development and upon which the military had pinned much of its future fighting strategy. A small group of three analysts started with wide search strings, looking for pairings of their target technology with "China," "espionage," "export." They stretched digital reapers through the classified databases and across the fertile field of the Internet, pulling in thousands of Web pages containing potentially relevant information. They retrieved an enormous harvest.

Next, Kleinsmith and the analysts took a first pass with their mining tools, separating potential leads from dead ends, wheat from chaff. Typically, some connections just seemed implausible on their face, or obviously coincidental, and the analysts used their common sense to help them sort things out. The initial take showed tantalizing correlations among universities, national laboratories, and Chinese nationals, all of which popped up as references in news articles, intelligence reports, and other sources in the harvest. This was just a first step, but it hadn't taken Kleinsmith very long.

The beauty of the IDC's approach, Kleinsmith had always thought, wasn't its ability to collect information. Vacuuming up the Internet or a database was a crude technique compared with what he did next: convert all that information into a picture.

Kleinsmith ran a collection of now filtered information through a "visualization tool." In a matter of seconds it read all the information, which consisted of news stories, Web pages, classified cable traffic, and other documents, and then pulled out pieces of information such as names, places, and actions. Something discernible, with a clear point of reference in the harvest.

Then the tool plotted each document as a small point on a graphic map. A trade press article about satellite acquisitions by the Chinese military, say. Or a cable from the embassy in Beijing about a space research delegation visiting universities in California. Documents with similar subjects appeared close together. Then the tool created peaks, signaling a high concentration of documents about a specific topic. This was the visual component. The distance between two peaks showed how closely those topics were related.

As Kleinsmith stepped back and took in the entire map, he could see the landscape of information. And with that, he could start to ask questions. What does the harvest say? Who are the most important people? Where were the gaps in his intelligence base? The tool let an analyst click on a specific data point and pull up the underlying report, to read it in full and put it in context. One could suddenly not just see the forest but zoom in on a single tree.

This kind of production, from beginning to end, would have taken large teams of analysts weeks, if not months, to complete. They'd have to manually collect the data first, or use proprietary searching tools that only let them scan one or a few databases. Then they'd have to draw all the links themselves. And they certainly would not have used the Internet for source material.

Kleinsmith's approach offered liberation. It was as if he and his analysts had grown wings, and slipped the coil of gravity that kept their colleagues toiling in a vineyard of data. They soared over the terrain, dove down into the valleys, rested on peaks. Although Kleinsmith's rapid-fire version of analysis would, only a few years later, essentially be available to the masses through Internet search engines and online collaboration sites, at the time, in 1999, his approach was something marvelous.

And rather dangerous.

As Kleinsmith and his team worked through their China harvest, the pervasiveness of the espionage startled them. But the fact that they had discovered it with relative ease, that the clues were out there for the taking, surprised none of them.

The harvest had gotten them only so far. This high-tech analysis was not magic, as Kleinsmith often reminded his customers, particularly when they came calling in desperation. At some point the analysts had to put their own skills to work.

The analysis indicated that Chinese agents had access to the target technology through the labs and research facilities of a number of U.S. universities. Kleinsmith wanted to know which ones they should focus on first, as they might represent the weakest points. Armed with that threat-mapping model, as Hamre wanted, counterintelligence agents could get to work plugging leaks.

Kleinsmith and a colleague spread out a map of the United States on a table in the team's workspace. He scanned the terrain, not immediately sure what he hoped to find. Lots of cities. Lots of rivers.

Rivers.

Without saying a word, Kleinsmith grabbed a stack of yellow Post-it notes and a pair of scissors. He cut the notes into triangles and affixed them to apparently random points on the map.

"What are you doing?" his puzzled colleague asked.

"I'm marking the areas where they're stealing this stuff."

"How do you know?"

He drew a path down the St. Lawrence River from Canada, into New York, and onto the Great Lakes. Sixteenth-century explorers had used this route when they first came to North America, he explained. Invading French and British armies had used it. Even the Germans snuck U-boats into the river during World War II. The river was a natural entrance point to the continent, and on its banks, hubs of commerce and activity had sprung up. "If you go back and look at intel," Kleinsmith told his colleague, "you'll see that the pattern of theft fits the river."

She checked. Indeed, the intelligence indicated that the technology in question was either found at or associated with universities and corporate facilities located in the geographic corridor Kleinsmith had isolated. He never thought that Chinese spies were floating missile parts up the St. Lawrence River. But he knew that this place, over time, was a beehive of activity. People and goods moved in and out. They conducted trade. They waged wars. These were entry and exit points. People come in, they take things out, whether physical devices or useful information.

If the Pentagon wanted a way to model the espionage threat, here it was. Go back to history, formulate a hypothesis, and then see what the intelligence says. It all seemed perfectly logical.

To Kleinsmith and his tiny team, the conclusions of their analysis were inescapable. The Chinese had established a veritable underground network inside the United States. The analysis showed front companies probably controlled by government officials. Ostensibly legitimate Chinese academics, scientists, and businesspeople, some of them with contacts and even teaching posts at major research universities, were well positioned to send technology designs and other useful intelligence back home.

The leads needed to be vetted, no doubt. And as word of the China experiment spread throughout the intelligence community, Kleinsmith's team drew vehement detractors. One Defense Department analyst confronted Kleinsmith over his conspiratorial notions, the "connections" he had found sitting right out in the open: "You could find a connection between China and dog poop, the way you're representing this."

"You're right," Kleinsmith replied. "But that's not what we're showing."

Kleinsmith and his team, acting on their own and without prior knowledge of the threat, had demonstrated that the congressional commission on Chinese spying was essentially right. And they'd done it all in a matter of days, with relatively little effort. So, if an entire congressional investigation had now validated the IDC's methods, why wouldn't the Pentagon eagerly pour money into more advanced tools? Why wouldn't they build more IDCs to stop spies and counter a whole range of new threats that befuddled traditional agencies?

They were good and fair questions. But Kleinsmith and his supersleuths had raised another that was far more troubling to the senior officials who'd put them on the case: How did these techniques, impressive though they were, not violate almost every privacy law on the books?

Kleinsmith knew the regulation well. He could rattle it off as instinctively as his home address. DOD 5240.1-R:

> [T]o enable the DoD intelligence components to carry out effectively their authorized functions while ensuring their activities that affect U.S. persons are carried out in a manner that protects the constitutional rights and privacy of such persons.

Kleinsmith didn't have to be a lawyer to know what that meant. Regulation 5240 was the guardrail against domestic spying by the military. And he was bumping up against it.

The government had been down this torturous road several times. After World War II, the National Security Agency began collecting all telegram traffic leaving the United States, a practice that continued well into the 1970s. The FBI had set up a covert spying operation against the Black Panthers and other perceived "hostile" groups, including political opponents of various administrations. Critical journalists had ended up on enemies lists; their phones were tapped, their movements were tracked, and in some cases their finances were audited by the IRS. The exposure of those and other scandalous operations prompted a near full stop on domestic intelligence work. For decades, America's spies had kept their noses pointed overseas and had left stateside investigations of security threats to law enforcement agencies. They operated under crystal clear rules about what information the government could collect on American citizens.

The IDC's techniques muddied those rules. As Kleinsmith and his analysts harvested thousands of Web pages, they unavoidably vacuumed up the names of American citizens—probably thousands of them—who were mentioned in news articles, in chat rooms, or on electronic bulletin boards along with people Kleinsmith actually wanted to know more about.

They were the innocent bystanders of the investigation. Ordinary people who had done nothing wrong, and whom the government had no reason to believe were helping the Chinese or any other hostile service. Their connections to potential targets were coincidental. A college president mentioned on the same page as a visiting Chinese scholar. A U.S. executive who visited China on a trade delegation. Kleinsmith had plenty of logical explanations, but in order to verify them, he'd have to dig deeper into the connections. And that meant, in effect, investigating an American citizen without legal cause.

Even if he'd had the authority to vet these names, he didn't have the time. There were simply too many names to sift through without slowing down the rest of the analysis. But it wasn't just names that the IDC team collected. The harvest revealed facts about a person's life. His job. His hobbies. Any trivial fact mentioned in an online newsletter, an annual report, a transcript, became part of an ever-widening profile. What could an industrious snoop have found out about Kleinsmith just by scanning the Internet? That he was thirty-three years old. That he was a Cub Scout den leader. That he liked to play online war simulations in his spare time. It was all out there for the taking.

Only with a duly authorized warrant, issued pursuant to an official investigation, could an intelligence agency start building files on U.S. persons. And by law, that designation covered not only American citizens but also legal residents, American corporations, and even unincorporated associations substantially composed of American citizens or resident aliens.

Regulation 5240 was the Defense Department's legal guide. It specified what kinds of information an agency could collect (it must concern foreign powers and governments), under what circumstances (generally, with a warrant or pursuant to a legal authorization), how long it could be retained (if it had no demonstrable intelligence value, no longer than ninety days), and how widely the collecting agency could share it.

These were the rules, and people in Kleinsmith's business were trained to follow them. But technology had outpaced such restrictions. Now they were holding him back. His team had obtained no warrants because they weren't specifically targeting anyone. And their task was an experiment, not an operational mission. To confuse matters, the team was combing through publicly available information, which was not absolutely off-limits to intelligence agencies. But after they harvested those Web pages, they deposited them in storage with classified *government* data. The names of U.S. persons were being commingled with those of people actually under investigation.

Kleinsmith and his analysts risked breaking just about every rule spelled out in 5240 and the laws from which it flowed. They collected information. They stored it. They were searching it after they stored it. They intended to craft reports, which would be shared, perhaps widely. Their data mining was some bizarre hybrid of covert monitoring and public research. That's how the Army's lawyers saw it, and they conveyed that concern to the Pentagon's senior leadership.

But there was something else about the China experiment that proved far more troubling and politically perilous. The IDC wasn't just collecting information on ordinary people. The names of many prominent Americans popped up as well. For starters, there was Condoleezza Rice, the provost of Stanford University and a former member of George H. W. Bush's National Security Council. The hit was another by-product—Stanford, an elite research institution, hosted a number of Chinese scholars and delegations.

But the connections didn't stop there. William Cohen, the secretary of defense, also appeared. Was this the promise of "intelligence on steroids"? Condoleezza Rice and Bill Cohen implicated in a military smuggling ring? Hamre and other Pentagon leaders blanched at the political implications. The controversy over technology leaks to China had inflamed the White House. Republicans accused Bill Clinton of weakening U.S. export control laws in exchange for smoother diplomatic relations with Beijing and after generous campaign contributions from U.S. missile and satellite companies. The whole affair was radioactive. And so a chill shot through the Pentagon's upper ranks when Kleinsmith's China harvest churned up the name of First Lady Hillary Rodham Clinton.

The Pentagon placed an urgent call to the House Intelligence Committee. Hamre wanted to come up to the Hill and talk to the staffers personally. A number of them had heard of the IDC already, but they didn't know much more than that the analysts were using computers in new ways.

Hamre explained the problems the IDC had encountered with "U.S. persons" information. He wanted to know, Should the Pentagon shut down the program? The legal implications were obvious to everyone, but the IDC had shown real potential. They had to weigh the competing concerns of an intelligence breakthrough and privacy law. The Chinese were gaming the United States, but the country's laws arguably were making it harder to fight back.

The committee's lawyers had an easy gauge for deciding whether to continue a promising program like this or to kill it: Does it pass the *Washington Post* test? In other words, if the details of this operation ended up on the front page of the nation's most important political newspaper, would you—or more to the point, your boss—feel comfortable explaining it? Could you live with the headline "Defense Department Collecting Information on Americans in Espionage Investigation"?

No way. Even if the IDC analysts operated in a legal gray area, and there was some indication they did, this operation would never pass the test. The committee staff also wondered why the IDC was on this job in the first place. The National Security Agency was the expert in handling U.S. persons information. The Army intelligence command didn't have a clue about this stuff. It seemed to some staffers, as they listened to Hamre and worked through the legal implications, that the IDC team was utterly unaware that they even had a legal problem.

In October 1999, two months after the IDC had started the China experiment, the Department of the Army sent down new orders to the team. They should conclude the experiment and then purge all the data from their systems. That included the harvest and any reports they'd created, with visualization tools or by hand. The IDC must also return all information obtained from other agencies. And under no circumstances could they retain any nonessential U.S. person information for more than ninety days. Since they had no time to vet, everything would have to go.

Kleinsmith tried not to fret. Hamre was just one of many customers, he told himself. The IDC was still a hot ticket across the military commands. They had plenty of work to keep them busy.

Kleinsmith wasn't oblivious to the lawyers' concerns. He knew that the IDC's methods skirted the edge. But he also knew that most of his customers weren't bothered.

Over the next several months Kleinsmith gave more than one hundred briefings on the IDC to members of Congress, generals, and senior government officials. He could tell almost immediately whether someone got it. The look in his eyes. How he leaned forward. If he nodded as Kleinsmith elaborated on the technology's potential. Hamre got it, he thought. And so did two officers from the Army's Special Operations Command, who showed up at the IDC in December 1999 looking for information about a little-known terrorist organization called Al Qaeda.

CHAPTER 9

ABLE DANGER

A pair of officers showed up unannounced, a Navy commander and a Marine captain. Ordinarily, military visitors got the VIP reception, with a formal welcome and nickel tour. But these two had meant to come in quietly.

They explained that Special Operations Command, headquartered in Florida, had heard about the IDC's work on the China experiment. People were impressed. Word was that the analysts here had developed some unique capabilities. Could they ask Kleinsmith some questions about that?

Kleinsmith brought the officers into the IDC's main conference room. He was used to the dog and pony show by now, and the China presentation was as good a way as any to introduce people to his new breed of analysis. But as he walked the officers through those results, they interrupted him with pointed questions that had nothing to do with tracking military hardware.

These men wanted to track people. And, presumably, kill them. They never revealed a specific mission, but Kleinsmith knew that Special Operations guys were hunters. Their elder brothers had taken down the hijackers of *Achille Lauro*. Special Ops went places no one else would, or could. And based on the places that seemed to interest these officers most—"Can you track a vehicle moving real-time through the streets of Karachi?" one asked—Kleinsmith got the drift. They were hunting terrorists.

Kleinsmith always cautioned his audience that he didn't have superpowers. (Some of his more enthusiastic colleagues were less restrained.) The IDC could not direct spy satellites, and they certainly couldn't implant tracking devices on people or their vehicles. "No, we can't do that," Kleinsmith replied to the Karachi question. But, he explained, the IDC could provide new insights. They could help answer questions. If these two had shown up at Kleinsmith's door, then the establishment intelligence agencies probably had failed to do that.

The officers thanked Kleinsmith for his time, and then they left. Kleinsmith understood that Special Ops worked that way. They gave you nothing until they let you in. The past hour wasn't a presentation. It was an audition.

When it came to Al Qaeda, Special Operations most wanted one thing: Boots on the ground to go after the terrorists where they lived, trained, and planned. Al Qaeda had burst onto the scene a year earlier with a brazen, simultaneous attack on the U.S. embassies in Kenya and Tanzania. The military hadn't seen anything comparable since the bombings in Beirut fifteen years earlier. This new generation of extremists seemed equally bold but somehow more unmanageable. Al Qaeda, unlike the ideologues who had dogged Americans in Iran and Lebanon, appeared uninterested in negotiation.

The Special Operations officers who'd sought out Kleinsmith were given a straightforward yet utterly perplexing task: Draw up a military campaign plan for dismantling the Al Qaeda network. In October 1999, the chairman of the Joint Chiefs had directed Special Operations to map out Al Qaeda and all its support mechanisms, including its linchpin members.

Precisely how they should do that, no one knew. Al Qaeda wasn't a country. It had no obvious infrastructure and an opaque command and control system. It seemed to have a reach beyond Afghanistan, where the intelligence agencies knew Osama bin Laden, the Al Qaeda leader, kept his base of operation. But Special Operations could only judge that reach after an attack. If the military wanted to destroy Al Qaeda, then it had to understand it inside and out, just as it would a foreign army. How did the members communicate? How did they move money around? Who gave the orders to cells in the field? These were the weak spots. Disrupt those functions, and Al Qaeda would find it difficult, maybe even impossible, to launch attacks. Special Operations was given clear instructions: Identify the key players, roll them up, and bring down the network. It was more like a hit list than a blueprint for invasion. Death by dismemberment.

The planners kept their work close to the vest, but they gave their mission an oddly conspicuous code name: Able Danger. The word "Able" had been used to describe military exercises for more than two decades. But it was the second word of the nickname that revealed the planners' view of their target and the sense of urgency they attached to the mission.

Special Operations had ideas about how to hit Al Qaeda. First, they'd strike the terrorists' redoubts with AC-130 gunships, fearsome birds of prey armed with a bewildering array of guns and cannons. Alternatively, or perhaps in concert, commandos and elite special forces could stalk and eliminate individual Al Qaeda members on the ground. Special Ops had plenty of fire and manpower for the job. But they lacked an essential ingredient—specific, "actionable" intelligence that showed them where to aim.

For years now the military had depended largely upon the CIA for that information, and commanders had grown impatient with the paucity of results. The CIA had practically no presence in Afghanistan since the Soviets had abandoned their occupation in 1989. The agency had reestablished contacts more recently, and they were paying some dividends. But these sources were mostly tribal chiefs and rebels trying to oust the Taliban regime. They had their own agenda.

The CIA's counterterrorist center, along with a unit at headquarters solely devoted to tracking bin Laden, believed their Afghan sources could say reliably when he was on the move, where he might be on a particular day, perhaps even where he planned to spend the night. Locating bin Laden, and either killing or capturing him, became the agency's chief strategy for undermining Al Qaeda. The CIA had devised a dramatic plan in which the tribes would pounce on bin Laden in the middle of the night and then move him to a hiding place. They'd hold him there for a month or so while things quieted down and any suspicion of U.S. involvement wore off. (The agency and the White House were deeply concerned about antagonizing extremist elements in neighboring Pakistan, a key domino in the unstable region.) Once the tribes had an opening, they'd spirit bin Laden from his secret location and then put him on a U.S. aircraft, which would take the terrorist leader back to America for trial, or they'd hand him over to a friendly government. The chief of the CIA's bin Laden tracking unit thought it was a solid plan, the best anyone had devised so far. And the agency's chief Afghan field operative cabled headquarters that it was "almost as professional and detailed . . . as would be done by any U.S. military special operations element."

Special Operations begged to differ. This looked like amateur hour. A half-cocked, risky scheme that relied far too heavily on unreliable locals. In the time they wanted to hold bin Laden, he could die, be discovered, escape, or make a deal with the tribes. The commander of the military's Joint Special Operations forces said the CIA wanted results "on the cheap." The senior military leadership refused to outsource bin Laden's capture and then risk American lives when it came time for U.S. forces to extract him. Memories of another failed attempt to snatch a wanted terrorist loomed in their calculations: the disastrous Black Hawk Down incident of 1993. Then, nineteen soldiers died in an ambush in the streets of Mogadishu, Somalia. Warlord loyalists dragged their burned corpses through the streets. The military blamed the disaster in large part on poor intelligence gathering before the strike.

So it was under this umbrella of mistrust and hesitation that the Able Danger team tried to develop another way forward. They wanted to broaden their focus beyond bin Laden, and to think about Al Qaeda more systematically. Kleinsmith's presentation had made a deep impression on the two officers. Perhaps he had something they could use. In mid-January 2000, Commander Scott Philpot, the lead in the pair, called Kleinsmith and asked him to attend a special all-hands planning session, to be held at the Joint Warfare Analysis Center in Dahlgren, Virginia. Able Danger was going back to the drawing board, and he wanted Kleinsmith's ideas.

Kleinsmith was unsure what to expect. He'd never sat in one room with so many emissaries of the big three-letter agencies. The CIA sent a team. The National Security Agency and the Defense Intelligence Agency also sent their reps. As Kleinsmith sized up the gathering, he thought that they didn't seem especially collegial. He guessed that this might have been the first time they'd ever come together in one place.

Philpot hadn't asked Kleinsmith to give a formal presentation, or even to ask questions. Instead, he should be the fly on the wall. Were the group's methods sound? Were they overlooking anything?

To start things off, a CIA analyst, billed as the leading expert on the life and times of Osama bin Laden, laid out what he knew, or believed, about the terrorist leader. Most of what Kleinsmith knew about Al Qaeda came from the news. And he knew nothing of the agency's arduous slog to track bin Laden, or that they'd come closer to him than anyone else. But what the analyst had to say just didn't make any sense: Bin Laden would be dead within six months. According to intelligence, he was suffering from pancreatic cancer.

You've got to be kidding me, Kleinsmith thought. He couldn't imagine that the start point for a major campaign plan began and ended with the death of one man. Even if bin Laden had cancer, what about his second-tier leaders? Wouldn't they just take his place? And if the CIA had this kind of specific intelligence, then why wasn't it enough for the Able Danger team to act upon? Kleinsmith had been in the room for only a few moments, but he could see things didn't add up.

The analysts from the other agencies each gave their assessments of Al Qaeda. And in their often emphatic presentations, Kleinsmith recognized a certain myopia. This was the kind of narrow analysis produced by people who relied mostly on one kind of information. For the CIA, it was human spies on the ground. For the NSA, intercepted phone calls and communications. The satellite guys had their photographs, and so on. They all had gotten too close to the target. And in the process they'd let their own parochial biases guide them.

Kleinsmith considered himself a member of a new generation. These guys were the old guard. They'd become powerful, and they forgot to question their own assumptions about how the world worked. Or maybe they couldn't. Maybe that would undermine their dominance. Maybe that was why they were starting to yell at one another now.

Kleinsmith recognized that he was an outsider. And he wasn't so impolitic as to apprise the group of his candid assessment. At least, not without an invitation.

During a lunch break Kleinsmith buttonholed Philpot and gave him his assessment of the group's dynamic, as he'd been asked. These analysts were basing their conclusions on hardened assumptions, he said. Maybe those assumptions were good ones, but the analysts had closed themselves off to alternatives. They weren't fusing their ideas; they were bickering. And by his read, the course of action for Able Danger was being dictated by whoever could yell the loudest. About the only thing they could agree on was that the United States should hit Al Qaeda in Afghanistan. But here too they seemed to have excluded other options. How could they be so sure that would do the job? Hadn't the network demonstrated a reach far beyond its remote head-quarters?

Kleinsmith didn't think he was being especially insightful—just observant. He made Philpot an offer. "Let me do a quick, preliminary run on the data sets we have at the IDC and see what the picture is. I'll call my guys right now." Philpot agreed; he seemed equally unimpressed with the results so far.

Kleinsmith told two of his analysts to start with a broad, keyword search involving Al Qaeda. They ran the usual sources—public information on the Internet, as well as the Joint Worldwide Intelligence Communications System, a private network that the Defense Department used to transmit classified messages.

Ninety minutes later, the analysts passed the results back to Kleinsmith. They startled him. The IDC had found Al Qaeda "footprints" around the world, in the form of news reports, cable traffic, and other sources that when viewed collectively showed the network hardly was confined to its base in Afghanistan. Hits popped up around the world, and a lot of it came from open sources. The information the intelligence community lacked could be right at its fingertips.

Philpot asked Kleinsmith to present his findings to the group. To make it more intelligible, he ran the data through ThemeScape, one of the mapmaking tools that displayed information as a series of peaks and valleys. Al Qaeda seemed to have four major centers of gravity, he explained, indicated by the high volume of reporting pointing to Europe, North Africa, the Middle East, and the Far East. Everywhere he looked, there were mountains waiting to be excavated. Nuggets to be discovered. Leads to be followed. *Here*, he seemed to be saying. *Don't you see?*

Kleinsmith read the faces in the room. *Now who was kidding?* they appeared to be asking

"Centers of gravity"? In practically every major hot spot around the globe? This was absurdly broad. Useless. *Who is this kid?* he imagined them thinking. *Some punk major from an intelligence outfit no one's ever heard of? You've spent an hour on this. We've spent years. And where did you find this stuff again? The Internet? You're wasting our time.*

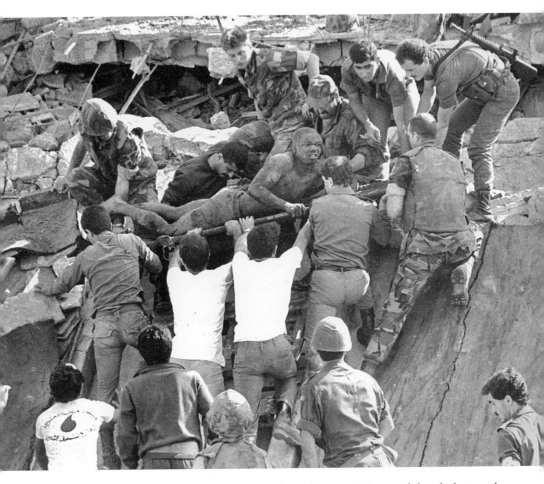

On the morning of October 23, 1983, a truck bomb destroyed the barracks of the Twenty-fourth Marine Amphibious Unit stationed at the Beirut International Airport. The attack killed 241 men, most of whom were asleep when the terrorist struck, and introduced America to the religious "suicide bomber."
(Associated Press/Bill Foley)

The Beirut attacks spurred Admiral John Poindexter (head of table) to organize the government's unwieldy approach to countering terrorism. As national security adviser to Ronald Reagan, he connected intelligence and security agencies with new technologies and used their collective skills to predict and manage crises. Here, Poindexter heads a Situation Room meeting of the National Security Planning Group, a committee of Cabinet secretaries and the CIA director. *(Ronald Reagan Presidential Library/Bill Fitz-Patrick)*

In 1986, Poindexter struggled to control a secret arms-for-hostages swap with Iran. At the same time, he authorized the diversion of funds from the arms sales to support anti-communist rebels in Nicaragua. The ensuing Iran-Contra affair was the most explosive political scandal of the Reagan administration. Poindexter resigned. Here, he sits before a congressional inquiry placidly smoking his trademark pipe, while he considers how to answer lawmakers' questions. *(Associated Press/Scott Stewart)*

Analog phone equipment, like this cross-bar switch, made it easy for law enforcement and intelligence agencies to monitor individual phone lines. But an explosion in digital technology in the 1990s threatened to put the government out of the wiretapping business. The FBI and the National Security Agency pushed for expansive changes to surveillance law and set their sights on the Internet as a valuable intelligence source.

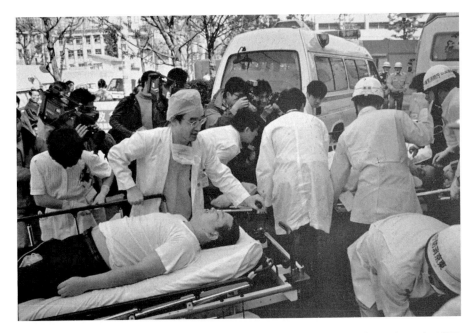

A series of suspicious events preceded a sarin nerve gas attack on the Tokyo subway in 1995, but government authorities had never connected all the clues. John Poindexter studied the attack while developing a computer program called Genoa, which aimed to detect the warning signals of crises, especially acts of terrorism. He pushed officials on Bill Clinton's National Security Council staff to adopt the program. *(Associated Press/Chiaki Tsukumo)*

Enter Al Qaeda: The shadowy terrorist organization exploded onto the international scene in 1998 with the twin bombings of U.S. embassies in Africa. The embassy in Nairobi, Kenya (pictured), was devastated by a truck bomb. More than two hundred people perished, most of them local embassy staff. *(Associated Press/Franco Pagetti)*

To halt Al Qaeda's advance, U.S. Special Operations Command launched a classified plan called Able Danger. Thirty-five-year-old Army major Erik Kleinsmith led a team of maverick analysts that used "data mining" tools to find valuable intelligence on the Internet. Kleinsmith discovered disturbing evidence of a terrorist presence inside the United States more than a year before the 9/11 attacks. *(Associated Press/Dennis Cook)*

Kleinsmith's methods alarmed Pentagon officials. In an earlier investigation of Chinese industrial espionage in America, his team had turned up the names of Stanford University provost Condoleezza Rice and defense secretary William Cohen. The connections were innocuous by-products of the massive Internet sweeps Kleinsmith conducted, but they appeared to violate privacy laws.

(Left: National Journal/Richard A. Bloom; Right: Department of Defense)

When Pentagon lawyers discovered that the Able Danger program had also collected the names of American citizens, they ordered Kleinsmith to destroy all of the information his team had compiled. Otherwise, "you guys will go to jail," an Army lawyer warned him. Any evidence of terror cells in America was lost. Rep. Curt Weldon (pictured), a longtime critic of the intelligence community, was incensed. In 2005, he showed members of Congress re-creations of the massive link charts the Able Danger team used to understand terrorist networks. *(Associated Press/Dennis Cook)*

After the 9/11 attacks, John Poindexter returned to government as the head of the Information Awareness Office. Housed in the Defense Advanced Research Projects Agency, the Pentagon's futurist brain trust, its centerpiece was an ambitious and controversial program called Total Information Awareness. Poindexter aimed to identify unknown terrorists by examining the everyday transactions of the general public. He hired computer scientist Bob Popp (left) as his deputy. *(Leanne K. Wiegand)*

When word spread that Poindexter was building an intelligence super-system, military officials came calling for help. Analysts used experimental data analysis tools to try and make sense of interrogation reports on the detainees held at Guantánamo Bay, Cuba. They discovered that some of the men in the island prison *weren't* terrorists.
(U.S. Navy/Shane T. McCoy)

Poindexter enlisted the help of Jeff Jonas, an eccentric software genius who'd developed a system for spotting card cheats at Las Vegas casinos. Jonas was impressed by Poindexter's vision, but he was skeptical of his ultimate goal: finding terrorists in a sea of anonymous people. In time, Jonas became convinced that "total information awareness" and protecting personal privacy were incompatible goals. *(Michelle Jonas)*

Poindexter thought that the logo for his Information Awareness Office reflected the power of his idea. But its Masonic design and ominous motto, "Knowledge is power," enraged those already leery of the Bush administration's expanding surveillance power. The logo offered potent evidence that Poindexter didn't see the world their way. He left government in 2003, after civil libertarians and privacy activists excoriated Total Information Awareness and Poindexter's idea for a "futures market" to predict terrorist attacks. *(Department of Defense)*

While Poindexter toiled away on Total Information Awareness, Air Force general Michael Hayden was secretly building his own early-warning system for terrorism. As the director of the National Security Agency, he obtained authorities from President George W. Bush to monitor phone calls, e-mails, and other telecommunications into and out of the United States without a warrant. The program was code-named Stellar Wind. Hayden was also keeping an eye on Poindexter's efforts, and the two discussed how they could work together.

(National Journal/Liz Lynch)

The BAG: President Bush walks past a "big ass graph" at NSA headquarters. The agency's terrorist hunters used a computer program like this one to display connections among people, places, and events. It was the core of the agency's early-warning system, but critics complained that it churned up dense, impenetrable "hairballs" that couldn't dependably locate or identify terrorists. *(Associated Press/Evan Vucci)*

In 2007, former NSA director Mike McConnell put a lucrative business career on hold and became director of national intelligence. Years earlier, he had met with John Poindexter and offered to help him find support in Congress for Total Information Awareness. By the time McConnell returned to government, Poindexter's programs had been secretly taken over by the National Security Agency. *(Associated Press/Charles Dharapak)*

After the NSA's warantless surveillance was exposed in the press, Bush became a vocal defender of the agency's work. Here, he speaks after a briefing at the agency's headquarters in Fort Meade, Maryland, joined by (from left) Homeland Security adviser Fran Townsend, Vice President Dick Cheney, spy chief Mike McConnell, and NSA director General Keith Alexander. *(Associated Press/Charles Dharapak)*

Global panic: In August 2006, British security officials disrupted a plan to smuggle liquid bombs onto trans-Atlantic airliners. The attack could have eclipsed 9/11 in lives lost. The National Security Agency obtained e-mails that traced the plot's suspected mastermind to Pakistan. Passengers were stranded at airports as flights were canceled; when they finally boarded, they were prohibited from carrying liquids. *(Associated Press/Rebecca Reid)*

In December 2007, John Poindexter joined several former national security advisers for a dinner at Blair House to celebrate the sixtieth anniversary of the law that created the position. After leaving the government, he transformed into an agent provocateur and a gray eminence of American spycraft. He maintained professional and personal ties to senior officials in government. *(Photo by Joyce N. Boghosian, courtesy of George W. Bush Presidential Library)*

As a senator, Barack Obama initially was opposed to expanding surveillance law and granting legal immunity to companies that helped the government spy without warrants. But as his nomination for president appeared certain, Obama changed his mind, saying that he'd been told the NSA's surveillance program was actually useful. He voted for a new law that granted many of the same broad powers that Bush had authorized in secret.

(Associated Press/Charles Dharapak)

In moments like this, the dutiful Boy Scout gave way to the petulant up-start. The analysts' hostility emboldened Kleinsmith. These were the guys who didn't "get it," he told himself. And not because they couldn't comprehend the technology, but because it threatened them. He threatened them. This nobody was pointing out, on a map, where the nation's most exalted spies had failed to look.

If Able Danger wanted to understand Al Qaeda, he declared, if they wanted to attack it on all fronts, then they had to plunge deeper. They should start here, in this ocean he had collected. Why did the big letter agencies presume the government had the best information? Clearly, a lot of journalists, aca-demics, and others grazing on open sources had come up with some powerful insights about the network. He had just demonstrated that. With more work his analysts could suss out meaningful signals in this noise, separate the real leads from the garbage, and come back with what the military wanted: a list of Al Qaeda's weak spots, the keys to its demise.

Philpot had seen enough. As the meeting concluded he announced that Kleinsmith and the IDC would take the lead on the Al Qaeda mapping plan. Able Danger would shift its attention and support to a wider campaign. The new guys were in charge. And Kleinsmith was a marked man.

A few weeks later, in February 2000, Able Danger gave Kleinsmith his first marching orders: "Start with the words 'Al Qaeda,' and go."

The IDC team worked as it had during the China experiment. A small group of analysts, never more than four, started broadly. They reaped a har-vest of Web pages and classified reports, then got their hands dirty sifting the pieces. They worked quickly, and under pressure, since demands from the IDC's other clients—the various military commands—hadn't abated.

Kleinsmith drew up an ambitious wish list of more than one hundred military and intelligence databases that he wanted to access in addition to the sources already available. He thought that the richness of the harvest, and therefore the analysis, would increase as he fed more data into the system. The new sources ranged from the merely "classified" to those designated so sensi-tive that access was given only as needed.

About half of the data owners rebuffed Kleinsmith's requests. Many feared that sharing secrets would reveal how they acquired them. A breach like that could put an agency out of the intelligence business. They jealously guarded their sources and methods, and Kleinsmith knew that even if he was allowed to brief them in detail on Able Danger, the gravity of the mission alone could not persuade others to cooperate with him. He'd have to rely on sheer persuasion.

It wouldn't be easy. Law enforcement agencies, in particular, resisted his requests. They were in the business of keeping records for criminal prosecutions, not freewheeling intelligence missions. By design, their databases were full of U.S. persons information. "There's no way in hell you're getting this," more than one official told Kleinsmith.

He had anticipated roadblocks like this. So, as Kleinsmith made the rounds, he set his sights on sources he thought would pose the fewest hassles. He was particularly interested in a database of foreign students maintained by the Immigration and Naturalization Service. These people were in the United States on temporary visas. They were here legally, but they weren't permanent residents—a key distinction. Kleinsmith was learning to think like a lawyer.

When he sat down with immigration officials and explained that he wanted temporary access to the visa data, they seemed supportive. His legal rationale was sound. But, the officials explained, they simply couldn't assist him, because their database was rife with U.S. persons.

Kleinsmith was perplexed. "What do you mean, U.S. persons?" he asked. Weren't these foreign students?

Well, the officials explained, INS employees manually entered visa forms into the system. It was a painstaking process, and the agency was short staffed. Currently, they had a six-month backlog of forms waiting to be processed. So they couldn't guarantee that, by the time they got around to a particular batch, the students' legal status hadn't changed. Statistically speaking, they were certain, some people in the database were now citizens or permanent residents. They just weren't sure who.

Able Danger, like the China experiment, revealed just how disconnected and convoluted the government's intelligence systems really were. The community was anything but a community. Some sources thankfully were not off-limits, Kleinsmith discovered. The IDC could still tap the classified Defense Department network they'd used in previous harvests. Finished reports in that system often yielded productive nuggets, including bank account and phone numbers.

Of course, the Internet provided the most productive source of all. It gave him the best leads. And, as far as he understood the law, public information was free for the taking. In February, the IDC conducted its first harvest for Able Danger—it was, as Kleinsmith had expected, huge.

The cache totaled roughly 2.5 terabytes, equal to about one-tenth the number of printed pages held in the Library of Congress. In that single harvest Kleinsmith guessed they'd pulled in about sixteen thousand names. It was all a mile wide and an inch deep. But what he saw unnerved him. Recurring names connected to one another, linked by geography, by intermediaries. A spider's web of suspicion. What did it all mean? It couldn't be good, he told himself. He saw associations coming into focus. A global spread. Were these communications channels? Money exchanges? It was all so much vapor, contrails left in the wake of fast-moving bodies. But the picture was there, taking shape. There were signals in the noise. If only a tenth of them were meaningful, it was enough to lose sleep over. And he did.

He wasn't alone.

Less than a month later, the staff of the House Intelligence Committee learned that Special Operations had tapped the IDC for data analysis, the same kind they'd done for the China experiment. The committee lawyers' first call went to the Pentagon.

The committee presumed that the Army had established significant oversight procedures for this. These guys in the IDC weren't out there on their own again, were they?

Word came back from the Army lawyers to the committee staff director: "We'll have to check on that."

In the winter of 2000, with the IDC several weeks into its Able Danger work, no one in the senior ranks of the Army or the Pentagon realized that Kleinsmith's team was once again pulling in thousands of names of U.S. persons. Senior Army intelligence officers had asked the Pentagon for guidance on how to assist Special Operations with Able Danger, but while the lawyers were still deliberating over some new "methodology," Kleinsmith and his colleagues were off investigating specific leads generated by the harvest.

Army lawyers were eager to protect the service from a repeat of the China fiasco. They wanted senior-level cover this time. Rear Admiral Michael Lohr, the legal counsel to the chairman of the Joint Chiefs of Staff, got involved. His boss had ordered Able Danger in the first place.

As Lohr examined what the IDC was up to, he grew increasingly troubled by its novel approach of mining government and public information. He fired off a memo to the Army enumerating his concerns. The IDC could "pull together into a single database a wealth of privacy protected U.S. citizen information, in a more sweeping and exhaustive manner than was previously contemplated." The message was unmistakable. The Joint Chiefs and the Army must "think carefully how we want to deal with a capability which can gather such information into one cross-referenced super database." If the Department of Defense planned to maintain such a system, that decision should be made "at a very senior DOD policy level," Lohr wrote.

Then, in a note that surely shot fear through the military's legal corps, Lohr indicated that he had consulted with both a lawyer in the Pentagon general counsel's office and the United States attorney general. They all agreed that, at least in the short term, the IDC should only be allowed to mine Defense Department databases. That the Internet was off-limits.

Able Danger was not a law enforcement mission. It was effectively an assassination campaign. The military planned to eliminate these terrorists, not try them in court. The *Washington Post* smell test would have registered off the charts with this. But as the attorneys closed ranks, and congressional staff hyperventilated, Kleinsmith and his team started passing along information to Able Danger. Weeks before Lohr wrote his memo, Philpot briefed General Peter Schoomaker, the U.S. Special Operations commander, on the progress Kleinsmith had made. He showed the general some of the intriguing discoveries the analysts had produced using their new tools. Schoomaker liked what he saw. The IDC should keep up their good work.

Kleinsmith and his team worked at a fast clip. Connections became stronger. Signals came in clearer through the noise. Kleinsmith could see that

Al Qaeda had evolved from an ideological movement into an operational network—and a formidable one. Names, locations, capabilities, and even financial sources were converging. But the harvest was still too unruly to give Special Operations the precise information they needed. The team had to dig deeper.

The computers could get Kleinsmith only so far. Now was the time to put them aside and rely on his own mind. Kleinsmith liked to characterize analysts using the Myers-Briggs Type Indicator, which divided people into one of sixteen personality types based largely on how they processed information and made decisions. The best analysts, he thought, excelled at "sensing." They focused on what they could see, what they could touch. The physical world. They solved problems by working through facts. Kleinsmith was a sensor, as were most of the analysts on his team, who were also mostly women. Most of the women he knew were sensors, and he'd always ended up working with them. Once, in an Army training class, Kleinsmith and his fellow students were divided into two groups based on their Myers-Briggs results. He and the women ended up on one side of the room. From the other side, his male colleagues ribbed him mercilessly.

In Kleinsmith's experience, a lot of male analysts were judgers. They added their own values and insights to a problem. They interpreted, and in the process, they made too many leaps in logic. That was a risky approach with Al Qaeda, especially since what the intelligence community did *not* know far outweighed what they did.

Kleinsmith and his team sat around the IDC talking their way through the rich data harvest. They started with what they knew: Certain names popped up more than others, and often there were links between them. The obvious question was, How were they actually connected? Not by coincidence in a set of news articles. But by real people? Who were the intermediaries? Was there a human chain? Did it connect person A in Yemen to person K in Germany? The tools indicated that it might. Person K was showing up in other connections too. He seemed . . . prolific.

As the analysts pondered the possibilities, one of them noted the striking similarity between this puzzle and a favorite party game—Six Degrees of Kevin Bacon. The object was to connect the actor, who seemed to have worked with everyone in Hollywood at some point, to any other actor through six steps or less. Kevin Bacon to Tom Cruise. Bacon starred in *Flatliners* with Julia Roberts, who was in *The Pelican Brief* with Denzel Washington, who was in *Courage Under Fire* with Meg Ryan, who was in *Top Gun* (as Goose's wife) with Tom Cruise. Three degrees of separation. The best players could nail it in two or less. Kevin Bacon to Arnold Schwarzenegger: Bacon starred in *Apollo 13* with Bill Paxton, who played the bumbling con man in *True Lies* with Schwarzenegger. One degree. Of course, sometimes the obvious connection was staring you in the face. Kevin Bacon to Tom Cruise? Hello. *A Few Good Men.* Direct connection.

If the Kevin Bacon game worked for movie actors, why couldn't it work for terrorists? The team spent hours sitting around the IDC trying to pare down the number of connections between names they'd never heard before and to countries they'd never visited. Their critics thought the analysts had surrendered all logic to machines. They just had to laugh at that.

Working the problem over, the analysts helped Able Danger planners isolate some twenty individuals they thought merited further scrutiny. The Kevin Bacons, Julia Robertses, and Arnold Schwarzeneggers of Al Qaeda—maybe. Philpot and a handful of his colleagues had camped out at a nearby hotel, so they were on hand to watch the IDC churn out results. They fed the analysis back to Special Operations headquarters, and campaign planners there gave the thumbs-up: Zero in on these people. Find out everything you can about them.

The target sets narrowed. That made Kleinsmith happy. But he had a much bigger problem.

Each of those targets required a new harvest. And any names connected to them, any new links, had to be harvested too. The analysis tools were designed to find connections in contained sets of information. But on the Internet, one page linked to ten others, which in turn linked to ten more. The tools couldn't handle exponential growth.

Each target created more noise. In a desperate attempt to simplify the analysis, the team constructed rudimentary charts—nothing but boxes containing names connected to each other with straight lines. But the charts ended up twenty feet long and covered with small type. They were so big that the team had to hang them on a wall just to read them.

The deeper they dove, the more they questioned their own results. Could the data play tricks on them? A line between two people looked so convincing. But what did that line really mean? What relationship lay underneath it?

"Do you have any idea how many people on the planet would go to jail just because they *knew* somebody bad," one woman asked the group.

It wasn't just a good question. It was *the* question. Guilt by association was a useless standard, at least for Able Danger's purposes. They had to know, for sure, that the targets actually mattered to Al Qaeda, or were Al Qaeda. They were grabbing at smoke. They needed hard information.

They knew that intelligence reports from the classified systems often came with an especially useful lead—telephone surveillance logs of suspected foreign targets. Connections through phone numbers offered a more concrete basis of suspicion than much of what the team had pulled in so far. Target X called person Y. On this day. At this time. They wouldn't call each other if they didn't know each other.

One of the analysts meticulously combed through the phone logs. She'd pick a target, then pull out all the numbers that he had called, entering the information as a series of "to" and "from" fields in a spreadsheet.

Now the analysis tools became useful again. They could crunch all those confusing numbers lightning fast. The team ran the phone number spreadsheet through a visualization program, called Parentage, which created link charts based on phone and Internet logs. At the time, the NSA was using Parentage to trace attacks on computer networks back to a discrete Internet address.

Parentage created a link chart, and the analysts gathered around to examine it. As Kleinsmith scanned the results, one node caught his eye. He had to check himself to make sure he was reading it correctly. "Plymouth, Michigan."

One of the analysts noticed the fixated expression on Kleinsmith's face. "What's the matter?" she asked.

"That's my hometown," he said.

Kleinsmith quickly retrieved the original report containing the numbers listed in the node. As he read the synopsis of the calls, he realized that this wasn't incidental traffic. This wasn't someone calling to order pizza or to make a doctor's appointment. This looked, to him, like people making plans.

Kleinsmith had been losing sleep, but now he was deeply frightened. Until this moment terrorists had existed as some far-off menace, in a place that couldn't touch him. Now they were here. Where he had lived. He was looking right at them.

CHAPTER 10

"YOU GUYS WILL GO TO JAIL"

Kleinsmith and the team worked from the dark early morning until they couldn't keep their eyes open. They'd spent February of 2000 peeling back layers of a digital onion, and they were amazed at what they found. New connections. New leads. New sources. They couldn't possibly vet it all. In addition to the signals in Michigan, the team had picked up intelligence on other potential terrorist cells—one in New York, another in Florida.

Kleinsmith was vaguely aware that lawyers well beyond his pay grade had been fretting over the collection of information about U.S. persons. But he had no idea just how high the concern had reached. The Pentagon's top lawyers had weighed in. Even the attorney general. The only higher legal authority was the president.

The IDC was pulling in thousands of names with every harvest. Once again, the names of prominent politicians were in the mix. The analysts had to be reined in. In May, about three months after the team had started work on Able Danger, Colonel Tony Gentry, the top lawyer for the Intelligence and Security Command, had paid Kleinsmith a visit. He found him in his office just off the IDC's main floor. Gentry said that he wanted to deliver a message personally. Kleinsmith had never found Gentry especially unsympathetic to what the analysts were trying to do. But as a rule, when the lawyer showed up, it wasn't to deliver happy news.

Kleinsmith had a ninety-day window to delete all the data his team had collected in support of Able Danger, Gentry said. And not ninety days from now—the clock had started back in February, with the first data harvest. Kleinsmith knew the rules. Army regulations, per DOD 5140-R. And who knows how many other laws he risked breaking. Unless Kleinsmith could verify that U.S. persons information embedded in his work had legitimate value, then it had to go. That included not only the harvest but the link charts, the Parentage records, and any other products the team had created.

Ninety days. Kleinsmith counted backward in his head. He guessed that he had about ten days left. Ten days to separate the few dozen bad guys from tens of thousands of the good guys. Ten days to make sense of the often insensate. Ten days to unlock Al Qaeda. He couldn't do it.

Gentry wanted to impress upon Kleinsmith what he already understood— that he and his team were personally bound to follow the rules. "Remember," Gentry said, in an easy tone that suggested he might be half-joking, "delete this stuff, or you guys will go to jail!"

This was the most direct warning the IDC had received, but it wasn't the first. In recent weeks lower-level lawyers had showed up to "remind" the analysts about privacy rules. They asked them to sit through a privacy briefing that they'd heard so many times by now they could probably give it themselves. The lawyers had wanted to send a message and to cover themselves.

They had also set new restrictions on what the IDC could do with its harvested data. Anytime the analysts came upon a potential U.S. person, they had to stop work and call a lawyer. The Pentagon feared that the names of Americans would get passed on to Special Operations, or end up in reports circulated throughout the intelligence community. The privacy protections reached levels of absurdity when the analysts started tacking Post-it notes over the names and faces of individuals who appeared in the link charts.

The pressure had mounted on the analysts before Gentry delivered the ultimatum. The constant briefings. The lawyers standing over their shoulders. One of the analysts came to Kleinsmith in desperation, demanding that she be let off the team. They were trying to do a job. They would go to jail for that?

Kleinsmith had pleaded his case to lawyers with his command, Special Operations, and the Defense Department. The restrictions were stifling. "You might as well assign a lawyer to sit behind every one of us!" he vented. Colonel James Gibbons, Kleinsmith's boss, had tried to run interference. The IDC's raison d'être was to support troops in the field. The Able Danger mission was vital, and obviously Special Operations thought so. Kleinsmith and his team had built something that didn't exist anywhere else, Gibbons told the lawyers. "You're asking us to take this race car and drive it around the track at twenty-five miles per hour. We might as well get out and walk."

As ten days turned into one, Kleinsmith assessed his options. He pulled one of the analysts into his office. Were they really going to destroy everything? They might get authorization to start again for another ninety days. In that case, reharvesting the information was easy enough. But they weren't sure they could re-create all the products, the charts and reports that showed Al Qaeda's global footprint. This was the preliminary blueprint for the campaign plan. If they deleted it, it would be gone forever.

The pair discussed conveniently forgetting to destroy everything. Maybe a few essential files could be left behind. Or perhaps they could send as much raw data as possible to the Able Danger team now, then delete the rest tomorrow. But the truly useful sets were too big to send in an e-mail. And besides, Special Operations headquarters didn't have the analytic tools. Even if they had pieces of the harvest, they couldn't make much use of it.

Kleinsmith wondered if they should just copy as much as possible onto portable hard drives, and then hide them. But ultimately, his inner Boy Scout prevailed. He would follow the rules. He consoled himself that he really had no choice.

They divided the work. Kleinsmith deleted all the files on the IDC's main system—the raw intelligence from Internet page harvests, as well as intelligence reports and messages, along with the analytic reports contained in Microsoft Word documents, PowerPoint slides, and link charts. Point. Click. Delete. All the folders, and everything in them, disappeared.

Kleinsmith's partner collected all the removable hard drives and electronically wiped them clean. She also gathered up all of the hard copies of the analysis lying around the office and put them into burn bags, which were collected later and incinerated.

Kleinsmith never thought it would come to this. He honestly believed that the IDC could work through the legal nettles with the command lawyers. But every day he pushed to get over one hurdle, only to find another in his path.

He felt thrown into a fight with his hands glued together. The day he spent destroying months of work was just the latest in a string of agonies.

When they finished, Kleinsmith phoned Philpot to tell him what they'd done. He seemed not to believe it at first. Like Kleinsmith, he had thought they might navigate the legal channels. But he knew the odds, and so he'd been crafting a backup plan in case the IDC was pulled off Able Danger. The analysis would move to a private facility, an intelligence operations center owned and operated by Raytheon in Garland, Texas. Raytheon was a titan of the Beltway. The company ran so many military and intelligence programs that it might as well have been a federal agency. Among its tens of thousands of employees were former high-ranking officials and a cadre of program managers, all with the necessary security clearances for the job. The company also had its own suite of analytic tools. Able Danger could try to replicate the IDC in Texas.

Kleinsmith's life returned to what passed for normal before Special Ops had shown up. A few weeks after he ended his work, he hopped a flight to Fort Huachuca, Arizona, to teach a class for military intelligence officers. While changing planes in Dallas, he ran into two senior officers from Special Operations Command. These were the men up the chain who ultimately ran Able Danger and were responsible for presenting a campaign plan. They'd both been visiting the Raytheon facility in Garland and were on their way back to command headquarters in Florida.

One of the men, Major General Geoffrey Lambert, confronted Kleinsmith. He ran policy and plans for Special Operations Command, and he demanded to know if it was true what he'd heard, that Kleinsmith personally had made the decision to destroy the analysis.

Kleinsmith confirmed that he had, and Lambert proceeded to chew his ass in the middle of the terminal, as dozens of curious passengers walked by.

Kleinsmith pleaded. He knew Lambert was upset. So was he. But he was following orders. "I was directed to either delete the data or go to jail!"

Lambert had heard enough. He gave Kleinsmith a piercing parting glance, then carried on with his fellow officer, as if Kleinsmith were no longer there.

Kleinsmith went home that night to his wife, two-and-a-half-year-old son, and month-old baby girl, crushed by the realization of what he'd done. *We failed them*, he thought. He knew that for certain now.

A year passed. A new administration took over. Special Operations commanders remained on edge trying to track the elusive Al Qaeda network. And they weren't alone. Back in the White House, Dick Clarke and the other career NSC staffers had been working furiously, and now they were in panic mode.

In the spring and summer of 2001, intelligence reports on bin Laden and Al Qaeda were coming faster than ever, but with no corresponding rise in clarity. The National Security Agency and the CIA, among others, reported an increase in "chatter," coded communications among terrorists. There was a plot in the offing, but no one could say where or when it would happen.

Mary McCarthy was fielding the daily barrage of chatter. She had moved into the top intelligence job on the NSC staff in 1998. Whatever she could do to help John Poindexter and his Genoa project find a home had to wait now. Every day McCarthy and her colleagues sat in their offices scratching their heads and pounding on tables, trying to make sense of the alarming traffic they saw. *What is it that fits?* she asked herself. *What is it that matters?*

McCarthy wished that someone was arranging these pieces of data somewhere, scrubbing them, looking at what they all meant. Heading into the summer, the FBI was being led on wild-goose chases and goat ropes by hard-to-trust sources, whose information often turned out to be bogus. At one point the bureau got spun up over rumors of an attack on shopping malls; it turned out to be baseless.

Signals were everywhere. But the noise was deafening. Genoa was still too young and unproven a system to run against the problem. And Able Danger was guarded so closely that no one in McCarthy's office, or anyone on the NSC staff, knew that a team of Army analysts was living the same nightmare as them. *What are they up to?* McCarthy asked herself as she puzzled over the vague terrorist intelligence. *What could it be?* Looking back on that time years later, she thought it was crazy that the NSC staff had worked so unsystematically.

In June 2001, the intelligence community issued a warning that a major Al Qaeda attack would occur within the next several weeks. Officials weren't sure where but suspected that the target might be in Saudi Arabia. Clarke and his colleagues on the NSC staff asked whether Al Qaeda might strike within the United States. Intelligence officials replied that they couldn't rule it out.

Clarke held a meeting in his office during which CIA officials briefed domestic law enforcement agencies about the possibility of an attack in America. Representatives from the immigration service, the Federal Aviation Administration, the Customs Bureau, and the Coast Guard attended. And so did FBI agents, who agreed with the CIA's assessment that there was now a high probability of a major terrorist attack.

That summer was also a tumultuous period of transition. George W. Bush had taken office only six months earlier. McCarthy, as part of the professional staff, agreed to stay on board temporarily. But as she prepared to head back to the CIA, she worked up a memo for the new national security adviser, Condoleezza Rice. She wanted to document the lessons she had learned in her years at the White House and to suggest changes that would improve the intelligence process, changes that Rice, by dint of her position, might be able to effect.

McCarthy asked Poindexter whether he had any advice for Rice, one adviser to another. He had one suggestion, which McCarthy included in the memo: The national security adviser should have one deputy who focused on nothing but strategic and long-term approaches to improve the national security process. The big-idea person. Ideally, he, or she, would be technologically oriented and would have the political backing to bend people to his will. The strength of Goliath and the wisdom of Solomon, in a perfect world. But failing that, just a position that was freed from the day-to-day grind that kept so many eyes off the horizon.

McCarthy submitted her memo; Rice never replied. McCarthy returned to the CIA later, in August 2001.

Kleinsmith tried not to think much about Able Danger. He hoped that the team could start up again, and at that rarified level of officialdom that had so disappointed him, talks were under way.

Special Operations commanders were furious at the lawyers for impeding their mission. The Garland facility wasn't going to cut it. Eventually, the analysts there had to destroy their data too. They needed the IDC back in play.

In late September 2000, the Pentagon had cleared the IDC to go back to work for another ninety days. But before the team could ramp up, a new crisis took hold of their attention. On October 12, while USS *Cole* docked in the port of Aden in Yemen, Al Qaeda suicide bombers rammed the ship with a small explosive-laden boat, killing seventeen sailors and wounding thirty-nine. At that moment, U.S. Central Command, which was responsible for military operations in the Middle East, became the IDC's primary customer, and the analysts assisted with the massive investigation of the bombing. For months they'd been working to stop this kind of thing from happening. Now they were working cleanup.

The next year, Kleinsmith left the Army. He'd been planning to take a white-collar job, and now he had more reason than ever. He went to work for Lockheed Martin, another massive defense contractor, heading up an intelligence training program. He figured he could do more good wearing a private-sector badge than a military one. Like so many, he found the pay superior, the hassles fewer, and the work just as rewarding. Maybe even more so.

Some of his analysts stayed, and under a new leader. Keith Alexander, a seasoned military intelligence officer, took over as commander of the Intelligence and Security Command. Alexander was a close friend of Jim Heath, the "mad scientist" of the IDC. The pair had worked together for years; wherever Alexander went, Heath usually followed. Both were fervent evangelists for the transformative power of technology. They would make a formidable team.

The Pentagon chiefs had assured themselves that the IDC's methods were unsound. Their reports to Able Danger certainly weren't actionable. The technology needed more time to evolve. It showed great promise, but so many of the links and connections the analysts had made were just goofy. Terrorist cells in Europe. In the United States. Kleinsmith never doubted that much of what he'd found was misleading, and maybe wrong. But he could never shake the thought of what more he might have found had he only been allowed to look.

Some months later, when the seemingly unthinkable happened, Kleinsmith wasn't at all surprised. As he watched buildings fall and burn, he thought to himself, *So it begins.*

And so it did.

ACT THREE

I recall that within days of the 9/11 attacks, I addressed the NSA workforce to lay out our mission in a new environment. . . . I tried to comfort. Look on the bright side: Right now a quarter billion Americans wished they had your job. I ended the talk by trying to give perspective. All free peoples have had to balance the demands of liberty with the demands of security. Historically we Americans had planted our flag well down the spectrum toward liberty. Here was our challenge. "We were going to keep America free," I said, "by making Americans feel safe again."

—*Michael Hayden before the Senate Judiciary Committee*
in 2006, recalling an address he gave on September 13,
2001, as director of the National Security Agency

We did not want to make a trade-off between security and privacy. It would be no good to solve the security problem and give up the privacy and civil liberties that make our country great.

—*John Poindexter, in a letter to the director of the Defense*
Advanced Research Projects Agency, August 12, 2003

CHAPTER 11

ECHO

At a quarter to ten on the morning of September 11, 2001, John Poindexter was stuck in traffic. Every morning he followed the same slow crawl from his home in suburban Maryland to his offices at Syntek, in Northern Virginia. He drove down the congested 270 corridor, rolled onto the bustling Beltway that encircled Washington, and then crossed the Potomac over the Chain Bridge, a lushly tree-lined expanse that, at this time of day, bore an unfortunate resemblance to a parking lot.

This was the least favorite part of his day, caught helplessly in the downstream of a chain reaction. Some fender bender, probably miles away and an hour earlier, set off a domino of brake pushers and rubberneckers, disrupting the rush-hour flow for millions of harried commuters. Poindexter blamed highway engineers. He thought they should have lined the roads with sensors to monitor vehicle movements, weather patterns, accidents, all the information motorists needed to plan their route and avoid the hassles. He thought it seemed obvious.

Poindexter liked to drive with the radio off. The lengthy commute gave him plenty of time to think in silence. Genoa was never far from his mind. Half a decade later he was still at work on the elusive crisis management system, as well as on related technologies that for all their initial interest had yet to catch fire among the intelligence agencies. Their methods had not changed, and they continued to resist new ideas. Moving the agencies to change had been an arduous slog, with little success. The world was still noisy. Deafeningly so.

Poindexter's furrowed hands rested on the wheel of a leased Acura Legend. The customary spoils of a retired flag officer had eluded him. No lucrative

positions on corporate boards, no six-figure executive salaries at defense contractors, no speaking tours and book deals. Poindexter still worked for a living. His job at Syntek kept him in the game, and it helped pay for his sailing
habit. Poindexter kept a forty-two-foot sloop named *Bluebird* moored in Annapolis, not far from the Naval Academy. It was practically criminal not to
pass a morning like this on the water. But he kept his eye on the road. He
didn't see the smoke cresting on the horizon, just a few miles south.

His cellphone rang. It was Linda.

"Turn on the radio!" she insisted. "They're saying planes flew into the
World Trade Center."

"I'll call you back."

Poindexter tuned the radio to a news station. He caught a live, on-the-
scene interview with an eyewitness to a plane crash. Poindexter presumed that
they were talking about the Twin Towers. But then the eyewitness said he'd
seen a plane come in low, over the highway, and crash into the Pentagon.

The reporter said he saw smoke and flames pouring out of the building.
Poindexter listened for clues about their positions. Based on the vantage point,
he surmised they were standing near the Navy annex, on a slight rise that
overlooked the Pentagon from across the highway. The plane must have
hit near the helicopter landing pad, on the west side of the building, he
thought. Poindexter knew the spot well. That's where the chief of Naval Operations kept his offices.

Mark, one of Poindexter's five sons, was a Navy commander working on
the chief's staff. He'd graduated from Annapolis in 1985, seven years before
his brother Tom. Poindexter had been the CNO's executive assistant in the
late seventies and had held ambitions of rising to that highest of uniformed
Navy posts. The detour to the White House had changed all that. Poindexter
remembered those days as fondly as any of his time in the service. Now the
son was following in the father's footsteps.

Linda rang again. "Mark called," she told her husband. "He said that he's
safe." Linda was confused. "Why is he calling?"

She hadn't heard the news about the Pentagon yet. Poindexter explained
what had happened. Then they remembered that Mark had no reason to be
anywhere near the Pentagon that morning. The staff had cleared out for tem-

porary quarters while their offices were renovated. Some part of the Pentagon was always getting a face-lift. This time it was Mark's. He was safe.

Poindexter's relief quickly faded, washed away by the bitter swell of frustration he'd felt that predawn morning of October 23, 1983. Another sudden phone call had delivered the news that he found all too predictable. It was happening again.

He pushed on toward the office. The radio was now reporting that both of the Twin Towers were ablaze. He stayed tuned for the rest of the trip.

The morning commute was still his thinking time, and Poindexter wondered if the intelligence community ever had considered terrorists using commercial airplanes as weapons. He could imagine the plot from beginning to end, and he ticked off the list of discrete actions one would have to take in order to enter the country, slip past airport security, and commandeer a jetliner. Purchase a plane ticket, for sure. Probably rent a car. Find shelter. Did the hijackers rent a hotel room? When did they get here? Did they live here for weeks? Months? Did they know one another? Whom did they call? How did they get money? What did they buy? Phone calls. E-mails. Credit card purchases. Money transfers. The digital footprints of a mass attack lined up in his mind, and he could walk them backward, all the way to the day, time, and place where these people first set foot on U.S. soil. The start of their mission.

Poindexter arrived at Syntek and found his colleagues huddled silently around a television in the conference room. One of the towers had fallen already. A smoky apparition hung next to its burning twin. Debris and people fell away from a fiery scar cut into the upper floors, belching jet-black smoke from an insatiable furnace. The unmistakable white radio antenna, rooted defiantly atop the building, seemed to reach upward for clean air, like the proud mast of a ship. Below, all fire, thick with madness. But above, all quiet. And blue.

The mast stayed fixed. Strong. And then, as if cut loose from its moorings, it started to float. To bob and roll. It looked like the whole top of the building might sail away, just break clear of the fire and drift to safety.

But then a gush of ash from below. The snare of gravity. And the mast slipped down. It became an outstretched arm, extending shoulder to fingertip as it reached for some tiny bit of sky, something to cling to before disappearing in the cascading black.

The building peeled away and evaporated into a billion flickering bits of glass and paper, metal and steel that shimmered in the bright sun, emitting indecipherable messages as they fell to the ground. They rose again in a pale torrent of ash, turning everyone in its path into raceless, sexless phantoms. Poindexter watched. The signals. The seeds of the undoing. They were in there. And out there.

We weren't watching.

Television images from Lower Manhattan showed dazed pedestrians covered from head to toe in a ghostly film of powdery debris. In appearance and demeanor, they resembled those dust-coated survivors from Beirut nearly twenty years earlier, as they struggled to comprehend what had happened and what they should do next. Across Washington millions of workers and tourists retreated via the only mode of transportation still functioning dependably—their feet. Government agencies sent their employees home. Soldiers wielding automatic rifles cordoned off whole blocks of the downtown area and directed human traffic via the wide streets and avenues that ran north into Maryland and south to the Virginia suburbs. Amid frantic news reports of a fire on the National Mall, a car bomb in front of the State Department, and another plane heading for Washington, the Secret Service evacuated the White House. Agents screamed at the crowd to run, take off your shoes if you have to, but run, as fast as you can.

At Syntek, most of the staff gathered their personal belongings and headed for home, unsure when they might return. But Poindexter stayed. As he had on that October morning eighteen years earlier, when the world spun so wildly around him, he went to work.

In 1983, Poindexter was one of the few men in the country with a laptop computer, encrypted phone line, and data connection in his home. Now the cellphone in his pocket packed more computing power than the GRiD Compass he'd kept locked up in his basement. Technology had become ubiquitous. Invisible. And for most, an afterthought.

The spy agencies had been reluctant to adopt Poindexter's Genoa system, or some of the newer tools from his workshop that he thought showed real promise. But their indifference was not directed just at him. The agencies spent secret billions on systems to *collect* data—plucking signals out of the air, snapping photos from hundreds of miles above the earth—but a comparatively paltry sum trying to make sense of it all. This had been their problem two decades ago, and nothing had changed. The world around them had evolved. But the system—that slippery, bureaucratic nemesis that Poindexter had tried to defeat, and that ultimately bested him—had stayed the same.

Around town that morning and afternoon, the kindred spirits of Poindexter's tribe lamented their perceived personal failures. As Erik Kleinsmith watched the towers fall, the seeming inevitability of the moment could not assuage his profound regret. Mary McCarthy would not forgive herself, then and years later, for not finding the right signal in that ceaseless chatter that crossed her desk in the summer of 2001. Poindexter stewed privately, looking for a channel to vent his annoyance. He recalled a meeting years earlier with a senior intelligence official who'd dismissed the forecasting powers of the Genoa system. His comments struck Poindexter now with forehead-slapping ferocity: "John, all I want to know is, on the morning after, who knew what, when."

That time had passed.

Poindexter sat at his desk watching an old world fade around him. He'd weathered enough crises to know what came next: the mad reshufflings of agencies; the blue ribbon committees; the recriminations. "Nothing will ever be the same," people would say. And they'd be right. But there were constants. And for a student of crisis, one was never so true: From chaos comes opportunity.

People would say that the world changed on September 11. But for Poindexter, as buildings and bodies burned, the world became a much clearer place.

CHAPTER 12

A NEW MANHATTAN PROJECT

Poindexter worked all day at his desk, convinced that the morning's events were an opening salvo, not a final shot. Outside, the country braced for a follow-up attack. The Federal Aviation Administration grounded all air traffic in the United States. The stock market closed. Soldiers and policemen patrolled the streets of New York and Washington, keeping close watch on subway trains and government buildings. Initial estimates put the death toll at the Pentagon as high as eight hundred. In New York, where the casualties at the World Trade Center were yet unfathomable, a Navy aircraft carrier and warships took up defensive positions off Long Island. America was at war.

As he sat in the nearly empty office, Poindexter cleared his mind, pushing aside the noise that surrounded him even now in such a quiet space. What signal had been missed? What clue? What moment? But more important, how could he catch it next time? What did he have to do now to preempt that second wave he was certain crested just beyond his line of sight?

He worked the puzzle over all day and at home that night. It waited for him when he woke up the next morning and when he piled into his car again, the radio turned off. Poindexter had just driven out of his quiet, tree-lined subdivision when the answer hit him.

He pulled his car over to the side of the road and grabbed his cellphone, scrolling through his contacts list. He found the number of the one man he knew was knocking around in the same headspace that morning.

"That's funny," Brian Sharkey told his old friend when he rang. "I was just thinking about calling you."

Sharkey and Poindexter had been waiting for this day. And this conversation, where they'd commiserate over lost chances. Poindexter vented about how slowly the intelligence community had accepted the Genoa program, and how few tools he and Sharkey had developed had actually been implemented. Poindexter thought DARPA management had been too stingy, allocating a mere $40 million over the past five years to advance and sustain his research.

Poindexter had plenty of reasons to condemn those he'd tried to persuade. But at that moment he saw a window, and he decided to jump through it.

"We need to talk to Tony," he said.

Tony Tether, the new director of DARPA, had been on the job only three months. Poindexter didn't know him well, but Sharkey did. Poindexter wanted a chance to get in front of Tether with an idea that had been gelling in his brain that morning but that both he and Sharkey had been nurturing for some time.

They called it "total information awareness." Sharkey had introduced the phrase two years earlier in Denver during a speech at the annual DARPATech conference. The event brought out all the big names in the military R&D world, and Sharkey had told them what they already knew: The world was awash in information, and every day valuable intelligence was lost in the deluge. The sources of information seemed to expand at uncontrollable rates. It was clear that without some intervention the momentum of data would outstrip the government's ability to keep up with it.

Sharkey had imagined a comprehensive system to collect all this diffused data about real world events and then assimilate them in a process of "collective reasoning," which would be conducted by human analysts linked together through their computers. This was the heart of Genoa, but the concept of total information awareness took things a step further. This system would collect information too and vet it against known types of crises. If it could be trained in what signals to look for, then the system might identify an impending crisis early and increase the chances of preempting it.

It was a fanciful notion, one that, Sharkey admitted, tested the boundaries between human reasoning and computer automation. Sharkey was still a DARPA employee, and he reminded the crowd that total information awareness was a concept, not an active program.

Poindexter wanted to change that. It was time to bring TIA to life.

He told Sharkey that DARPA needed a new program office, a place to harness Genoa and a slew of other technologies into a large system, like the one that he'd outlined two years earlier. Poindexter could think of several tools under research that would fit logically into this new portfolio. There was one aimed at reaping rich data harvests from large information sources and making meaningful connections. Another area that Poindexter thought received far too little funding was automated translation, computer programs designed to convert foreign languages, whether written or spoken, into English. Also, he was keen on a program that DARPA had neglected that could use facial recognition technology from a distance, and in crowds.

These ideas were force multipliers—each would make the other stronger when used in concert. Poindexter wanted to bind them all. To create a superstructure, a "system of systems." A single, automated design to discover information, to mold and shape it. It would see what human eyes could not. And perhaps to finally, truly, understand the world around them.

Though Poindexter had imagined such a grand apparatus from his earliest days in the White House, the technology to build it didn't exist then. Times had changed. Now the physical constraints were the least of his concerns. People had to change. That was the hardest part.

Fortunately for Poindexter, people were scared now. And that meant they'd be ready to take risks. Sharkey agreed to call Tether and arrange a meeting. Poindexter went back to his office and spent the rest of the day sketching the first draft of his plan.

In all his years of thinking about preempting terrorism, Poindexter had fixed his eyes abroad. Even at the height of the terror wave in the eighties he had never contemplated a massive assault on U.S. soil. Terrorism was a foreign problem, and more specifically, a foreign intelligence problem. Vast and nebulous though his work was, those factors gave it a useful frame. It told him, and told the government, where to look, what kinds of information to gather.

Whatever signals pointed to the catastrophic events of September 11, they were most certainly not to be found exclusively abroad. Poindexter reasoned that unless these men had slipped into the United States only days before their mission—and that seemed implausible—they would have left many traces here. They made phone calls. Probably sent e-mails. They bought merchandise with credit cards. They made plane reservations. Perhaps they'd lived here a long time, leased apartments, maybe bought property. They would have gone to grocery stores, meandered through shopping malls, dined at restaurants. People would have seen them. But more important, and more dependably, computers would have seen them and kept tiny memories of the encounter. Everywhere they stepped these men left digital footprints, the permanent markings of where they'd been, what they'd done, and what they might do next. These were their signals.

Poindexter had a theory. Just as submarines emitted a unique sound signature in the ocean, terrorists emitted a unique transaction signature in the information space. If he could pick it out, then he could find the goblins hiding in that noisy sea.

The idea departed radically from every other counterterrorism program to date. The intelligence and law enforcement agencies had always hunted for terrorists by starting with a known target. They'd get a name, or a phone number, and then scan their databases for any mention of the quarry. Working step by step they could link the target to other people and places, or to known events. This was shoe-leather investigation. Excavating a terrorist network one data point at a time.

Technology had sped up the process, but the end results were limited. As Kleinsmith had learned in Able Danger, sometimes the mass of links and connections was so dense, so crisscrossed, that it was unintelligible. But terrorists were hiding in that mass. As investigators located the 9/11 hijackers' electronic transactions, surely they would find overlooked clues, dots unconnected. But for present purposes, the CIA, the FBI, everyone had obviously been blind. How was the intelligence community expected to find men who it didn't know existed? That, Poindexter thought, was the crux of the new problem. Terrorists were not about to signal their intentions. The government would have to find them first. But in order to find one man's digital footprints, he decided, you had to look at everyone's. The innocent and the unknown guilty. Total information awareness.

Instead of asking airlines to raise a red flag whenever a suspected terrorist purchased a ticket, Poindexter wanted to look at all passenger reservations for anomalies. There were patterns of transactions he thought might indicate terrorist activity. People buying one-way airline tickets who also entered the country together, or near the same time. Maybe they stayed in the same hotel together, or shared a credit card account. Maybe they rented a car together. He decided that the best way to find these phantoms was to look for evidence of their activity first—and decide later whether the people in question were truly innocent.

Before September 11, he would never have dared propose such an idea, much less have any confidence that anyone would back it. But the old method of tracking known targets had obviously failed. Now pattern-based searching of everything, of everyone, of all that was known or knowable, seemed to him the only logical choice.

Sharkey called Poindexter back. Tether was willing to meet and hear about his idea. Given their personal history, Poindexter thought that Sharkey should make the first, broad pitch. He arranged for the two of them to have lunch at a quiet restaurant a few blocks from DARPA headquarters. Poindexter had spent most of September 12 crafting a set of talking points, enough to give Tether the essential elements of the plan.

Tether liked what he heard. All across the government agencies were revving up for a new kind of war. Previously "risk averse" organizations, as critics liked to think of the CIA and others, were now desperate for ideas. Tether would back Poindexter's program, he said, but on one condition: Either he or Sharkey had to come back to government to run it. This was far too complicated a task to leave to anyone other than the experts, and clearly, they were Poindexter and Sharkey.

Sharkey left the luncheon and relayed the bad news to his friend. Neither of them wanted to return to public life. Since his speech in Denver, Sharkey had left DARPA and joined a boutique technology and consulting firm, Hicks & Associates. He enjoyed private-sector work, both for the intellectual freedom and the financial reward. Hicks's parent company, Science Applications International Corporation, was one of the largest employee-owned companies in the country, and Sharkey had amassed considerable stock options. The company's business would boom as government agencies planned to spend billions on new technology for counterterrorism. If Sharkey returned to public service, he might have to give up his options. He'd certainly have to take a substantial pay cut.

Sharkey was a younger man than Poindexter. He had different obligations. He just wasn't prepared to come back, and Poindexter didn't want to force him. Besides, Poindexter was the mastermind. He could see the system from end to end. And he knew how the bureaucracy worked. Few DARPA program managers had ever been national security adviser to the president. Poindexter's return was the agency's gain.

All that was true, but Poindexter had his own reasons to turn the job down. Along with his résumé came his baggage. How big a distraction might that be? He and Linda weighed the options together. He had the bureaucratic expertise, the technological fluency, the vision. He also still had the highest level of security clearance, owing to his work at Syntek.

He also weighed the financial concerns. Poindexter was not a rich man. But his children were grown. He owned his home. The boat was the biggest expense, yet a manageable one. There was really only one question: Was John Poindexter his plan's best asset or its worst liability?

Though he'd been a master of casuistry in his dealings with Congress, Poindexter had always been honest with himself. His association with an ambitious and controversial counterterrorism program would cause trouble. He had no doubts about that. The moment he stepped back onto the public stage he could become a lightning rod atop his provocative venture.

Poindexter had long thought that if he had it to do over again, he would have devised a public relations strategy for the "Iran-Contra business," as he preferred to call it. He had warned his cohort then that if the convoluted operation ever became public, they'd have a very hard time explaining it.

Washington was a town of institutional memories. Many of his oldest allies in government were back in power, in senior positions within the Bush administration. And his oldest foes had remained in Congress. Poindexter wasn't sure now how, or if, he could avoid the lightning. But he figured it would come eventually.

He thought about it for a few days, then picked up the phone and called Sharkey. *Okay. Let's do it.*

———

A month later—a quick turnaround by government standards—Poindexter found himself sitting in Tether's office, suit-clad, a PowerPoint briefing on his laptop, ready to explain TIA. He'd taken to calling total information awareness by an acronym, which he pronounced like a woman's name, "Tia."

Poindexter had always prided himself as a superb briefer, and this time he'd come armed with the goods. Tether donned his big wire-rimmed glasses and pulled up to Poindexter's laptop. It wouldn't be hard to sell him on the technology. He had a PhD in electrical engineering from Stanford and had spent a career in the private sector as a high-level program manager for defense contractors. Rather, Poindexter wanted to impress upon his future boss, from the outset, that this was no ordinary research project.

Poindexter called up the title slide: "A Manhattan Project on Countering Terrorism."

He couldn't have chosen a more powerful allusion. Likening TIA to the construction of the first atomic bomb, Poindexter immediately conjured up the forces of war, ingenuity, and dynamism. He was telling Tether that he sensed a historic opportunity, and that, like the original Manhattan Project, TIA would require an extraordinary combination of research, science, and money. DARPA was the only agency Poindexter could imagine taking on such a futuristic and risky concept.

Beneath the title, Poindexter excerpted a passage from a *New York Times* article that had run a few days earlier, which crystallized the nascent critique of the government's pre–9/11 failures now taking hold.

In hindsight, it is becoming clear that the CIA, FBI and other agencies had significant fragments of information that, under ideal circumstances, could have provided some warning if they had all been pieced together and shared rapidly.

That was TIA in a nutshell. And from then on, even if Tether didn't grasp the technical esoterica that riddled Poindexter's presentation, he would get the essence of it.

The quote was appropriate for another reason. The article from which it came led with news of a bracing memo sent to senior officials at the CIA from the director of central intelligence, George Tenet only five days after 9/11. Tenet had made it clear that the government was less interested in assigning blame for the attacks than in radically departing from the culture that had allowed them.

"The agency must give people the authority to do things they might not ordinarily be allowed to do," Tenet commanded. "If there is some bureaucratic hurdle, leap it." Tenet titled his memo simply "We're at War."

Poindexter showed Tether the leap he wanted to make. He called up a world map peppered with red dots and accompanying text labels. Each one hovered over some disaster-prone part of the world and asked an expansive question. Over the Middle East, "What do we know about terrorists like Osama Bin Laden?" Next to New York, "How do we prevent another World Trade Center Disaster?"

But elsewhere around the map, Poindexter placed questions that had nothing to do with religious terrorism. "What should the U.S. do about China?" "How can we fix Colombia?" Clearly he thought TIA had applications beyond just the current crisis. Poindexter had been traveling this road for decades, and in a way, 9/11 was merely a catalyzing event.

"It's all about information," Poindexter told Tether. "We are swimming in data but still need more." But not general information, and not the kind that was easy for the intelligence community to get. Right now they needed transactional information—about people. What they bought. What they read. Where they traveled. Whom they talked to, and what they said.

Terrorists worked in cells, and those cells represented nodes in a large global network. The government might not always understand its reach, but they could grasp its structure by pulling apart the transactional bonds between nodes and among clusters of them. This was the best way to disrupt terrorists and prevent their attacks: to unlock the design of the network.

What Poindexter was proposing now went far beyond the traditional boundaries of law and policy. "Our focus has to be on individual people," he told Tether.

"Focusing on People . . . Extremely Sensitive," Poindexter titled a subsequent slide. It featured a flow chart, bland and undecipherable at first, but that, upon closer examination, revealed a basic structure for how information about people might flow through a TIA system. First, Poindexter listed a dizzying array of sensitive data to access. "Transactions: Communications, Financial, Education, Travel, Country Entry, Place or Event Entry, Medical, Veterinary, Transportation, Housing, Critical Resource, Government."

This was the raw material of a total information awareness system. But it was just a first step. The chart showed how this stream, along with covertly collected photographs and "biometric" information such as fingerprints and image scans, would comprise "dossiers" used by multiple government agencies to develop models of terrorist attacks. The TIA system would use this information to help analysts predict "plausible futures," or terrorist scenarios that were likely to occur. The analysts, not the system, would then suggest to national leaders how they might mitigate or prevent that crisis.

Poindexter described the entire process in four discrete steps: "Detect, Classify, ID, Track." And, he told Tether, an analog for this kind of hunt already existed—antisubmarine warfare.

"This is not business as usual," Poindexter said. "We must put introduction of new technology on a wartime basis." He wanted only the brightest program managers and researchers. He told Tether he'd like to cordon them all in a secret facility outside Washington, some massive complex surrounded by high fences and concertina wire with "No Trespassing" signs prominently displayed. This was mostly theater, he explained, set dressings meant to impress upon those inside the gravity and consequence of their historic mission. It was a "patriotic duty," Poindexter said. "We should not waste time."

Poindexter would only design TIA. It was up to the intelligence agencies, or maybe the FBI, to use it once the prototype had been built. That was not his call. In the meantime, though, Poindexter wanted to do something that DARPA managers had never tried before—he wanted to ignite a policy debate.

Poindexter suffered no illusions that a large portion of the public—maybe the overwhelming majority—would find his ideas not only distasteful but unconscionable. He wanted a chance to change their minds. And he would do it, unsurprisingly, in a technical fashion.

Poindexter told Tether that he would build "privacy-protection" technologies into TIA's design. He showed how the system could encrypt each one of the millions, perhaps billions of discrete data points it inspected, so that all a human analyst ever saw was a series of numbers—no names, no faces, no identifying information. The identifier could contain all the information an analyst needed, including its source, which agency collected it, its relationship to other data, and the time and place it was captured. But it need not contain a name or any other clue that would give away the true identity of the person who had created that tiny ripple in the digital ocean. As his thinking evolved, Poindexter imagined an entire "privacy appliance" built into the system that would lock private information away in a kind of electronic safe that might only be opened upon order of a judge. The judge would have to find that the government had a reason for thinking this anonymous person might actually be a terrorist. Poindexter called this case-by-case approach to putting names to data "selective revelation."

Poindexter emphasized that the research in this area was distressingly scant. He wanted Tether to include funding in the TIA budget for new research, which he also hoped might inspire discussion about the merits of the concept, and therefore the entire system. Poindexter believed that if he could prove a privacy appliance worked, people might strike a bargain between their privacy and their safety.

That meant taking his idea public. He'd first imagined TIA as a "black program," veiled behind a classified budget and rings of secrecy. But he wondered if this would slow his progress and lead people to think he had something to hide.

Tether also said keeping TIA classified would slow Poindexter down. Time was not on his side. Poindexter wanted to assemble a team quickly, and he wanted to gather ideas from thinkers and tinkerers well beyond the security-cleared confines of Washington. If he kept TIA under wraps, he was bound to get many of the same tired ideas he'd seen in the past five years. He wanted to blow the doors open.

"Don't worry about the dollars," Tether assured. "I'll give you all the money you need." DARPA would pool all the existing funds for the various programs Poindexter planned to acquire, the ones he'd mentioned to Sharkey when they first talked after 9/11. And Tether would throw in some start-up capital. The pool came to about $100 million. And Tether agreed to increase that budget to at least $150 million the following fiscal year.

Poindexter had gotten what he asked for. He had planned. He had executed. He had succeeded. Strong winds portended smooth sailing. He hadn't any clue that thirty miles away, at the headquarters of the greatest signals-catching apparatus ever devised, another fleet was preparing to sail.

THE BAG

It was October 6, two days before Columbus Day. The holiday passed unnoticed and uncelebrated by most, but Washingtonians coveted it: For thousands of federal employees and Capitol Hill staffers, it was the one day each year when they got the day off and their kids still had to go to school.

Mike Wertheimer was looking forward to some quiet time with his wife. They both needed the break. Wertheimer, a PhD mathematician and the National Security Agency's top technologist, had spent the past few weeks climbing out of a profound depression.

When the planes hit the Twin Towers and the Pentagon, the shock wave resonated uniquely with Wertheimer and his colleagues. It was their job to build the tools that the NSA's terrorist hunters needed to stop a cataclysm like this. The agency had paid for Wertheimer's university education, and in return, he'd given the place twenty-one years of his life, putting his prodigious technical skills to work as an electronic monitor in his country's secret service. Yet he seemed to have missed the signals emitted right in front of him. The 9/11 hijackers, it turned out, had been plotting their attack within miles of the NSA's headquarters at Fort Meade, Maryland. They'd been here all along, and Wertheimer never knew it.

Wertheimer had risen through the ranks to become the agency's top techie. On paper, he fit the stereotype captured in an old joke traded among the NSA lifers: "How can you tell an extroverted analyst? He's the one who looks at *your* shoes when he's talking." But Wertheimer, over six feet tall with deep, searching eyes, defied the image. He looked in people's faces when he spoke, undistracted.

The arch of his eyebrows and the glint in his eyes gave everything away—when he was listening, when he disagreed, when he was afraid.

And so he couldn't conceal the depth of his regret from his wife, his family, or his coworkers. He was convinced that he hadn't fought hard enough for those things that might have made a difference. Haunted by three thousand ghosts, he wondered what he had missed. What he had left undone. What trick he hadn't tried or what argument he'd conceded when he should have shouted louder. Wertheimer drifted about his house, inconsolable, until one day his eighty-year-old father pulled him aside.

"What are you doing? I lived through World War II, through the Depression, through Vietnam," Wertheimer's father said. And now terrorism. He looked his son in the eyes, those eyes that revealed all. "I don't hold you responsible," he said. "I sleep better with you back at work trying to solve these problems."

Wertheimer had long since concluded that he and his father had little in common beyond lineage. But now the man was breaking through to him in a way no one else had.

The lecture was like an antidote. It snapped him to life. Wertheimer renewed himself to the fight, but he vowed never to let it into his home. He would do his job, and keep his family safe.

His newfound resolve was tested that Saturday before Columbus Day, as Mr. and Mrs. Wertheimer made plans for a solitary retreat. The phone rang. An emergency call from the office. "You need to come in."

Wertheimer found himself in a large conference room in the NSA's headquarters building, along with about eighty of his colleagues. Standing before them was a man who had made his own resolution in the weeks since 9/11: The next attack was not going to happen on his watch.

Wertheimer had worked closely with Mike Hayden since he took over the agency in March 1999. They and a band of senior officials had been shaking up the place from the inside out. Hayden, a lieutenant general in the Air Force and a career intelligence officer, knew that the NSA was being overtaken by the digital revolution. The biggest threat came from global telecommunications networks, which the agency's eavesdropping systems, largely designed to intercept satellite transmissions, were not prepared to address. Hayden, Wertheimer, and others had done yeoman's work bringing the agency into the twenty-first century and realigning its post–cold war mission to deal with terrorism and other asymmetric threats. But now they could wonder if it was all for naught.

Hayden was a football fanatic and often liked to tell stories about the NSA using sports metaphors. After 9/11 it had become clear to him that the agency played too much defense. President Bush agreed. The NSA had a formidable capacity to detect terrorist threats, but it had gone largely unused in the United States, owing largely to legal restrictions over when and how the agency could monitor targets inside the country. Now it was clear that the strategy of fighting a war "over there" had been upended. The targets the NSA needed to track now were in the United States, or on their way. It was time to change the game plan.

Hayden explained to his employees that four days earlier the president had granted the agency new authorities that allowed the NSA to greatly expand its surveillance net. The agency could now target the communications of anyone reasonably suspected of being a terrorist, or those associated with them, without a warrant. Whereas once the agency would have had to get permission from the secretive Foreign Intelligence Surveillance Court to conduct intelligence surveillance inside the United States, now they could bypass that requirement, so long as the surveillance complied with a few simple yet utterly new rules.

First, there was a question of geography. Say someone in Pakistan called a phone number in San Francisco. That would be considered a foreign communication, well within the agency's traditional surveillance domain. If NSA analysts reasonably believed the target in Pakistan was a terrorist or associated with terrorists, then the agency's eavesdroppers could monitor both the target in Pakistan and the person he called in San Francisco. Under ordinary circumstances the NSA would have either stopped that surveillance or erased records of the San Francisco person's name and identity. But now the analysts could listen in and determine if the conversation, or the parties involved, had any "nexus to terrorism."

This would be the new watch phrase. The analysts would have to study up on Al Qaeda and other terrorist groups, learn their calling and e-mailing patterns, and their code words, to determine whether that nexus was real or if the call they were tapping was entirely benign. The same went for e-mails. The analysts would have to read the messages to determine whether it contained potential intelligence or something useless—a fruitcake recipe, a lame joke, a chain letter. But after digging into the phone call or the message, if the analysts determined that the communicant in San Francisco was in the terrorist nexus, then the NSA could begin targeting him directly, without a warrant. That was the major new change. Such surveillance was supposed to require a warrant under the Foreign Intelligence Surveillance Act, the 1978 law enacted to prevent unchecked domestic spying. But the president had determined that if anyone in the United States was in contact with known or suspected terrorists, then they too could reasonably be suspected of involvement in terrorism. The agency could start monitoring that person's phone number, or his e-mail account, in order to find out whom else he was in touch with. And then whom *those* targets were talking to and e-mailing. And on and on and on, until the agency had a map of what this global nexus of terrorism really looked like, and where it touched the United States.

The employees listening to Hayden could have been forgiven if they swore they'd felt the ground moving beneath them. This was a seismic shift—in law, in policy, in culture. Hayden was saying that the president had just given the NSA permission to go on the offense against terrorists. And on a new playing field—the United States. Only one category of communications was off-limits: those conducted entirely within the country. If the target in San Francisco called someone in Brooklyn, the agency could not monitor without a warrant from the judges on the FISA court—which, if the target in San Francisco really was a suspected terrorist, would not be hard to get.

The agency's global monitoring system certainly had the technological capacity for this new play. It snatched satellite transmissions out of the air, gobbled up overseas phone calls and faxes as they traversed massive undersea cables, snooped on military communications and diplomatic correspondences. If it traveled on a wire, a fiber-optic cable, or on a wave through the air, the NSA could grab it. But this new monitoring would require significant assistance from the companies that controlled the telecommunications system. Fortunately, because of the midnineties surveillance law that required those companies to build equipment that could be monitored, the new targeting procedures could be implemented rather easily. The NSA would soon tell the phone companies to load targeted phone numbers and e-mails into the international gateways through which all foreign traffic entered the United States, and from which U.S. communications were routed onto foreign destinations. Tracking suspected terrorists would be as straightforward as waiting to see when the number in Pakistan made or received a call. The telecom companies could also be accommodating in other ways. International gateways could be created if a phone company or Internet service provider rerouted traffic through a "point of presence" in the United States, a physical location with access to a network. That point of presence needn't be at the company's offices. If the company was willing to assist, it could also reside in a government facility.

Wertheimer had spent his career at the agency. Like every employee, he received training in the tenets of privacy and surveillance law that controlled the NSA's spying activities. And every refresher course reminded him that the laws governing what the intelligence community did with U.S. persons information were criminal statutes. People went to jail for breaking them. Congress had not changed these laws in the past three weeks. The authority to recalibrate the NSA's electronic sights had come from the president. There was no higher authority.

"We're going to do exactly what he said," Hayden told his staff, referring to Bush. "Not one photon or one electron more."

To Wertheimer, it seemed like the right thing to do. At least for now. Just how long the agency would be able to stay within the boundaries of the president's admonition no one could say. But as far as Hayden was concerned, he was going to play right up to the line until someone told him to stand down. For years he had lingered in the backfield, and clearly to his peril. The country had been attacked on his watch. He wouldn't let it happen again. As Hayden would say more than once in the months and years to come, "I will play in fair territory. But there will be chalk dust on my cleats."

On the morning of 9/11, Hayden had been working for two hours already when news reached him that a plane had struck the North Tower. Security procedures at the NSA were tighter than at most agencies, and almost immediately submachine gun–toting guards and bomb-sniffing dogs fanned out across the vast Maryland campus. As the other planes struck their targets, Hayden ordered all nonessential workers to evacuate the grounds. He called his wife, Jeanine, asked her to find their three children, and headed to the counterterrorism center, home to the signals experts and linguists who tracked Al Qaeda's foreign communications. Hayden knew that the chatter level had been high lately, and now he could see why.

The center's offices were located near the top floor of a high-rise. Hayden had tried to move as many employees as possible out of these vulnerable buildings. But he couldn't let the counterterrorism center stand down now. When he arrived, he found staffers crying, and yet defiantly hanging blackout curtains over their windows, a wartime measure to mask their location from future attackers.

The attacks were personal for the staff and for Hayden. In his two and a half years as director he had devoted extraordinary amounts of time and personal political capital to burnishing the agency's image. He defied the popular conception of the NSA as a stealthy, all-knowing, and conspiratorial government organ, so secret that employees joked its acronym stood for "no such agency." The image popularized in Hollywood productions like *Enemy of the State*, which premiered the year before Hayden took over, had made the agency seem stronger and more independent than it really was. Hayden wanted to educate the public about what his staff did every day. He courted outsiders. He spoke candidly about global eavesdropping. He invited journalists to the agency's annual holiday party. And most important, he nurtured personal relationships with his key overseers on Capitol Hill.

Hayden's public relations had spooked a lot of the NSA lifers. This was not business as usual. But his dedication to their mission, and to their protection, was indisputable. His employees could trust that the boss had their back, as surely as he covered his own.

In a town full of self-promoters, Hayden had mastered that delicate art better than most. He possessed the requisite cunning for a high-level existence in Washington, but also the chops, a rare combination. In a twenty-one-year military career he'd held a series of increasingly demanding intelligence jobs, most bearing titles that began with "director" and "chief." Hayden was a born manager. He had survived, and excelled, by exhorting people to follow his lead.

Hayden was an unlikely public face for a secretive spy agency. He *looked* shady. With his shiny bald head, wire glasses, and hooded eyes, he bore an uncanny resemblance to the character actor Kurtwood Smith, who played the villain in *Robocop* and a double-crossing FBI agent on *The X-Files.* But Hayden played against type. He was charming. Ebullient. He was as polite and deferential to journalists as to members of Congress. It worked. Hayden turned the agency's image around and was without question its most vocal supporter.

In the first day's after the 9/11 attacks, Hayden hadn't waited for permission to act. While the agency had held off from any kind of domestic mission in the past, the fact was, Hayden had a number of arrows in his quiver that he had yet to use.

Immediately after the attacks he ordered the agency to "go up on," or monitor, a set of hot targets, foreign entities that the agency believed were connected to terrorism. Hayden didn't wait for a court order to do this. Just how broad that target set was remained a closely held secret. But even if the targets turned out to have connections inside the United States, the NSA would not shut down its surveillance. Hayden wasn't out on a limb here. Under the banner of a twenty-year-old executive order, enacted by Ronald Reagan, the NSA was authorized to collect, retain, and disseminate foreign intelligence as part of a terrorism investigation. Clearly, one was afoot.

Hayden broadened the reach of his signals-gathering agency in those first days after 9/11. The surveillance extended not just to those foreign targets but to the individuals they were communicating with inside the United States.

As Hayden's monitors listened, they did something else extraordinary: They handed over leads about potential targets inside the country to the FBI. Hayden flooded law enforcement agents with anything that might lead to a sleeper cell or help detect a future attack. Again, that same presidential order covered him. Executive order 12333 (or "twelve triple three," as it was known in the trade) was the intelligence community's set of operating authorities. Their playbook. Some believed that Reagan had issued it as a kind of counterweight to the Foreign Intelligence Surveillance Act, which the president and some of his national security aides saw as a blatant attempt by Congress to interfere with the spy agencies. Hayden, ever the lover of football metaphors, had now turned to the order as a source of new offensive tactics, and well before the current president gave him a new set of rules.

In the course of this immediate post–9/11 surveillance, U.S. persons— which included citizens and legal residents—were being caught up in the NSA's electronic nets. These were the people in communication with those hot targets already on the agency's radar. But the agency's terrorist hunters could not know whether that secondary ring was composed of conspirators or incidental bystanders in the hot targets' communications chain. Were they bomb makers or pizza deliverers?

The FBI agents who received the tips were often unsure, but it was their job to run those leads to ground. And the leads piled up quickly. As agents fanned out around the country, they were unaware of how the information in their hands had been obtained. Even in an emergency, the NSA assiduously guarded its sources and methods.

While the FBI agents were equally concerned with finding the next terror- ist cell, they had their own careers to worry about. If the NSA had captured these communications illegally, they might be unavailable to federal prosecu- tors hoping to build cases against terrorism suspects. A judge could dis- miss them as fruit of a poisonous tree. What's more, if the agents themselves were seen as complicit in illegal spying, they could be prosecuted. These were criminal statutes, after all, something the cops at the FBI knew as well as their cousins in the spy world.

It might have seemed like the NSA had crossed a threshold. Here was Hayden, rushing the field in a moment of crisis. But even this bold play was insufficient. As Hayden laced up his cleats, he knew that if he really wanted to score, he'd need a whole new strategy.

As Hayden saw it, all these hot communications constituted *foreign* intelli- gence. If a terrorist in Islamabad called someone in Brooklyn, that was an international phone call. And it was the NSA's job, legally, to collect such foreign intelligence. Had the agency turned its monitors loose solely on Amer- ican citizens, or started tracking their constitutionally protected political activities, Hayden likely would have turned himself in, handcuffs already affixed. But by his reading he was adjusting the scope of the NSA's collection, not changing the rules governing it.

Nancy Pelosi, the top Democrat on the House Intelligence Committee, wasn't so sure. On October 1, Hayden briefed the California congresswoman and the full committee on what the NSA had been doing over the past few weeks to prevent another attack. Hayden brought up Executive order 12333. Pelosi and the other members knew it well. But 12333 was an order, not a law. Only Congress wrote those.

The same was true for the litany of regulations and operating procedures that had trickled down from 12333 over the years. They couldn't trump legislation—especially the Foreign Intelligence Surveillance Act. Congress had meant that law to be the exclusive means by which intelligence collection inside America was authorized and controlled. It was the same kind of collection that Hayden was engaged in now.

Hayden knew that FISA warrants weren't handed out freely. They required thick sets of paperwork accompanied by sworn statements from lawyers at the Justice Department. And if said officials thought that a surveillance request didn't meet the muster of the law, they would never argue for it in front of a judge. To do so imperiled their career, maybe even their ability to practice law.

But most of the NSA's activities weren't covered by FISA. The agency's surveillances were directed overseas and usually against foreigners. It wasn't unusual for the NSA to scoop up the communications of some protected Americans in the course of monitoring foreign targets, but when that happened the agency replaced their names in its reports with anonymous markers such as "U.S. Person 1." This privacy protection, known as minimization, kept the NSA from incriminating presumably innocent people. And as long as the NSA was fighting foreign wars, that worked just fine.

Congress and the intelligence community both understood FISA. But their interpretations differed markedly. Some of the authors of Reagan's executive order saw it as a marker against Congress after it passed the surveillance law. They saw FISA as an unjust limitation on the president's *inherent* authority to collect foreign intelligence. The lawyers at the NSA saw 12333, not FISA, as their agency's marching order. (After all, the NSA didn't routinely spy on Americans, and so the law bore less day-to-day relevance to their operations.)

As Pelosi and her colleagues listened to Hayden talk about the NSA's new counterterrorism activities it was unclear whether what Hayden authorized after 9/11 was permissible, or whether it fell into some murky gap between a law and an order. Pelosi was concerned that Hayden had crossed a line. Whether that was true would not be resolved during his appearance on the Hill.

After the briefing wrapped up, Pelosi thought about what Hayden had said. She still wasn't sure she understood, or agreed, that he had the authorities to expand his agency's mission. She told her staff to do some digging.

What little they could pry out of the administration, which had clamped down on the flow of national security information to Congress, didn't satisfy Pelosi. She wasn't sure if Hayden needed, or had obtained, specific authorization from the current president to conduct these new activities. Hayden had a difficult case to make, she thought.

Hayden seemed to agree. Not long after the attacks, George Tenet made the rounds to the various intelligence agency chiefs, and he asked Hayden a question: "Is there anything more you can do?"

"Not within my current authorities," Hayden replied.

Hayden had in mind a far more aggressive role for his agency, and one that mirrored the plan Poindexter was hatching at precisely the same time. Hayden wanted to build an early-warning system for terrorist attacks.

He knew as well as Poindexter, as well as anyone, that the keys to terrorist planning lay in their electronic transmissions. So it was before 9/11; so it was before the Beirut bombing. And he knew that law, policy, and culture had impeded his efforts in the past. But technology was not one of his big problems. In fact, it could save him.

Well before the attacks, Hayden understood his agency was still collecting intelligence with a cold war mind-set. So he tasked a team of senior managers, including Wertheimer and another NSA lifer named Maureen Baginski, to reshape signals intelligence for the digital age. They put a premium on analysis, and on targeting the right sources of intelligence, instead of on just vacuuming up as much information as the agency's computers could stomach. Baginski liked to call it "hunt, not gather," and that mantra was reflected in the agency Hayden was trying to build.

By the time terrorists invaded America, the NSA had come a long way. In October 2001, when CIA and military forces deployed to Afghanistan to hunt Al Qaeda leaders, Wertheimer and Baginski had so improved the agency's global tracking systems that the NSA could identify human targets for soldiers and airmen in the theater, telling their precise location within a few yards. The agency had learned to find people through their communications devices, and through the signals they emitted and the traces they left. Hayden understood the power of this technology—conceivably, the NSA could have more awareness about terrorists than they had of themselves.

But to accomplish that feat the NSA would have to collect more—a lot more—in places that had traditionally been out of bounds.

Tenet asked Hayden to brief Bush administration officials, including the president and vice president, on what more he needed, and wanted. Hayden explained that any effective system for spotting terrorists before they struck had to meet three criteria: It must be technologically feasible. It must produce useful intelligence. And it must be lawful. Hayden spoke to the first two elements; but he left the last for others to decide.

Technology was the part Hayden knew best. Since the attacks the NSA had been tracking suspected terrorists using the traditional model, starting with a known target and then branching out through their associates. This was not pattern analysis, like what Poindexter wanted to pursue, at least not in the purest sense. Hayden's electronic sleuths might start to notice suspicious indicators in the way terrorists used phones—maybe they used intermediaries or limited their calls to under a certain number of minutes. But this wasn't the start-from-scratch concept behind TIA, in which a system would ingest every piece of data and look for patterns in it without known targets. At least not yet.

In order to build an early-warning system, the NSA would need access to the customer records of the phone companies, Internet service providers, and other purveyors of electronic communications. In the case of the phone companies, call detail records—or logs that showed who called whom; from where to where; when; and how often—constituted a valuable potential resource.

They also would need access to a source that the NSA had not been collecting systematically in the past: e-mail. Despite the agency's reputation for collecting anything and everything electronic, the agency had shied away from this increasingly common medium. One reason was parochial—the agency's terrorist hunters simply didn't believe their targets were using e-mail. They were holed up in caves and dusty campsites, after all, and had seemed to get by just fine with telephones.

But there was also a legal rationale. E-mails, unlike phone calls, were not transmitted point-to-point between two parties. Instead, an e-mail message was broken up into pieces called "packets," each of which traveled different routes through the Internet before being reassembled at a destination. Most packets traveled through the United States, home of most of the world's Internet infrastructure. So the NSA could not be sure that even a foreign e-mail wasn't passing through America. Furthermore, the agency couldn't know for sure whether the sender or receiver was a protected U.S. person. In the face of these uncertainties, the NSA left e-mail alone.

In early 2001, the NSA had begun experimenting with e-mail as an intelligence source, but not against Arab terrorists. Wertheimer had led an exercise to find out whether Russian mobsters were supplying weapons of mass destruction to Iran. He told his team to pull in a variety of data sources, including e-mail, from different agencies. Here too the analysts weren't sold on the idea that Russian organized crime figures were logging on to the Internet to send messages. After 9/11 he told his team to operate as if the terrorists were doing just that. "You are now to presume they use e-mail. Find it," he instructed.

As Hayden set up the new surveillance program, it was increasingly clear to NSA officials that e-mail, not phone calls, would constitute the bulk of their collection. It made sense. Terrorists had to presume that their phone calls were being tapped, or could be easily. But e-mail allowed for a certain amount of stealth. One could open a new account, use it to send a few messages, and then never return to it again. An Al Qaeda operative could log on from different Internet cafés so that he never used the same service provider. He could mask his physical location by using an Internet address that was actually based on a server in another country. As analysts began to study terrorist e-mailing habits more closely, they came to believe that members of a cell actually were sharing a single e-mail account and writing all of their messages to one another as "drafts," which were actually stored in a folder within the account and never sent over the Internet. It was the electronic version of a drop site.

But no communications system, no matter how complex, offered total anonymity. The NSA hunters understood, as did Poindexter's team, that terrorists were susceptible to detection every time they used a phone, sent an e-mail, or made a credit card purchase. Every move left a trace, and though it might be hard to find, it wasn't impossible. But Hayden's system lacked a key component of Poindexter's brainchild—privacy protection. The NSA had no appliance of the kind Poindexter envisioned. No agency did. In this new and treacherous realm of domestic communications, the best assurance that Hayden could provide that he was playing by the rules was his word.

Hayden had come up with a plan, and Bush personally felt it was a good idea. The NSA director's system was technologically feasible. He felt it would produce useful intelligence—perhaps the most useful intelligence the government could expect, since it had so few human spies on the ground in Afghanistan and throughout the Middle East. One question remained: Was Hayden's system legal?

The crux of the answer actually preceded Hayden's pitch. Yes. The president of the United States had the authority to order electronic surveillance of foreign terrorists. And he didn't need a court's permission.

That was the conclusion of John Yoo, an expert on presidential war powers who found himself in high demand after the terrorist attacks. Yoo worked as a politically appointed attorney in the Justice Department's Office of Legal Counsel, the font of wisdom to which all presidents turned when they needed to know if a particular course of action was, in fact, legal. On September 25, Yoo sent a memo to a senior official in the Justice Department, who had asked whether the administration might change some language in FISA in such a way that made it easier for the government to secure warrants in terrorism cases. (That question was up for public debate as Congress and the administration hammered out major changes to surveillance rules in the USA PATRIOT Act.)

Yoo, who had no experience arguing cases before the court that granted FISA warrants, determined that it was not unconstitutional to change the wording of the law. The administration could propose that "a purpose" of surveillance was to collect foreign intelligence, as opposed to "the purpose," which was what the law required. The administration wanted to lower the bar, and Yoo said that was fine.

But then Yoo offered an unsolicited assessment. The president didn't really need to go through FISA at all. The nation was at war, and the president had to gather intelligence to fight that war. "The Fourth Amendment declares that '[t]he right of the people to be secure in their persons, houses, papers, and effects, against *unreasonable* searches and seizures shall not be violated.'" The emphasis was Yoo's own.

"Thus, the touchstone for review is whether a search is 'reasonable,'" he continued. And the Supreme Court had made clear that the government didn't always need a warrant in order to conduct a reasonable search, Yoo noted. Quoting a case that upheld the constitutionality of an Oregon school district's program of random drug testing, Yoo wrote that "a warrantless search can be constitutional 'when special needs, beyond the normal need of law enforcement, make the warrant and probable-cause requirement impracticable.'"

Yoo was going well beyond the question that had first been posed—whether or not FISA could be amended. Now he was articulating a basis for warrantless surveillance conducted "beyond the normal need of law enforcement" because the Fourth Amendment's requirement of probable cause to search was "impracticable."

The president could decide whether those conditions existed, Yoo determined. And the commander in chief should rest comfortably in his authorities: "[T]he Court has found warrantless searches reasonable when there are 'exigent circumstances,' such as threat to the safety of law enforcement or third parties."

Yoo was a scholar, and had pulled only a few previous stints in Washington—in the midnineties, as a general counsel to the Senate Judiciary Committee, and in a clerkship for appeals court judge Lawrence Silberman, who happened to be the presiding judge on John Poindexter's appeal of his

Iran-Contra convictions. Yoo had come to Justice shortly before the 9/11 attacks. But in this memo and others he wrote in coming weeks, he laid the
foundation for a sweeping new regime of warrantless electronic surveillance.
From these memoranda, President Bush justified his decision to grant Hayden
the authority for his new mission.

The key question hanging over Hayden's surveillance system was whether
or not it touched the arch of FISA. Yoo had concluded that that didn't matter.
Even if the NSA's surveillance targeted U.S. persons, including those inside the
United States, the administration decided that any communication involving
foreign parties made the entire communication "foreign intelligence." The president's authority here was unchallenged, Yoo concluded in a later memo. "Unless Congress made a clear statement in the Foreign Intelligence Surveillance
Act that it sought to restrict presidential authority to conduct warrantless
searches in the national security area—which it has not—then the statute must
be construed to avoid [such] a reading."

Yoo apparently had overlooked both law and the legislative history of
FISA, which clearly established that Congress had intended the law to be a
check on the president's surveillance powers. A separate wiretapping statute
declared that when it came to foreign intelligence gathering, FISA was in
control. Transcripts of the debates about the law, as well as statements by
lawmakers at the time, affirmed this was their intention. Whether or not Yoo
grasped this history, or whether he was acting as a zealous attorney looking
for the narrowest and still reasonable interpretation of the law for his client,
the White House determined that Bush had the authorities he needed.

That fit squarely in the worldview of both Dick Cheney, the vice president,
and his chief legal adviser, David Addington. Both men believed that since the
Watergate scandal, Congress had slowly but successfully chiseled away
the president's most fundamental powers. They'd nurtured that view throughout the crucible of the Reagan years, when Congress and the executive had
gone toe to toe in that most sanctified of presidential domains, national security. Addington, then a congressional staffer, and Cheney, a congressman
from Wyoming, articulated their philosophy in the "minority report" of the
congressional Iran-Contra commission, of which they were among the principal authors. Both men believed that lawmakers once again had strayed well
beyond their brief in trying to micromanage the executive:

Deeper than the specifics of the Iran-Contra Affair lies an underlying and festering institutional wound these committees have been unwilling to face. In order to support rhetorical overstatements about democracy and the rule of law, the committees have rested their case upon an aggrandizing theory of Congress's foreign policy powers that is itself part of the problem.

President Bush didn't need FISA, and he didn't need Congress. The FISA warrants process would impede the swift, hot pursuit approach that Hayden had laid out. The NSA would be bogged down in paperwork while potential terrorists slipped through their digital nets. They would bob and weave through the network, switching phones, using different e-mail accounts to cover their tracks. If the agency had to wait for a federal judge to issue a warrant for each and every suspect who appeared, the NSA might as well just stop trying to track them at all and devote its resources to more productive ends.

On October 4, just three days after Hayden appeared before Pelosi and the House Intelligence Committee, Bush granted the authority for the NSA to design the surveillance system Hayden had described. The NSA now had the power to target anyone it reasonably suspected was a terrorist, or their associates, regardless of their location. One rule applied: At least one party to the communication must be located outside the United States. Under these new orders the NSA had the power to target Americans inside the country without warrants. The lines on the field had just been redrawn. The definition of foreign intelligence now encompassed Americans' phone calls and e-mails.

Hayden had gotten what he asked for. The three pillars were aligned. The math added up. He had a chance to say no, to send the authorities back. It was his call. But given the stakes, and the backing he'd received, he decided to proceed.

Hayden was a Catholic, and he believed in the proportionality of war. There was a balance to strike between force and the good that could come of it. He laid the facts as he knew them on the table. The United States had been savagely attacked. He believed he could take reasonable action to stop another atrocity. And the president had given him the authority to act.

I can't not do this, Hayden told himself.

Whether he needed the commander in chief's blessing or could have continued working under his existing authorities, probably only a judge could decide. But that was a question Hayden didn't need to answer. The president of the United States had just given him the ultimate cover.

In time, the NSA's surveillance system went by various names within the tiny circle of officials who knew it existed. Officially, it was code named Stellar Wind. Some just called it the president's program. But inside the labs and idea factories of the agency's formidable technology team, the terrorist hunting machine had another name.

They called it the Big Ass Graph.

CHAPTER 14

ALL HANDS ON DECK

Bob Popp had always wanted to work for DARPA, but the right job had yet to come along. In January 2001 he joined a smaller version of the futuristic brain trust—the Pentagon's Advanced Systems and Concepts Office. It was full of big thinkers, people of outsized intellectual ambition, like him. But they set their sights on more practical ideas than their fellows at DARPA. More near-term payoff, less pie in the sky.

For Popp, a thirty-eight-year-old technologist and freshly minted civil servant, it was a respectable position with a résumé-burnishing title—assistant deputy undersecretary. In Washington, that counted for something.

Popp's new job put him at the center of the action. Each year the advanced systems office vetted roughly a hundred new research proposals for concepts and technologies that needed Defense Department funding. Popp was asked to "rack and stack" the proposals, vetting and ranking them to help his bosses decide on a final list of candidates that should be considered for precious dollars. But to his great disappointment, the current stack was bland and conventional.

Popp saw plans for making airplanes fly faster and for making tanks more rugged. But there was no novelty to any of it. He had spent the past three years with a defense contractor, helping the Air Force develop new tracking methods for ground targets, creating "situational awareness," in military parlance, for airborne missions. Far more ambitious stuff, he thought. Just making things go boom and bang gave him limited satisfaction.

As Popp read the hundred or so proposals, he also saw nothing that rose to the challenge just put forward on January 31 by a blue-ribbon panel of experts. The group had been convened to draft a road map for national security in the twenty-first century. Chaired by former senators Gary Hart and Warren Rudman, it bleakly concluded that the country had overlooked the dangers to the American "homeland" in the fallout of the cold war.

"The combination of unconventional weapons proliferation with the persistence of international terrorism will end the relative invulnerability of the U.S. homeland to catastrophic attack," they wrote. "A direct attack against American citizens *on American soil* is likely over the next quarter century." Their italicized emphasis was a clarion call: If you read nothing else in the report, read this.

The authors recommended that the recently inaugurated President Bush create a national homeland security agency to harness the nearly two dozen federal entities that played a role in domestic protection. Popp thought it was a brilliant idea, and something that his office should pay attention to. Finding nothing with a homeland angle in the pile of proposals on his desk, he decided to write one himself.

Popp took his cues from the Hart-Rudman commission, dubbing his idea "Homeland Security Command and Control." He had three goals, all aimed at deficiencies the commissioners had identified: expand the flow of security information between foreign and domestic counterterrorism agencies, especially the FBI and the CIA; create better command and control systems for federal, state, and local governments, since the latter two were really the front lines of domestic defense; and beef up communications for so-called first responders—police, fire, and rescue personnel who'd be sent into the breach during an emergency.

Popp was a systems thinker, and he intuitively grasped that all those moving parts had to move together. He thought that one new tool, or an improvement on an existing technology, would yield but incremental progress. What the world needed now was a big step forward. He threw his proposal into the mix. And after others winnowed down the list to about twenty ideas worthy of funding, his ranked near the top.

In early September 2001, near the end of the government's fiscal year, the candidate proposals were circulated among potential sponsoring organizations throughout the Defense Department. Only a few days later Popp's idea looked eerily prescient. After the disaster of 9/11, the phrase *homeland security* quite suddenly was in vogue.

A few weeks later, in mid-October, Popp showed up for work one morning and found an e-mail from a name he vaguely recognized—John Poindexter. Why did it sound so familiar? he wondered. Popp searched his memory; the best he could recall was something about a political scandal. Years ago, maybe.

In his e-mail Poindexter explained that he had read Popp's proposal. He was setting up a new program at DARPA that would be involved in similar research, and he needed a deputy. Someone to help him run the office. If Popp was interested in the job, they should meet.

Before he responded Popp tapped Poindexter's name into a search engine. He tried "Poindexter and Watergate," and although that string came up empty, he eventually landed on the correct inglorious chapter of history.

In 1981, the year Poindexter went to the White House, Popp was nineteen years old. He joined the Air Force, and while the admiral was fighting for his future in a congressional hearing room, Popp was repairing airplanes. He was a kid at the beginning of his career, with a blossoming family. Looking back on Iran-Contra, Popp only recalled seeing some of the hearings on television, and he couldn't remember many of the details.

Popp replied to Poindexter's e-mail. "I'd love to meet."

Mary McCarthy told Poindexter he was nuts. In the kindest way she knew how, of course. But what was he thinking?

McCarthy was one of the first to hear of Poindexter's return to government, after so many years on the outside. He was going to DARPA, he said, to lead a new group called the Information Awareness Office. TIA would be the centerpiece but not the only research thrust.

McCarthy was incredulous. "No, John! *You're* going to do this? No."

"Yes, I am," Poindexter replied resolutely.

She couldn't shake the feeling that her friend was heading for rough water.

McCarthy and Poindexter were cut from distinct partisan cloths, but she had come to admire him, even emulate him, and she wanted to protect him. Power had changed hands in Washington, back in Poindexter's favor. But old memories persisted. She feared that his past would catch up with him and overshadow all the good she thought he could do with TIA.

Still, she could hardly fault him for fighting. McCarthy had not, and would not, forgive herself for what she thought she'd failed to do before the attacks. Her brightness and her smile were thin gauze on a deep wound. Now Poindexter intended, in some way, to make amends for all that. How could she tell him not to try?

McCarthy considered herself an ardent civil libertarian, and she held out the possibility that her friend's work on behalf of the free world might constitute a threat to freedom. But there had to be a way to balance security and liberty, she thought. There was a rational answer to this equation. If anyone could find it, she believed it was Poindexter. He had the will. Once he set his mind to a problem, he wouldn't be dissuaded. McCarthy hoped that those who didn't know him as well as she would view him as charitably. At the very least, she thought, he needed a major public relations campaign.

Poindexter didn't want to hang around DARPA for long. He planned to serve as director of the Information Awareness Office for about a year, enough time to get TIA and its related programs on their feet. Then he'd hand it all over to a permanent manager. Maybe Popp would be that man; Poindexter had to meet him first.

Poindexter thought Popp had crafted an exceptional proposal. A bit more geared toward crisis management than preemption, but he found the writing so superb that he wanted to meet the man behind it. Two weeks after their first e-mail contact, Popp came to a job interview at DARPA headquarters. Their scheduled one-hour meeting stretched on for two more.

Poindexter didn't fit Popp's expectations at all. He was warm, courteous, easy to talk to. After he'd boned up on Poindexter's past, Popp imagined an imposing giant, quick to cut him down. But instead he felt that he'd found a reflection of his own father. As a child, few things made Popp happier than to build something with his dad. "Let's go build a porch," his father would say. The elder Popp drew up the plans and his son did the hammering. One designer, one implementer. Popp sensed that Poindexter needed someone who was good with a hammer.

Poindexter liked what he saw. Popp was a young hard charger, with a palpable energy. He was bright and came equipped with a military background and a PhD in computer science. This wasn't so far afield from Poindexter's own experience, even if Popp was an Air Force man, a sin for which the admiral agreed to forgive him. Poindexter had always trusted his sense about people, and now it told him he'd found a winner.

Poindexter wasted no time bringing Popp into the fold. He pulled out his TIA presentation materials and described how he wanted the overarching Information Awareness Office to function. Popp thought that it all looked strong, but certain words Poindexter used to describe his efforts seemed politically supercharged.

In one chart Poindexter used "profiling" to describe a method of screening particular individuals for terrorist characteristics. "That seems to be a little delicate," Popp said. "That word 'profiling' is a hot button, loaded term. We may want to consider not using it."

Popp was unsure how Poindexter would react to such a presumptuous remark. He hadn't even landed the job yet.

But Poindexter seemed to take the point. He didn't agree that the term was loaded, though he granted that another could find it so.

This made Popp wonder: Did Poindexter have a political blind spot? He didn't dismiss concerns about semantics, about how others might *perceive* his intentions. But he did seem to think he was above their judgments, Popp thought. As if the world was full of petty people, and he just wasn't one of them.

But Poindexter got the message. It was a delicate word. Much as he might like to change people's minds, he knew that some never would.

In all their time together Popp never heard Poindexter use the word "profiling" again.

Poindexter called Popp two days after the interview and offered him the job. Tony Tether, the DARPA director, still had to bless the arrangement, but that was a perfunctory gesture. Popp was now the number two.

On January 14, 2002, Poindexter reported for duty. He and Popp spent the unseasonably warm day "in-processing," an administrative routine that reduced human beings to the sum of their paperwork. A day spent filling out personnel forms overshadowed its exquisite uniqueness. Today was John Poindexter's return to government after fifteen years in the wilderness. His curious pariah existence ended now. Poindexter was back.

The welcome was unceremonious. DARPA's building managers, lacking enough offices for Poindexter's new venture, stuck him and Popp in closets. The pair set up camp in a sliver of tiny niches on the tenth floor of the headquarters building. Poindexter took the biggest of the group; Popp ensconced himself in a slightly smaller space, barely big enough to turn around in. A team of four support contractors eventually would cram themselves into the middle alcove.

Time, not space, was of the essence. Poindexter had spent the holidays laying out his strategy to quickly award a raft of TIA contracts, so that experiments could be under way and have achieved some measure of progress by the end of the year. He articulated his plan in a formal solicitation to potential researchers, known in government parlance as a "broad agency announcement."

A mere pamphlet by procurement standards—it totaled only twenty-five pages—the document was chock-full of insights into Poindexter's mind. He described the motivation behind TIA and made clear his ultimate goal: "to predict and hence preempt future terrorist actions against us."

Anyone who hadn't known of Poindexter's relentless technological pursuit over the past decade would be brought up to speed quickly after reading the first few paragraphs of the announcement.

> Currently, terrorists are able to move freely throughout the world, to hide when necessary, to find unpunished sponsorship and support, to operate in small, independent cells, and to strike infrequently, exploiting weapons of mass effects and media response to influence governments. This low-intensity/low-density form of warfare has an information signature, albeit not one that our intelligence infrastructure and other government agencies are optimized to detect. In all cases, terrorists have left detectable clues that are generally found after an attack.

He continued.

To fight terrorism, we need to create a new infrastructure and new information technology aimed at exposing foreign terrorists and their activities and support systems. This is a tremendously difficult problem, because terrorists understand how vulnerable they are and seek to hide their specific plans and capabilities. Terrorists' use of camouflage and deception reduces their signature and introduces great uncertainty in the interpretation of any data collected. Once an information leak is discovered, terrorists can adapt quickly to stop it, either by changing tactics or re-organizing in some way.

The key to fighting terrorism is information. Elements of the solution include gathering a much broader array of data than we do currently, discovering information from elements of the data, creating models of hypotheses, and analyzing these models in a collaborative environment to determine the most probable current or future scenario.

So there was his vision—laid bare for all to see. The unclassified document ended up in the hands of Beltway contractors, university researchers, and, eventually, a small number of trade journalists. Poindexter had meant to assert a grand challenge, proposing a broad, scientific problem and inviting solutions to address it. Cost was not the deciding factor. Broad agency announcements also were governed by separate regulations different from traditional procurements, so Poindexter was free to evaluate each proposal separately, and with criteria based on his own scientific judgment. He and his crew would award contracts to the companies they felt showed the most promise, even if it meant risking the taxpayers' money. Indeed, at DARPA the managers believed they hadn't achieved success unless some of their ventures failed. They often learned the most from their biggest mistakes.

Poindexter hand selected the managers for his research programs. A team of warrior geeks, each one possessed bona fides in the fields of high-end, high-risk technology. And fortunately for Poindexter, most of them already had been working on the very projects he planned to incorporate into his new office.

Among this elite, esoteric band were people like Ted Senator, an MIT graduate who'd spent fourteen years building computer programs to detect fraud and illegal activity in financial systems. Senator was managing DARPA's Evidence Extraction and Link Discovery program. Poindexter assigned him the crucial task of developing automated tools to extract, or harvest, data from large information sets. By design, the tools were not so different from those the Able Danger team had used a few years before, but the state of technology was advancing rapidly, as Senator knew well. Before coming to government he founded an analysis group at the National Association of Securities Dealers, where he built a system that monitored the NASDAQ stock exchange for improper trading activity. He'd also pulled a stint as the chief of artificial intelligence with the Financial Crimes Enforcement Network at the Treasury Department, one of the most advanced and successful data-tracking operations in government. FinCEN was tapped to monitor and shut down terrorist-funding streams immediately after the 9/11 attacks.

Each manager brought his own narrow focus to Poindexter's broad task. This was a researcher's dream—to have his pet project lifted up to national policy status, and by none other than a former presidential adviser. Scientists like Jonathon Phillips, who'd spent the bulk of his career developing automated face recognition technology, were now let loose on a wartime effort. Phillips assumed command of a Poindexter program dubbed Human Identification at a Distance, which aimed to verify people not only by their unique facial characteristics but by their particular gait or the way they held their bodies. Such a tool would be a boon to surveillance and had applications on the battlefield as well as the home front.

Poindexter eventually chose half a dozen men to join him. Perhaps most important among them was an ex–CIA officer named Tom Armour, who'd worked on the original Genoa program. Poindexter prevailed upon him to launch a new effort, aptly, albeit unimaginatively, named Genoa II. Armour had been chief technologist for the CIA's nonproliferation center. An expert on nuclear weapons systems and Soviet missiles, he and Poindexter shared a cold war pedigree. Armour was also a warrior. Before his career as a spook he'd flown combat missions in Vietnam aboard AC-119 gunships. To Poindexter, Armour was one of the few bright lights in the dim CIA.

Poindexter told his managers to think about the counterterrorism mission at hand but also to design with future leaders in mind. Think about the commander in chief ten years from now who will have grown up with the Internet, he liked to say. "That president is going to expect the best technology and will be really pissed if she doesn't have it."

Along with data extraction, human identification, and the Genoa follow-on, Poindexter carved out three other research thrusts. One would create a kind of database dashboard, a tool to manipulate and explore far-flung, massive databases as if they were a single information repository. With so much data at an individual user's fingertips, the program also conducted parallel research on privacy protection mechanisms that would shield the human identities behind all those faceless data points. Second, Poindexter launched research on software to translate foreign languages into English text automatically. Arabic translators were most in demand, though Chinese would not be far behind on the intelligence community's priority list. And finally there was a war-gaming component aimed at the core question Poindexter had posed with TIA: Could the government identify a "terrorist signature" that would allow it to predict human behavior? This was perhaps the most crucial research of all. If TIA couldn't identify the terrorists' codes, it would never work.

To catch terrorists, TIA had to think like them. Poindexter was no database expert. But he understood that detecting terrorist signatures was as hard as finding a needle in a stack of needles. In antisubmarine warfare, goblin hunters had certain advantages. They knew what materials they were looking for, what sounds a submarine generally made in the water. They knew where to focus their searches. There weren't many known characteristics for terrorism, particularly in the information space. Poindexter's team would have to discover them.

Several months after he'd set up his new office Poindexter asked Steve Lukasik, a former DARPA director and a self-described political liberal, to form a special "red team" of experts on terrorism. Lukasik assembled a group of academics; authorities on special operations; security and aviation specialists; and experts on terrorist tactics, including the finer points of bomb making. The red team met separately from the other TIA researchers to marshal their collective wisdom. They pretended to be a terrorist cell.

If they were going to attack America, and kill huge amounts of people and do massive damage, where would they strike? The red team concocted different attack scenarios to help TIA narrow down the kinds of signals it needed to detect. There were a seemingly infinite number of possibilities, so the red team devised a kind of generic attack sequence, broken down into a number of essential movements.

First, the plotters had to get organized: rent safe houses; construct their communication systems; make contacts. The team determined that this took up about 20 percent of the cell's time. Next, the attackers would make a list of targets and winnow that down to whichever were the easiest to hit or the most advantageous. And finally, there'd be a reconnaissance phase.

That was the movement to watch, the red team agreed. Based on their collective study of terrorist operations, they estimated the attackers would spend about 40 percent of their time physically scouting out targets, sending small teams to take photographs, case the security in place, and generally get the lay of the land. The experts also agreed this was the time when the terrorists would be most exposed—they'd be out in the open, traveling, making purchases, and sending messages to one another and their handlers. If TIA were trained to monitor the transactions that occurred in the reconnaissance period, it stood a better chance of spotting the signs of a plot, they theorized.

The team ran an imaginary attack on a shopping mall, which seemed an obvious target for inspiring mass panic, creating economic shock, and claiming large casualties. Lukasik went online to find the biggest malls in major cities, which presumably would have the most customers. He looked only at indoor malls; outdoor venues seemed less attractive targets, since they offered shoppers more avenues of escape from attackers.

The red team had started to define a pattern: Reconnaissance requires travel to the site, usually by two people. So look for the simultaneity of travel. Search airline databases for two people arriving in a known target city on two different airlines but who stay in the same hotel. They leave a few days later—

presumably after casing the mall—and then move on to another location, home to the next potential target. They stay there a day or two, and then they leave again.

This sequence of events—which the red team regarded as suspicious—became one terrorist signature. With enough signatures the team could build a template, which would be fed into the TIA system. Using the template as a guide, TIA would scan airline, hotel, and rental car databases looking for the data points that matched up to the preselected picture. If the system returned a huge number of matches, that meant the signatures weren't specific enough. The template hadn't filtered out the noise of innocent travelers who happened to have similar schedules. TIA would have to look for more attributes, more signals. So the red team would have to devise a more detailed template. Were there certain materials the terrorists would have to buy? Modes of transportation they were likely to use? Whom were they calling while they made these multicity hops?

And on and on the iterative process went, until the red team came up with viable templates that detected more signals than noise. The team examined a gruesome range of scenarios. In addition to attacking a mall, they plotted how to destroy a nuclear reactor. The team's aviation expert sat down with flight charts and topographical maps to come up with the best approach for flying an airplane into the reactor complex. Reactors that had a minimum of obstructions from surrounding hills, bridges, or power lines were the easiest targets. He rank-ordered 103 reactors in 63 different locations, from the easiest to hit to the hardest. Topping the list was the San Onofre Nuclear Generating System, perched right on the edge of the Southern California coastline, with the Pacific waves lapping at the facility's outer walls.

The team also took their attacks underground, when they looked at flooding New York City by blowing holes in the tunnels under the Hudson and East rivers. All of their devious scenarios rested on a simple concept. Red teaming was nothing more than the common sense of experts. It should come as no surprise to anyone that a nuclear reactor on a beach was vulnerable to aerial assault. TIA was not so simple, but Poindexter reasoned that if it could be calibrated based on these known, or knowable plots, it would stand a far greater chance of detecting them.

Poindexter spent the winter of 2002 gathering his fleet and assembling his officer corps. They were a fine lot in his estimation, as committed to the challenge as they were to the cause. But before Poindexter could set sail, he needed allies, well-placed officials who could provide safe harbor when the seas turned rough. Above all others, one man could give Poindexter that kind of protection. He was at the top of his list of calls.

CHAPTER 15

CALL TO ARMS

Poindexter had known Donald Rumsfeld as long as anyone in Washington. They'd met almost twenty-five years earlier in the Ford administration, when their meteoric career paths crossed at the Pentagon. Rumsfeld was the new secretary of defense, the youngest in the department's history, and Poindexter had come to work for Admiral James Holloway, the chief of Naval Operations, as his executive assistant and all-around right-hand man.

Years later Poindexter and Rumsfeld met again at the White House. Poindexter was on Reagan's NSC staff when Rumsfeld was the president's chief emissary to the Middle East during the hostage crisis. They had battled the fires of suicidal terrorism, each from different positions. And while their professional courses had diverged after that, Poindexter and Rumsfeld had remained in similar orbits.

A few weeks after Poindexter moved into his new office, he dropped in on Rumsfeld, who was back at the Pentagon, this time as the oldest defense secretary in history. Poindexter had been there for the welcome-back ceremony some months earlier, but they hadn't had much time to chat. Rumsfeld arranged for a private luncheon in his office, so they could catch up.

It was a friendly meal, and mostly a social call. Rumsfeld asked after Linda and Poindexter's boys. They reminisced about Holloway, who, like Rumsfeld, was a wrestler, the former for Navy, the latter at Princeton. Rumsfeld liked to bring Holloway into his office for beers and bull sessions; they'd prop their feet up on the furniture and relive favorite matches while puffing on cigars. Poindexter enjoyed being near those casual moments and such men of great institutional power and professional wisdom.

Poindexter had appraised Rumsfeld early on as a sharp bureaucrat and a climber, but one who possessed a refreshing genuineness that Poindexter found lacking in so many of his civilian superiors. These men merely played the part of statesman, he felt. Like John Warner, for whom Poindexter had worked when he was secretary of the navy. These were the days before Warner married Elizabeth Taylor, and before Virginia sent him to the Senate; and while his political future seemed momentous, Warner once confided to Poindexter that what he really wanted to be was an actor. *Well, sir*, the young officer had thought, *you're doing a pretty good job.*

Rumsfeld was a lot like Poindexter. In the crucible of the Pentagon they'd forged a mutual distrust of the military and intelligence bureaucracy, which so often resisted the president's policies. And it extended to the Congress, whose incursion into the commander in chief's sacred realm of national security had been on a long and steady march since the fallout of Watergate.

The suspicion culminated in political warfare during Iran-Contra. Poindexter believed that congressional Democrats had set their armies on him personally as an avenue to the president. And when they could not breach his wall—"The buck stops here with me"—they hated him for it. The sentiment was mutual, though. Poindexter despised Congress for launching the attack in the first place.

Over lunch, Poindexter and Rumsfeld remembered the caldron of Lebanon and the attack on the Marines, the first shot in the intermittent series of battles that had brought them to their present positions. And they uttered the old lamentations—how the intelligence agencies had too long demurred in the fight over the years, hadn't embraced the expansive powers that presidents had meant to give them. Look at how they'd failed to use Executive order 12333, Poindexter said. "By the time that policy gets down to the working level, every layer of command has backed away from the edge a little bit, to make sure that nobody stepped over," Poindexter said. "They're overly cautious," he told the secretary.

"You're absolutely right," Rumsfeld replied. And, he said, he'd had a similar problem trying to promulgate combat rules of engagement. Bush would agree to one set of rules, but when Rumsfeld asked the spear-carriers in the field what those rules were, their version bore no resemblance to what the president had agreed to.

Poindexter and Rumsfeld both thought people were backing off, playing too cautiously, when they should have seized their hard-won authorities, unbowed and unafraid. The attacks of 9/11 were as much a result of weakness as they were a chance to erase it. Now each man, in his own way, was seizing the moment to bend the system to his will and toward the end he thought it ought to run—Poindexter in quiet, studious steps, Rumsfeld in cage-rattling bursts of bravado, as he sought to transform the military for the war on terror. The bookworm and the wrestler. But they were heading down the same path.

Poindexter didn't lay out all the technical details of TIA for Rumsfeld. But he gave the secretary the overview, explained the concept and his goals. He wanted Rumsfeld to understand what he was up to, why he had returned. Rumsfeld expressed his support for the research and affirmed to Poindexter that it was a good idea. And that was enough for him. Poindexter left lunch feeling that he had an ally, an old and faithful friend, in the highest place.

Poindexter launched a broad campaign among the intelligence and national security agencies to enlist support for TIA. Rumsfeld had given his verbal support, but Poindexter wanted more. He thought that individual agencies should join in his research, by experimenting with the data collection and analysis tools that his team soon would be fielding. As they brought new tools onboard, Poindexter hoped that the agencies' own analysts would put them through their paces. Only agencies like the CIA, the FBI, or the NSA could truly discover what worked and what failed. After all, they were Poindexter's ultimate customers. Once he built a TIA prototype, it would be up to them to use it in the real world.

Although Poindexter distrusted what he saw as the bureaucracy's calcified traditions and narrow mind-set, he knew that without broad support TIA would languish on a shelf. Yet he was not prepared to let them tinker with his masterwork in a vacuum. And so, Poindexter hatched a plan to enlist the agencies in his effort and, at the same time, influence them.

Any agency that wanted to test-drive the TIA tools would have to install a special node on a data network he set up exclusively for that purpose. It was a digital laboratory where the agencies could tinker and toy, then share their results. The tools lived on the network. But the nodes—consisting of little more than a laptop computer—would sit at the agencies themselves.

Poindexter would install the central node for the network in a place of his choosing. When the time came to pick it, Tony Tether suggested that Poindexter go meet with a technologically astute Army general named Keith Alexander to ask if he could borrow space in his facility outside Washington. Though not well known to Poindexter at the time, the place shared TIA's spirit of rebellious innovation. It was the Information Dominance Center, former home of Erik Kleinsmith and the Able Danger team.

Alexander, the commanding general of the Army's Intelligence and Security Command at Fort Belvoir, was a career military intelligence officer and West Point graduate. He was a warrior geek like Poindexter and his crew. Alexander earned two master's degrees from the Naval Postgraduate School, one in systems technology, with a specialization in electronic warfare, and the other in physics. He was also the intelligence officer for the 1st Armored Division during the 1991 Gulf War.

Poindexter had come to know Alexander during the Genoa years. The general had attended the technology demonstrations, so he was already up to speed on Poindexter's thinking. Alexander agreed to give Poindexter and his team some space on the sci-fi set of the IDC, and to let them use its existing data network, which ran on the Joint Worldwide Intelligence Communications System. This was the same information source that Kleinsmith and his analysts had tapped to harvest classified messages and traffic during Able Danger, and the intelligence agencies already had access to it.

Above all, Poindexter wanted real users and real data to run his experiments. The IDC gave him both. It already had the physical infrastructure to link agencies together and let them share intelligence. More nodes could be installed as more agencies joined. The IDC provided a natural setting. But there too space was scarce. Within feet of where Kleinsmith had worked two years earlier, Poindexter and his team received an office about the size of the broom closets they were working in back at DARPA headquarters.

But again it wasn't physical space that Poindexter was after. Now he had his virtual lab. He called it the TIA network. And as winter melted into spring, Poindexter enlisted many agencies to join it.

He made a sales tour. He felt that he couldn't emphasize enough the urgency that propelled him. He evangelized about TIA, delighting his audiences with both his enthusiasm and the thoroughness of his approach. He seemed to have thought of everything. Poindexter remained convinced that another attack was either imminent or already well along in the planning sequence. Fortunately for him, the senior officials he was meeting with were gripped by the same fear, and they were primed for new ideas.

Langley, Virginia, was on Poindexter's whistle-stop tour. He knew the CIA's capabilities intimately, and its limitations, and so he felt particularly emboldened to tell the agency's top men why they should join his quest.

Poindexter drew an impressive crowd for his first TIA briefing. The agency's executive director, the third in command, convened the meeting. A. B. "Buzzy" Krongard was a former Marine and longtime executive banker who'd only joined the CIA a few years before the 9/11 attacks. He was the top-ranking official there, joined by John Brennan, the deputy executive director and a onetime station chief in Riyadh. (Brennan spoke passable Arabic and recently had served as CIA director George Tenet's chief of staff.) Donald Kerr, the deputy director of the agency's science and technology directorate, and Alan Wade, the chief information officer, rounded out the group. Since the CIA was spydom's central management office, Wade was also the top computer systems official for the entire intelligence community.

This wasn't the first time Poindexter had been to Langley since the terrorist attacks. Before the Information Awareness Office was formally established, Kerr had set up a special committee on science and technology and asked Poindexter to talk to the members about Genoa. As he listened to them kibitz, his frustration swelled. These were the same people who had failed to adopt his ideas years earlier. Now they'd invited him out to give a speech he'd made countless times. Poindexter pounded his fist on the table. "We have got to change the way we do business!" he boomed.

It was a rare and notable venting from the usually placid admiral. So, a few months later, when Poindexter was back at CIA headquarters briefing Kerr and several of his senior colleagues on his new vision, he had their attention.

Poindexter talked about TIA, its animating concept and its goals. This was bold stuff by any agency's standards. But Poindexter's expansive view of the terrorism intelligence problem struck Wade in particular as unique. Indeed, Poindexter was one of the only people Wade had heard talk about the challenge in such broad terms, and as an end-to-end concept. He'd thought out how to obtain information, how to use it, what limits to place on that use. In the first, urgent days after the 9/11 attacks, Wade mostly had heard his colleagues discuss just the first part—how to obtain information, and *more* of it. With the threat of another attack looming, the agencies began to covet one another's most precious resource—their secrets—and to resent one another's stinginess when so many refused to share. They could justify holding back out of an overabundance of caution; they didn't want to expose vital sources and methods for acquiring intelligence lest they be lost forever. But in truth, information was one of Washington's most valuable currencies. The intelligence agencies measured their status by it and were loath to diminish their influence by spreading the wealth.

But Poindexter had figured out a compromise. He explained to Wade and the others that he would let the agencies come to the TIA network and bring as little or as much information as they wanted. In exchange they would be the first to experiment with his new tools. As the agencies' haul of intelligence piled ever higher, they became desperate for ways to make sense of it. Poindexter could fill that need, with his test bed for the electronic war on terrorism.

Wade liked the idea, but he heard something even more intriguing in Poindexter's pitch, a concept that he hadn't heard in any of the tech briefings he'd sat through since 9/11: the words "protect privacy." Wade thought that Poindexter's was the first ambitious information architecture that included privacy from the ground up. He described his privacy appliance concept, in which a physical device would sit between the user and the data, shielding the names and other identifying information of the millions of innocent people in the noise. The TIA system would employ "selective revelation," Poindexter explained. The farther into the data a user wished to probe, the more outside authority he had to obtain. An intelligence analyst mining and moving information would only encounter individuals represented as numbers, or as some anonymous marker. Poindexter also proposed an "immutable audit trail," a master record of every analyst who had used the TIA system, what data they'd touched, what they'd done with it. The system would be trained to spot suspicious patterns of use: say, an analyst poking around in domestic data sources that had no bearing on a terrorism investigation. Poindexter wanted to use TIA to watch the watchers.

The CIA team liked what they heard. "Alan, you follow this," Krongard advised. As TIA evolved, Wade and Poindexter held several more meetings, and the agency eventually installed a node on the TIA network.

Poindexter was glad for the enthusiastic response. But he wanted someone to challenge him. To poke holes in his theory and his reasoning, particularly his novel concept of selective revelation. He wanted someone to tell him he was wrong.

Fran Townsend seemed like she would know for sure. The senior official in charge of intelligence at the Coast Guard, which now played a pivotal role in homeland security, she was already on Poindexter's list of potential TIA participants. But he was most intrigued by her previous jobs and her peculiar area of expertise. Townsend was an authority on surveillance law.

Townsend had spent much of her career at the Justice Department. She started out in 1988 at the U.S. attorney's office for the southern district of New York and then spent the late 1990s working for Attorney General Janet Reno in Washington. Townsend had worked most of the major terrorism cases of the decade, including the Africa embassy attacks and the USS *Cole* bombing. She was among the few career officials in Justice who were following Al Qaeda and increasingly worried that law enforcement alone was ill equipped to halt its advances.

Like Poindexter, Townsend was seared in the early fires of the terror wars. She had been in law school at the time of the Beirut bombing, and as a prosecutor she became convinced that Hezbollah was responsible for the attack and had never paid for its crimes. At the tail end of the Clinton administration, Townsend oversaw the preparation of warrant applications to the Foreign Intelligence Surveillance Court, the secretive panel of judges that oversaw the wiretapping of suspected terrorists and spies. Townsend was in charge of making sure the government's requests complied with the letter and spirit of FISA. She knew the ins and outs of the law, as well as the temperament of the judges and the strict barriers that had been imposed between the law enforcement and intelligence arms of government. (Foreign and domestic. Those same bright lines that had kept the NSA outside America.) By the time Poindexter sought out her counsel, Townsend was one of the few people alive who legitimately could call herself a FISA expert.

When she got the phone call, Townsend was taken aback. She had known Poindexter only by reputation. The idea that a former national security adviser would want a meeting with the intelligence director of the Coast Guard struck her as flattering and unusual. She wasn't about to say no. Townsend invited him to Coast Guard headquarters to brief her personally, as well as the service's intelligence and legal experts.

Poindexter gave the standard TIA presentation. Townsend could tell that he'd already anticipated having to cross a variety of legal hurdles. There was a gap between what Poindexter envisioned and what was doable under current law. But his proposals, specifically selective revelation, appealed to her. If TIA could actually "anonymize" the data it examined, and only reveal names through a legal process, then Townsend thought it would be an extraordinarily valuable intelligence tool. She imagined that it could help FBI agents find the most valuable leads to investigate, filtering out the dead ends and the background noise. That made TIA a worthwhile experiment, she thought.

But she knew that Poindexter wanted advice, not plaudits. So she tallied up a list of his vulnerabilities. "You're going to need advocates on the Hill," Townsend said. The right staffers on the key committees, and he'd need enough face time to fully explain what TIA was and wasn't. Nothing in his proposal struck her as legally problematic for the moment, since it was still just a research project. But Poindexter was thinking years into the future, to a day where perhaps the government would have access to now off-limits sources of information.

Townsend knew how seriously the Justice Department and intelligence community obeyed "the wall" that separated their two worlds, in which information was acquired under different legal standards and used for different ends. Poindexter's vision would merge those two worlds. He was taking on two cultures at once.

Townsend had seen others try that, and the public reaction was explosive. She shared a cautionary tale with Poindexter. During the Clinton administration the FBI had launched a new e-mail monitoring technology named Carnivore. It was a packet sniffer, a tool that could track a surveillance target's online messages. But a combination of factors, not least of which was its unfortunate name, overwhelmed any chance for widespread acceptance. The public harbored abiding suspicions of law enforcement in general. Now the FBI wanted to read people's e-mail? Technological privacy activists were also outraged. Throughout much of the 1990s the Justice Department and the National Security Agency were making big public power plays to control the emergence of new Internet technologies. They'd pushed through a law that required all telecommunications companies to build their network in such a way that they could be instantly and secretly tapped. To a lot of people Carnivore was one more instance of relentless government excess. It attracted all the wrong kinds of attention. And Townsend had a front-row seat to what she considered a public relations train wreck.

"Learn from their example," she told Poindexter. Don't make the same mistakes. Think about how people react to names, to perception.

"That's why I'm here," he said. "Help me figure out how to avoid that."

Townsend said that to win over lawmakers, privacy advocates, and individual citizens Poindexter would have to persuade them not only of TIA's value but that he had truly thought through the privacy protections. He'd have to convince them that selective revelation and privacy appliance weren't just buzzwords, lip service to the critics. If he couldn't do that, Townsend warned, "the public would react badly."

Though she didn't say it, ultimately, TIA's fate all depended on Poindexter. Before the public could accept the idea, they first had to accept the man.

Townsend was taken aback by Poindexter's willingness to listen. She had imagined that he'd do most of the talking. The gentle, almost excessively deferential "gentleman" that she saw before her defied her expectation of an imposing, strong-willed military man toughened by Washington warfare. It was all so disarming.

Poindexter likewise knew Townsend only by reputation. She was an assiduous lawyer and had worked on terrorism cases for years. But he knew nothing of her thinking. Now he could see she was spirited and whip smart. And while he couldn't say the same for himself, she could cuss like a boatswain's mate.

Townsend was one of the few senior officials in Washington to have worked counterterrorism for both the Clinton and Bush administrations. Poindexter had a way of gravitating to these careerists, people like Mary McCarthy and Richard Clarke. It was no accident. In his relationships, professional and personal, he made no partisan distinctions. As long as someone was loyally committed to the fight, he didn't much care how they cast their votes. It didn't hurt that Townsend was politically more aligned with the current president than the last one, but it didn't particularly matter to Poindexter either way. That meeting at Coast Guard headquarters was the first of many, and their relationship accrued new value when, several months later, Townsend took a pivotal job at the White House.

As Poindexter shuttled around Washington in the winter of 2002, he left every meeting with the feeling that his audiences understood his approach and were generally supportive of it. At least outwardly. What they said when he wasn't in the room, he didn't know. And indeed, many of those supportive officials had deep misgivings about the idea and the man in charge.

For the moment, Poindexter opted for a low public profile. No big speeches. No unveilings just yet. But with him making the rounds of so many chiefs of the spy community, word about his radical proposal to mine private information was going to get around on Capitol Hill. And when it did, Poindexter would find himself in combat, once again, with his oldest nemeses.

Perhaps no one understood that better than Mike McConnell. As a former director of the National Security Agency, and he knew firsthand the extraordinary problems Poindexter would encounter trying to expand the government's access to data on American citizens.

Poindexter wanted McConnell's advice. He was a fellow admiral, and Poindexter had followed his career admiringly over the years. During the Gulf War McConnell was the top intelligence officer to then chairman of the Joint Chiefs Colin Powell. Poindexter thought he'd performed superbly, and he'd came to value his opinion when McConnell, after leaving government, attended the Genoa demonstrations and became a major player in the world of intelligence contracting.

The two met in McConnell's office at Booz Allen Hamilton, a brand name inside the Beltway. McConnell had led the intelligence business there since leaving the NSA in 1996. McConnell was frank in his assessments of what Poindexter was up against. He was heading for a political buzz saw.

Both men could see it. McConnell was concerned that Poindexter would end up creating dossiers of innocent people, and he wasn't sure that Poindexter appreciated just how disastrously that would play out with Congress and the public. Lawmakers would give Poindexter his biggest grief, but McConnell was prepared to provide "top cover" by talking to senior members and committee staff about TIA, with an eye toward supporting it. McConnell knew how to reach all those key influencers that Townsend had said Poindexter should seek. He would emphasize that TIA wasn't an operational system (that dirty little word again). McConnell also told Poindexter that he mustn't portray TIA as a domestic intelligence program.

McConnell could broach the subject of surveillance laws and regulations with far more credibility and less drama than Poindexter. He had enjoyed an impeccable Navy career, and his name counted for a lot in Washington, particularly among senior members of the Bush administration. He could clear Poindexter's path. That sounded, to Poindexter, like an excellent idea.

But McConnell didn't want to stop there. He told Poindexter that he should award Booz the entire TIA contract, letting the company effectively take over the research, testing, and construction of the prototype, a soup-to-nuts arrangement.

McConnell and his team arguably possessed the technical expertise and the manpower to handle the entire "system of systems" effort. And he thought he knew how to weather the political controversy. But Poindexter was reluc-

tant to give one company—one man—so much influence over TIA's development. Business was booming after 9/11. TIA would hardly be the only jewel
in Booz's crown.

"I'd like for you to participate in some way," Poindexter said, leaving the
door open. He could sense McConnell's disappointment. "I hope that you'll
propose under the BAA," he added, referring to his broad agency announcement out on the street.

McConnell would have to settle for less than the full project. Yet his ultimate prize was a handsome one. Under a contract Poindexter awarded later
that year, worth more than $8 million, Booz was tapped to help bring a pro-
totype TIA system to life. McConnell and company would get TIA out of the
lab and into the hands of government users, a process that Poindexter dubbed
"assured transition." Poindexter would create the system, but McConnell
would spread it around. His connections, and those of his company, would
pay off after all.

McConnell's offer of top cover was not part of the final deal. When Tony
Tether reviewed the provisions of the contract, he struck that portion. "We
don't need this," he told Poindexter.

Poindexter pushed back, arguing that DARPA needed McConnell's influence. The agency only had one full-time legislative affairs specialist and one
PR person. Tether was not persuaded.

Poindexter had worried since coming to DARPA that Tether wasn't facing
up to TIA's political realities. It wasn't that he didn't want to address the controversy, Poindexter thought. He just seemed not to imagine there was one.
"They haven't come up over the hill at us yet!" Tether was fond of joking. But
Poindexter knew that if TIA exploded onto the national scene in the wrong
light, he'd be left to defend it on his own.

Bob Popp sat at his desk, thinking about a sandwich. It was nearly lunchtime,
and he'd spent much of the day reviewing sketches for the Information Awareness Office's new logo. Every DARPA office had its own custom design that
was supposed to convey, elegantly and concisely, its animating ideas. Poindexter had asked Popp to hire an artist, who came up with several conceptual,

abstract drawings. Popp thought they would look more at home in a modern art museum than a Defense Department office. "Go look at the other logos," he told the artist. "They have three letters, with a little leaf, or a lightning bolt." Nothing exotic.

The artist took Popp's conservative approach to the other extreme, returning some sketches that used nothing but the office's initials: IAO. This was harder than it needed to be, Popp thought. As he sat at his desk struggling to make the image work, his secretary came and asked if he wanted lunch from the deli. Perfect timing. Popp handed her some cash and returned to the sketches.

A few minutes later the secretary returned with Popp's lunch and put his change on the desk. As he reached for the loose bills, he stopped short. A one-dollar bill had landed a few inches from one of the drawings. Popp stared at the great seal on the back of the note, a pyramid topped by a shining, all-seeing eye.

"Hey!" he yelled out to his secretary. "Look at that!"

"The eye. Like the letter *I*," he said. And the pyramid, an A shape. IA. What could he think of that looked like an *O*? He thought about it for a few seconds, and then it came to him. "A globe!"

IAO. Information Awareness Office. Popp would take the eye and pyramid of the great seal but have it cast a gaze across a picture of the world. Information awareness. Total information awareness, in fact. It was perfect.

He took five minutes to sketch out a rough version. Then he showed the mock-up to his secretary. "Oh, very clever!" she said. He asked a few colleagues around the office, which by now had grown in size and moved into more substantial quarters. People seemed to like it. Popp had the sketch artist do a more polished job before showing it to Poindexter.

He had the same reaction. What a neat idea. Poindexter had long thought of the perfect information system as a pyramid, with a decision maker at the top able to reach down to the base of the structure for the information he needed. The logo conveyed just the right idea, he and Popp agreed. And it was provocative. It would get the public's attention, Popp thought. For him, "the public" was the agencies and scientists with which DARPA did business. It was not the man on the street. He never imagined that the *general* public would see the logo, and so he never dreamed anyone would react unfavorably.

Popp and Poindexter noted that the great seal on the dollar bill incorporated some Latin phrases: *Novus ordo seclorum,* "New Order of the Ages," and *Annuit coeptis,* or "He approves of our undertaking." Could they work some Latin into the IAO seal? they wondered.

Poindexter had a favorite Latin phrase, and it seemed a perfect choice: *Scientia est potentia.* "Knowledge is power." He placed it underneath the all-seeing eye, which in the final version of the logo cast an enormous searching beam of light over an image of the globe.

The people who knew DARPA, they told each other, were going to love this. The logo was published on the office's Web site in April.

The Information Awareness Office came together in the span of a few months—a breakneck pace for the government, even at crisis tempo. Poindexter added more staff. The TIA network attracted new members every month. By year's end Poindexter would award tens of millions of dollars in research contracts to more than two dozen companies. Some were big, well-known Washington players, others were smaller shops located far outside the Beltway.

At the beginning of his research experiments Poindexter drew a bright line in the kinds of data he would use. On the TIA Network, which was classified and restricted to intelligence and military agencies, he would tap into real intelligence, collected through foreign operations. This was the daily take of the intelligence community, and as far as Poindexter knew, it was all obtained legally.

But he needed a source of domestic intelligence as well. Something akin to the mounds of corporate and personal information that TIA was meant to mine. Unable to obtain these kinds of databases legally, Poindexter decided to build them. His team constructed a repository of simulated intelligence reports about terrorists, including fake accounts of their daily activities that left transactional footprints. The red team would use these synthetic worlds to run their exercises. In these virtual realities hundreds of thousands of innocent and ordinary electronic people would mix among a few bad actors. It was here that Poindexter would truly discover whether TIA could detect terrorist patterns. Whether it could distinguish signals from noise.

Two paths of research—one foreign, one domestic. Poindexter had no idea that at the NSA, an agency he wanted with him on his quest, the line between those two worlds had practically disappeared.

CHAPTER 16

FEED THE BAG

They called it the BAG. As in black bag. Grab bag. Bag of tricks. And while it was all those things, the acronym that the National Security Agency's techs used for their terrorist hunting machine stood for something unexpected: Big Ass Graph.

In the late 1990s the engineers and systems gurus at the NSA became enamored of computerized graphs to display huge sets of information. Graphs were simple, and elegant. A set of axes and plotted points. Inasmuch as data was a collection of points—events, people, places—they too could be displayed on a graph in a comprehensible or meaningful form.

That was the idea, at least. Not unlike the data harvesters of Able Danger, who displayed names and events on link charts, or those of Poindexter's Genoa team, who sought to diagram information as a series of questions and answers, the graph builders of the NSA wanted to turn raw data into visual knowledge. Graphs became their favored method.

The BAG, as its name implied, was big. Enormous. It compressed mounds of data into their linear essence. The BAG could show how swarms of people were connected to different places by displaying each set of data on its own axis. The graph could turn a seemingly random pile of information into a more complete explanation of relationships. Put enough names, phone numbers, and e-mail addresses into a graph, and it might illustrate an entire social network, which in the global terrorist hunt was indispensable intelligence. (The way to roll up a cell was to pick off the members.)

The BAG was the ultimate manifestation of graph theory. And its ultimate aim was to reveal suspicious linkages. Immediately after the 9/11 attacks, with the NSA frantically searching for the next sleeper cell poised to attack, the BAG became one of its favorite tools. But it was not entirely the agency's invention.

The BAG was created by a computer scientist who perfected his craft far away from the gates of Fort Meade. Dr. J. C. Smart started his technical career at the Lawrence Livermore National Laboratory, about a half hour's drive east of San Francisco Bay. Smart joined the lab in 1980, after graduating from Northwestern University with a degree in electrical engineering and a specialization in computer science and logic.

Few institutions in the world could offer a bright, enterprising computer geek such a rich history of technological innovation, and a bounding professional playpen, as Lawrence Livermore. The lab played a central role in the evolution of computing in America. A year after its founding, in 1952, it purchased the UNIVAC, the country's first commercial computer. Year after year it bought the prototypes of the most powerful computers in the world and helped turn a generation of experimental machines into viable, marketable systems that changed the face of science, communications, and business in America.

Livermore, founded at the height of the cold war, had developed nuclear warheads and made early breakthroughs in fusion energy. The line between computer research and warfare was a thin one. In fact, each fed the other. As the nuclear arms race speeded up, the government's requirement for ever more sophisticated and powerful simulators to help design nuclear weapons fueled the private sector's construction of new supercomputers. At Livermore, Smart sat at the crossroads of American technology and national security.

Smart worked at the lab for nineteen years. He completed his graduate and PhD work in computer science at the University of California at Davis. In his studies and at work, Smart became an authority on graph theory and its application to national security problems. In 1996, he founded a new center at Livermore dedicated to "information operations, warfare, and assurance." IOWA, as it was called, put Smart at yet another crossroads—the converging worlds of computer security, espionage, and digital war. Those were the NSA's sweet spots, and so it was perhaps inevitable that Smart would make the trip east and end up at the agency's doorstep. He brought the BAG with him.

In 1999, Smart became the technical director of the agency's signals intelligence program. Four years later, amid the heat of the terror war, he took the same job in the agency's National Security Operations Center. This was the heart of the agency's early-warning system, a fitting place for a scientist whose creation was put into service for that purpose.

The center was manned around the clock, and its sole purpose was to alert the president and the national leadership to an unfolding crisis. Blue lights flashed whenever the agency picked up emergency signals traffic from its worldwide stations, sometimes within minutes of the event. In 2000, the center was the first unit of the intelligence community to alert the White House that USS *Cole* had been bombed. By the time Smart arrived it was a beehive of intelligence activity, central and vital to the war.

As was the BAG. The terrorist hunters poured signals into it, in the hopes of finding those hidden connections that would bring down a terrorist network. But if the BAG was a useful tool, it was also a demanding one. For the BAG to tell them things, the hunters had to fill it. Constantly. There was only one source that might satisfy its appetite.

The nation's phone companies and Internet service providers owned a rich set of details about the people who used their networks. In order to hone their marketing campaigns, companies studied whom their customers called and how long they spoke, and then developed service packages to attract new business. They also used this data to create monthly phone bills. The companies would watch for communications surges at a particular time of day in order to manage the traffic on their networks. All of this data constituted a valuable repository of corporate knowledge. It was also a potential gold mine of terrorism intelligence, and after the 9/11 attacks, the NSA asked the companies to share it.

This wasn't wiretapping as usual. The agency didn't just want to target individual people's communications. They wanted blanket access to the information about the network as a whole. It was an extraordinary request, but it wasn't the first time the spy agency had made it. Indeed, Mike Hayden himself had proposed the idea on February 27, 2001, nine months before the terrorist attacks.

On that day James Payne, the head of Qwest Communications' federal government business unit, accompanied the company's chief executive to a business meeting with Hayden at his Fort Meade headquarters. The CEO, Joe Nacchio, wanted a piece of a new NSA contract called Groundbreaker, a multibillion-dollar program to outsource maintenance of the agency's nonclassified technology systems, such as desktop computers. Several Washington mainstays were vying for a piece of the deal, forming large teams of companies. Payne had made plenty of drop-in calls like this before to discuss potential business with large, important clients. Indeed, he was an old hand in the close-knit club of federal telecom contractors and agency executives.

A lifelong Washingtonian, Payne had mastered the ins and outs of the government market. He knew how to build relationships not just with agency chiefs but with the program managers and contracting officials underneath them who had the final say on how dollars were spent. They were the seldom seen bureaucrats who ultimately decided which companies rose and fell.

Payne's impeccable dress, polished demeanor, and practically antebellum gentility seemed outwardly at odds with the bureaucrats and bean counters of the federal contracting market. But his refined style masked the heart of a bare-knuckled businessman. Payne had grown up in the government telecom space, a viper pit in its own right where executives hopped among companies and found themselves fighting alongside a friend one day and bidding against him the next. They understood the bottom line—the federal government was, by far, the largest single buyer of telecom services in the United States. Payne fought for the business he won; the NSA was no exception.

Qwest already had an in with the NSA, having worked on agency projects for a few years. The company had allocated portions of its telecom network for the agency's exclusive use. Payne and Nacchio wanted to expand the business relationship. And so did Hayden.

In the meeting Hayden told Payne and Nacchio that he wanted information about Qwest's customers, as well as the flow of traffic across its network, in order to track computer hackers and foreign intelligence services trying to penetrate U.S. government systems, particularly within the Defense Department. The agency was going after digital spies, not terrorists. Part of the NSA's charter included the defense of government secrets. And by 2001, outside forces were trying to capture them with alarming frequency and some success.

Government officials had also begun to fear a "digital Pearl Harbor" if intruders were to seize control of sensitive military systems or other key U.S. infrastructures, like power grids or the financial system, via the Internet. Hayden couldn't let that happen.

The agency didn't need to target individuals to look for anomalous behavior. It could monitor—or rather, have Qwest monitor—an entire network for suspicious patterns of activity. Maybe it was a particular Internet address probing a government network or a series of bogus information requests pinged off a server indicating the preparation for some massive electronic attack. Faceless signals, but signals nonetheless.

Telecom carriers routinely monitored their networks for fraud and hacking activity, so they had an enormous amount of intelligence capability already deployed. And Qwest was well positioned to help the agency. Perhaps even uniquely so.

The company was building a new and much heralded high-speed network for phone and Internet traffic. It promised faster, more powerful data flows, and it caught the attention of senior U.S. military officials. They worried about how it might be exploited by hackers, but they also wanted to use it themselves. Qwest was a darling of the Internet Age. Philip Anschutz, who owned the Southern Pacific Railroad, founded the company in 1988, and it eventually built the first all-digital, fiber-optic network by laying lines alongside railroad tracks. Those lines linked to terminals in key geographic locations, from which Qwest provided high-speed Internet and data connections to its customers. The company was based in Denver and was the largest carrier in the Rocky Mountain corridor, home to some of the military's most important command-and-control facilities. U.S. Strategic Command, which oversaw the country's nuclear arsenal, was a neighbor. And Buckley Air Force Base, in Aurora, Colorado, was a major downlink facility for U.S. spy satellites, including "eyes in the sky" that detected foreign missile launches.

The military and intelligence community needed what Qwest had: its network, its agility, and its information. In late 1997 a three-star general had met with Nacchio at his Denver office and later told one of Nacchio's associates that he wanted to use the company's network "for government purposes." After that meeting Qwest chased after a pair of potentially lucrative deals to build private, secure networks for defense and intelligence agencies. So on that February day in 2001, when Hayden asked Qwest for its assistance monitoring cyberthreats, he had plenty of reason to think Nacchio would comply.

But he didn't. Hayden's proposal struck Nacchio, Payne, and Qwest's lawyers as potentially illegal. If the company were to hand over customer information to the NSA without a lawful order, it could violate the Electronic Communications Privacy Act (ECPA), a 1986 statute that extended the wiretapping restrictions on phone calls to electronic information transmitted and stored in a computer. Though it might sour the company's friendly relationship with the NSA, Qwest said no.

It was hardly the last Payne would hear of the matter. Time and again the agency raised it in meetings. Payne had a feeling that the NSA wasn't just asking for the information for its own use; they also appeared to be acting on behalf of other government agencies. As the company continued to vie for the NSA business, the request hung unresolved in the air.

It was still unresolved as planes crashed into the World Trade Center and the Pentagon. The NSA quickly came calling again—on Qwest, as well as on its competitors, the country's major telecom carriers and Internet service providers. Except this time the agency wasn't hunting for hackers.

In the weeks after the attacks the NSA asked telecom executives for access to their customer records as well as direct, physical access to their data. The NSA specifically asked companies for their call-detail records, the logs of whom customers had called, on what days, and how long they had talked. Companies kept these records for routine billing matters. The NSA wanted them to feed the BAG.

If analysts started with a list of phone numbers, they could find all the other numbers called from those phones, and so establish the close circle of people in the targets' daily lives. From there it was just a matter of exponential analysis. The NSA could look at all the numbers called from the second layer of phones, and all the numbers that those numbers called, pushing out until they'd identified a vast network of callers. Then, they could layer it over with e-mail information, financial reports, any kind of transaction the hunters could get their hands on to add meaning to the lines and dots that the BAG spit out.

Considering that terrorists often talk and write in code, this transactional data, or "metadata," if properly exploited could yield more valuable information than recordings of the phone calls themselves. The same was true for e-mail messages, though establishing who actually sent an e-mail and where it came from was technically harder to do.

In any case, the NSA would have to collect huge amounts of metadata in order to capture specific communications and to establish patterns of activity among terrorist groups. Analysts had to set baselines about what constituted "normal" versus "suspicious" behavior. To make any reasonable determination the agency needed thousands, potentially even hundreds of thousands or millions, of customers' call records. Analysts needed a thirty-thousand-foot view of the battlefield before knowing whom to target, which phones to tap, and which e-mails to snatch. And they needed those metadata preferably as soon as they were created, since call-detail records were not real-time accounts of who had called whom. The NSA needed a way to tap into the network at the source. It needed the kind of access that Qwest had refused to give almost a year earlier.

But once again, when the NSA came calling, Qwest said no. This time the agency seemed to have a new argument: The USA PATRIOT Act made it easier for the government to obtain certain private communications. But still Nacchio declined. The company decided it would violate the privacy requirements of another law, the Telecommunications Act. Try as they might, NSA officials could not convince Qwest's executives and lawyers that their requests for customer information passed legal muster. Agency officials rebutted by questioning the company's patriotism. They let it be known that Qwest's competitors were already on board. All around Washington the message to the companies whose assistance the NSA needed was clear: You *must* help us. Many executives agreed willingly. Others held out. Nacchio was one, and as far as the government was concerned, he was on the wrong side.

Lawyers for telecom and Internet companies were working overtime to comply with the government requests. Some came in the form of traditional warrants. But the emissaries of the most secretive terrorist surveillance programs carried only the assurances of the president of the United States and the attorney general. They averred that these untraditional requests were lawful and necessary to protect the nation.

Telecom data was only a part of the trove. In the first weeks after the 9/11 attacks, the Treasury Department formed a new investigative unit tasked to disrupt the routes of terrorist financing by monitoring bank transactions and money transfers. Al Qaeda and other groups had made brilliant use of the global financial system and its ability to move money effortlessly from one country to another. The government wanted to know how they did it.

The Treasury team, dubbed Operation Green Quest, was specifically interested in a money-moving system called *hawala*. For decades, *hawala* dealers had helped clients around the world quietly move money without the aid of electronic requests or even bank accounts. *Hawala* dealers didn't actually transport currency. Instead, they arranged for cash pickups with other dealers, and their clients paid a fee for the brokering service. A cabdriver in the United States could find a local *hawala* dealer and ask him to get a thousand dollars to his brother in India. The dealer would contact another in Mumbai, who would then get in touch with the brother and pay him. *Hawala* dealers were constantly giving money out and taking it in, along with their cut. They managed their own books, which were kept in balance by trust and tradition. It was quick, discreet, and largely untraceable.

It was also generally unknown to U.S. investigators as a terrorist funding mechanism. In fact, before the 9/11 attacks, the Treasury Department and the FBI had never mounted a task force investigation into terrorist financing and assets at all. As Operation Green Quest and a partner group at the FBI got up to speed, however, they became quick studies on *hawala* as well as on overt mechanisms that terrorists used to move money, often in sums that avoided detection by banks and government regulators.

The FBI unit, called the Financial Review Group, set out to discover the financial linkages that tied the nineteen hijackers to one another and to their sources. Agents, some of them working out of the bureau's crisis management center in Washington, pored over credit card statements, ATM transactions, and wire transfer receipts like auditors trying to reverse engineer some fraudulent scheme. Their work eventually led to the indictment of Zacarias Moussaoui, who the FBI suspected would have been the twentieth hijacker aboard a doomed airliner on September 11 had he not been detained earlier on an immigration violation.

FBI agents also dove into credit and debit card histories housed at First Data in Colorado. The huge company processed almost half of all card charges in the United States and ran payments for customers located around the world too. The agents were there at the company's request. Like a number of American businesses large and small, First Data voluntarily handed over its data in the days after the attacks, a patriotic and perhaps legally risky gesture that was driven by the same fear of an impending follow-up attack. First Data also owned Western Union, which meant that the government's terrorist trackers were now tapped into two vital streams for moving money.

The FBI and Operation Green Quest weren't alone in sniffing out terror-ists' money trails. The Treasury Department's Financial Crimes Enforcement Network also spun up into wartime tempo. FinCEN was one of the most sophisticated electronic intelligence units in the government, with a solid reputation for catching money launderers, organized criminals, and drug traf-fickers exploiting the U.S. banking system. A unit at the Customs Bureau in Northern Virginia also joined the fray. Agents there built dummy Web sites, hoping to snare people donating to terrorist groups. Agents loaded the sites with code words that frequent *hawala* users would recognize, as well as with other terms meant to entice terrorism funders.

Based on all this financial intelligence, law enforcement agents launched raids on Islamic charities suspected of backing Al Qaeda and affiliated groups. It was also vital to CIA agents as they tracked suspected terrorists and their middlemen in Pakistan, Afghanistan, and the Middle East.

As Treasury, Customs, and FBI agents probed electronic and underground financial mechanisms, they unearthed evidence that terrorists were supported through a vast network of wire transfers as well as cash funneled through long-standing money-laundering rings run by groups posing as legitimate businesses. These were located in the United States and overseas. The terror-ist financing machine was a global enterprise, the investigators realized. If they could disrupt it, they might prevent more attacks. But if they knew where the money was coming from, they also might find out where the terrorists, and their backers, were hiding.

That's what the NSA wanted to know. Owing to an unprecedented level of cooperation among law enforcement and intelligence agencies, as well as new financial reporting requirements placed on banks and money transfer services, the NSA became privy to a wealth of financial intelligence, including wire transfer records, credit card transactions, and "suspicious activity reports," which financial institutions were required to file anytime their customers moved a certain volume of money. In effect, the NSA turned banks and transfer services into their eyes and ears on the financial networks. The agency set up financial watch lists—whenever a particular target used a credit card or moved money, a red flag went up. But financial data was also poured into the BAG and overlapped with phone and e-mail communications in an effort to dig deeper into terrorists' social networks. The tiniest bit of information might be the key clue that put the agency on the terrorists' trail, and ultimately led to his brothers in arms.

Throughout 2002 the NSA sated its analysts' ravenous appetite for more intelligence. Phone calls, e-mails, metadata, financial transactions. Anything that could serve the agency's twin goals of tracking terrorists and disrupting their plots.

The NSA was hardly alone in this quest. Nor was it the sole collector of intelligence. But those presidential authorities that allowed the agency to sidestep the Foreign Intelligence Surveillance Act also came with new responsibility. For years the NSA had played a supporting role, providing tactical intelligence to the military in wartime or responding to requests from national leaders. Now the agency was on point. It plugged into an array of data sources, including those at AT&T, one of the oldest and most important telecom providers. The agency made arrangements to siphon phone and Internet traffic off the company's network. The NSA was also privy to financial intelligence streams coming out of the Treasury Department and the FBI. And, of course, its traditional foreign intelligence mission continued unabated.

But for all its riches of data, the NSA was still starving. Access to information wasn't the challenge. What to do with it—how to make *sense* of it—that's what mattered most. And as it sucked in more and more data, the NSA started to choke.

The agency could store terabytes of intelligence in its vast databases, but it couldn't analyze it fast enough before the mounds piled ever higher. Despite its vaunted, almost mystical reputation as an all-seeing eye, the NSA was physically incapable of analyzing all of this information in real time as it coursed through the world's networks. Analysts could only search digital archives after information was collected.

That wasn't their only problem. Once they obtained the information from their data banks and fed it into the BAG, the resulting analysis overwhelmed them. The BAG's very design, the way it compressed information into more manageable forms, actually diluted nuance. The graph might only reveal how many times a particular word appeared in a conversation, not necessarily the significance of the word or how it related to other words. The same could be said for a lot of mining tools, but the BAG had another particular handicap. When it displayed those connections as lines, they could be so dense as to be indecipherable. A mishmash of lines, dots, and intersections, weaves and lattices. To some of the analysts and techies at the NSA it looked like the BAG had taken the information and twisted it up into a sickening, knotted jumble. They named these unhelpful diagrams after another tangled mess they'd seen their pets cough up at home—hair balls.

And that was how the hunters learned a painful lesson about the BAG: For it to tell them things, they had to feed it. But the more they fed it, the less it actually told them.

They were going to need help.

CHAPTER 17

SHIPS PASSING IN THE NIGHT

Since September 11, John Poindexter and Mike Hayden had been sailing the same noisy ocean, searching for the same signals. But they hardly recognized the other's presence. They were ships passing in the night. Sooner or later, they were bound to collide.

Poindexter had never met Hayden. On paper the pair seemed natural competitors. Poindexter was the elder, by nearly ten years. He was Navy, Hayden was Air Force. Poindexter came up through the academy, Hayden was an ROTC graduate from Duquesne University. But in one important respect—and for their present purposes, maybe it was the most important—they were identical. Each man was a brilliant technocrat.

They knew the system. They knew its limits. They had built their careers pushing them, and they regretted the times they hadn't. They were survivors. And now each man had come to a crest. Not by virtue of his status or position but because of the job each one believed he'd been called to do.

Poindexter made his first approach to the NSA in February 2002, when he was making the rounds of the other intelligence agency heads. Poindexter wanted the NSA to join his network, based at the Information Dominance Center. The agency was the biggest signals collector out there—he thought it was only natural they should participate.

Poindexter secured a meeting with Bill Black, Hayden's number two and a career NSA employee. When Hayden took over as director, he brought Black out of retirement to help him run the agency. Black had taken a post at SAIC, the California contractor so intrinsically linked with the agency that employees called it NSA-West. He knew the agency in ways that his new boss didn't. The NSA was run by middle management, the career establishment that caustically referred to any chief as "the current director." They were the permanent class. And within their ranks, the lawyers held particular sway. Without Black, Hayden might have found the agency too inhospitable to carry out his broad agenda.

Poindexter showed up at Fort Meade on the morning of February 2. Officials had a whole day of events planned for him. He started out at a ten o'clock meeting with lower-level officials and then sat down with Black after lunch. Poindexter gave him the same TIA briefing he'd presented to others. But he didn't find Black as talkative and agreeable. He was in listening mode, Poindexter thought. He took more than he gave.

Poindexter wasn't completely in the dark about what the NSA was up to. Based on those prelunch meetings, he understood that the agency was in the midst of a much broader intelligence-gathering effort. He could also tell that to preempt terrorism the NSA was expanding the scope of its activities. Poindexter was never read into the warrantless surveillance program, now known internally as Stellar Wind. Nor was he ever told that the agency was operating under new presidential authorities. But he could see that the tempo had changed. And why wouldn't it? he figured.

Black and his underlings didn't tell Poindexter about the agency's work with telecommunications companies. But again, he knew from his own career what a long history the NSA had with the intelligence agencies. The phone companies were indispensable partners, something Poindexter had been reminded of on a recent visit to an AT&T laboratory in New Jersey. There he learned that a large percentage of phone calls, no matter which carrier generated them, passed through AT&T circuits. Clearly, he thought, of all the telecom companies, AT&T was the most important. Had someone at the NSA said they were working with the company to divert their network traffic to the agency, Poindexter wouldn't have blinked.

Poindexter told Black that he wanted the NSA on his network. Black seemed supportive, Poindexter thought. But he made no promises. Poindexter had a hard time deciding how impressed Black was with the TIA concept. But he thought that they surely needed it.

Indeed, as the agency amassed more stores of telecom metadata, its approach started to look like Poindexter's. Instead of just monitoring individual targets, the terrorist hunters began to look for patterns. They timed series of phone calls, measured the waves of e-mail traffic emanating from particular corners of the world, and examined the conspicuous but still vague overlaps of phone calls and credit card purchases. These patterns told the agency whom to zoom in on, whose phone to tap and e-mails to read. It was the best method they had, but all too often, it led nowhere.

The FBI was discovering that firsthand. The torrent of leads that Mike Hayden let loose after 9/11 more often than not led agents on wild-goose chases. Rather than leading them to sleeper agents, the NSA's intelligence usually led them to the doorstep of an innocent American, or a Pizza Hut.

FBI agents weren't the only ones frustrated by the NSA's lack of specificity. At the CIA, the senior officials in charge of tracking Al Qaeda members overseas were less impressed by social network models, and the insights they could provide into terrorist behaviors and organizational structures. They wanted to know whom to kill. In one meeting at Langley, a senior CIA official looked across a table at an NSA analyst, who'd shown up with a nebulous link diagram. "I don't need this," the official said. "I just need you to tell me whose ass to put a Hellfire missile on."

The NSA wanted that too. "Geo-location" was the trade term for locating a target based on his signals. And the analysts could do that. But still, they were overwhelmed by the amount of information they had to process. The data was piling up.

Poindexter knew that had long been the agency's problem. And he knew about the BAG. He thought it was a blunt instrument compared to the precision tools he was testing. Poindexter distrusted graphs in general. He abhorred how they watered complex information down into a bland stew.

Poindexter left Fort Meade feeling moderately successful. Black hadn't made any promises, but having spent nearly the entire day there, Poindexter felt confident that he was on the right track.

Exactly seven weeks later, on March 25, Poindexter went back to the fort and sat down with Mike Hayden. TIA was the topic of discussion once again.

He didn't give Hayden the full briefing. Poindexter presumed that Black, who was also there, had given his boss the highlights. Poindexter heard a lot of the same talk about the NSA's new challenges. He explained to Hayden how he thought TIA could help.

It was hard to get a read on the NSA director. Did he grasp the concept? Was he willing to experiment? Poindexter had a long-standing bias against Air Force officers, so he was perhaps skeptical about Hayden going into the meeting. He also knew the NSA's reputation as a reluctant partner with other intelligence agencies. The fort took in a lot more than it gave out.

Poindexter and Hayden had a polite if cool exchange. It was the first and last time that they ever sat down face-to-face.

Over the next several months, the two ships passed each other more frequently, closer each time. They watched each other. And in time, they stalked each other. Neither man could have predicted how it would all settle out. But in the end, the NSA would own TIA.

CHAPTER 18

FULL STEAM AHEAD

Once the first node was installed on the TIA network, in early 2002, Poindexter set out an ambitious schedule to enlarge his laboratory and build a working TIA prototype. Every three months he would conduct an analysis experiment on a particularly challenging problem facing the network's members. The idea was to test a set of tools in a real-world environment. The members brought the problems, Poindexter provided the tools.

Each experiment received a code name that, to a landlubber, might seem obscure. "Mistral," "Sirocco," "Rafale," "Noreaster." The names paid homage to Poindexter's other passion—sailing. Each one referred to a type of wind.

The first experiment began in May. And with each new test Poindexter made more tools available to the members of the network. Some performed well. Others the members junked.

It wasn't hard to find real-world intelligence problems. With the government's fear of more attacks spreading at a relentless pace, there was always more work to be done. The list of experiments reflected some of the worst fears and toughest challenges that military and intelligence agencies were facing.

Domestic military planners creating a new homeland defense command were worried about nuclear, biological, or chemical weapons attacks against a U.S. city. Collaborating on the TIA network with analysts in different agencies, they devised a rank-ordered list of targets, starting with the most likely and working down to those at less risk. Over the course of the experiment, the analysts swapped classified documents, posed competing hypotheses, and employed an audio search tool that let them find keywords in spoken recordings. This was the kind of information sharing that the 9/11 Commission called for years later in its final report. In the end the TIA team produced the analysis in one-tenth the amount of time it had taken another set of analysts to do the same work by hand.

Word of the experiments spread. Like Kleinsmith's analysts on steroids, Poindexter's researchers were offering faster and potentially better ways of doing business.

Analysts poring over interrogation reports from detainees held at Guantánamo Bay, Cuba, wondered if Poindexter's new system might help them. Hundreds of men captured on the battlefields of Afghanistan and Pakistan had been flown to the island jail, often with little attempt to discern whether they were actually members of Al Qaeda. The Pentagon's Criminal Investigation Task Force, which was trying to sort the prisoners, asked the TIA team to use their data extraction and linking tools on a set of interrogation reports. These were the end result of lengthy, often coercive sessions with the detainees, and they contained hundreds of references to other people, places, and groups. As the stacks of reports piled up, the interrogators struggled to make sense of what was in them.

Some detainees frequently mentioned the same names or places. Some claimed to know one another. Others said they didn't. The Pentagon task force wanted to know which men were real terrorists and which were just "dirt farmers," innocents caught in the fog of war who had no useful intelligence to offer.

The TIA team ran their tools, looking for interesting and nonobvious relationships among the prisoners. What they considered to be valuable leads they passed along for use in follow-up interrogations. But the tools also revealed that some of the detainees were certainly not terrorists. Far from speeding their release, this new information became a kind of baseline for what a "nonterrorist" looked like. The data tools were then recalibrated to disregard certain attributes and search for others that were germane to the interrogators' work.

Throughout 2002, anywhere Poindexter turned he could find agency chiefs and cabinet secretaries trying to carve their own counterterrorism niche. Intelligence was the best game in town, and Poindexter was in demand. Paul Polski, an old Naval Academy classmate, called Poindexter for help on an ambitious project to screen millions of airline passengers against terrorist watch lists and intelligence databases. Polski was working with the new Transportation Security Agency, set up swiftly after the 9/11 attacks, on a system that could assign risk levels to each flier. Like Poindexter, Polski was an old counterterrorism hand. In the late eighties he had directed a team of engineers at a Federal Aviation Administration research lab set up in the wake of the Pan Am Flight 103 bombing. Polski called his technicians, who invented bomb-sensing equipment and other countermeasures, the "Green Berets of science." Poindexter's team helped Polski vet ideas and proposals for the passenger-screening system.

Attorney General John Ashcroft also came calling. Shortly after 9/11 he set up a new terrorist-tracking task force to find suspects using public records. The FBI hired ChoicePoint, a data-aggregation firm based outside Atlanta, to give agents access to billions of records on nearly every person inside the United States—everything from their driver's licenses to marriage records to the forms they filled out to open post office boxes. The company made millions of dollars off its federal government sales, which became an indispensable part of the business, and designed systems specifically for use by the FBI and the intelligence agencies. Poindexter's team helped the FBI trackers devise new ways of sifting through hoards of information without hitting dead ends.

As the TIA experiments continued apace, Poindexter's team made more data available to the network members. They already had access to the database of simulated intelligence reports about terrorists, including fake accounts of their daily activities. The TIA researchers nicknamed the database Ali Baba, after the Arabian folk character who opens a cave full of hidden treasure with the magic words "open sesame." (The name Ali Baba was also becoming a sobriquet in military circles for all suspected terrorists.)

Simulated intelligence was also used to create ever more complicated synthetic worlds for testing the red teams' attack templates. The first world consisted of two million individuals. Their names were randomly assigned by mashing together real first and last names, and each person was assigned to an actual address somewhere in the United States. But their attributes were manufactured—age, gender, nationality, whether they paid with cash or credit for purchases. The synthesized people took trips on airlines, which created travel records. Poindexter's database builders called this alternate reality Vanilla World, because it was so plain. As more sophisticated attributes were added, and new transactions, the flavor names changed.

Cherry Vanilla World emerged when a separate red team covertly added terrorist sleeper agents into the mix. *Their* travel records were the signals that the templates were supposed to spot. Poindexter thought that the TIA analysis tools did a respectable job, and he hoped that Strawberry World and Chocolate World were not far off. But there was no denying that the system was primitive. It took a week to successfully identify some suspicious individuals in the fake world, and a lot of manual labor on the part of the researchers. Still, it was a start.

The TIA network also added real databases of known or suspected terrorists as well as the people, places, and activities that had been linked to them. These "entity databases" were highly classified and were restricted to agencies with nodes on the network. Critics of the intelligence failures that had preceded the 9/11 attacks lambasted the intelligence agencies for not sharing enough information about terrorism. But on the TIA network partners were swapping leads and finding ways to give one another access to their secrets. The network was quickly becoming the most active experiment of its kind. By the end of 2002 the number of individual users at agencies increased more than 35 times, from 7 to 250. By August 2003 the network had 23 nodes and 320 users.

By far, the NSA was the biggest presence on the network. The agency eventually installed 15 nodes, eclipsing all other organizations. The NSA seemed intensely interested in collaborating. But that struck Poindexter as rather odd, since the agency still had never participated in a single experiment.

The rules of membership on the TIA network were simple. Each agency brought its own problem set and could bring its own data. But participation in the experiments wasn't required. And there was also no rule against an agency taking any of the tools off the network to use within the walls of their own organization. Poindexter and Bob Popp both expected that the NSA was moonlighting, but neither could be sure.

Their suspicions were well founded. In fact, the NSA analysts did remove the experimental data crunching, linking, and extracting tools from the TIA network and quietly put them into service as part of the agency's warrantless surveillance regime. While Guantánamo interrogators and homeland defenders nibbled at the edges of the signal-in-the-noise dilemma, the NSA set off on a new course. And the agency's terror hunters put Poindexter's creation through an ordeal of size and strain that not even he could have devised.

Behind the blackout curtain that enveloped Fort Meade, the TIA tools were used on the massive flow of data that the NSA was now receiving from U.S. telecommunications companies—that stream of metadata that included phone numbers called, length of calls, the "To" and "From" lines of e-mails. There had never been a noisier ocean that demanded such immediate, careful attention.

The BAG was failing. The constant hair balls aggravated analysts, and technicians started to doubt whether or not graphs were really up to the challenge. Though its proponents within the agency—and there were many—saw graphing analysis as the new wave, others knew the awful truth. The NSA was churning out charts and diagrams, but it still hadn't created the early-warning system that Hayden had envisioned. It had still not achieved total information awareness.

When the time came to put Poindexter's tools to the test, the NSA was disappointed again. The TIA tools crashed. They were simply incapable of processing so much information in real time. Like balloons affixed to a fire hydrant, they burst.

Technologists liked to say that the TIA tools were "brittle," that they weren't ready for prime time. And certainly that was true. But for present purposes, that didn't solve the NSA's problem. They'd have to tack a new course.

Yet, all was not lost from the TIA experiment. Poindexter had hit the nerve. What the NSA techies knew, what anyone who watched what he was up to in his workshop knew, was that Poindexter had just broken through a wall. He had dared to suggest, and then envision, that the government could tap into information at its source, that it could find signals in noise the moment they were created. Poindexter had articulated a data philosophy. He was H. G. Wells and Albert Einstein in one package. The imaginer and the creator. Fiction become reality.

In the months and years to come this glimpse of the future, of what was possible in spite of overwhelming odds, would become Poindexter's legacy. More than any tool, clever experiment, or acronym, his ambition became a beacon. It called to others, and it drove them.

It was time for a break. Summer was descending upon Washington, and Poindexter was looking forward to getting out of town. He wanted to talk up TIA to a wider audience. The Highlands Forum in Carmel Valley, California, seemed the perfect place.

There were few more exclusive tickets in the circuit of the Big Thinkers, the high priests of academia, government, and industry who relished an opportunity to marinate in one another's ideas. The Highlands Forum was created in 1994 when a Defense Department strategist named Dick O'Neill decided he couldn't do his job locked inside the Pentagon. O'Neill was puzzling over how war would break out in the information age. But roaming the fluorescent and concrete halls, he couldn't find a soul to talk to. Those who did approach him said something he already knew. O'Neill was uninspired.

And that was a problem, because O'Neill's job was to find unconventional answers to big, amorphous problems. He decided to get out of town. With the checkbook of the secretary of defense in hand, he called a dozen bright lights in government and academia, ditched his suit and his tie, and bought plane tickets for the Left Coast, as he and his Pentagon colleagues liked to call it.

They landed in Carmel Highlands, on the Monterey Peninsula, at O'Neill's brother-in-law's house. It was a glass-walled showcase perched atop a rocky tower overlooking Big Sur. There, over good wine and perhaps better cheese, the merry band of boondogglers thought their big thoughts and invented a tradition. Every year the Highlands Forum convened to recapture that magic. The bar was high. In that first meeting atop the precipitous cliffs of Carmel, with otters' tails lapping in the crashing waves below and the giant sun melting into the Pacific, the gatherers invented the concept of information warfare, which then defined how the military conceived of twenty-first-century conflict.

Eight years later leaders from industry, academia, government, and the arts convened on the rocky cliffs to imagine the future of fighting terrorism. Amid the backdrop of playful otters and solar splendor, and wine, Poindexter had come to talk about TIA. But for the presentation O'Neill had paired him up with an outsider, a thirty-eight-year-old computer software designer from Las Vegas named Jeff Jonas.

Jonas had been making the rounds in Washington recently. He'd designed a computer program that he thought might be useful to intelligence agencies trying to detect suspected terrorists. Jonas had hired some seasoned Washington trail guides to show him around town and make introductions. He'd managed to land an invitation to the forum, as good a sign as any that he was meeting the right people. Jonas was a techie like Poindexter, and so they made a logical pair for a panel.

But Poindexter had never heard of Jonas. And when he saw him in person, he could see why. This guy would never fit in among Poindexter's crowd.

Jonas showed up in black pants and a tight black T-shirt in a room full of khaki-clad wise men, sporting blazers and loafers. His clothes showed off a torso well trimmed by Iron Man triathlons and power bike rides. Jonas might have looked like the entertainment. Was he a dancer? A magician? When it came time for Jonas to speak, Poindexter thought he might be a comedian. Everything about Jonas—his dress, his casual manner of speaking, and his wild eyes—told Poindexter he was nutty.

But the more Poindexter listened, the more he heard a familiar refrain.

From an early age, Jonas was a dabbler, and directionless. Growing up in Healdsburg, California, north of San Francisco, in the late 1970s, Jonas had been exposed to all manner of techie innovators. His mother was a lawyer, and once she let him tag along to a demo of the TRS-80, one of the first desktop computers, which had just been released by the Tandy Corporation. His mother hoped it could help automate her legal billing process. But during the demo Jonas watched the computer connect to other machines used by academic researchers around the world. It instantly downloaded abstracts of papers in the researchers' files. Years later Jonas decided that the computer was probably communicating via the primordial Internet, developed by researchers at DARPA. But at that moment, standing there next to his mom and an inventor friend who had joined them, he thought this was magic.

Jonas was hooked. *I get this,* he thought. A singular obsession gripped him, and it ruined him for any other pursuit or profession. How could vast seas of information be harnessed and made useful?

At Jonas's high school computer lessons were reserved for upperclassmen, but he requested an exception. Soon the sophomore was learning how to use the new Personal Electronic Transactor, or PET, a personal computer released the previous year by Commodore.

Jonas's computing skills seemed preternatural. Over the summer he wrote a word-processing program for extra credit, which an instructor thought was so good that he sold it on Jonas's behalf to the Los Angeles Unified School District. The budding programmer was paid two hundred dollars. He had never considered that he could make money off a hobby.

After Jonas had taken the only two computer classes in the high school curriculum, he dropped out. He took his GED and enrolled in a local community college so he could take more courses. During his second semester the owner of a computer consulting firm gave a guest lecture, and he said he was looking to hire someone to write custom software. Jonas asked for the job.

He came on as a subcontractor, and before long had hired twenty-one employees to keep up with his workload. Jonas's business was growing faster than his boss's. He built customized software for local companies—a chain of shoe stores that needed an inventory tracking system, a newspaper that wanted to keep track of billing for its advertisers. It was all data management work. And it was always over budget. Even what appeared to be the simplest of projects, Jonas never finished.

He amassed $200,000 in debt. Creditors called. When the checks bounced, the employees left. He worked off half the debt but thought the balance looked insurmountable. It was Christmas 1984. Jonas filed for bankruptcy.

His father kicked him out of the house, so Jonas moved into his car. He kept the bankruptcy notice with him as he drove around, a kind of talisman on his road to reinvention. It named each of the creditors he vowed to one day pay back.

Jonas was twenty years old. He was broke. As he sat in the corner of an empty office, it hit him. He needed a plan. A blueprint, in fact. For designing computer systems.

This was where he'd gone wrong, he decided. He was trying to build complex structures without specifications. (The same was true for his life.) He vowed that from now on he'd only take on custom software work when he had a detailed plan, depicting every step needed to finish the job.

Jonas sought out software customers who'd been disappointed by over-budget and undelivered products—the kind that he used to build—and he made them a deal. He offered to build the software in a fixed period of time and according to a blueprint. They would pay him six hundred dollars a day. When he saw his potential customers' jaws drop and sensed he was being moved toward the door, Jonas finished explaining the offer. If he didn't do the job on time, he would pay the customer a hundred dollars a day for as long as it took him to finish.

The business took off. In time, Jonas was building software systems faster than his competition, and for companies whose businesses had nothing to do with one another. He made a financial management system for the Fresno airport, a labor management program for a local fruit grower, and a genealogy system for a North American association of llama owners. And then, while still in bankruptcy, he hooked up with another unlikely customer—a credit bureau and collections agency.

The credit bureau of Tulare County was looking for a way to improve its operations. Rather than sending out five collections notices to the same person, the company preferred to send one past-due notice listing all of the debtor's outstanding obligations.

But that wasn't so easy. The owner explained to Jonas that debtors evaded the collections agencies by making subtle alterations to their identities. They might change one letter in their name (Smith became Smithe) or invert two digits in their Social Security number. These people weren't untraceable, but they were more difficult to find. The credit bureau needed a way to match up the conflicting records, to predict that Smith was Smithe. Sure, Jonas said. He could do that. He called it "debtor matching."

The credit bureau was very clear: Jonas's system must not accuse the wrong person of owing money. If it simply merged John Smith, Jr., and John Smith, Sr., assuming they were one and the same, he could be sure that the elder Smith would start making irate phone calls, demanding to know why he was being blamed for his son's debts. These erroneous matches, what data engineers liked to call "false positives," would undermine the entire system and invite a slew of complaints or, worse, harassment claims.

Jonas perfected a technique for resolving people's true identities. His system could see past the smoke screen of aliases and forged numbers. The credit bureaus loved it, but they weren't the only industry troubled by masquerading clientele. After Jonas moved his company to Las Vegas, he discovered that casinos were having a problem keeping certain undesirables off the gaming floor.

Under state gaming regulations casinos were required to bar anyone who appeared on an official "exclusionary list," a kind of all-points bulletin of people often known to use fake identities. These listed people ran the gamut, from scamsters to money launderers. The casinos also had their own no-entry lists, which included gamblers who stole chips from other players on the floor and gambling addicts who had explicitly asked the casino management not to let them play. While crooks and junkies were bad for business, the casinos had a second problem: casino employees who started working against the house. That kind of behavior was potentially costly and hard to detect. The management needed a way to cover themselves, finding threats from the outside and within their own organization.

In 1994, Jonas built a new software program that discovered watch-listed gamblers as well as latent connections among casino workers and gamblers. He called it Non-Obvious Relationship Awareness, or NORA. He sold the program to the Mirage, whose corporate security department fed it watch-listed parties as well as information about their employees and their customers.

Players often didn't realize how the data they voluntarily handed over to the casino was being analyzed. Whenever they registered with the hotel, signed up for a frequent player card, and especially when they asked for credit, they left a trail. It included names, Social Security numbers, phone numbers, dates of birth, addresses. NORA went to work, ensuring the watch-listed parties weren't the same as the trusted people—employees and customers.

The tool succeeded because it placed bad guys, like card cheats, in the exact same database as those trusted individuals. This was a kind of shortcut, and

Jonas realized that it actually made the tool smarter. NORA found many interesting connections that the casinos had missed. Once NORA discovered that a pay clerk's personnel record matched up with information about a vendor working for the casino. This meant one of two things. Either the clerk was being repaid for work performed for the casino or the employee was stealing, by setting up a dummy account for a company that didn't exist. NORA couldn't say which story was true, but it compelled the management to find out.

Jonas had found his direction. Years passed. He made money. He ran in marathons. He was a single dad to three kids. His life was normal. He hadn't planned to start working for spies.

Around 8:30 on the morning of September 11, 2001, Jonas was in a cab headed to a meeting in uptown Manhattan. His hotel was next door to the Twin Towers. "Is there time to stop so I can go up to the observation deck?" he asked the cabbie. Jonas had seen the view from the top only once.

"Not if you want to make your meeting," the driver said. They drove north. In hindsight Jonas recalled seeing people standing gob-smacked in the streets looking back behind him. He never turned around to see what had caught their attention. Over the din of the city and his own preoccupations, he hadn't heard the explosions behind him.

Jonas rented a car and headed for home. During the drive he recalled how only a few days before the attacks he'd paid a visit in New York to the top security official for one of the stock exchanges. He had a picture of Osama bin Laden hanging behind his desk. When Jonas asked why, he replied, "This is what I'm most afraid of."

A day into the car ride home, Jonas got another idea.

Maybe I can help, he thought.

Poindexter listened to Jonas's entertaining stories about catching casino cheats. He told the one about seven employees who also turned out to be vendors. About some high rollers who one casino flew out to Vegas, only to find out they were scammers. The more Jonas talked, the less Poindexter noticed the black pants and T-shirt. He stopped noticing how different Jonas was from most people in the room.

Poindexter believed that the casino and the government had essentially the same problem. They were both looking for hidden connections, both on the watch for threats in their midst. Poindexter knew technology better than he did gambling, and in NORA, he saw potential.

When Jonas stepped into Poindexter's office at DARPA headquarters, his eyes went immediately to the large photographs of Poindexter and Ronald Reagan hanging on the wall. Candid shots of an abundantly confident president and his obviously enamored aide. The pictures, snapped by the White House photographer, were a point of pride. Poindexter had hung similar photos on his family room wall, where he kept his most cherished memorabilia.

Poindexter was enamored of Jonas already. Bob Popp could see that. The question now was how to get NORA into some experiments. After a few minutes listening to Jonas's Vegas cops-and-robbers stories, Popp could see that he was living in a world of information. Jonas spoke with a fluency and ease that Popp had never seen. He rose up and sketched out examples on a whiteboard hanging on Poindexter's wall. He wrote names, jotted down imaginary phone numbers, and worked through the mechanics of connecting them.

Neither Popp nor Poindexter was a database expert. They understood concepts and systems. But Jonas was into the inner workings, the gears and sprockets. And he was intense. His eyes lit up and his voice took on a contagious eagerness. Jonas was like a frenzied car mechanic, hauling everyone under the chassis to explain how the engine worked. Soon they all wanted to be mechanics.

Jonas was also guileless. When someone used a word he didn't know, he asked what it meant. He confessed that he didn't read books and that he never finished college. No question, even the impertinent ones, stayed locked inside his head for very long. And when it came time to listen to Poindexter and his vision for TIA, Jonas didn't bother hiding his skepticism.

In the casinos, NORA started with known bad guys and tried to sort out their relationships. The tool didn't do pattern analysis, which was, at least in part, what Jonas believed Poindexter was after. Jonas had done that kind of work for corporate marketers, building them giant databases of consumer behavior so they could better model consumer buying habits and interests. Companies could lay their hands on reams of personal information—people's hobbies, their income, what sports they preferred, what magazines they read—all from public sources or surveys. But even with all that raw material, Jonas knew that the ability to predict whether someone would subscribe to *Golf Digest*, or was likely to travel to Ireland, or would buy a brand of soda was incredibly low.

That was fine for companies making money on the margins. Even a 1 or 2 percent success rate correctly predicting someone's shopping list could translate into millions of dollars in extra revenue. But to catch terrorists the government had to be right every time.

NORA was an investigative tool and, Jonas thought, had a much narrower application than what Poindexter seemed to envision. It started with a bad guy. But Poindexter wanted to find bad guys who no one knew existed yet.

"I don't think you're going to get it to work the way you want to," Jonas said.

But the admiral was willing to roll the dice. Jonas might not have built the most sophisticated or elegant program. But at that moment, no one had come up with a better way to catch terrorists. And there was the obvious fact that Jonas understood how to live in data better than anyone. He'd come along at just the right time.

Poindexter brought Jonas on board as a consultant. He eventually put NORA into service, testing whether it could connect entities in those synthetic worlds, Ali Baba and Vanilla. Poindexter and Popp both thought the program showed promise, although it didn't perform as well as they'd hoped. Still, Jonas was full of ideas, and those could be more valuable than any one tool. For the next several months Poindexter and Jonas stayed close. Jonas had good thoughts, and Poindexter admired his unconventional spirit. They were an unlikely duo. The Wizard and the Wild Man. But somehow, they worked.

By the summer of 2002, Poindexter had been getting ready to award a set of new contracts and looked forward to a series of new experiments. He was also approaching the halfway point of his presumed one-year tenure. In August, TIA would have its official "coming out," at the annual DARPATech conference in Anaheim, California. It was Poindexter's first big public appearance since returning to government.

But something was missing. On the critical question of privacy protection in the TIA system, he still had little to show. Just a few proposals had come back from the broad announcement. A scientist at the Palo Alto Research Center, a storied facility, had returned a promising plan, and Poindexter intended to give her a contract. But he still wasn't making enough headway in building a privacy appliance and incorporating it into his prototype.

There was, however, a development brewing on the sidelines. Before Poindexter returned to government, DARPA was considering whether to convene a study group to look at the balancing act of privacy and security, from a technical perspective. Every summer the agency sponsored inquiries on a range of big topics, all run by outside experts. They volunteered their time to do the research and write a final paper. (The suggestion for the privacy study came from a senior researcher at Microsoft, who'd been part of the previous summer's round.)

When Poindexter opened the Information Awareness Office he learned that the privacy study was up for consideration. He immediately agreed to sponsor it.

The final report was due out in December, but the panel held a number of meetings to generate ideas. It gave them a chance to put Poindexter's concept through closer scrutiny.

That summer the panelists invited Fran Townsend to attend a meeting. Poindexter was pleased to have her, since she'd been frank about the legal hurdles he faced yet generally agreed that his concept was solid. But the group also brought in some sharp skeptics, a pair of noted electronic privacy experts, including one of the toughest Poindexter would ever face.

His name was Marc Rotenberg, and he had an abiding institutional memory of the government's historic forays into citizens' private lives. A graduate of Harvard College and Stanford Law, Rotenberg cut his teeth as counsel to Senator Patrick Leahy on the Judiciary Committee. He was currently the president and executive director of the Electronic Privacy Information Center, EPIC, which had been at the center of the privacy debate since 1994. The group was established to alert the public to emerging threats against the Constitution, particularly those rising from the ever-expanding stores of personal data compiled by corporations and the government. EPIC had a broad mandate, and at times it seemed kept alive solely by Rotenberg's unceasing and humorless work ethic. He was a tireless activist and frequent speaker, as at home providing congressional testimony as he was giving sound bites to reporters. If Poindexter really wanted to be challenged, there was no one better for the job.

The meeting convened at the Institute for Defense Analysis, a Washington think tank. Poindexter noticed that Rotenberg didn't say much during the formal discussions. So he approached him during the breaks.

"We need your help thinking about how to provide security and privacy," Poindexter said. Rotenberg said he understood, and he thought increased oversight would help. Poindexter seemed to think they were on the same page there, since he wanted TIA to monitor its own users. That was a kind of oversight, he thought.

Poindexter wasn't sure Rotenberg was with him on that. And he didn't think Rotenberg had given him, or the panel, any constructive suggestions.

The meeting lasted several hours. No one shouted. And no one told Poindexter to scuttle his project. But it was hard to imagine how anyone could. The privacy study was restricted to the question of whether technology could protect privacy. It didn't ask whether the government *should* build the ever more powerful data aggregators that, everyone agreed, posed a threat to privacy in the first place.

As far as Poindexter was concerned, he had opened the floor to debate. But the panel's final report suggested that it was already on his side. "Our thesis is that technology can allow us to make substantial progress towards supporting *both* privacy *and* national security," the authors wrote, placing special emphasis on the win-win approach that Poindexter himself had advocated. The study recommended "key technical strategies" for protecting innocent people's data.

They were all concepts that Poindexter had been pitching for months. Selective revelation and the immutable audit log topped the panel's list.

The panelists were genuinely qualified to assess the concepts. Poindexter believed that he had invited criticism; Rotenberg had the chance to chime in. As far as Poindexter was concerned, he had made the effort and the overture. He was sparking the policy debate he wanted to have.

The report's authors noted that policy questions came up in their meetings, but that they had been a peripheral matter. The group was convened only to assess technology, not the larger questions that people like Rotenberg had been debating for years. "Our policy discussion should be understood with caution—we have no special expertise in policy."

One could ask why the panel had convened at all if they weren't prepared to tackle the controversy head-on. It wasn't in their charter. But in the months to come Poindexter would cite this review as a kind of vindication. Experts—technical experts—had weighed in and found that his ideas had merit.

Rotenberg didn't see it that way. He might have kept his powder dry in that private meeting, but on the outside, he and his cohort were preparing for battle. And several months after the meeting, when TIA suddenly caught the attention of the country's most important newspaper, the war cry sounded. That's when things started to fall apart.

CHAPTER 19

THE UNRAVELING

On November 14, 2002, Bob Popp sat down at his desk, opened his e-mail in-box, and found a string of panicked messages from friends and colleagues. They all asked the same question: "Did you see the following?"

It was Bill Safire's weekly column in the *New York Times*. Safire, a former speechwriter for Richard Nixon and one of the country's most widely read conservative libertarians, had just gotten wind of Poindexter's new project. And under the headline "You Are a Suspect," he sounded an alarm.

"The supersnoop's dream," Safire called it. "'Total Information Awareness' about every U.S. citizen." The Pentagon was building "a computerized dossier on your private life," he wrote, the likes of which battle-worn privacy activists like Safire had never seen. The *Times*'s John Markoff had first reported about TIA less than a week earlier; he had quoted Marc Rotenberg, who called the system "the perfect storm for civil liberties in America." The *Washington Post* followed with a story. But Safire felt that editorial writers had not fully grasped the ramifications of Poindexter's new undertaking.

Every purchase you make with a credit card, every magazine subscription you buy and medical prescription you fill, every Web site you visit and e-mail you send or receive, every academic grade you receive, every bank deposit you make, every trip you book and every event you attend—all these transactions and communications will go into what the Defense Department describes as "a virtual, centralized grand database."

"This is not some far-out Orwellian scenario," Safire cautioned his readers. "It is what will happen to your personal freedom in the next few weeks if John Poindexter gets the unprecedented power he seeks."

Popp's first reaction was not to worry. He thought Safire was full of crap, that he'd got his facts wrong and mischaracterized TIA. And of course he'd seized on Poindexter's checkered history. ("This ring-knocking master of deceit is back again with a plan even more scandalous than Iran-contra," Safire wrote.) Nothing to fear, Popp told his worried friends. It will all blow over.

But over the next few days Poindexter was flooded with interview requests from reporters. All the major media outlets. The morning talk shows. They all wanted to put the elusive admiral on television. *Maybe this was a bigger deal than I thought*, Popp told himself.

Poindexter and his staff started living day to day, waiting for the news cycle to burn itself out. But the further reporters dug, the more incriminating evidence they found to support Safire's allegations. It didn't matter if he had mischaracterized Poindexter's intentions, or even that he'd gotten some of the facts wrong in his column. They had Poindexter's own words to use against him.

At the DARPATech conference in Anaheim Poindexter talked about treating distributed stores of information "as if they were one centralized database." People seemed to think he wanted to hoard private information in a single government warehouse. And then there was the logo, with the intimidating Latin motto *Scientia est potentia* emblazoned under an all-seeing eye. The illustration, with its Masonic overtones, appeared on dozens of Web sites within days. It was mocked, reviled, and instantly turned into a weapon. Privacy activists could scarcely believe their luck. Was Poindexter really so politically tone-deaf? He had practically handed them a sword to cut his legs out from under him. The *Washington Post* editorial board observed, "Anyone who deliberately set out to invent a government program with the specific aim of terrifying the Orwell-reading public could hardly have improved on the Information Awareness Office."

Poindexter and Popp knew things had taken a bad turn when, in addition to press calls, inquiries came in from the Pentagon. Congressional oversight staff had been calling. Lawmakers had sent over lists of questions. They wanted details. Just what in the hell was Poindexter doing over there at DARPA?

He decided to tell them in person.

"I cannot stand confusion." Truer words Poindexter never wrote.

He offered that candid assessment in a personal essay penned as a midshipman at Annapolis. The three-page reflection, audaciously titled "Portrait of the Ensign as a Young Man," was Poindexter's attempt to explain how a rural kid from the Midwest, with no knowledge of military tradition, had not only chosen to attend a service academy but excelled there. There was no simple answer, he concluded. It had a lot to do with discipline. He knew when to work, and when to play. He was a fast learner with a good memory, which made coursework easy. And he thought he was a born leader. But above all those traits, "order and organization" had gotten him this far. They were his "guiding principles," he wrote, and probably the biggest reason why he found the Navy so appealing.

As Poindexter sat before fifty or so curious, skeptical, and undoubtedly confused members of Congress and their staffs, he hoped his guiding principles would keep him afloat. He had prepared a three-hour presentation for an audience that demanded quick answers. After about fifteen minutes Popp, who had accompanied him, realized that Poindexter hadn't used the word "privacy" yet. The audience was getting restless.

"Hey!" a Senate staffer piped up, interrupting Poindexter. "When are you going to start talking about the reason you're here?"

Poindexter was taken aback. "Get to the data mining!" the staffer insisted. He'd read the news reports, he said. He knew what Poindexter was after. Personal information. Financial transactions. That was the issue.

Poindexter assured the staffer he would get to the privacy components, in due course. But first people needed context. They needed the full picture.

The staffer pushed back. He said that he wanted answers now. That's what these people had come to hear.

"Will you sit down!" Poindexter snapped. Popp was shaken. He'd never seen his boss lose his cool. He didn't know he could. "I'll get to it. But I'm not going to let you drive the agenda!"

The staffer stayed quiet, and Poindexter continued with his presentation.

The last time he had squared off against a room like this he was sitting behind the witness table. Things hadn't gone much better in this repeat performance. Word of his outburst filtered back to the Pentagon, and to the office of Donald Rumsfeld. There would be no more speeches. No interviews. The secretary of defense ordered Poindexter gagged.

The assault came quickly. Calls for Poindexter's resignation emanated from Capitol Hill. A few days after his appearance Senator Charles Schumer sent a letter to Rumsfeld, urging him to fire Poindexter. Appearing on a Sunday morning talk show, Schumer called TIA the latest example of intrusive and excessive counterterrorism policies concocted by the Bush administration. The Patriot Act, military tribunals for terrorist suspects, Attorney General John Ashcroft's idea to enlist postal workers and electricity meter readers as neighborhood lookouts. They were all building toward a disturbing end, Schumer said. "If we need a big brother, John Poindexter is the last guy on the list that I would choose."

The next day Rotenberg called a press conference to raise awareness of TIA. He called it the "hub" of a far-reaching effort by the government to "extend surveillance of the American public." And Poindexter was "the architect of a program to extend surveillance of private databases" that went back almost twenty years. Rotenberg pointed to that 1984 policy directive on computer security that Poindexter had written in the White House, the one critics said would establish a powerful "computer czar" in the government. Poindexter had been Big Brother all along, Rotenberg seemed to say. TIA was merely the fulfillment of a dream. When the Pentagon refused to turn over documents about Poindexter's program, Rotenberg sued the government under the Freedom of Information Act.

In the withering critique of TIA, two themes emerged. First, there was the program itself, the latest example of the Bush administration's excess and zeal in the war on terror. More than a year had passed without another act of terrorism on U.S. soil, and yet the government was relentlessly determined to expand the corners of the battlefield. Total Information Awareness, with its creepy logo and absurd premise, was hardly a surprise.

But the man behind it. He came with a longer history. Poindexter was a liar. A shill. One couldn't utter the words "total information awareness" without mentioning Iran-Contra as well. It was only fitting that Poindexter, the poster child of governmental overreach, should be in charge. People worried about TIA. But they distrusted Poindexter. And why not? After all, as Safire pointed out in his column, "a jury found he spoke falsely before."

Poindexter emerged as a caricature. A boogeyman. Two days after Rotenberg's press conference, a columnist for the independent *San Francisco Weekly* turned the tables on the supersnoop, publishing Poindexter's phone number, along with satellite images of his house, all of which the writer found on the Internet. Why, he asked, was Poindexter's "$269,700 Rockville, Md., house covered with artificial siding, according to Maryland tax records? Shouldn't a Reagan conspirator be able to afford repainting every seven years?" The columnist also published the names and addresses of Poindexter's neighbors, demonstrating that innocent people could be ensnared in a dragnet flung at one man.

Strangers started calling the house. Poindexter installed a call-blocking device. Unable to speak for himself, he waited for someone to defend him.

But the White House deflected inquiries about TIA and what the president knew about it. Only Bush and a few senior staff knew that over at Fort Meade the kind of snooping machine being pilloried in the press was actually cranking away. The White House stayed quiet, even after Poindexter personally briefed the vice president's staff on TIA and his intentions.

The Defense Department had authorized TIA and committed nearly a quarter billion dollars in funding over three years. Some in Poindexter's office hoped that Rumsfeld or his lieutenants, some of whom had known Poindexter for years, might set the record straight.

A few days before Schumer called upon Rumsfeld to fire Poindexter, the defense secretary gave an in-flight press briefing en route to an international defense ministerial meeting. He took questions about his old friend's new work, which they'd discussed over lunch earlier that year.

"I don't know much about it," Rumsfeld said. "And what I do know, I'm not sure I understand completely, which is not surprising." He threw water on the "hype and the alarm" over TIA, and said he hadn't seen much negative press on it. It was just a research program, not an intelligence-gathering operation.

So much for the program. How about the man? In one deft move, befitting a champion wrestler and Washington knife fighter, Rumsfeld dispensed with that problem too.

"I have met Poindexter. I don't remember him much, though. I had known him years and years and years ago when he was in a junior position. And he explained to me what he was doing at DARPA, but it was a casual conversation. I haven't been briefed on it; I'm not knowledgeable about it. Anyone who is concerned ought not be. Anyone with any concern ought to be able to sleep well tonight."

Poindexter's junior position was as the assistant to the head of the Navy. That casual conversation was a private luncheon during which both men fondly reminisced about glory days and shared their ideas. If Rumsfeld didn't remember much about Poindexter, perhaps it was because he had only recently forgotten it.

CHAPTER 20

GOING BLACK

They're not after you, John. They're after Rumsfeld and the president.

That was the message that John Hamre brought back to his friend Poindexter after a scouting mission on the Hill. Not long after the Safire column appeared, Hamre, the erstwhile deputy defense secretary, had tried to discern what lay underneath the outrage over TIA. It was pretty grim, he reported, but it wasn't just about the program. Poindexter had become a lightning rod for Congress and the public's growing frustrations with the Bush administration. Attorney General John Ashcroft had publicly told members that they emboldened America's enemies by questioning the president's policies, which included some increasingly invasive counterterrorism measures. The administration had publicly toyed with the idea of enlisting mail carriers and electricity meter checkers as citizen "tipsters." They were building airline passenger profiling systems and watch lists. The components of the Big Brother society were falling into place. People were afraid. They were angry. And then along came Poindexter. He was an easy target.

And a legitimate one. Poindexter had hit a nerve, much like Hamre's experiments with the Information Dominance Center years earlier. The China experiment and the Able Danger program had all gone down amid howls about domestic spying, privacy infringement, and illegal data collection. Hamre, now the head of a renowned Washington think tank, the Center for Strategic and International Studies, had been advising Poindexter, trying to help him avoid those pitfalls. But the furor over Able Danger had been confined to a small circle of insiders. TIA had enraged an entire public.

Poindexter thought that his critics had condemned his idea simply because he was in charge of it. His history and his ambition were locked in a grudge match. With "he lied to Congress" as a perennial footnote, Poindexter could not escape himself. As one senior fellow at the libertarian Cato Institute put it at a press conference in December, "The concern is not that he is not the right man for the job. The problem is that he may be the right man."

Poindexter's original fear had come true. He had become the center of attention.

Doubts about TIA's feasibility also mounted. Technology experts who scrutinized the idea thought it couldn't avoid rampant false positives. As one skeptic put it during a congressional hearing, a system designed to flag people who rent vehicles and purchase fertilizer might catch "not only Timothy McVeigh," who bombed the Murrah Federal Building in Oklahoma City, "but most farmers in Nebraska."

Poindexter had tried to explain that TIA was more sophisticated than that. It would never be used to label someone a terrorist. Human analysts, law enforcement officials, and judges would have to make that call. TIA was just a tool.

But civil libertarians wanted to know: Were the current laws for wiretapping and surveillance really so inadequate that the country needed Total Information Awareness to protect itself? This was the response to terrorism? Sweeping up the digital detritus of ordinary people?

Poindexter wasn't allowed to give interviews, but the gag order didn't apply to his number two. As the scandal swelled Popp invited two noted privacy experts over to the office at DARPA, for a firsthand look at Poindexter's work.

Barry Steinhardt, the lead technology and privacy expert for the American Civil Liberties Union, and Jim Dempsey, from the Center for Democracy and Technology, were curious to hear Popp's case. They had run into each other a few weeks earlier at a conference in Florida, and Popp could see that they had more questions than he could answer there.

When Steinhardt finally saw the TIA PowerPoint presentation, he thought that Poindexter had clearly been thinking about privacy protection. But he wasn't at all satisfied that he'd gone far enough. The presentation lacked details, Steinhardt thought. It hinted at a role for privacy but didn't spell it out in detail.

Midway through the meeting, Poindexter popped into the office unannounced. He introduced himself to the visitors, his pipe dangling from his mouth.

Steinhardt had never met Poindexter. All he'd ever heard came from Ollie North, whom the ACLU had actually defended during his Iran-Contra trial. (The group argued that North's testimony to Congress was used against him improperly; the same argument had helped keep Poindexter out of prison.) North had painted Poindexter as a technological genius, a man who kept a "supercomputer" in his basement, Steinhardt recalled.

Whatever his technical bona fides, nothing that Poindexter said during his short visit put Steinhardt at ease. The retired admiral struck him as a modern-day Dr. Strangelove. Popp's briefing, which lasted several hours, also didn't convince Steinhardt that TIA was a benign program, much less one that the ACLU should support. Popp could call it research if he wished. But this wasn't science fiction, Steinhardt thought. This was doable. Poindexter's team was building something that would gather reams of real information on millions of real Americans.

Steinhardt was unnerved—by the briefing, by Poindexter, by the rigorous, suffocating security in the building. He was escorted by a DARPA employee whenever he wanted to use the bathroom. Steinhardt and Dempsey left the meeting unconvinced that TIA could do all Poindexter claimed.

But worse than that, Steinhardt thought that TIA was a harbinger. Left unchecked it led to one awful place—a total surveillance society.

Poindexter endeavored to carry on. The wind experiments were still on course; another, Noreaster, was slated to begin in March 2003. And even amid the roiling controversy, the TIA network kept expanding, with the NSA adding nodes faster than any other agency.

The more Poindexter tried to mitigate concerns by explaining the most rational aspects of TIA—the red teaming, the privacy protections, the fact that it was "only research"—the more desperate he sounded. Those jesuitical strains emerged again. People thought he was hiding things, proffering explanations only when asked, only after he'd been caught.

Poindexter's defense relied mostly on intermediaries like Hamre, or on

Tether, the DARPA director, who insisted on personally giving briefings to members of Congress. But Tether wasn't versed in the details of every office under his management. He had a hard time explaining the complexities. Whenever Tether went to the Hill, he brought Popp along for backup.

At times Tether forgot names of specific technologies within the Information Awareness Office portfolio. The office itself and TIA seemed to blur together, into one menacing concept. In those fumbling moments Tether turned to Popp to fill in the gaps. He was mortified. The briefings felt like a shtick. Tether, Popp thought, was just making an awful situation worse.

With the Hill and the press on watch, Poindexter now sailed under a different kind of all-seeing eye. The Defense Department inspector general launched an investigation. And in January the Senate voted to block all funding for the TIA project until the Bush administration produced a detailed report on how it would affect individual privacy.

As far as Washington horse trading went, that was the nuclear option. If Congress was really prepared to pull the plug on funding, few avenues of escape remained for Poindexter.

All those allies he had spent months courting remained conspicuously silent. He had been in talks with the FBI to be the first adopter of a TIA prototype. Now that plan was put on ice. To forestall a showdown on the Hill, Poindexter wrote a detailed review of TIA and the Information Awareness Office. When the hundred plus–page report went to Congress, in May 2003, Poindexter felt he'd given it his best shot. Ever the proud briefer, he considered the paper one of the best he'd written in a long time. He'd turned out every drawer, opened every file. What was left?

Quite a lot, apparently.

In the report's lengthy appendix, which listed every program in the Information Awareness Office's portfolio, lawmakers found one they hadn't heard of yet: Futures Markets Applied to Prediction, or, as Poindexter dubbed it, FutureMAP.

The idea wasn't so far-fetched. Gather a pool of experts on terrorism, foreign policy, and military tactics and let them place educated bets on when terrorists were next likely to strike.

"Will terrorists attack Israel with bioweapons in the next year?" To find out, Israel and Middle East analysts would trade contracts in an online "market"; one contract would pay out one dollar if an attack occurred, and the other would pay out the same amount if the attack never materialized. Prices and spreads would indicate the likelihood of each prediction.

Futures markets like this had been used, with remarkable accuracy, to predict commodities prices, the outcomes of elections, and even Oscar winners. And experience had shown that unless real money was at stake, the predictions were less accurate. The incentive nature of the market compelled people to sharpen their focus and make better calls.

When news of FutureMAP became public, economists and financial experts praised its application to the terrorist problem; indeed, the *Economist* magazine's business intelligence unit had signed on to help run the program.

But for some lawmakers FutureMAP was a ghastly step too far. As they saw it, Poindexter wanted to make money off terrorism.

"The idea of a federal betting parlor on atrocities and terrorism is ridiculous and it's grotesque," Ron Wyden, a Democratic senator from Oregon, announced in a press release in late July, almost three months after Poindexter's report had gone to the Hill. Wyden had emerged as TIA's most visible opponent in Congress. Earlier in the year he had introduced legislation to ban all "data mining" projects at the Defense and Homeland Security departments until Congress had reviewed TIA fully. Wyden had also introduced the legislation that required Poindexter to write the full report.

Before the FutureMAP debacle DARPA had made desperate attempts to dampen the controversy. The agency even changed TIA's name to "Terrorism Information Awareness." The eye-popping pyramid logo was yanked offline, replaced by an innocuous red triangle with a zippy yellow ribbon winding through it. The new logo looked like a piece of corporate stock art, as easily applied to a discount airline as a line of diet foods. It was meaningless.

All attempts to save TIA had failed. "Changing the name doesn't change the concerns," a spokeswoman for Wyden declared. The senator was neither a powerful member of his caucus nor a particularly well-known national figure. But with the kind of material Poindexter was handing over, and the public relations tornado he created, a rank amateur could have taken him down.

Poindexter, who'd been telling Tether that he wanted to resign since the spring, now said he would leave by the end of August. Tether didn't protest.

But when word got back to the Pentagon, rumors started circulating among the press corps that Rumsfeld had fired Poindexter, dumping him over the FutureMAP fiasco. Poindexter's plan for a graceful exit evaporated.

On the Hill congressional appropriators began the process of zeroing out his budget. Poindexter was ready to leave, but he knew that this could be the end of TIA too.

It was time for Plan B.

"I'm going to turn SAIC loose," Poindexter told Tether. The intelligence contractor with deep roots at the National Security Agency also had a seasoned lobbying shop. Tether was getting nowhere with skeptical lawmakers on the Hill. It was time to bring in the big guns, Poindexter decided. Tether agreed.

Poindexter asked Brian Sharkey to make the call, since he had the closest business contacts at the firm. Popp had told Sharkey about the awful Hill briefings, and he urged Sharkey to intervene for his own sake. "You've got a $20 million contract on the line," Popp said. "They're gonna shut everything down because they don't understand what we're doing."

Sharkey contacted SAIC's legislative affairs office in Washington and explained that they needed backup. But the lobbyists rebuffed his request, afraid that if they got on the wrong side of a losing battle members might exact their revenge on other SAIC contracts. It was too risky.

Sharkey decided to bypass the Washington office and go straight to the top. He called his friend Bob Beyster, SAIC's legendary founder, chairman of the board, and chief executive, who was based in California. Beyster had built his company by taking chances on employees' ideas, especially the wild ones that seemed never to have a chance.

Sharkey had briefed Beyster on TIA already. He explained that the project was on the ropes but that Beyster's lobbyists were afraid to go up to the Hill and save it.

That was going to change. Beyster told Sharkey that he'd call the legislative director. Rest assured, SAIC's team would give Poindexter all the assistance he needed.

Sharkey and SAIC's lobbyists fanned out on the Hill, canvassing the key staffers and members of the Appropriations and Armed Services committees.

This time they used descriptions of TIA and the Information Awareness Office that Poindexter and Popp had written themselves, like the ones Poindexter used in those early rounds of ally-building talks with the intelligence agencies.

The presentation was straightforward. Sharkey wanted to show the lawmakers what TIA was, and more important, what it wasn't. It was tailored for the casual observer, someone who might have read about Poindexter's superspy machine in the newspaper but not much else. TIA had pursued two research paths, it said, one using legally obtained, foreign intelligence and the other using "synthetic data"; the words were underlined and in boldface.

On a slide headlined "TIA is <u>NOT</u> . . ." the notes stressed that "data mining on U.S. citizens" wasn't occurring, nor was TIA "searching credit card histories/library records/gun ownership records, etc." TIA wasn't "developing a Big Brother system to invade privacy," the slide proclaimed. "Only foreign terrorists need fear its capabilities."

While Sharkey and his team mounted the defense, Poindexter called in a heavyweight. Through a DARPA contractor, Poindexter had a connection to William Perry, the secretary of defense under President Clinton. Perry was known for taking a bipartisan approach to national security, a kind of peacemaker for the warrior set. At Poindexter's request, he came down to Fort Belvoir, to the TIA network hub. There Popp explained Poindexter's research goals. The team wanted his advice. But more important, they wanted him to make some phone calls.

Perry obliged. He contacted the staff of two powerful lawmakers with their hands on the Defense Department's purse strings—Senators Ted Stevens, an Alaska Republican and the chairman of the Appropriations Committee, and Daniel Inouye, a Democrat from Hawaii. Congressional appropriators were in the process of eliminating Poindexter's budget when Perry intervened. The irony was of a uniquely Washington variety.

Inouye had chaired the Senate committee investigating Iran-Contra. When the embattled national security adviser appeared before him, Inouye called Poindexter's testimony, in which he acknowledged withholding information from Congress and even the president, "incredible, mind-boggling, chilling." Almost two decades later Inouye was effectively passing judgment on Poindexter again.

Word came back that the appropriators were prepared to make a deal. Sharkey and his team had been making progress with their efforts too. Those in a position to save TIA from the chopping block understood that some of Poindexter's ideas were worth keeping.

Popp was relieved. He had planned to remain at DARPA and take over as director when Poindexter resigned. From the signals he'd received via Perry and the SAIC lobbying teams, it was clear he would have to come up with some kind of peace offering. A way for the Information Awareness Office to remain intact but perhaps not with all of its most controversial research. But it must stay at DARPA, he thought. Nowhere else in government had the vision and the discipline to see TIA through properly. Take it away from the original team and the program could fall apart.

The Hill got the message. Except for the last part.

TIA had to change homes. Tether in his awkward briefings had failed to make the case that his agency was capable of handling the program. Popp's sources reported back that the lawmakers were in no mood to let DARPA hold this hot potato. The agency seemed to have strayed well beyond its normal boundaries. They were getting dangerously close to the red zones of policy, of intelligence operations.

Popp hadn't planned for this. In his mind he had worked out a way to keep the research alive, but he had to keep his hands on it to do that. It had come to an unthinkable decision, befitting Solomon's court. Would he let TIA go in order to let it live?

Perhaps it was best that he didn't have to decide. In the flurry of backroom conversations and brokering over TIA's fate, one candidate came forward to take over Poindexter's programs, to pick up the shattered pieces and rebuild them. Most agencies would have shied away from such a task. But the NSA was no such agency.

If Poindexter and Popp really thought about it, the NSA was a logical place for TIA to go. They were a signals agency, and their ears were filled with noise. Poindexter knew from his meetings with Mike Hayden, Bill Black, and others at Fort Meade that they were on similar quests.

But Poindexter had misgivings about Hayden. He'd been picking up signals from the Hill that senior NSA officials were bad-mouthing TIA. Whispering that Poindexter's idea was far-fetched, that it wouldn't work. Poindexter had always suspected Hayden was personally behind the rumors. Maybe it was jealousy. Maybe ignorance. He wasn't sure.

Still, the NSA was full of kindred spirits. People like Poindexter who put their faith in technology's power to solve the big problems, to protect the nation. They were true believers. The agency had a special R&D unit that could handle the work and that stood a good chance of eventually building a prototype that could actually be put to use.

It was called the Advanced Research and Development Activity, and in theory it was a lot like DARPA. Its charter was to field new technology for all the intelligence agencies, just as DARPA was supposed to work for the entire Defense Department. In fact, though, the group was an NSA-owned operation. The director of ARDA reported to the director of central intelligence *through* the director of the NSA. On paper the line of demarcation seemed inconsequential. In practice it meant everything. ARDA was the agency's property. It was even housed in a building at Fort Meade.

Popp focused on working out a deal with Congress over which programs to keep and which ones to kill. The decision would not be based on merits. He knew that Congress wasn't interested in debating the finer points of data mining versus pattern analysis or listening to lengthy explanations about synthetic data worlds. It was time to make sacrifices.

Popp drew up a simple list, dividing the office's many programs into two buckets: those that were so controversial as to arouse continued debate and press attention, and those that were less likely to attract unwanted attention. FutureMAP went in the former column, no question. So did the research on identifying people at a distance based on how they walked. Useful? Yes. Creepy? Absolutely.

Popp went through all the programs, applying this brutal calculus. He boiled everything down to a sound bite and asked himself whether it passed that critical "*Washington Post* smell test."

Then it was time for the privacy research. TIA's critics had largely glossed over this part of the program, and Poindexter's assurances about selective revelation and audit trails had rung hollow. For Popp it was an obvious choice what to do with this research. Though he might wish otherwise, it belonged in the kill bucket.

Privacy had become the third rail. It wasn't just controversial in its own right. The subject created *more* controversies. Popp thought that if he tried to save the research, people would ask why: What are you doing that requires such strong safeguards? We thought this was just research. You aren't poking around in off-limits information . . . are you?

Popp had no reason to know that the NSA already was. His team had unwittingly assisted them by inviting them into the experimental network. And while TIA prepared for its new home, members of Congress were making a connection: John Poindexter and Mike Hayden's work sounded terribly similar.

In July 2003, with the controversy over TIA about to hit the boiling point, Hayden sat down with the Democratic and Republican heads of the House and Senate Intelligence committees. They were his legislative overlords. George Tenet, the director of central intelligence, and Vice President Dick Cheney joined Hayden for the meeting at the White House.

Porter Goss, the Republican chair of the House Intelligence Committee and a former CIA officer, had attended five briefings on the NSA's secret surveillance program already. Only his Democratic colleague, Nancy Pelosi, had received as many. But that day they were joined by three relative newcomers. California congresswoman Jane Harman, a Democrat, had taken over the ranking House committee slot from Pelosi. And on the Senate side, Pat Roberts, a Republican from Kansas, and John Rockefeller, a West Virginia Democrat, had been made aware of the NSA's new orders only recently. This was only the second briefing they'd ever received on the program from administration officials.

And brief was the operative word. Harman thought that the PowerPoint presentation she saw was pretty thin stuff and didn't constitute full disclosure. These presentations, led mostly by Hayden, had been limited almost entirely to the intelligence committee heads—four people at any given time. The administration had still never briefed the four party leaders from the House and Senate. Together, these members constituted the so-called Gang of Eight and were customarily let in on sensitive operations like this.

Hayden, Tenet, and Cheney gave the four intelligence overseers a glimpse into the NSA's world, but they forbade the lawmakers to speak publicly about it. They couldn't talk to their staff members or the committees' lawyers. Rockefeller was troubled by the presentation. The details weren't entirely clear to him. What exactly had he just heard?

Later that day, he penned a letter to Cheney. "I am writing to reiterate my concerns regarding the sensitive intelligence issues we discussed today," Rockefeller wrote. "Clearly, the activities we discussed raise profound oversight issues." The senator confessed that he was "neither a technician nor an attorney." And since he couldn't discuss the program with his staff, he could not "fully evaluate, much less endorse these activities."

But there was something else. "As I reflected on the meeting today, and the future we face, John Poindexter's TIA project came to mind, exacerbating my concern regarding the direction the administration is moving with regard to security, technology, and surveillance."

What Rockefeller heard sounded familiar indeed. "Without more information and the ability to draw on any independent legal or technical expertise, I simply cannot satisfy lingering concerns raised by the briefing we received."

Rockefeller signed the note, put a copy in a sealed envelope, and filed it in a classified facility in the Senate committee's offices.

Poindexter packed his bags in early August. The press seemed to say he'd been forced out. He was in no position to say otherwise. Even if FutureMAP hadn't blown up on him, Poindexter was well past his self-imposed one-year tenure. It was time to leave.

Before he headed home for good, Poindexter stopped in at the Pentagon, to say good-bye to Rumsfeld. He walked into the office, and the secretary came straight for him. Before Poindexter could say a word, Rumsfeld apologized. "John, I think we overreacted on the FutureMAP thing."

"Don," Poindexter said, "I agree. It's a good idea."

That was the last time they spoke.

Popp took over at the office for the next couple of months. His sole job was to salvage Poindexter's work, managing the transition over to ARDA. It was a quiet, last-ditch effort, conducted entirely out of the public eye. The move itself was classified. As far as civil liberties activists were concerned, Poindexter's brainchild was imploding. He had left. Congress was going to pull the funding. TIA was on its deathbed.

Not quite. Buried deep within the massive Defense Department spending bill for the coming year, cobbled together by the powerful senators and staffers that Popp had been courting, TIA found an escape hatch.

> None of the funds appropriated or otherwise made available in this or any other act may be obligated for the Terrorism Information Awareness Program. [The congressional appropriators used the program's old and new names interchangeably.]

That was the pledge. As far as the Defense Department's budget was concerned, not a nickel would go to TIA.

But then, a caveat.

> Provided: That this limitation shall not apply to the program hereby authorized for processing, analysis, and collaboration tools for counterterrorism foreign intelligence, as described in the classified annex.

It was the black budget. An underground river of undisclosed billions flowing directly into the spy agencies. It would carry the program formerly known as TIA. With a pair of obscure yet legally elegant sentences, Poindexter's vision was given a second chance.

The compromise for keeping TIA alive in some form was that it not be used for domestic counterterrorism or against U.S. persons. But that was a flimsy rule, and one easy to break, since the lines between foreign and domestic were getting blurrier all the time. And the prohibition technically only applied to the current fiscal year. If a TIA system was ever up and running, the rules could be changed. But lawmakers had struck a compromise, one that sustained a research program some considered vital, but blocked it from being unleashed on the American public, at least for now. Each side had gotten what it wanted.

Now, a black veil descended over Poindexter's program. Every dollar once spent on TIA in the open now was spent in the dark. Every experiment conducted outside the wall of secrecy now went to the other side. As far as the public knew, TIA was dead.

But as Poindexter drifted back into his private world and watched his enemies declare victory, he comforted himself with the secret. TIA lived.

ACT FOUR

Too often, privacy has been equated with anonymity; and it's an idea that is deeply rooted in American culture.... But in our interconnected and wireless world, anonymity—or the appearance of anonymity—is quickly becoming a thing of the past.

> —Donald Kerr, the principal deputy director
> of national intelligence, speaking to an
> intelligence symposium on October 23, 2007

I once asked someone in the diplomatic corps, What do you think about intelligence as a professional? . . . The answer was, Well, let me tell you what a diplomat is. A diplomat is someone that can tell another person to go to hell and make them look forward to the trip. An intelligence officer is someone who can tell another person to go to hell and has the means to deliver them to that track.

> —Mike McConnell, the director of national
> intelligence, speaking at a military
> communications conference, November 17, 2008

CHAPTER 21

BASKETBALL

Poindexter's crew waited for news of his next move. One Tuesday morning in early December 2003 word arrived: They were back in business.

Brian Sharkey sent an e-mail to firms working with his company, Hicks & Associates, to build the TIA prototype. He explained that an organization had come forward to sponsor their project. The precise scope of work going forward still needed to be sketched out, but Sharkey confidently reported that there would be a lot of it.

TIA had barely skipped a beat. Even the contract used to pay Hicks remained in place. Besides the new sponsor, only TIA's name would change.

"We will be describing this new effort as 'Basketball,'" Sharkey wrote.

Sometimes one could only guess what inspired the vague, innocuous code names attached to secret government programs. The fact that they *were* vague and innocuous counted for a lot. Basketball was no different, although the image of TIA simply bouncing from one agency to another was apt. One of Sharkey's colleagues sent a follow-up message to Hicks employees, instructing them not to use the name of Poindexter's old program: "TIA has been terminated, and should be referenced in that fashion."

Sharkey's contract wasn't the only ball passed. Appropriators spelled out in the classified annex which elements would continue to receive funding. Genoa II was saved, and it reappeared with a name that harkened back to its nautical creator: It was now called Topsail.

Along with Basketball and Topsail, the evidence extraction and link discovery research also survived. This was the area where Jeff Jonas's NORA system had been tested. The new program was code-named Eagle.

Finally, the TIA network, with its central node in the Information Dominance Center, remained intact. Now known as the Research Development and Experimental Collaboration, or more simply, "the RDEC," it continued the wind-themed experiments. In August, the very month that Poindexter resigned and Congress began to hammer out TIA's secret compromise, the network was in the thick of "Sharqi," named after a persistent, dry Saharan wind that kicked up a thick cloud of dust and sand.

Poindexter had reason to celebrate. Not only had core elements of his research remained intact, but the vast network he'd established continued to grow. By the end of 2003 the RDEC—pronounced phonetically as "r-deck"—boasted more than 27 nodes and 350 individual users. An entire community had grown up, and it continued to flourish.

But he regretted that the privacy research had been tossed into the dustbin. He'd never felt that the idea got traction, and what little research there'd been would wither without funding. It was a fateful decision, since the agency inheriting TIA would soon enough find itself accused of a massive and illegal incursion into Americans' private lives.

Few officials in government actually knew how far the Bush administration had gone. More than two years after 9/11, headlines about the Total Information Awareness program obscured the real story playing out just below the surface. The NSA had already plumbed the depths of the global communications system. The agency was the nerve center of a new war. The analytic engine, the hub, the place where all those dots that the government had failed to connect were now coming together. More than any single agency, the NSA had become the all-seeing eye.

The war took its toll. In late 2003 Mike Wertheimer left the agency that had reared him. He took a job with a high-end technology company that mostly worked for the intelligence agencies. Washington's revolving door was well oiled. Senior officials routinely took more lucrative jobs in the private sector and ended up under contract to their old bosses. But when Wertheimer left the NSA, he left more than his job behind.

It had been two years since President Bush granted the agency extraordinary authority to monitor Americans' communications without warrants. In the beginning Wertheimer supported the move. It was the right response to a crisis, he thought. But those authorities, and the surveillance they unleashed, went on too long, Wertheimer decided. As the threat of another terrorist attack on U.S. soil diminished, so too should have the NSA's special powers.

"When I walked away from that program," he would recall years later, "I wanted nothing to do with it ever again."

The agency's relentless pursuit to comprehend the once unknowable continued without him, and without customary restraints. Officials across the government saw that firsthand. One senior CIA official who was privy to the security agency's reporting routinely saw American citizens and other U.S. persons directly named in its reports without the minimization procedures that had once shielded their identities. It was a clear indication that the president's authorities really had pushed the agency into new territory—they could spy directly on Americans now.

After the TIA programs moved into their new home, Popp tried one last time to revive the privacy research. He spoke with ARDA's director about what funds were in the pipeline. Fortunately, the budget was laid out through the 2007 fiscal year. If the research group were looking for new areas to fund, Popp suggested, they might consider privacy research.

"Thanks, but no thanks" was the message Popp received. ARDA wanted nothing to do with all that.

CHAPTER 22

RESURRECTION

John Poindexter had already proven F. Scott Fitzgerald wrong. There were, in fact, second acts in American life. And he was about to have his third.

He had held off on calling Fran Townsend. In May 2003, before he left government in a firestorm, she'd taken a new job in the White House. Townsend was now the deputy national security adviser for combating terrorism, working under Condoleezza Rice. She wasn't exactly the new Ollie North, or the new Dick Clarke, but she did have the terrorism brief. If Poindexter hadn't already admired her since their meeting at the Coast Guard, he might well have sought her out anyway.

Poindexter hadn't been far from Townsend's mind. When she read the first news reports about TIA, and the *New York Times* column, she felt a pit forming in her stomach. *This is exactly what I was afraid of,* she thought. Townsend had worried that Total Information Awareness would follow the path of Carnivore, the FBI's e-mail surveillance tool. She hadn't spoken to Poindexter since she took the White House job. But a few months after he left government, Townsend received a message that Poindexter had called. She contacted him right away.

Poindexter said that he'd like to get together. "Sure," Townsend replied. "Why don't you come see me?"

He was cautious. "Why don't I *not* come to the White House?" he suggested. "Why don't we meet for lunch?"

A few days later Townsend walked across Lafayette Park to the Oval Room. The restaurant was a power stop for politicos where food was an afterthought.

Poindexter thanked her for coming, and said it took some courage. Townsend felt a mix of admiration and sympathy. She thought that Poindexter had been taken to the Washington woodshed, for the second time. As they dined together she considered that for John Poindexter to thank her for coming said more about him than about Fran Townsend.

There was no doubt about it. They were kindred spirits.

Poindexter wanted to explain what had happened. He made it clear that the government was still going to get something out of his presumably defunct program. The baby had not been thrown out with the bathwater. After they finished lunch Townsend walked back to the White House with a comforting thought. *All was not lost.*

From then on, Poindexter and Townsend kept in closer touch. They swapped ideas, discussed current events. She revered him, and he admired her tenacity and her thoroughness, two qualities that could endear just about anyone in his eyes. Poindexter had a powerful ally now in the heart of the White House.

Poindexter also reemerged quietly in TIA's new home. He got the word out to the new crew of program managers who'd taken over his research that he was available for consultations. Some of them called on him. They wanted his guidance, and he gave it. TIA was not gone, nor was its creator.

Poindexter spent seven months underground reforging his alliances with key administration officials and the career class. Then, one chilly afternoon in March 2004, he reemerged in public.

Syracuse University had invited him to debate the prominent privacy advocate and legal journalist Jeffrey Rosen on the subject of privacy and security. A small, invitation-only crowd attended—mostly current and former intelligence officers. Rosen had a new book out, *The Naked Crowd: Reclaiming Security and Freedom in an Anxious Age*. In it he decried Total Information Awareness and related programs that seemed to feed off the public's fear about terrorism.

Poindexter gave his trusty PowerPoint briefing. It was precise, thorough, and tedious. Rosen delivered a more passionate address, with no notes or slides. The two men were a discordant pair.

When it came time for rebuttals, the audience was primed for a verbal brawl. But Poindexter and Rosen hardly threw a punch. Each conceded points to the other. They kept eye rolling and groaning to an acceptable minimum. Rosen also acknowledged Poindexter's long career of public service and steered clear of the obvious targets—Iran-Contra, lying to Congress, spying on Americans. They argued over policies, not personalities. This was the kind of intellectual pugilism that Poindexter liked and hadn't gotten much of in a while. It was civil. Tidy.

After a spirited hour-and-a-half discussion, Poindexter appeared satisfied. He had wanted to test public reaction to his ideas—and to him—in an intimate setting before heading out for a broader campaign to salvage his concept. The members of the audience, several of whom knew Poindexter and had worked with him over the years, seemed intrigued.

When it came time for questions, the moderator called on a young, bespectacled man, apparently a student, sitting in the middle of the small crowd. Amid the gray suits and jackets and the neatly trimmed haircuts, his baggy clothes and shaggy mop quickly raised eyebrows.

Sam Alcoff opened with the obvious and indelicate question. How could the public be sure that TIA wouldn't be incorporated into some larger, unchecked "domestic spying" program?

A few people in the audience winced at those two dreaded words. Others toward the front row craned their necks to see who was talking.

Simple, Poindexter declared. TIA would be used to monitor the people using it—watching the watchers, logging all abuses. Poindexter looked mildly annoyed. Hadn't Alcoff been listening to his speech? But he also looked cautious. How had this young man gotten into the room? This wasn't a public event.

Alcoff considered Poindexter's response. "I guess we'll have to take your word for it," he said, his voice rising. "But how can we, Admiral Poindexter, when you lied to Congress and the American people!"

Poindexter sighed.

"You're a liar!" Alcoff shouted. "You authorized death squads in Nicaragua, who raped and murdered people!" A few gray-haired spies in the crowd shot Alcoff pointed looks. "Why don't you shut up?" someone grumbled.

"Do you have a *question*?" the moderator interjected.

"Yes," Alcoff said. "Admiral Poindexter, if your system is so good at catching terrorists, how long will it take to catch you?"

The room froze. Poindexter's eyes narrowed. Everyone turned to face him.

"Young man," Poindexter said, "you were probably in grade school when all that happened. You have a limited view of those events." Poindexter waved his hands dismissively and signaled for another question.

Alcoff stayed quiet for the rest of the session. Later Poindexter learned that his was a familiar face around Syracuse. The campus chief of police, who provided security for Poindexter during his visit, told him that Alcoff's mother was a liberal psychology professor.

Figures, he thought.

Poindexter flew back to Washington that afternoon.

Alcoff was an outspoken campus activist. He had disrupted the visits of other prominent national figures. When Syracuse announced former New York mayor Rudy Giuliani as its 2002 commencement speaker, Alcoff handed out flyers at a "teach-in," enumerating several controversies of Giuliani's tenure. Racial profiling. Police abuse of prisoners. And the mayor's use of a "homeless army," Alcoff told the student newspaper, to move the city's "undesirables" out of public view.

There was a saying in the Poindexter household: "No one is obliged to be ignorant." If Poindexter had been quicker on his feet, he thought later, he might have shared that bit of wisdom with Alcoff. But the chief of police's report on the young man and his mother confirmed what Poindexter had already suspected—Alcoff wasn't worth the effort. There was no time to educate him.

And yet Poindexter didn't grasp, and didn't care to consider, how Alcoff was a proxy for so many reasonable people. What would it take, they wondered, for one such young man to be deemed a public threat rather than a private nuisance? A public outburst? A few suspicious purchases? Some phone calls to the wrong kind of people? This was the subtle equation that produced such anxiety among ordinary people. They might not comprehend the complexity of Poindexter's mind. But this much they knew for sure: If information was power, then Poindexter, with all the information, would have all the power. That, they thought, was untenable, and fundamentally un-American.

Poindexter himself was a proxy. Total information awareness looked dangerous regardless of who had it. But he thought that most of his strongest opponents were motivated by politics, not principle. Many of the same foes who'd come after him in the eighties were at his throat again now. He accepted it. But he refused to let them attack him without all the facts.

He thought it was time to set the record straight. After that bruising debut in Syracuse, Poindexter felt emboldened. Far from dampening his spirits, the fight had lifted them. He wasn't going to let the Sam Alcoffs of the world direct his agenda. No one was obliged to be ignorant. He'd have to teach them.

For his third act Poindexter fashioned a new public role. Part agent provocateur, part gray eminence of spy craft.

As he reestablished his ties within the government, he became a closer, and in some cases indispensable, adviser. Around Washington insiders started talking about Poindexter in a new light. People said he got a raw deal, that some of his ideas were actually pretty good. Poindexter started giving interviews with influential national magazines. He posed for photographs, something he never felt comfortable doing in the White House. Few rushed to his defense within range of a television camera or a reporter with a pen, but the ones who did tried to rewrite Poindexter's narrative.

Two months after the Syracuse visit, former Navy secretary and 9/11 Commission member John Lehman gave a little-covered speech before the U.S. Naval Institute. Lehman had known Poindexter since the Reagan administration, and he summed up a feeling taking hold not just among Poindexter's supporters but among more detached observers as well.

"In our government bureaucracy today, there is no accountability," Lehman said. "Since 9/11—the greatest failure of American defenses in the history of our country, at least since the burning of Washington in 1814—only one person has been fired. He is a hero, in my judgment: Admiral John Poindexter. He got fired because of an excessive zeal to catch these bastards."

The following month Poindexter emerged fully from his brief self-imposed exile. A prestigious conference series sponsored by the McCormick Tribune

Foundation asked him to join about forty other luminaries for a meeting on the day's hot issue: "Counterterrorism Technology and Privacy."

The participants gathered at Cantigny, a sprawling five-hundred-acre estate not far from Chicago, replete with intricate gardens and capped by a handsome Georgian mansion. In addition to Poindexter, John Hamre was there, as was Mike McConnell, the former director of the National Security Agency turned Booz Allen executive and TIA contractor. Spike Bowman attended too. He was the FBI's senior counsel on national security law and a friend of Poindexter's who had attended the speech at Syracuse.

Michael Chertoff, then a judge for the U.S. Third Circuit Court of Appeals, also came. Only six months later Chertoff would step down from the bench when President Bush nominated him as the Secretary of Homeland Security. A pair of key NSA officials also showed up—Joel Brenner, the agency's inspector general, and Vito Potenza, the deputy general counsel. As the agency's top watchdog and its number two lawyer, respectively, both men had been informed about the NSA surveillance program.

Representatives from prominent government watchdogs and security experts also attended. There was Kate Martin, the executive director of the Center for National Security Studies, an authority cited frequently in the national media. Lara Flint represented the Center for Democracy and Technology; her colleague, Jim Dempsey, had met with Bob Popp in his office not long after Safire's *Times* column appeared. And Dempsey's partner that day, Barry Steinhardt of the ACLU, also came.

The gathering at Cantigny erased any doubts about John Poindexter's status. He was a player. He'd been a part of the terror war since its inception. And now, when the brightest minds of the day pooled their collective perspectives, he was at the table.

The discussion lasted for two days, with a dinner and overnight stay at the estate. Passions ran hot. The participants argued about public expectations. Could people reasonably expect the same level of privacy today as they did in an era without the Internet? No one could argue that technology hadn't influenced, and changed, their assumptions. But the government had redrawn the baselines. What were the new limits on its ability to spy on people in the name of protecting them?

Steinhardt and Poindexter hadn't seen each other since that meeting in

Popp's office, when he popped in midway through the briefing. Cantigny might not have been the optimal setting for a reunion. During a break in the discussion, Poindexter approached Steinhardt. He'd been itching to tell him something since their last encounter.

"At least I was doing this in public!" Poindexter jabbed. He wasn't hiding from the debate. He'd encouraged it.

Steinhardt admitted that Poindexter was right. He ran TIA in the open. But his indignation was unjustifiable, Steinhardt thought. Poindexter had invited ridicule with that preposterous logo and his visions of virtual databases and all-seeing systems. Steinhardt was sure that TIA's gaze would not be limited to "foreign" targets. It would be turned on ordinary criminals—deadbeat dads, men beating their wives, tax absconders. There was a term for this—"mission creep."

But Poindexter was no longer interested in Steinhardt's critique. He thought that he'd had his chance, and missed it. He scolded Steinhardt for not providing "constructive ideas about privacy and security."

"The nation faced a grave threat," Poindexter said. Steinhardt should have tried to help him instead of tear him down.

Poindexter pointed his finger at Steinhardt and got up close to him, so that he was almost poking him in the chest. Steinhardt might think that he'd won, but this wasn't over.

"It's all secret now," Poindexter said, another reference to TIA. "You forced me to take this underground."

Steinhardt wasn't entirely sure what he meant. Ever since the program was officially shuttered there had been rumors about some lingering pieces still in operation. But nothing was ever confirmed. The ACLU had helped get language in the defense bill to shut TIA down, but they were unaware of what the classified annex contained.

TIA wasn't gone after all. Steinhardt knew it now.

Looking back, Steinhardt still felt that killing TIA—at least in one form—counted as a win. There was a public debate, and his side prevailed. But had the program not gone away, had it remained in DARPA's purview with Poindexter at the helm, Congress, Steinhardt, and the entire civil liberties community might have kept the admiral under their collective thumb. He would have lived under the microscope. All his funding would have been visible, all his research too. If TIA worked, there'd be another debate over whether to use it. But now, with the program in the black and consumed by the NSA, its onetime watchdogs would lose track of it. For Steinhardt and his colleagues, whose struggles were far from over, a question remained unanswered: Had they won a battle over TIA only to lose a bigger war?

The conference wasn't all fireworks. After two days the attendees drew up a lengthy set of principles that they hoped would offer some way forward. At the top of this list was an urgent call to Congress and the administration to face the privacy debate head-on, publicly and honestly. "Government should infringe on privacy only as an imperative to protect the safety of U.S. citizens and resident aliens," they wrote in a formal report. "The legislative and executive branches share the fundamental constitutional responsibility to protect the privacy and safety of all U.S. citizens and resident aliens—and should act in partnership."

That wasn't happening. Only a few months before the group gathered the administration gave its first briefing on the NSA's warrantless surveillance program to the full Gang of Eight—the congressional leaders and the top members of the intelligence committees. The briefing itself was prompted by a crisis.

In March, the warrantless surveillance program was up for a required forty-five-day renewal by the attorney general. Since October 2001, John Ashcroft had regularly averred to the legality of the agency's covert activities. But now his deputy, James Comey, had brought to light disturbing details about the breadth and scope of the NSA's spying.

It wasn't warrantless "wiretapping" that had senior lawyers at Justice on edge. Rather, it was the layer of surveillance that often preceded it—the massive sweep of telecom metadata. This included information on Americans collected from U.S. companies inside the country without a warrant.

What started as a program of *targeted* surveillance now included collection and analysis of huge amounts of metadata, unfathomable by human analysts. Jack Goldsmith, the newly installed head of the department's Office of Legal

Counsel, had first spotted the trouble when he read John Yoo's memos on warrantless surveillance. Goldsmith found the analysis both indefensible and illogical.

The conclusion was shattering. The attorney general had been signing off on illegal domestic spying ordered by the president of the United States. Now the administration wanted Ashcroft to sign off on the program again.

With the deadline upon him, Ashcroft was bedridden in hospital fighting an acute pancreatic disease. He'd already been complaining that the White House so obscured the NSA's various activities, setting them up in different security "compartments," that he couldn't see the full picture. The "program" had evolved, and grown new legs.

Comey had taken over as the acting number one while Ashcroft recuperated. He refused to sign the forty-five-day authorization, and a scene of Washington drama for the ages ensued when Alberto Gonzales, the president's lawyer, and White House chief of staff Andy Card showed up at Ashcroft's hospital bedside, pressuring him to sign the authorization instead.

Ashcroft unceremoniously sent them packing. Comey, along with Goldsmith, was prepared to resign if the NSA's activities weren't brought under legal control. Ashcroft would join them, along with FBI director Robert Mueller.

President Bush personally intervened to avert a mass resignation of his entire law enforcement leadership. That spectacle, coming without warning, would have so rocked the corridors of Washington that the NSA's spying would not stay secret for long. It would also have marked an irrevocable downward slide for Bush, who was campaigning for reelection. Such a mass exodus would constitute a vote of no confidence in his leadership of the war on terror.

Tensions were high inside the NSA as well. Brenner and Potenza—the two officials who went to Cantigny—had assured Hayden he could rely on those presidential authorities that Ashcroft was supposed to review. But the White House had forbidden the NSA men from seeing the underlying analysis, prepared by Yoo, that defined the legal supports for the program. As long as they were blocked, Brenner and Potenza could not render a fully informed opinion on whether the president's program was legal. That put Hayden in a tight spot, since he'd spent the past few years telling congressional officials, in his limited briefings, that the NSA's lawyers had signed off on the program.

In the end, Bush acquiesced to certain changes that Justice wanted to get the surveillance activities on legal ground. The chief judge of the Foreign Intelligence Surveillance Court had been rattling cages, upset that information from warrantless interceptions might find its way into legal warrant requests before her court. The program was also modified to keep that from happening.

The upper echelon of power breathed a quiet sigh of relief. Crisis averted.

But the surveillance did not stop. And neither did the NSA's quest to overcome another major handicap. Legal obstacles were trivial in comparison with the technological barrier that the agency was struggling with in 2004. And unless the agency's technicians could overcome it, the early-warning system that Hayden had envisioned would never materialize. They needed a big idea.

CHAPTER 23

THE BREAKTHROUGH

The NSA was coming up with weak links. Stellar Wind and the BAG might have provided new insights into terrorists' social networks, but they had failed to find any blockbuster revelations, much less intelligence that actually had preempted an act of terrorism. This was no early-warning system.

To build one, the agency had to acquire and then analyze information quickly, while it was still fresh enough to produce useful leads. Hayden wanted to engage terrorists in hot pursuit, as they jumped around the global communications grid using disposable cellphones, different phone lines, and ever-changing e-mail addresses to cover their tracks. To catch them before they disappeared, Hayden had to be able to react to new intelligence within minutes, not hours or days.

And that was very hard to do. The NSA could consume seemingly limitless amounts of data, but everything that its electronic vacuums collected went into huge databases. If analysts wanted to look at a day's or a week's catch, they had to retrieve it from storage. By then the information might be outdated. Intelligence in the global terror hunt had a short shelf life.

The agency could monitor individual phone numbers or e-mail addresses in real time, but it could not take an expansive view of an entire communications network and know, at any moment, what was happening everywhere. It could not see all the patterns forming in the noisy ocean of metadata. In that sense, the NSA did not truly have a real-time system for detecting terrorists, at least not before it knew who the terrorists were.

The agency wasn't the only large organization looking to crunch data in real time. Banks wanted that power to detect fraud. Hedge funds dreamed of capitalizing on minute movements of the stock market. And energy companies building seismic models to discover new sources of energy needed this kind of hypercomputing. Throughout the entire history of computers, the answer to dealing with big sets of data was to build very big databases to hold them all, and then to go to work with sophisticated tools. Luckily, mass storage was relatively cheap, and there was no shortage of it. But this approach didn't help information mammoths like the NSA achieve their real-time ambitions.

The techies and computer programmers at Fort Meade, along with their army of contractors, needed another way. And in 2004, with the privacy debate flaring, they hit upon a counterintuitive and elegant idea.

Maybe the agency had been thinking about the problem all wrong. What if the response to the constant flow of communications the NSA sucked off the global communications network was to not store them all?

This was a radical notion. The database was the backbone of the NSA's intelligence operations, and the source of its power. (Information was currency in the spy game, after all.) The NSA was essentially a big library. Every record, every bit and byte it collected, was like a book. And the books were stored on vast, deep shelves. The agency could categorize those books and cross-reference names, places, and events like some sophisticated card catalog. But that didn't change the fact that the books were still sitting on a labyrinth of shelves, waiting for someone to retrieve them.

The analysts were the library patrons. And when they needed something from the shelves—an intercept, a recording—they put a request into their computer terminals. Then, an unseen team of electronic librarians took over. They disappeared into the shelves to find the requested file. Then they presented it to the analysts.

These librarians didn't work quickly. They followed a rigid, inflexible approach each and every time they fetched a book. They walked back to the stacks, found the book in question, pulled it off the shelf, put it on a cart, logged it out, handed it to the patron, and then waited for the return, at which point they put the book back on the cart, walked it back to the shelf, and put it in the proper place.

This wasn't an abstract process. It was physical. This was how computers retrieved information from databases. Information was stored on a physical medium—a disk. That disk was no different from the bookshelves. Each piece of information resided in a specific location on the disk. And when the computer wanted to find it, the disk had to spin to just the right point, and another mechanism had to retrieve it so the user could see it. The process was essentially no different for an NSA analyst than for an ordinary home computer user calling up a document from his word processor. That document was stored on a hard drive, which was just another disk. Behind his simple point and click, a set of electrical and mechanical steps played out. People saw something similar when they played a jukebox. They fed the machine a dime and selected a song, then watched the gears spin as a metal arm dropped down, pulled the right record out of a rotating stack, grabbed onto it, and then set the record on the turntable.

The computers at the NSA—the giant library, the big jukebox—spent a lot of time and energy fetching and reshelving information. It could take several minutes, if not hours, for analysts to call up all the data they needed. This was where the real-time aspect of terrorist hunting broke down. This was the bottleneck.

But there was another way to store and retrieve information, and it was also well known to anyone who'd ever used a computer. A word processor, an e-mail in-box, a Web browser, any application used to perform work, was made possible by something called random access memory. RAM was a storage system too, but it was nothing like a library. It didn't rely on the physical sequence of moving parts to deal with data.

RAM, as its name implied, used a "random" structure to organize information. Once something was put into RAM, it was simply *there*, available for the taking. It was as if all the books in the library had been put in one big room instead of being dispersed to far-flung stacks. And unlike the disk-based librarians, with their inviolate sequences, the librarians in RAM were all on speed, zipping around and grabbing books in an instant compared with their slower counterparts. If disk world was like a jukebox, RAM was an iPod.

But RAM had its problems. For starters, it was highly "unstable," from an engineering perspective. RAM could not save information without a constant source of electricity. Turn off the computer, or lose power, and anything stored in RAM was lost. This was why home computers and databases alike used disk-based storage; it retained information regardless of whether the machine was on or not. RAM was also more expensive than disk memory. Its market price could fluctuate wildly, depending on global demand. That was one reason why computers mostly used RAM to run applications—word processors, Web browsers, or the tools that intelligence analysts used to work on stored information. Its random structure gave these memory-intensive programs the running room they needed to operate smoothly, without having to rely on those pesky, slow librarians. RAM was not a storage mechanism.

But the NSA thought it could be. From the agency's perspective, RAM's instability and cost were surmountable obstacles. Money was no barrier for an agency with a multibillion-dollar annual budget. And as for the power supply, the 350-acre Fort Meade campus was the single largest customer of Baltimore Gas & Electric, consuming the same amount of electricity as the city of Annapolis. Back in the late 1990s officials had started to worry about whether the power would run out. But in the heat of the global terrorist hunt, the issue slipped down the priority list. As far as the agency was concerned, electricity constraints were not going to stop technological progress.

And so, beginning in 2004, the NSA began a shift toward "in-memory" databases that were built entirely with RAM. The agency would place oceans of telecom data into these new systems and hope at last to have their real-time terrorist tracker. It was an unprecedented move for such a large organization. It was extravagantly expensive. And the agency protected its new approach like a national secret.

The NSA had found its breakthrough.

Though they were expensive and unstable, in-memory databases had one undeniable advantage over their disk-based cousins—speed. And that was just what the NSA wanted.

In-memory databases were experimental, contemplated mostly within the cloisters of computer geekdom. But early on, engineers could see their promise. In 2001 a group of database builders in Washington State decided to test the speed of a disk-based database and one built entirely in memory. Each system was told to retrieve and store thirty thousand individual records, a straightforward and simple computing task. It was a mere sliver of the NSA's workload, but the test yielded staggering results.

While the traditional machine took sixteen seconds to retrieve, or "read," the records, the in-memory version did it in one second. But more stunning, it took the traditional computer almost one hour to store, or "write," the records onto its disks. The in-memory machine stored the information in 2.5 seconds.

In-memory databases were the NSA's best shot at real-time analysis. So how to build the system? Simple enough. Just construct a computer with lots and lots and lots of RAM. Or harness together many computers with the same attributes.

Simple in theory. Even the most opaque computer engineers didn't mince words about what this amalgamation of hardware would look like. Huge. A supercomputer in Maryland, which comprised more than a thousand linked machines and was used by the National Weather Service to predict hurricane paths, took up seven thousand square feet of floor space. And that machine wasn't working in memory. Who could say how much real estate this NSA supereye would need?

Few agencies had the tens or hundreds of millions of dollars required to install giant computer farms in their basement, much less pay the power bill for cooling them. (From its previous experiences with supercomputers and large databases, the NSA engineers knew that a horde of machines in one room generated extraordinary amounts of heat. The agency had to design specially cooled rooms to keep the machines from melting down.)

But the in-memory system had another flaw. One that the BAG and all other terrorist-hunting devices shared.

It lacked what data engineers called a logic layer, a kind of vocabulary that told a computer what the cacophony of phone records and e-mails, words and numbers running through its brain actually meant, and more important, what they meant in relation to one another.

In the human world objects had names, and names had meaning. There was something called a plate. It sat on a table, and a person ate food off it. One could teach a computer to recognize "plate." It was flat, often white, usually round. Its edges were slightly curved. But how did a computer know that "plate" had a relationship with something called "silverware" that was actually a set of dissimilar-looking objects that for some reason seemed to pop up next to plate all the time, and always in a group? And what was this thing that looked like "plate" but was called "platter"?

Humans understood plates and silverware perfectly well, what they were used for and how they worked together. They knew why a knife wasn't a spoon, and when a plate was actually a platter. And they understood why those distinctions mattered. But a computer had to be taught all of this. It could not learn on its own. A machine had no experience, no residual memories. So the NSA would have to create them.

Computers needed this human logic layer. Without it the NSA could never achieve the kinds of early-warning insights Hayden had dreamed of, or Poindexter for that matter. The switch to in-memory computing was a legitimate breakthrough. But on its own it could not produce better analysis. The NSA might be able to swallow the ocean. But what good was that if it could never digest it?

Consumer marketers had been grappling with this problem for a generation. In their trade there was an old story, probably apocryphal, that seemed to illustrate the holy grail of insight that the NSA was reaching for. Clerks in a convenience store, the story went, noticed that men often bought beer at the same time they bought diapers. And the clerks noticed that they usually came in at night, alone. They started to wonder whether the men had been sent out by their wives for an emergency diaper run and decided they might as well pick up a six-pack for their trouble.

The store manager went through his receipts and confirmed that the clerks' observations were correct. Sales of beer and diapers were higher later at night, when men did the shopping. After dinner or later in the evening, sales of both products rose.

The store manager had just discovered a logic layer, the connection between two distinct objects. He started stocking diapers next to the beer. Sales of both skyrocketed.

At the most basic level, this was the NSA's quest. This was the end state of total information awareness. A set of rules, a pattern, that defined human behavior.

The richer the logic layer, the more patterns it could detect. And the more patterns, the more relationships. Did a man arrested for cocaine possession in Los Angeles have any connection to a suspected terrorist recently stopped at the Mexico border crossing? Did a man buying five hundred pounds of fertilizer need them for his gardening business or to build a bomb?

As the NSA forged ahead with in-memory databases its counterterrorism experts, as well as those in other agencies across the government, set out to try to answer these questions. They chased the same elusive dream as Poindexter's red team.

They had a slim chance of success. How could one account for the variances of human behavior? People were logical creatures—most of the time. But they often behaved illogically, and in ways that confounded explanation. Was there really a model for terrorism like there was for a hurricane, or a cold front, or the sales of beer and diapers? Detecting terrorism wasn't purely science. It was also an art.

Poindexter knew that. So did his critics. They vilified him for asking whether such a system could work. But at the NSA, Hayden and others were listening. And they quietly followed suit. They picked up where Poindexter had left off.

The result was chilling. Even without a logic layer, NSA's technological breakthrough meant the agency could see an entire network, and everything moving on it, in real time. They were one step closer to total information awareness.

CHAPTER 24

EXPOSED

In May 2004, Fran Townsend celebrated her first anniversary at the White House. She'd been the president's point person on terrorism, but always as a deputy to Condoleezza Rice, whom the president cherished not only as his national security adviser but as a personal friend. That immovable layer had separated Townsend from the commander in chief. But she was about to move up. That spring Bush tapped her as his assistant for counterterrorism and homeland security. She reported directly to him now.

Not long after Townsend moved into her new West Wing office, an NSA employee came to see her, someone she knew from her days working surveillance warrants at Justice. But this wasn't a social call. It was time to clear Townsend into the program.

Up to now she had only a notion that the NSA was working outside its customary boundaries. The first clue came from her old friend Jim Comey, the deputy attorney general. He approached Townsend at the White House during the crisis over the spying program's legality. Before a meeting in the Oval Office, which was also attended by Mike Hayden, Comey asked Townsend, who was still a deputy, if she had ever heard of the code name Stellar Wind.

Townsend said no, she hadn't, which Comey found deeply unsettling. The White House had, indeed, kept the circle tight, so tight that the president's terrorism adviser sat outside of it. Townsend had never seen her friend so ashen, so worried. She knew that Comey met with the president, but she didn't know what they discussed.

It became much clearer after the NSA employee brought Townsend into that tiny circle. After she'd been read in, Townsend had only one question about the program: "Has the Department of Justice said it's legal?"

Yes, the NSA employee replied.

That was good enough for her.

One of Townsend's new duties was playing intelligence traffic cop. She had to make sure that the information the NSA collected from the surveillance program made its way to the FBI. If the program was legal, then Townsend was less concerned about the details of what the NSA gathered, or how, than about what the agency did with that information. Were the leads getting passed on to the appropriate domestic law enforcement agency for follow-up?

Townsend also understood how important the program was to the intelligence community. That fact would be driven home repeatedly over the course of the next year, and particularly when the new head of the NSA, Lieutenant General Keith Alexander, started showing up at the White House for daily briefings on what the agency was learning about terror networks.

Alexander took over at the agency in August 2005. His experience overseeing the Information Dominance Center and the intelligence command at Fort Belvoir made him a natural choice for the signals job. Alexander had deep technical expertise and long-standing contacts within the community. (He'd also attended those Genoa demos put on by Poindexter years earlier.)

But Alexander also had a contentious relationship with Mike Hayden, the man he was replacing. The two had sparred over how much access Alexander's analysts, particularly those working in the IDC, should have to raw signals data. Alexander wanted Hayden to bend the pipes toward his people, but Hayden had resisted. Now Alexander was the head plumber.

Hayden had left Fort Meade earlier in the year, moving steadily and considerably up the bureaucratic ladder, as was his way. In April 2005, he became the principal deputy director of national intelligence, the number two man in the community. He was the first person ever to hold the post, which was part of the new Office of the Director of National Intelligence, created in response to the 9/11 Commission. It had recommended a new upper management to corral the restive agencies and force them to cooperate.

Depending on how one chose to view the assignment, Hayden had either been handed the keys to the kingdom or been made to walk the plank. The deputy slot was a political post and required the Senate's approval. That would mean public hearings in which the dirty laundry of the war on terror might have an airing. Still, the fact that Bush had tapped Hayden, his leader in the digital global terrorist hunt, was a clear signal of the president's confidence and his approval.

Even if Hayden made it through confirmation unscathed, he'd be taking on a thankless job. As the deputy, he was guaranteed to spend most of his tenure warring over budgets as the new office asserted its dominance. Congress might have slapped the word "director" onto Hayden's forthcoming title, but that didn't make it so. The defense secretary still controlled the vast majority of all intelligence dollars, and the new DNI's office didn't have the authority to overrule him. Indeed, the new law didn't give the DNI the necessary authorities to enforce the policies he might choose to implement.

Still, Hayden was getting a promotion and, with it, a huge boost to his military clout: Bush put him up for his fourth star, the highest rank that the service could bestow. That made Hayden not only a full general but the highest-ranking military intelligence officer in all the armed forces. And Hayden could claim one more bragging right: He was the first career Air Force intelligence officer ever to earn a fourth star. Hayden didn't resign from the Air Force, and that troubled some lawmakers. The new national intelligence office was supposed to be independent. In Washington that usually meant run by civilians. As if to ease concerns about militarization, the Bush administration picked a counterweight of sorts for the top slot.

John Negroponte, a career diplomat whose only experience with intelligence was reading it, seemed an unlikely pick. Negroponte had been the U.S. ambassador to Iraq and had previously represented the country at the United Nations and in Honduras. The Central American post, which he held in the first term of the Reagan administration, had endeared him to John Poindexter, who thought that Negroponte was one of the few people in the State Department who supported the president's goals in Nicaragua. Negroponte carried his own stains from the Iran-Contra affair, but they were insufficient to derail his nomination to the top intelligence job.

Though a capable diplomat, Negroponte was out of his depth in his new role. He quickly developed a habit of leaving the office early. It was customary for a deputy to take over day-to-day management of any large organization. But Hayden was no ordinary backup man. He brought an incomparable résumé and deep institutional knowledge. Negroponte might have been at the top on paper, but there was no mistaking who was really in charge.

Hayden had a new job. Townsend a promotion. Poindexter had begun his third act. The spring of 2004 kicked off a game of musical chairs that lasted well into the next year. This was a predictable and time-honored Washington custom, particularly heading into a second presidential term. But 2005 would be a year of surprises. The first one came in June, when news broke of an intelligence program that few had ever heard of and that those in the know presumed was dead and buried.

Able Danger had surfaced.

Congressman Curt Weldon had been hearing things. There was a lot more going on at the Information Dominance Center than even he, its biggest supporter in Congress, had known.

The first hints came in May. Weldon had a meeting with an Army reserve officer working at the Defense Intelligence Agency named Tony Shaffer. He'd been asked to meet with the congressman to help drum up funds for a new data analysis program the Navy wanted to launch. But once Weldon had Shaffer in his office on the Hill, the conversation turned to Able Danger.

Weldon had heard about the program a few days earlier, from Scott Philpot, the Navy officer who had first brought Erik Kleinsmith into the secret operation and tapped his team of analysts to run intelligence on Al Qaeda. Weldon wanted to know what happened to all the work the team had done. He asked Shaffer to fill in some details. So he gave the congressman the briefing he'd presented two years earlier to staff members of the 9/11 Commission.

Weldon was surprised to hear this. He had read the report, and he didn't recall a word about Able Danger. His chief of staff grabbed a copy, scanned through it, and told his boss that this code name was nowhere to be found in the pages.

Shaffer said that he had contacted the commission staff and offered to tell them what he knew about Able Danger. In October 2003, some staffers flew to Bagram, Afghanistan, where Shaffer was stationed, and they interviewed him. It was late in the commission's work, and back in Washington, members were writing the final report. The commission found Shaffer's interview unsatisfying; he hadn't provided enough definitive information, or proof, about Able Danger's activities, and so the report never mentioned it.

Weldon was baffled. As he'd just learned, Able Danger was the Special Operations Command's program to hunt down and kill Al Qaeda members. It had been reviewed and approved by the top echelons of the military. How could this narrative be left out of the final accounting of the 9/11 terrorist attack, particularly since it appeared to show the military was moving in to thwart Al Qaeda? Weldon had no immediate explanation, but his confusion was turned into rage over what he learned next.

Former members of the Able Danger team now claimed that they had identified the ringleader of the 9/11 hijackers, Mohamed Atta, more than a year before the attacks. Using the IDC's advanced analytics, they had zeroed in on a sleeper cell in New York. When team members tried to approach the FBI with the information so agents could investigate, they said, they were shut down by higher authorities. Eventually, all the intelligence Able Danger had collected was destroyed.

It was a bombshell. Weldon had spent a fair share of his career in Congress railing against the intelligence and military bureaucracies. He had pitched the Information Dominance Center as a novel, cutting-edge capability for preventing acts of terrorism like the 9/11 attacks. Now he discovered that when the center had a chance to do just that, no one had lifted a finger. The Able Danger team had apparently been stymied by higher-ups in the Pentagon and dismissed by the FBI.

Over the next few weeks Shaffer gave Weldon more details about Able Danger. It turned out that Weldon had actually become aware of the program much earlier, without fully realizing it. Two weeks after the 9/11 attacks, staff from the IDC had brought Weldon a smaller version of one of their massive link charts. It measured only two by three feet and was a mock-up prepared by a contractor that had once worked for the center.

Weldon had acted as if it were a smoking gun. He'd left his office and headed for the White House. He had brought along Eileen Preisser, an analyst who had worked with Kleinsmith. She had become one of the congressman's "friends" in the intelligence community.

Weldon had shown the chart to Stephen Hadley, President Bush's deputy national security adviser. It was a frantic time, with officials bracing for another attack. Weldon had been driven to show Hadley that the very capabilities he'd been promoting all these years had, in fact, revealed something remarkable—an Al Qaeda presence inside the United States.

Hadley had taken a look at the chart, and he seemed impressed. "I have to show this to the big man," he said, meaning Bush.

It was the last Weldon ever saw or heard of that chart. Perhaps the congressman had believed that the NSC staff would investigate, and that he'd learn the truth eventually, because after that meeting with Hadley, Weldon didn't speak publicly about the chart. Not until he learned that it was the product of a secret program that apparently had identified Atta.

Throughout the spring and early summer of 2005 Weldon spoke with others who'd worked on the classified program. A new narrative emerged. These bright, innovative analysts from Army intelligence and at Special Operations had zeroed in on the 9/11 hijackers, and in the United States, possibly in Manhattan or Brooklyn. But, true to form, the recalcitrant and hidebound bureaucracy had failed to act.

Weldon screamed cover-up. In June he took to the House floor in a forty-five-minute address. "For the first time, I can tell our colleagues that one of our agencies not only identified the New York cell of Mohamed Atta and two of the terrorists, but actually made a recommendation to bring the FBI in to take out that cell," Weldon declared triumphantly. "Why, then, did they not proceed? That is a question that needs to be answered."

Weldon went to the press. In August the Able Danger story went national. Weldon was quoted by the wire services and the major papers, and he appeared on the news networks. Shaffer came forward with his own account. He said that he'd tried to alert officials at the FBI, and that he'd even set up meetings, but he was thwarted by senior Pentagon officials. The nation was gripped by this latest twist in the 9/11 saga. Had the United States government actually missed the chance to prevent the mass murder of nearly three thousand people?

Weldon launched a crusade to expose the FBI and the Pentagon for covering up Able Danger's discoveries. For him, that was the unforgivable sin. Weldon blasted the 9/11 Commission, which he thought had failed to see the program's significance because it only conducted limited interviews with the former team members. He declared that the Bush administration's efforts to dismiss Able Danger amounted to a scandal "worse than Watergate."

Weldon was raving. He looked unhinged. He made long, bombastic speeches, extolling the IDC and Able Danger but also rubbing the intelligence community's nose in their own undeniable failures. He wanted to remind the world that he'd been clamoring for intelligence reform, and of how he'd told many administration officials to look closely at the IDC's good work. Along with "cover-up" came another refrain: "I told you so."

Had a calmer voice spoken, the public might have learned the real truth about Able Danger. The story was far more complex, and more disheartening, than the one Weldon was telling.

Erik Kleinsmith sure thought so.

When Kleinsmith finally went public, in September, it was under oath before a Senate panel. He had ceded the media field to Weldon, who sucked all the oxygen out of the story anyway. For weeks Weldon had been raging over destroyed evidence and deleted charts. He railed against the Pentagon lawyers who got in the Able Danger team's way. "I'll tell you how stupid it was," Weldon told the Associated Press during an interview in his office. "They put stickies on the faces of Mohamed Atta on the chart that the military intelligence unit had completed and they said you can't talk to Atta because he's here [legally]."

The kernel of the story was correct. The lawyers did intercede over privacy regulations and concerns about U.S. persons. And the team did stick Post-it notes over the faces of people on the link charts. But Kleinsmith didn't believe that Atta was among them. And he said so at the hearing.

"I myself do not remember seeing either a picture or his name on any charts," Kleinsmith told members of the Senate Judiciary Committee.

The chairman, Arlen Specter, a Republican from Weldon's home state of Pennsylvania, asked Kleinsmith whether he could corroborate the accounts of Preisser, Philpot, Shaffer, and now two others who also claimed they saw Atta.

"I cannot corroborate them completely and say that, yes, they saw it,"

Kleinsmith replied. He tried hard not to refute them. He was sure that they *thought* what they saw was real. "I believed them implicitly," Kleinsmith said. But he wouldn't and couldn't back up their story.

Specter asked Kleinsmith whether Able Danger had identified a specific terrorist operation in a U.S. city.

"No specific operation in the United States," Kleinsmith said. "Only a presence that was known."

Kleinsmith was in the best position to know. And sitting before the imposing dais, he described how he'd personally destroyed all the evidence about Al Qaeda's global and U.S. presences.

"We were forced to destroy all data," he said. All the charts, all the reporting. Anything related to Able Danger was gone, he told the senators.

They seemed incredulous, as if Kleinsmith was surely mistaken when he said everything was gone. "What kind of information was deleted?" Specter inquired.

"*Everything,*" Kleinsmith replied. "Everything that we had." How could he say it more clearly? There was nothing left.

Kleinsmith spelled out how Able Danger progressed, how it moved from an information harvest into a painstaking but technologically enhanced phase of analysis. "We were trying to get a worldwide perspective of exactly where Al Qaeda functioned and operated," he said. "We were unable to get to the details for specific persons or information in the United States before we were shut down."

If Shaffer or Preisser or anyone else had actually seen Atta on the charts, they had only their memories to back them up. All the physical evidence was gone.

Specter had a report in front of him with a particularly dramatic statement from Kleinsmith. "I want to know if this is an accurate quote, that every night when you go to bed, you believe that if the program had not shut down U.S. intelligence on these subjects, that 9/11 could have been prevented."

"That's not completely accurate," Kleinsmith replied. "What I have said is, yes, I do go to bed every night, and other members of our team do as well, that if we had not been shut down, we would have been able to at least present something or assist the United States in some way."

"Could we have prevented 9/11?" he continued. "I don't think—" But then he stopped himself. "I can never speculate to that extent we could have done that."

Specter followed up. "But you think you might have been able to glean some intelligence that could have been helpful along that line?"

"Yes, sir," Kleinsmith replied.

His was a more nuanced and ambiguous answer. And it was the one ultimately borne out by the record and an extensive investigation. The Defense Department's inspector general interviewed all the relevant witnesses and found no evidence to corroborate any claim that Able Danger members were prohibited by the Pentagon from contacting the FBI. Officials reviewed more than eighty thousand documents still in the department's possession. No one found a chart or any record from Able Danger with the name Mohamed Atta.

If such evidence had existed, the odds of investigators finding them were unlikely, since they'd probably have been destroyed. But in interviews with the investigators, team members who claimed to have seen Atta contradicted themselves, and at times appeared uncertain about what they'd actually seen or could remember years later. The Pentagon's final report concluded that Able Danger never identified Atta, or any of the other 9/11 terrorists, as possible threats.

Kleinsmith wanted the senators to understand that it wasn't his call to destroy the intelligence cache. He had fought against it. But when it came time to sit at his computer, point at the toxic documents, and eradicate them he was doing just as the Army had trained him.

"I understood that the regulation was written before the Internet, before data mining," Kleinsmith said. "Yes, I could have conveniently forgotten to delete the data, and we could have kept it." He had contemplated doing just that. "But I knowingly would have been in violation."

Kleinsmith was no hidebound bureaucrat. He was torn up over what had happened. It was his analysis, after all. Weldon later dismissed Kleinsmith as a know-nothing. His version of the narrative didn't fit with Weldon's cover-up story.

Kleinsmith didn't believe there was one, at least not the conspiracy Weldon was peddling. And he also thought the Atta question was an utter distraction.

The bigger story—the real scandal, he thought—was why the Pentagon had shut down a unit that made more progress on a national security threat of historic proportions than even the best analysts in the intelligence community. Kleinsmith thought that officials made their choices out of fear and ignorance. The Pentagon saw "data mining" as a dirty term. It portended an invasion of privacy, a waste of time and money. Kleinsmith thought that the lawyers had missed what it was really all about, from an analyst's point of view: making connections, finding anomalous patterns, working faster and more accurately.

But there was another question no one wanted to ask. Even if Able Danger had identified Atta . . . so what? How would the analysts have known who he was? Or why he mattered? Clearly, those who believed *now* that they'd seen his face *then* didn't know Atta's plans. Able Danger couldn't draw the contours of a plot. The analysts couldn't pinpoint the day and time of an attack. And that was the most maddening part of it all. Kleinsmith got nervous when he saw the presence of terrorists in the United States, but he was nearly petrified when he realized that he couldn't do anything about them.

Even with the IDC's hyperanalysis, Kleinsmith simply didn't have the information he needed. The real travesty, to him, was that he hadn't been allowed to go look for it.

Not long after 9/11, Kleinsmith left the military. He took a job with a big Beltway firm teaching intelligence analysis. There his services were more in demand than ever.

A long list of federal employees wanted to learn his craft. Kleinsmith's former employer, the IDC, became his biggest customer. It was a poetic twist that never failed to amuse him.

But feds weren't the only ones lining up for Kleinsmith's lessons. State and local police forces and corporate security officials clamored for the intelligence on steroids that he had practiced in government. In an age of terror, everyone wanted to see what was coming. Knowledge had never been more powerful.

Kleinsmith led a team of more than two dozen instructors. After the U.S. invasion of Iraq in 2003, five of them deployed to Iraq to run data analysis on the burgeoning insurgency there. Unbeknownst to Kleinsmith, John Poindexter's technology had played a role there as well. He sat on the board of a start-up firm called Saffron. It was building a tool used by forces in Iraq to help identify "entities," which were defined as people, places, and things involved in insurgent networks. The tool mimicked human memory by recalling associations among those people, places, and things. Most tools looked merely for the occurrences of words, but Saffron was focused on their context and the frequency of association. Each word representing an entity in a set of data had its own "memory" about all the other words it had ever been associated with. In this way the tool could learn as it ingested more information, the way humans did.

Like Poindexter, Kleinsmith had become part of an expanding private intelligence industry. A new wave of anxiety swelled as data collection firms like ChoicePoint, which had been hired by the Justice Department after 9/11 to help track terrorist suspects, worked more closely with the government to amass information about individuals. But when news about Able Danger broke, no cries of "domestic spying" were heard.

Few were concerned that a secret Army team had conducted intelligence operations inside the United States. Indeed, that part of the story—the one that Pentagon lawyers, congressional staffers, and Kleinsmith himself thought would fail the *Washington Post* smell test—barely played. Instead, people were outraged, and deeply confused, over how the government might have found evidence of the 9/11 plot and done nothing about it—except to destroy all the records. The lesson of Able Danger was the opposite of Total Information Awareness. If data analysis actually could find terrorists, then the public would embrace it. They might even demand it.

That theory was about to be tested with yet another blockbuster revelation of work done in shadow.

CHAPTER 25

REASONABLE BELIEFS

Mike Hayden was going to stop the *New York Times*. And the big man was going to help him.

In early December 2005, the former director of the NSA, now the second most senior spy in government, joined President Bush in an Oval Office meeting with Bill Keller, the *Times*'s executive editor. The paper's publisher and Washington bureau chief came along. Two *Times* reporters had been working up a story on the warrantless surveillance program, after mining a network of sources for months. They had satisfied Keller that the story was solid enough to run. Bush told Keller that was a very bad idea.

The *Times* was about to blow the cover on one of the most vital weapons in the war on terror, the president argued. Bush said he regarded the NSA's surveillance as one of the crown jewels of national security. If the targets knew that they were being watched, and how, they might be able to evade detection. If that happened, a vital stream of intelligence could dry up.

Keller had faced questions before about whether to report on intelligence sources and methods. It was a tricky issue, almost always fraught with tension between the government's need for stealth and the public's right to know. This story posed all those challenges.

But Bush had another message for the newsman. This was no ordinary program. If the story forced the NSA to shut it down, or gave the terrorists enough insight to reverse engineer the government's surveillance strategy, then the newspaper should feel responsible. "When we're called up to explain to Congress why there was another attack you should be sitting beside us at the table," Bush said. The president of the United States was warning him: If we get hit again, you'll have blood on your hands.

Keller took the president seriously. He sat on a couch only a few feet from Bush, who was seated next to Hayden. Stephen Hadley, now the national security adviser, was also there, as was Harriet Miers, the president's counsel. (Alberto Gonzales had become attorney general after Bush won reelection.) Prior to the Oval Office meeting senior-level and cabinet officials had tried to convince the *Times* not to run the story. The debate had dragged on for more than a year now. Keller had been persuaded to hold off, but now he felt that the reporters had brought home the evidence that this was a good and important story. Keller had pondered it. In the end, he decided that this wasn't a story about sources and methods but about warrants. It was about the law.

Keller and his two colleagues left the White House and went to catch taxis. He told the publisher, Arthur Sulzberger, that he wanted to sleep on it, but that he didn't think anything the president said would change his mind. On December 16, the *Times* published the story on the front page. The program was in the open.

Hayden had failed. The *Times* story exploded, sparking a national debate of surprising ferocity considering that it was moored in FISA, a law that even the foremost experts acknowledged was too dense for most people to comprehend. The administration had already faced accusations of illegal detention, torture, and falsifying intelligence about weapons in order to take the nation to war with Iraq. But the surveillance story offered the most concrete argument to date that in the war on terror ordinary Americans had been lumped into a pool of suspects with the terrorists.

Now, lawyers, technologists, and journalists endeavored to reverse engineer the administration's legal rationale. How, precisely, had the president of the United States violated the law and conducted a covert, multiyear surveillance program?

It was Hayden's job to explain why the administration had taken such extraordinary steps, and why they were legal. On January 23, 2006, he addressed a crowd of journalists and a few activists at the National Press Club, in Washington. Just four days earlier the Justice Department had published a lengthy white paper on the legal authorities supporting the NSA program, chock-full of footnotes and references to case law. But Hayden was going to put a human face on that logic and explain it all in basic terms. This was the job he excelled at from his early days at the NSA, when he courted remarkably favorable coverage of his secretive agency. Hayden was a top-notch salesman.

His opening lines left little doubt about his strategy. "I'm happy to be here to talk a bit about what American intelligence has been doing and, especially, what the NSA has been doing to defend the nation," Hayden said. "There's a lot of information out there right now. Some of it is, frankly, inaccurate. Much of it is just simply misunderstood. I'm here to tell the American people what the NSA has been doing and why. And perhaps more importantly, what the NSA has not been doing."

For present purposes, the second part was indeed more important. Bush had already acknowledged that targeted surveillance without warrants was occurring—what most people commonly referred to as "wiretapping." But what lines were Hayden going to claim, here in public, that the agency hadn't crossed?

"The program," he said, "is not a drift net over Dearborn or Lackawanna or Freemont grabbing conversations that we then sort out by these alleged keyword searches or data-mining tools or other devices that so-called experts keep talking about."

Somewhere between the lines of that statement there were bits of truth. Maybe the drift net wasn't over Dearborn or Lackawanna exclusively. But taken as a whole Hayden's remarks were inaccurate and misleading. There was, in fact, a drift net. It was cast wide, and it was grabbing metadata. Conversations were being snatched too, and all of this information was being sorted out using tools that Hayden's agency had built.

The public was still unaware that the government had engaged telecommunications companies to scoop up metadata, which might explain why Hayden tried to dismiss the notion of a drift net. But that part of the story would soon be exposed by the press as well. And when it was, the administration refused to acknowledge whether it was true or not. Maybe it was because the existence of a drift net hadn't been revealed that Hayden felt so emboldened to talk as if nothing like it existed. He kept his remarks tailored to the targeted surveillance that the *Times* had revealed and Bush had acknowledged. And the more Hayden talked, the more he sounded like a lawyer, not a spy.

"This is targeted and focused," he said. "This is not about intercepting conversations between people in the United States. This is hot pursuit of communications entering or leaving America involving someone we believe is associated with Al Qaeda. We bring to bear all the technology we can to ensure that this is so."

If ever there was "an inadvertent intercept of a domestic-to-domestic call," Hayden said, it was destroyed. "That's a normal NSA procedure," he noted.

Hayden was a gifted speaker because he knew how to hold a crowd. He could sense when he was losing them. And when that happened he turned on the common-man talk. The football analogies. The plain talking.

"So let me make this clear," he said. "When you're talking to your daughter at state college, this program cannot intercept your conversations. And when she takes a semester abroad to complete her Arabic studies, this program will not intercept your communications." No domestic-to-domestic calls. No calls solely among Americans. No spying because you're speaking Arabic.

Simple.

Hayden also played the cheerleader. "I recently went out to Fort Meade to talk to the workforce involved in this program," he said. "They know what they have contributed, and they know the care with which it has been done. Even in today's heated environment, the only concern they expressed to me was continuing their work in the defense of the nation, and continuing to do so in a manner that honors the law and the Constitution."

And finally, he was a storyteller. "As I was talking with them—we were in the office spaces there, typical office spaces anywhere in the world—I looked out over their heads—and this is the workforce that deals with the program the president discussed several weeks ago—I looked out over their heads to see a large sign fixed to one of those pillars that go up through our operations building that breaks up the office space. That sign is visible from almost anywhere in this large area. It's yellow with bold black letters on it. The title is readable from fifty feet: 'What constitutes a U.S. person?' And that title was followed by a detailed explanation of the criteria. That has always been the fundamental tenet of privacy for NSA. And here it was in the center of a room guiding the actions of a workforce determined to prevent another attack on the United States. Security and liberty. The people at NSA know what their job is. I know what my job is too."

Hayden looked confident. And pleased. But when it came time for questions, the audience was having none of it.

A man known for charm and aplomb became visibly agitated. Hayden batted away allegations that the Bush administration had reverted to the excesses that marred the intelligence community in the 1960s and 1970s. He seemed to think it was utterly illogical, even offensive, to draw comparisons between a war on terrorists and a time when the CIA and FBI monitored journalists, dissidents, and civil rights activists as political enemies. Hayden knew that ugly history. But that was another time.

"This is focused," he reiterated. "It's targeted. It's very carefully done. You shouldn't worry."

Maybe it had been focused once. But that was a long time ago. In the beginning, Hayden carefully had drawn out for the White House the three characteristics any good early-warning system must possess: It must be technologically feasible. It must produce useful intelligence. And it must be lawful. How solid were those pillars now?

What Hayden left out—the history, the technological challenges, the dead ends—told the whole story. His former agency had created something far greater than a neat, discrete capture of conversations. And it had taken them years to achieve a talent that could unashamedly be called "hot pursuit."

But Hayden had come to make other points, and one that he wanted to impress firmly upon his audience was this: The NSA surveillance program—at least the one that the president had acknowledged—did not violate the Fourth Amendment of the Constitution. No way, nohow.

A reporter in the audience tested Hayden's assertion. "I'm no lawyer," the reporter said. "But my understanding is that the Fourth Amendment of the Constitution specifies that you must have probable cause to be able to do a search that does not violate an American's right against unlawful searches and seizures. Do you use—"

Hayden cut him off. "No, actually," he gently instructed. "The Fourth

Amendment actually protects all of us against unreasonable search and seizure."

"But does it not say probable—"

"No," Hayden insisted. His eyes and mouth started twitching, a nervous facial tic that tended to flare up in tense exchanges. "The amendment says '*unreasonable search and seizure*.'"

Hayden emphasized the four words as if to say he knew perfectly well what was reasonable and what wasn't.

The reporter still pressed on the language. "Does it not say probable—"

"No. The amendment says—"

"The court standard. The legal standard—"

"—'unreasonable search and seizure.'"

"The legal standard is probable cause, General." The reporter raised his voice and sliced through. Hayden stayed quiet. "And a FISA court, my understanding is, would not give you a warrant if you went before them and say 'we reasonably believe.' You have to go to the FISA Court, or the attorney general has to go to the FISA Court and say, 'We have probable cause.' And so what many people believe—and I'd like you to respond to this—is that what you've actually done is crafted a detour around the FISA Court by creating a new standard of 'reasonably believe' in place of probable cause; because the FISA Court will not give you a warrant based on reasonable belief, you have to show probable cause. Could you respond to that, please?"

"Sure. I didn't craft the authorization. I am responding to a lawful order. All right? The attorney general has averred to the lawfulness of the order." (That was the order that Gonzales's predecessor, Ashcroft, had refused to sign almost two years earlier and in so doing had nearly brought down the Bush administration—a still unknown fact.)

Hayden continued, "I'm not a lawyer, and don't want to become one. What you've raised to me is, in terms of quoting the Fourth Amendment, is an issue of the Constitution. The constitutional standard is 'reasonable.' And we believe—I am convinced that we are lawful because what it is we're doing is reasonable."

For Hayden it was damn well reasonable to presume, on September 11 and after, that America's enemies were at the gate. Without another word, he stepped off the podium and left the building.

Many Americans agreed with Hayden. The government had an obligation to protect the country, and if that meant monitoring phone calls and e-mails, that's what had to be done. A *USA Today* poll taken not long after the *Times* story appeared showed Americans evenly divided between those who opposed warrantless surveillance and those who thought that the president should have the powers he deemed necessary to strengthen national security.

The Justice Department argued in its white paper that Congress had given him that power in the "Authorization for Use of Military Force" against terrorists, a joint resolution passed one week after the 9/11 attacks. Now officials claimed that the lawmakers had implicitly carved out an exception to FISA, even though the resolution never mentioned surveillance or intelligence specifically, and Congress had made clear, when it passed FISA in 1978, that the law was intended as a check on the president's authorities.

But in his Press Club speech Hayden said that "a serious and continuing threat to the homeland" had compelled the administration to give the NSA its new powers. Apparently, more than four years hence, the threat was still serious and continuing. Future events would tend to support that argument.

Two weeks after Hayden's speech Attorney General Alberto Gonzales appeared before the Senate Judiciary Committee, ostensibly to amplify Hayden's remarks. But Gonzales evaded senators' questions about the warrantless surveillance program and avoided many specifics about how it actually worked.

The president had the constitutional authority to order the secret surveillance, Gonzales insisted. It was necessary, and it still is.

"Well, then, let me ask you this," prodded Arlen Specter. He'd been a busy overseer lately. "Under your interpretation of this, can you go in and do mail searches? Can you go into e-mails? Can you open mail? Can you do black-bag jobs?"

"Sir," Gonzales replied, "I've tried to outline for you and the committee what the president has authorized, and that is all that he has authorized."

Gonzales didn't exactly say no. Patrick Leahy, the committee's top Democrat, tag-teamed the attorney general. "Did it authorize the opening of first-class mail of U.S. citizens? That you can answer yes or no."

"There is all kinds of wild speculation—"

"Did it authorize it?" Leahy persisted.

"—about what the president has authorized and what we're actually doing. And I'm not going to get into a discussion, Senator, about—"

"You're not answering my question! I'm not asking you what the president authorized. Does this law—you're the chief law enforcement officer of the country—does this law authorize the opening of first-class mail of U.S. citizens, yes or no, under your interpretation?"

Dianne Feinstein, a California Democrat, tried another tactic to pry information from the hedging attorney general.

"Has the president ever invoked this authority with respect to any activity other than NSA surveillance?" she asked.

"I'm not sure how to answer that question," Gonzales replied. "I am not comfortable going down the road of saying yes or no as to what the president has or hasn't authorized."

It might have been the most forthright statement Gonzales made all day. He carefully circumscribed his remarks—he was talking *only* about the surveillance activities that the president had authorized and that he confirmed existed after the *New York Times* published its story. This was becoming a well-worn refrain.

But Gonzales was still mostly opaque. He danced around the committee's questions. At times he almost seemed to smirk, as if he knew he was hiding a deeper secret. The lawmakers seemed to sense it and, of course, there were those in Congress who knew there was more to the story and couldn't say so publicly. But for the moment everyone knew that the Bush administration had been covering up and deceiving Congress for years. Anyone could see that there was more to "the program" than Gonzales was letting on.

CHAPTER 26

BETRAYAL

There was a lot more to say about another program too. On February 2, 2006, during a public hearing of the Senate Intelligence Committee, a secret the administration had tried to stuff in a black box started spilling out.

The committee had called up an all-star cast of intelligence chiefs for an annual hearing on global threats, a kind of panoramic view of the national security waterfront. Mike Hayden joined his boss, director of national intelligence John Negroponte, and the new head of the CIA, former congressman Porter Goss. FBI director Robert Mueller was also there, along with the chiefs of the Defense Intelligence Agency and the State Department's intelligence office. Rounding out the ensemble was perhaps the oldest senior spy in the United States—Charlie Allen. The onetime contact of Ollie North and John Poindexter, who'd helped set up those early links among counterterrorism agencies and the White House in the wake of the Lebanon bombings, was now the chief intelligence officer for the Homeland Security Department.

Negroponte gave opening remarks about global threats. But with cameras rolling and reporters jotting notes, the discussion quickly turned to the NSA's warrantless surveillance program.

The senators peppered the witnesses with questions about the program's legal underpinnings, which they were still struggling to understand. But they also wanted to know if the surveillance produced results. John Rockefeller, who'd written that note to Dick Cheney comparing the NSA's program to Total Information Awareness, asked whether the agency had actually detected terrorist plots and saved lives, as Cheney had claimed publicly after the program was exposed.

Negroponte took a shot. "Certainly it's been an effective and important program in dealing with the terrorist threat," he told Rockefeller. But rather than getting into specific examples, Negroponte turned to his number two. "If I may, I might ask—with your permission, Senator—ask General Hayden to elaborate somewhat in reply to the question that you have just directed to me."

"The program has been successful," Hayden insisted, adding, "We have learned information from this program that would not otherwise have been available." On that point, Hayden wouldn't waver. "This information has helped detect and prevent terrorist attacks in the United States and abroad."

But then Hayden went on the offensive. "The underlying basis of your question, though, Senator, is to put us in a position of proving a negative, proving that if we hadn't done this, if we hadn't had this knowledge, if these steps hadn't been taken, if these actions had not taken place, that something else would not have happened. That's very difficult to prove in a strict linear sense."

Rockefeller had limited time for questioning, and he wasn't getting anywhere with Hayden. He turned to Mueller, the FBI director. What was there to another *New York Times* article, he asked, about FBI agents being inundated by thousands of leads from the NSA, most of which turned out to be dead ends? Was the intelligence that Hayden had provided all that useful?

"We get a number of leads from the NSA from a number of programs, including the program that's under discussion today," Mueller said, widening the aperture of the lens. Unlike Gonzales, Mueller acknowledged that there was more to the agency's surveillance than this one sliver. "And I can say that leads from that program have been valuable in identifying would-be terrorists in the United States, individuals who were providing material support to terrorists."

Mueller had backed Hayden up on that score. But was *all* this intelligence valuable, in the aggregate? Hardly, according to the FBI director. "Most leads that we get, whether it be from NSA or overseas from the CIA, ultimately turn out not to be valid or worthwhile," Mueller said. "But in our view, any lead from any source, any legitimate source, is a lead that has to be pursued, and we pursue each and every one of them."

Senator Ron Wyden, Poindexter's old nemesis, was up next. He wanted to know what happened to the information the NSA collected on Americans who turned out to have nothing to do with terrorism. Were there restrictions on its use?

Again, Negroponte awkwardly replied. "Whether you're talking about one program or another with respect to NSA, those programs are under the strictest possible oversight," he said. "General Hayden may want to amplify."

Negroponte was treading water.

"Mr. Director, that answer isn't good enough for me," Wyden shot back, before Hayden could intercede. "That answer is, essentially, 'Trust us. The Congress and the public just have to trust us.' And Ronald Reagan put it very well. He said, 'Trust, but verify.'"

Hayden snuck in a few lines of support, once again averring, as he had at the Press Club, that the NSA had "lawfully acquired signals intelligence."

Wyden reminded Hayden that they'd discussed before how there were "virtually no rules on data mining" and that they could continue that discussion another time. Wyden moved on, but his next question came as a surprise.

"Mr. Director," he said, turning to Negroponte, "is it correct that when John Poindexter's program, Operation Total Information Awareness, was closed that several of Mr. Poindexter's projects were moved to various intelligence agencies?"

Negroponte seemed stunned, as if he didn't understand how the discussion had shifted so suddenly from the NSA to Poindexter. He offered only a sentence in reply. "I don't know the answer to that question."

"Do any of the other panel members know this?" Wyden asked. "I and others on this panel led the effort to close it. We want to know if Mr. Poindexter's programs are going on somewhere else. Can anyone answer that? Mr. Mueller?"

"I have no knowledge of that, sir," Mueller replied.

The room waited. And then Hayden leaned forward.

"Senator, I'd like to answer you in closed session."

Soon the secret was out. Later that month the first press account detailing TIA's transfer to the National Security Agency research shop appeared in *National Journal*, a nonpartisan Washington political magazine. The programs had moved, and their funding sources remained intact. As recently as October 2005 SAIC had won a $3.7 million contract for more work under Topsail, the new name for Genoa II.

The story quoted Tom Armour, one of Poindexter's former program managers, who said that the NSA unit absorbing TIA had pursued technologies that would be useful for analyzing large amounts of phone and e-mail traffic. "That's, in fact, what the interest is," Armour said. When TIA was still funded openly, its program managers and researchers had "good coordination" with their counterparts at the NSA shop and discussed one another's work on a regular basis, Armour said.

There was still one more step in the intricate dance between TIA and the National Security Agency. Its research unit was about to get a change in name and management. The Advanced Research and Development Activity would now report to the Office of the Director of National Intelligence. There it would be known as the Disruptive Technology Office, an allusion to a term of art for any new invention that suddenly, and often dramatically, upended established procedures.

John Poindexter's vision would soon be in the hands of John Negroponte. But not for very long. He too was on his way out. Within a year another, much closer ally of Poindexter's, and a true believer in TIA, would take over as the nation's top spy.

If 2005 had been a year of revelations, then 2006 was the time for retribution. Leaks about sensitive and classified intelligence programs sprang up across the government. Bush administration officials were outraged, and they were particularly aggrieved by secrets about the war on terror emanating from CIA headquarters.

The new director, Porter Goss, tried to round up the leakers by interrogating his own employees. Longtime officials were given polygraphs. The director wanted to know who was talking to reporters.

"Do you have any contact with journalists?" one interrogator asked a thirty-year intelligence officer working at the agency.

"Well, sure," he replied. "I just talked to one last week. Do you want his number?"

In fact, some senior officials were not only encouraged to reach out to the press but were told to, in order to defend agency policies. Where was this line of questioning going to get Goss? some of them wondered. Was he looking for leakers? Or for political detractors?

Perhaps both. Amid the internal probes Goss imposed new, tighter restrictions on the books, articles, and opinion pieces published by former employees who were still working for the agency under contract. They had always had to submit their work to a publications review board, which was supposed to ensure their writing didn't contain any classified information. But the new rules amounted to an unprecedented "appropriateness" test. The goal was not just to stop leaks but to suppress political criticism of the administration and the agency.

Relations between the CIA and the White House had soured when invading U.S. forces in Iraq failed to find any chemical, biological, or nuclear weapons stockpiles, as George Tenet had said they would. Careerists at the agency thought that Goss had been sent to clean house and to whip them into shape.

Goss was shaking up Langley, for sure. Although he was a former CIA clandestine officer and longtime chairman of the House Intelligence Committee, Goss was still an outsider. When he took over he brought along his Capitol Hill staff, rankling the old-timers. Some senior officials chose to resign rather than work under the new chief and his flock of "Gosslings."

Goss weathered a storm of leaks directed at him from many of those longtime employees turned disgruntled former employees. Still, the leaks about intelligence programs were his top concern. And Goss was particularly incensed by one that led to a story in the *Washington Post*.

In November 2005, more than a month before the NSA surveillance story broke, the *Post* revealed a global network of CIA-run prisons in foreign countries where the agency held certain terrorists the government thought had especially useful insights into Al Qaeda planning. These so-called black sites kept the suspects out of reach of the U.S. justice system and under the thumb of CIA interrogators.

Senior operations officials, the people using the intelligence gleaned from interrogations to target and kill other terrorists, were devastated by the leak. They thought the prisons were an invaluable resource, and now they'd probably have to be shuttered. The *Post* story also put on ice a plan to open a new, more sophisticated prison that the agency had built from the ground up in a friendly country.

Goss was incensed. He would send a message: Leak and you will be punished.

Goss's investigation of the prisons story led him to a longtime agency employee and an old friend of Poindexter's: Mary McCarthy, his chief advocate on the Clinton National Security Council staff. Now in her early sixties, McCarthy was back at the CIA, working in the inspector general's office and looking forward to retirement. She was also preparing for a new career, having recently graduated from law school. McCarthy passed the bar and planned to go into practice.

She'd already signed all the paperwork to leave the agency officially at the end of April 2006. But less than two weeks before her departure date McCarthy was fired and escorted off the premises.

Goss sent a communiqué to agency employees, never naming McCarthy but announcing that he'd found the leak: "A CIA officer has acknowledged having unauthorized discussions with the media, in which the officer knowingly and willfully shared classified intelligence, including operational information. I terminated that officer's employment with the CIA."

The first part was true. McCarthy had been in touch with journalists, most of whom she had known during her days at the White House. And technically that was a violation of the CIA's rules. But it was unprecedented to fire an employee over unauthorized contacts, particularly one so senior. McCarthy also thought Goss's move was petty, since she was already on her way out the door. Responding to Goss's second allegation, which was far more serious, McCarthy adamantly denied that she was the source of the information in the *Post* story. Friends and former associates said as much in the press on her behalf. The real reasons for her dismissal were more vindictive.

McCarthy's job in the inspector general's office was to oversee a criminal probe into the CIA's terrorist interrogation. From that perch she was privy to extraordinary information about what the agency was doing and what its intentions were as it subjected detainees to grueling physical and mental abuse. McCarthy was an analyst, not an operator. She came from the brainy side of the agency. That immediately put her at odds with those, like Goss, who had spent their careers in the field fighting bad guys.

What McCarthy learned in the course of her investigation made her a target. In June 2005 a senior CIA official had told senators in a classified hearing that the agency didn't break any laws or treaties banning the cruel, inhuman, or degrading treatment of the detainees. McCarthy thought that was patently false. She also believed that a senior CIA official hadn't given the full account of the agency's policy for handling detainees in a February 2005 appearance before the House Intelligence Committee. McCarthy also feared that agency officials would successfully bury the truth about the interrogation program. Officials were misleading Congress, probably breaking the law, and were prepared to cover it up. McCarthy was a Democrat. An unapologetic critic of the president. And she'd admitted talking to reporters. She was the perfect sacrifice.

A few days after McCarthy's dismissal she met her old friend Poindexter for lunch at the Tower Oaks Lodge, a robustly appointed establishment with hunting memorabilia hanging from the walls. Conveniently, it was just a short drive from Poindexter's house. (He'd finally given up fighting traffic, and these days he asked people to come to him.)

McCarthy told Poindexter she was not the source of that prisons story. She didn't even know where the prisons were located. The *Post* reporter had found out, but the paper had agreed not to disclose the names of the host countries in Eastern Europe after the administration said it could disrupt counterterrorism operations there and invite retribution. McCarthy insisted that CIA officials knew that she didn't have the information.

She wasn't sure, but McCarthy suspected that Goss's lieutenants had been telling reporters that she was the leaker. She knew Goss from her days in the White House and when he was on the Hill, but she told Poindexter she had no idea what Goss's people had told him.

Few things mattered to Poindexter more than loyalty. To a person. To an institution. To an idea. Poindexter had been on his boat, *Bluebird*, when several colleagues e-mailed him the first news reports alleging McCarthy was the source of the black prisons exposé. He never thought for a minute that the accusations were true.

Poindexter knew that McCarthy was a Democrat. And that she was a civil libertarian. And McCarthy knew full well Poindexter's colorful history running covert intelligence operations in foreign countries. But their political differences had never divided them from a shared sense of mission. They had come too far together. It would have been easy for Poindexter to accept the line of his party, take the CIA director at his word, and indict McCarthy as a treacherous leak. But he never considered it. A friend needed him, and he didn't turn away.

News reports indicated that McCarthy had failed a polygraph test about whether she'd had any contact with journalists. But contacts didn't equal a specific disclosure. McCarthy was hardly the only senior CIA official being questioned with a lie detector about talking to the press. And clearly other intelligence agency employees had leaked information about other programs, yet they hadn't suffered McCarthy's fate.

Some of her friends thought that Goss was looking to scare the spy workforce. If he was willing to ax someone who'd dedicated much of her career to fighting terrorism, then he would come after anyone.

If those were his intentions, they backfired. Goss and his staff's hard-charging management style had alienated the CIA lifers. Leakers or not, they knew how to run the traps at Langley. Two weeks after he dismissed McCarthy, Goss found himself sitting in the Oval Office with President Bush, who announced that Goss was leaving too.

Bush needed to reassert control over the CIA. He needed someone with a smoother style but still a firm hand. He needed someone he could trust.

The president turned to Mike Hayden, who took over the following month.

Since leaving government for the second time Poindexter had come to rely on his friends more than ever. Many of them, particularly Fran Townsend, still exerted tremendous influence in the administration. Some were at the peak of their power; some were in transition. Still others were about to embark on second lives of their own. While the admiral enjoyed his resurgence, and watched with quiet delight as his ideas were absorbed into the mainstream of American spy craft, one of his close allies came forward with an unexpected message: John Poindexter had it all wrong. His system of total information awareness could never catch terrorists.

Jeff Jonas had come a long way since Carmel. After meeting Poindexter at the Highlands Forum, his cheat-catching software had made the leap from Las Vegas to Washington. Poindexter's research team had put NORA through its paces with the experimental network. But the software required a lot of hand-holding. The TIA researchers weren't sure whether Jonas's program had flaws, whether they weren't expert enough to use it, or whether it was just ill suited to the task of catching terrorists—as Jonas had suspected from the beginning.

Poindexter ultimately decided that NORA was very good at sorting out aliases and finding connections among groups of people in discrete environments, like a casino floor. But it wasn't quite up to the task of finding bad guys in the vast unknown.

Jonas thought he'd tried to tell Poindexter that in their first meeting. But Jonas was open-minded by nature. He had come under Poindexter's spell—the White House photos on the wall, the high-level support for his idea from the Pentagon. Jonas was a patriot at heart. Poindexter became a catalyst for that emotion.

But Jonas had moved on since then. He'd made a lot more friends in Washington. With his compelling personal story and decidedly unstuffy charm, Jonas became a darling of the policy wonk crowd. He once threw a cocktail party for his new friends at the Ritz-Carlton, not far from the Pentagon, and entertained them with a professional "mentalist," who performed card tricks and sleights of hand. Jonas was unlike anyone they knew. And he was ceaselessly interested in whatever new idea someone wanted to plant in his ear.

After meeting Poindexter, Jonas had fallen in with the civil libertarian set. He'd never imagined that data privacy could be such a contentious issue, but he came to see the problem differently. The people he had spied on, if he could even call it spying, handed over their personal information willingly to the casino. But this new surveillance the government had enacted—this wasn't voluntary. And, he thought, it wasn't accurate.

In early 2005, Jonas attended a conference at the Heritage Foundation, a conservative think tank in Washington. During the lunch break he found himself standing in line for a sandwich next to a guy he'd never met, but who'd also grown up in the Bay Area.

Jim Harper was a conservative, of the libertarian variety. He had carved out a niche as a digital privacy maven, running a Web site called Privacilla that came at the issue from a free-market, pro-technology perspective. He viewed himself as a counterpoint to left-wing activists, whom he regarded as hostile to capitalism. These were the ACLU types and advocates like Marc Rotenberg, who'd been one of Poindexter's earliest critics.

Harper felt out of place at Heritage, which he regarded as a den of "terror warriors." He thought that these were the sort who, after 9/11, claimed the attacks had given the government permission to throw off law and custom. He thought that people had gone "tribal."

At lunch, Harper looked around the room for someone to talk to. That's when he spotted the guy who didn't look like anyone else. The one in the black pants and T-shirt.

Harper knew a bit about Jonas's story; he'd even come up in discussion that morning. People knew him as the Vegas data guru who had tried to help catch terrorists. Harper also knew that Jonas had written a paper with a Heritage fellow and wondered if he was just the go-along-to-get-along type with the terror warriors.

As they got to talking Harper saw that Jonas was open to new ideas. So over lunch, and in e-mails in the weeks that followed, they struck up a conversation that Harper was eager to have: Does pattern analysis of data really catch terrorists?

Harper believed that it didn't. Jonas agreed with him. And so another relationship blossomed. Harper suggested that they write a paper together, taking this flawed theory head-on. He knew that Jonas had worked with Poindexter, and he believed that killing TIA, while perhaps a pyrrhic victory, was still a victory for his side. Jonas didn't want to whack Poindexter in print. Harper didn't much care either way.

Perhaps owing to their shared geographical history, he and Jonas hit it off quickly. They traded coy e-mails. "Where's the love?" Harper would ask when he hadn't heard back on a recent round of edits to the paper.

Over the next several months, they hashed out their ideas, first in an outline, then in a draft. As they moved toward publication, Jonas emerged not only as a skeptic of Poindexter-style pattern analysis, but as an outright opponent. In December 2005 he spoke before a meeting of the Homeland Security Department's Data Privacy and Integrity Advisory Committee. Harper was a member, along with other prominent experts from academia, government, and think tanks, and they met periodically to discuss privacy with senior members of the department, including the secretary, Michael Chertoff.

The group gathered at a hotel a few blocks from the White House. Harper joined a team of questioners sitting before Jonas's panel, committee-style. He had a canned question at the ready, which would give his writing partner an opening to voice the ideas they'd been mulling over in print.

"I found it remarkable," Harper said, "that you, as an expert in this field and somebody who works for a company that would sell this product if it were viable, tells us that predictive data mining is not viable. I think that is an important thing to hear from you."

Jonas obliged. "While there's a large market for data mining, I'm suggesting that using data mining to predict the intent of a terrorist, where you're basically putting the finger on a trigger that is going to cause government scrutiny upon an individual, is where I see it as a bit problematic."

He didn't use the name, but Jonas had implicated TIA directly. "I consider my life's work in the area of knowing who is who and who's related to who," he said. But this kind of knowledge had limitations. The chances of finding one meaningful signal in the noise were almost nil. "One in a million things happen millions of times a day," Jonas said. "And bad guys don't leave as many transactional footprints."

Jonas had just turned his back on Poindexter. He declared that no one could detect terrorists by looking for patterns, not without ensnaring many more innocent people than guilty ones. When their paper was published a year later, Jonas and Harper warned against embracing technology. "Though data mining has many valuable uses, it is not well suited to the terrorist discovery problem," they wrote. "It would be unfortunate if data mining for terrorism discovery had currency within national security, law enforcement, and technology circles because pursuing this use of data mining would waste taxpayer dollars, needlessly infringe on privacy and civil liberties, and misdirect the valuable time and energy of the men and women in the national security community."

Poindexter read the paper and found it both flawed and misguided. He objected strenuously to any characterization of TIA as "predictive," and he took pains to tell people why it wasn't "data mining." He knew the difference, though most people didn't. Data mining was something that marketers used to sell more products—more beer and diapers. But Poindexter was chasing a deeper level of insight. He was after patterns and the ability to detect anomalies without any known starting point. He wanted to see the unseen. Not the future, just the present as it truly existed. He thought that Jonas's technology—which was more akin to data mining—was too simplistic. Just like his critique. While Jonas and Harper hadn't singled anyone out, the message was implied. Poindexter's grand vision would never work. The guru of data mining, Jonas, had said so.

The paper was only ten pages long, but it was a watershed. It became a pivot point in the debate over TIA, NSA surveillance, and the whole concept of using data to detect and preempt terrorism. Critics from the left and the right, anyone who'd harbored a grudge against TIA or even a sneaking suspicion that its powers were overstated, seized upon this new theory. Technologists without a dog in the political fight also thought highly of it, and many were inclined to believe Jonas because he was an expert and also had worked with Poindexter. Now he declared that this powerful, mystical, and artful science the man had employed could never do what he imagined.

Poindexter didn't take it personally. He moved on, confident that he could solve the problem eventually.

Jonas's admiration for Poindexter never dimmed. He still considered him a friend, and an unparalleled mind. But they had declared a war of ideas, and there could be no truce.

Elsewhere, a real war was on. And Poindexter's friends, along with his adherents, were arming their weapons.

CHAPTER 27

BOJINKA II

In the summer of 2006, the United Kingdom's warning system was blinking red with indications of new terrorist plots. Home Secretary John Reid, who, like some of his American colleagues, had been accused of exaggerating the danger, declared that Britain faced "probably the most sustained period of severe threat since the end of the Second World War." And most of the sources of this new wave, British officials concluded, traced back to Pakistan. There, in mountainous regions outside the government's reach, Al Qaeda's senior leadership had regrouped, after eluding U.S. forces in Afghanistan years earlier. They had recruited new operatives and were busy plotting more strikes on the West.

That's when twenty-five-year-old Ahmed Abdulla Ali appeared on British security's radar. Agents kept close watch on Ali, whom they feared had connections to the resurging terrorist network in Pakistan. Britain was still reeling from a coordinated bomb attack on its subway and bus lines less than a year earlier, pulled off by Muslim men living in the United Kingdom. Now they worried that Ali, who was born in Britain, had joined the growing ranks of homegrown radicals and could be searching for targets in a brazen new attack.

It wasn't hard under the circumstances to arouse the government's suspicion and for security officials to follow up on it. British law allowed for intrusive and secret surveillance of terrorism suspects as well as for preliminary detention before the government ever brought official charges. In June, after Ali flew back home from a trip to Pakistan, security officials covertly searched his luggage. What they found only heightened the government's concern: a container of powdered Tang, the neon-orange flavored drink, and a large number of batteries. Fine powders could be used as accelerants in bombs, and batteries were a common triggering device.

Officials began a massive surveillance campaign. They followed Ali on foot. They saw him using public phone boxes, mobile phones, and anonymous e-mail accounts. Undercover officers observed Ali as he paid cash for a £138,000 flat in the London borough of Waltham Forest. Then they bugged the apartment with a camera and microphone. On August 3, they watched him and another man construct disturbing-looking devices out of drink bottles. If Ali and his associate were building bombs, they were certainly small ones. Investigators could presume that they were meant to be hidden. Three days later, on August 6, officers followed Ali to an Internet café, and they watched him spend two hours researching airline timetables.

Back in Washington, senior intelligence and security officials had been watching developments across the pond since late June. The Brits had alerted the Americans, and for weeks no one was precisely sure of the suspects' intentions. But by August multiple streams of intelligence had helped bring the plot into sharper relief. Both sides were convinced that they were dealing with a terrorist cell that planned to go after civilian airliners.

Michael Jackson, the deputy secretary of Homeland Security, was used to a daily flow of threat intelligence. It arrived with the ferocity of a fire hose. Each day he and his boss, Michael Chertoff, examined a grid of known and suspected threats displayed as a collection of dots. Each dot represented a person or potential threat that the government was monitoring. It could be a known target of surveillance or a tip from a nosy neighbor about the suspicious guy next door. Sometimes the dots disappeared after a day or two. The target went silent or the tip turned out to be a bogus prank. But occasionally connections formed between the dots, an indication that intelligence had linked them together in some way. And sometimes clusters of dots formed. When that happened, Jackson and Chertoff knew to pay closer attention.

Throughout July Jackson had seen clusters forming with regard to the unfolding plot in Britain. The number of dots would swell and dissipate quickly, sometimes after a few days of probing specific individuals. From his office in Washington, Jackson watched the mass morph over time, and he grew increasingly concerned.

Only a small group at Homeland Security was apprised of the burgeoning plot. Along with Jackson and Chertoff, intelligence chief Charlie Allen and his deputy were aware. On the day that British authorities observed Ali building devices in his apartment, Kip Hawley, the administrator of the Transportation Security Administration, had still not been told. Hawley was in charge of protecting the entire U.S. aviation system. Jackson and Chertoff decided it was time to tap him in.

On Friday, August 4, they asked Fran Townsend to talk to the president. They wanted to tell Hawley to start making plans for protecting the airline system. Townsend had been monitoring the plot from the White House and was keeping the president up to date. John Negroponte, the director of national intelligence, and FBI director Robert Mueller were now involved as well. Negroponte was responsible for making sure all the components of the intelligence agencies worked together in a crisis—as they hadn't before 9/11. And Mueller's agency was the lead counterterrorism force in the United States, responsible for hunting down any terrorist agents and connections to the British suspects. Townsend got the president's go-ahead to tell Hawley. Jackson reached him by phone in California, where he was traveling with a congressional delegation. "I can't explain why, but I need you to get on a plane here tomorrow," Jackson said.

"You need me to take a red-eye?" Hawley asked.

"No, but you must get here by Saturday." Jackson knew Hawley well, and he told him to keep this under his hat. He should return to headquarters and come straight to Jackson's office. "Don't say why," Jackson said.

Hawley arrived the next day, and Jackson let him in on the details of what looked like a massive plot.

Over the past several days, anxiety had been building on the American side. Investigators still weren't clear they'd identified all the players involved in the plot. Jackson worried that the surveillance nets might have missed some operatives. If the Brits moved in to take down Ali, those unknown agents might get wind and move ahead with the bombing on their own. Officials kept the entire investigation compartmentalized. Only those who needed to know were let in. Any leak could blow the operation.

The intelligence agencies had seen a plot like this once before, in the mid-nineties. An Al Qaeda explosives expert had fashioned bombs out of liquid components, batteries, and a simple timing device built with a Casio digital watch. He and a team of operatives planned to assemble their bombs in flight on as many as a dozen trans-Pacific airliners. They would plant the bombs in the life vests under their seats, set the timers, and then get off the plane during a stopover. The aircraft would explode over the ocean simultaneously. Al Qaeda dubbed the plot Bojinka, and it was only disrupted when the bombers accidentally set fire to their apartment in the Philippines where they kept their materials.

Chertoff arrived at headquarters on Saturday and joined Jackson and Hawley. He would brief the president on Monday morning about what looked to be a repeat of Bojinka, and what steps his people were taking to stop it. The three men had to come up with a plan to keep bomb-making equipment, disguised as harmless liquids, off civilian airliners.

Jackson looked around for a laptop computer to start drafting a presentation. But he didn't have a machine handy with the requisite security devices installed to write such a sensitive document. He borrowed a laptop from Charlie Allen, who joined in the conversation. The group took the computer into Jackson's office, which was designated a secure facility, and spent Saturday night and all day Sunday writing a plan to keep liquid bombs off planes.

As soon as British authorities moved in TSA would announce a ban on all liquids and gels carried on to U.S. domestic flights and others bound for America. The prohibition would be just a stopgap. Eventually TSA would have to allow some items into the cabin.

Chertoff met with Bush on Monday morning. That night Jackson and Hawley discussed how to notify the airlines, once British authorities moved in and rolled up the suspected cell. They also prepared for the fallout of the raid—canceled flights, scared passengers, and massive confusion at airports.

Meanwhile, at the White House, Townsend had been trying to learn as much as she could about the suspects. Whom did they know? How were they connected? The NSA had some answers.

The NSA's terrorist surveillance efforts had not alerted U.S. officials to the planes-bombing plot. But once some of the suspects were on their radar, the agency provided new insights that Townsend thought were otherwise unavailable.

Keith Alexander, the NSA director, had been giving daily briefings at the White House that summer, talking about patterns of terrorist activity that analysts thought were important.

The UK plot had taken on such urgency that the president's top terrorism team officials held a weekly meeting in the Oval Office to update him on the situation. The director of national intelligence, the attorney general, the FBI director, Chertoff, and Townsend all chimed in. They called it Terrorism Tuesday.

Townsend could see that the NSA program wasn't going to solve all her problems. Some of the leads turned out to be garbage. In a crisis, that was expected, although the agency did have a reputation for turning out more noise than signals.

Still, Townsend thought the intelligence advanced the government's understanding of the plot. Because of its wide lens the surveillance revealed connections among the suspects that otherwise might have gone unnoticed. As she saw it, the United States could easily monitor calls between person A and person B. But unless the surveillance pulled back and examined the larger patterns of those two people, they might never see person C. And person C, it turned out, could reveal a lot.

Throughout the course of the investigation, Townsend came to rely on this wide-angle tool. The NSA was able to recalibrate when new targets were discovered and start collecting on them too. She believed that the only way to provide deeper insight into opaque terrorist plots was to collect a lot of information. The value of the NSA's analysis depended entirely on how much the agency collected. The program *had* to be big, or it wouldn't pay off.

From the moment she was cleared to know about the program, Townsend decided that if she was the one responsible for preventing an attack she didn't care how much information the agency gathered. The Justice Department, her old home, had said this was legal. She had struck her own balance. Massive surveillance for a modicum of insight—and the hope of more. This was one more tool in the kit. Why would she throw it out?

Jackson had not been read into the surveillance program, but he understood that the daily flow of intelligence coming into Homeland Security emanated from Fort Meade. And, like Townsend, he didn't want to go without it.

In Jackson's view it was as important to find meaningful connections among suspects as it was to find the gaps in his knowledge. He needed to know what he didn't know. And it was essential, he thought, to shake every tree in search of answers. He didn't want to learn *after* the attack that one of the bombers had a brother working in a secured area of the Washington national airport.

As the plot unwound, Jackson could see other clusters of dots on those daily grids. These were people of concern, at least, but Homeland Security officials weren't certain if they were related to one another, or how. The Brits wanted to keep their investigation confidential until the last moment, to ensure that they hadn't left any loose ends. That only added to the tension, and the sense of uncertainty, for Jackson and his colleagues.

Jackson considered it a grave responsibility to look at data and try to decipher it. That was his job. On 9/11 he was the deputy secretary of the Transportation Department, and he became the administration's point man on aviation security. It fell to him to set up the TSA, hiring tens of thousands of new security officers in airports. He lived each day not knowing whether this would be the one on which terrorists boarded planes again.

Jackson was also the government's liaison to the airline industry. After the attacks, on a plane ride home from Atlanta after meeting with the chief executive of Delta Airlines and a group of his employees, Jackson sketched out the first notions of a passenger-profiling system. He'd seen a test version of a data-mining tool in Delta's offices, and he was surprised by technology's power to collect vast amounts of personal information using one start point. Jackson volunteered his Social Security number and watched the tool retrieve his address, the names of his neighbors, his wife's name, and the date they were married, all from publicly available information. Some of the Delta employees had been test subjects already, and when his own personal data started popping up for all to see, Jackson joked that he'd seen enough. But the demo convinced him that the government had to have this capability. Not because he wanted it. But because he was afraid he couldn't do his job without it.

By the time Ali was spotted checking flight schedules at an Internet café the entire United States security apparatus was revving up to its highest alert. From the daily grid of dots, as well as other intelligence sources, Jackson and others could see this was potentially as big a plot as the United States had faced since 9/11.

But the public knew nothing yet. British forces continued monitoring the plotters. And within the Bush administration officials hotly debated whether to continue watching, in the hopes of learning who was directing the cell, and from where, or whether to shut the plan down before the bombers could purchase their tickets and board flights.

Precisely what prompted the Brits to make their move on August 10 would remain a subject of speculation. But early that morning, authorities fanned out and arrested two dozen suspects, including Ali. They found him carrying a blueprint for his alleged plot sketched out in a small, worn diary. On a portable memory stick in his pocket, police found details about airport security procedures and specific airline flights.

It was late at night in Washington. Chertoff's small office suite in upper northwest Washington was packed full of officials from across the department. Hawley and his team were joined by a communications officer, who'd been told to convey news about the liquids ban to the press. The various operational chiefs from across the department swung into play—the heads of border control and customs, as well as intelligence officials, who worked with FBI agents to run to ground any of the cell's connections in the United States.

As the cell was rounded up Jackson and Hawley held a conference call with the CEOs of the airlines that U.S. officials believed were targeted for bombings—American, Continental, and United. They kept the conversation at an unclassified level; no secret intelligence, and everything shared over an unsecured phone line. One of the executives was on vacation in the Caribbean, and he had to go to the other side of the island to find a decent connection. Chertoff and Jackson divided the task of calling key members of Congress, particularly those who ran the department's oversight committees. They woke them up one at a time and told them what was happening across the Atlantic.

The liquids ban would go into effect within hours. Headquarters blasted a message to the TSA officials who ran security at the nation's airports. The department had worked out arrangements with foreign airports to enforce the ban on all flights bound for the United States.

But the total ban would only last so long. Jackson and Hawley had to come up with a more permanent fix, something that would keep airplanes reasonably safe without imposing draconian rules on the flying public and further angering passengers who were already tired of the indignities of airport frisks and opaque security rules.

In the days leading up to the arrests Jackson and Hawley had consulted with explosives experts and tried to come up with an easy-to-remember formula for how much liquid was safe to pack in carry-on luggage. They determined what amount was necessary to build a bomb that could threaten an airplane, and they worked back from there. From now on passengers could carry on containers of liquids and gels measuring three ounces or less. They had to fit everything inside a one-quart plastic bag. And each passenger could bring on only one bag. TSA called the policy "3-1-1."

Jackson and Hawley presented the new rules at a press conference in Reagan National Airport, just outside Washington, in late September. By then the public was aware that an alleged terrorist cell intended to smuggle explosives disguised as juice and sports drinks onto several airliners bound for the United States and Canada.

Investigators believed that Tang—the powdered mix that the Brits had first found in Ali's luggage—was supposed to be used as a base ingredient that when mixed with hydrogen peroxide would form an explosive compound. The bombers would use a syringe to insert the compound into the drink bottles. Then the bombs would ignite with a small electrical pulse from a camera flashbulb. The terrorists planned to detonate the bombs simultaneously, midflight.

The chaos and panic that Homeland Security officials had predicted rippled throughout the aviation system. Flights canceled. Passengers stranded. Prosecutors in the UK later said the alleged terrorists had targeted airliners designed to carry upward of three hundred people each, and that they apparently intended to bomb anywhere from seven to eighteen specific flights. If those numbers were accurate, then at a minimum about sixteen hundred people might have died. If all the suspected flights were taken down, the fatalities could have exceeded five thousand, almost twice the number of people who died on September 11.

But the enormity of the plot was overshadowed by what lay behind it. U.S. and British intelligence officials agreed that the terrorist cell's command and control center was not in the UK, but in a remote, mountainous area of Pakistan. The terror gang that the CIA and U.S. soldiers had attacked in Afghanistan after 9/11 had slipped across the border and now found refuge in lands beyond the control of either country. There they regrouped, rejuvenated, and appointed new leaders. Al Qaeda 2.0 was in business.

After the British tipped off the Americans, the NSA was able to intercept e-mails that Ali sent to an apparent terrorist minder in Pakistan, an Al Qaeda operative named Rashid Rauf. The messages contained cryptic references to a plot, and that alarmed senior Bush administration officials. This seemed like proof that Ali's campaign was being directed from Pakistan. In Townsend's equation, Rauf was like that mysterious person C. And he revealed a lot, indeed. After the discovery of Rauf, U.S. officials leaned on the Brits to roll up the cell before it was too late. But the Americans refused to hand over the e-mails, which had been found on a Yahoo! server in the United States. These were the fruits of secret surveillance. And when Ali eventually went on trial, the British couldn't introduce the e-mails as evidence.

Had the attack succeeded, and been traced back to Al Qaeda in Pakistan, the Bush administration might never have survived the public condemnation. An inescapable narrative would form quickly and show that the nation's leaders were asleep at the watch: Al Qaeda terrorists, who had escaped U.S. military capture five years earlier, were allowed to gather their strength and form new contacts in the lawless regions of Pakistan under the noses of American intelligence officials and their allies. Their attack would have eclipsed 9/11 in scale and ambition, casting doubt on the Bush administration's conduct of a war on terror that had protected neither American lives nor American values.

This image of utter fecklessness would be compounded by the memory of the administration's dismal, at times unconscionable, response to Hurricane Katrina a year earlier.

Three months after the British authorities broke up the alleged cell, Dame Eliza Manningham-Buller, the head of Britain's MI5 security service, announced that officials were aware of nearly thirty active terrorist plots in the country. "These plots often have links back to Al Qaeda in Pakistan," she told an assembly at Queen Mary's College in London, "and through those links, Al Qaeda gives guidance and training to its largely British foot soldiers here on an extensive and growing scale."

A British army, trained by Al Qaeda in Pakistan to kill thousands, had turned its sights on the United States. That they actually had a chance to succeed was as terrifying as the plot itself. For all of the sacrifices of the past five years, all the risky, secret programs, the perilous authorities, and the moments when the government might break under the weight of a relentless war fought in the dark, the airline bombers could simply have gone undetected. Absent a tip, a gut-level suspicion, or a lucky signal, they could have slipped beneath the waves into the noisy depths, only to reappear in a fiery blast.

It took a combination of sophisticated surveillance and classic shoe-leather investigative work to untangle the bombing plot. Cameras, microphones, and the NSA's massive probe of the telecom system were merely tools. Effective though they were, machines could not solve problems without human ingenuity. It was another reminder of the limits of technology.

When the urgency of the moment subsided, some began to question how serious the threat had been. The CIA looked into Homeland Security's claim that the terrorists could bring down the planes with relatively small amounts of explosives. That was impossible, the agency's scientists determined. It would take a lot more material to down a jetliner. The Homeland guys were overreacting.

The seemingly arbitrary nature of the liquids restriction made airport security, already rife with inconveniences, appear even more pointless. And it reinforced the popular belief that the Bush administration was using fear of terrorism as a weapon, ratcheting up the nation's color-coded alert system whenever the public's overall confidence waned or its opposition to policies grew.

But for all that, the plot was still foiled. Luck and detective work might have played a bigger role than secret surveillance and technological wizardry. But who could say for sure? All anyone knew was that the bombs didn't go off. And as far as the U.S. government was concerned, that equaled success.

It was hard to argue that a disaster hadn't been averted. Ali, who denied the breadth of the plot at his trial, nevertheless admitted that he at least planned to set off a bomb in Heathrow Airport. He and two codefendants also admitted to planning a series of small-scale bombings in order to generate publicity for an Internet documentary he was making to protest British foreign policy in Iraq, Afghanistan, and Lebanon. A jury convicted Ali of conspiracy to murder, although they could not reach a conclusion on the major charge in the case, that he'd engaged in a conspiracy to destroy airliners.

Only after a second trial, in 2009, were Ali and two others finally found guilty of that crime. At this trial, NSA's intercepted e-mails were introduced as evidence, and they apparently persuaded the jury. Rauf, the terrorist minder in Pakistan with whom Ali corresponded, had reportedly been killed by a CIA missile strike in November 2008. Just two months later, the Justice Department issued a request for the e-mails with a court in California, where Yahoo! was headquartered. American officials then gave the e-mails to the British. Perhaps with Rauf dead, there was no longer any reason to monitor his e-mail account or to keep the messages secret.

The initial failure to convict Ali and his conspirators on the plane-bombing plot underscored the current of uncertainty that ran through any terrorist investigation. It could be difficult to prove an accusation that seemed so readily supported by the facts. And indeed, officials had falsely accused some people of horrific acts before. In 2004 the FBI incorrectly linked an Oregon attorney, Brandon Mayfield, to the Madrid train bombings that killed nearly two hundred people. And in June 2006, only weeks before the London plot unfolded, U.S. law enforcement officers arrested seven men in Florida on the dubious charge that they were plotting to blow up the Sears Tower. Investigators' own records showed that an FBI undercover operative, posing as an Al

Qaeda member, might have stoked the accused's appetites for violence, and that the men had few means of carrying out their fanciful plan. Two years later, all federal authorities had to show for their case was one acquittal and two mistrials after juries deadlocked. Ultimately, in May 2009, five of the original seven defendants were convicted of providing "material support" to a terrorist organization.

This was the nature of the game. A string of partially completed plays, the occasional fumble. And no one could say for sure who was winning. And where exactly the ball was on the field. When the rare victories came, when the hunters could claim a point, the celebration was ecstatic and fleeting. Though few would have heard it, the echoes of *Achille Lauro* bounced off the White House walls on the morning of August 10. People had worked. The system had worked. Not perfectly, just dependably. Maybe that's what John Poindexter had in mind all along.

But there was one final lesson. A harbinger, really. The UK was the closest thing to a surveillance state in the Western, democratic world. Perhaps no city in the world was more heavily monitored by security cameras than London. Citizens' every steps were recorded and monitored by an army of algorithms, which were in turn overseen by human officers. The cameras had started going up years earlier, after the kidnapping of a British child, a crime that both shocked and angered the public. Now, though, the cameras had been turned on another homegrown problem—immigrant Muslims and their children. Unlike such populations in the United States, who tended to assimilate into American life and culture, these new citizens were highly "disaffected," security officials liked to say, angry at the disparities in wealth and social mobility in a stratified British society. And their ranks were growing. The British had dealt with this kind of insurgency before, in Northern Ireland. There too the fight had been one of national survival, and the tactics and techniques employed far exceeded anything that the United States had ever countenanced in the name of homeland security. The fact was, the UK had established a domestic intelligence society, both in law and in culture. If the British rules applied in the United States it would be as if the CIA had supplanted the FBI. Customary standards of evidence and reasonable suspicion would no longer apply to investigations. You could be followed, bugged, and rounded up because someone *believed* you were up to no good. Given the UK's long history with domestic terrorism, it was perhaps easy to understand their fears of Muslim extremists. But the United States clearly didn't have the same level of homegrown threat. And yet, American intelligence agencies were moving closer to the British model. What would it take to finally tip the balance? In averting the planes' bombing, the United States had avoided more than just another massive attack. It had avoided the answer to that question.

CHAPTER 28

INHERIT THE WINDS

Technology had its limits. And every new battle in the terrorist war offered a palpable reminder of that unassailable fact. But that didn't stop agencies across the government from reaching for a brass ring.

Years after Poindexter had been pushed out at DARPA his system lived on, both in a physical sense and, more powerfully, as an idea. What had started as a research project in the Pentagon's think tank had morphed into operational systems being built on the fly in silos across the government.

Over at the Homeland Security Department officials had launched a new program with a curiously familiar pedigree. They called it ADVISE, for Analysis, Dissemination, Visualization, Insight, and Semantic Enhancement. It was a mouthful, and not especially catchy. Perhaps the program's managers would have had more luck with the original name—the BAG.

Back in early 2003, officials in the new Homeland Department's science and technology directorate went looking for data-mining and visualization tools to assist their counterterrorism mission. Poindexter was going through the wringer at precisely the same time, but the potential for political backlash didn't stop them. In fact, the law establishing the department had specifically required it to field new technologies for identifying terrorist threats within the United States, and it authorized officials to tap the expertise of the national laboratories.

Officials went to Lawrence Livermore, onetime home of Dr. J. C. Smart, father of the BAG and expert on graph theory. That's where they were first turned on to the power of graphing tools, and arguably they were oversold on their potential. Because at the same time that the Homeland Security Department was investigating the BAG, their fellow terrorist hunters at Fort Meade were struggling to make the recalcitrant technology work.

The BAG was simply ill equipped to handle the volume and complexity of information the NSA was dealing with; in technical terms, it could not "scale." But *any* government agency in the terror fight was going to be drowning in data. It was unlikely that the BAG, or tools like it, would solve their problem.

And yet it had been insinuated into other agencies in largely unseen ways. In September 2005 a team that had formed to run Homeland Security's ADVISE program and build a working prototype huddled at the Johns Hopkins Applied Physics Laboratory, in Maryland. There a new center had been created to help guide homeland security research. Steve Dennis, a technology official from Homeland Security, offered up the history of the program. Participants saw a diagram that conveniently illustrated how the work of Dr. Smart, mentioned by name, found its way into the present system's "architecture," or underlying blueprint. Smart's research had been part of an architecture called "Nebraska," which was eventually replaced by an updated version, dubbed "Kansas." This was the current plan that formed the core of ADVISE. (Technology researchers usually recycled one idea into the next and devised a consistent naming pattern to mark the evolution. The same way that Poindexter's team used the names of winds, the ADVISE builders used the names of states.)

The meeting participants saw the BAG labeled on their diagram. A simple flow chart showed it leading out of Nebraska and onto another pair of program names: "KSP" and "NSA Operational System." KSP stood for Knowledge System Prototype, a major initiative under way at the signals agency. The map showed a steady progression: What began at Livermore filtered over to the NSA, and now it had found its way to the Homeland Security Department. Lest there be any confusion about the roots that the department's data system shared with the terror-hunting apparatus at the NSA, the word "ADVISE" on the chart was followed by a big arrow pointing at "NSA Operational System."

The message was clear. *If this stuff was good enough for the NSA—well, it's surely good enough for the Homeland Security Department!* Never mind that the BAG had failed to identify terrorists dependably. The ADVISE team had been sold on the tool already.

Though it was still incomplete, ADVISE was no theoretical concept. So far versions had been deployed in support of four "mission areas" of the Homeland Security Department, including customs and border protection, biological weapons and disease defense, and weapons of mass destruction countermeasures. The fourth area, designed to protect critical infrastructure such as electrical grids, dams, and nuclear reactors, was also using the ADVISE architecture. Known as the Threat and Vulnerability Information System, it included a "threat mapper" that gave counterterrorism analysts a way to depict information geographically across the United States and then search underlying databases of information about possible terrorist actors and agents.

ADVISE's makers still hadn't achieved a system of systems, but that was their ultimate goal. Steve Dennis told the group that day that he was more interested in actual products than data "methodologies." The department had real work to accomplish. The meeting attendees debated whether there were any privacy constraints on information that the Homeland Security Department already had access to, such as immigration records. Toward the end of the discussion someone noted that Poindexter's old TIA network was testing components for the ADVISE system. That was helpful, since the team's approach had been to use "real data." The participants also discussed whether they should engage a red team that ADVISE had put together to help come up with ideas for what kinds of data they should be examining.

Had Poindexter been in the room he might have offered some pointers, since he'd been down all these roads already. ADVISE was the conceptual successor to total information awareness. But it was based on a failed technology, one that the NSA had already tried. The incestuous plot line would have made even the most jaded soap opera writer blush.

Poindexter had trouble keeping up with all the ersatz programs that rode his wake. He was familiar with ADVISE only in passing. He'd heard people mention it but had never looked deeply into the idea. And he was aware of others. The team representing the NSA at the meeting worked on a program run by a technologist named Art Becker, who had started up his own program that looked a lot like Genoa. Becker called his version "Geneva." Poindexter had heard it never amounted to much.

Just as ideas got recycled in the government research community, they also tended not to stay secret for very long. Poindexter had lit a match that even before this government meeting had spread into an untamable fire. It was only a matter of time before it spread beyond the Beltway.

On Wall Street, knowledge was power too. And for as long as anyone could remember, the kind of knowledge that could turn information into money was the province of a special few.

Traders, brokers, and dealers placed their bets on who was up and who was on the way down based on information that they swapped within a closed, elite, and jealously controlled network. Rumors, tips, and insider intelligence were the currency of the would-be Gordon Gekkos and Sherman McCoys. To augment their privileged sources they had high-priced newsletter subscriptions, Bloomberg computer terminals, and a chattering class of fellow pros to help them keep ahead of the masses.

And then one day that network was replaced by a new one. The Internet gave rise to a class of day traders, stock aficionados, and amateur investors. A proliferation of financial news sites rivaled what the rulers of the Street had been trading in person. Suddenly, and unceremoniously, the Masters of the Universe had been supplanted by bloggers.

Joseph Kennedy supposedly had warned that it was time to get out of the market when the shoeshine boy started offering him stock tips. But more than seventy years after the great market crash, Jeff Stewart sensed that this new whirlwind of corporate information was something to be embraced.

Stewart, a serial entrepreneur working in Manhattan, thought that if he could detect subtle changes in the market in real time, he might make a fortune. Conceptually, the idea was straightforward. Vacuum up corporate press releases, earnings reports, newswire stories, anything on the Internet that gave even the slightest hint of change in the status of a particular company. Then use that formerly privileged information to guide an investment strategy. But not for the long term. Just for the day. Maybe even for the minute, if making gains meant reacting on a moment's notice to even the slightest event that could spell big change in a traded company's fortunes.

Stewart wanted to build total information awareness for Wall Street. He was well aware of Poindexter's concept, having read about it in the press.

Technology made the idea doable. The Internet provided the data, so Stewart just had to build the system to vacuum it up and analyze it.

He might see an uptick in blog chatter about a particular product—rumors of a soon-to-be-released new version of the iPod, or an environmentalist backlash against paper products, like Kleenex tissues. If those signals could be tied back to a company, and thus to its stock, an investor could hedge his bets. He might be able to know whether the stock would rise or fall *before* the rest of the market.

That kind of information was golden. And if obtained in an instant, it could mean the difference between huge losses and huge gains. Stewart needed an early-warning system for arbitrage instead of terrorism. Really, were they all that different?

In 2004 he started talking to potential customers in New York, particularly hedge fund managers, who were crawling all over the city at the time. Stewart couldn't walk into a Starbucks without striking up a conversation with one of them, and so he started asking, would you be willing to pay twelve thousand dollars a year for this kind of early-warning and detection system?

He wanted to know if this was a reasonable fee. After a string of them answered yes, Stewart made hedge fund managers his exclusive target customer. He knew they would pay handsomely for anything that gave them the thinnest edge on their competitors.

When the time came to actually build the system, Stewart knew whom to ask. The government. And more specifically, researchers who had worked for the intelligence and national security community, who would know if something like this was feasible or had already been built.

In late 2004 Stewart met with scientists at the Lawrence Livermore lab. He'd been steered to them through his own connections in the New York venture capital set, which were never more than a degree removed from experts in academia and R&D. When Stewart met with the scientists he could see that they had the answers to his questions on the tips of their tongues. Clearly, he thought, they'd already been researching this question of how to harness penetrating insights from massive data. He listened to them, and then he incorporated their ideas into his product.

Stewart called his system Monitor110. He designed a prototype to gather all information about any changes in a company or product and then to display those changes as they happened. It was a hedge fund manager's dream.

Stewart learned that he wasn't the only one interested in monitoring huge data streams. From his conversations with people in the government, he understood that a big department was also interested in taking this approach—over at the Homeland Security Department. They called it "ADVISE."

It didn't surprise him. Stewart knew that the community of people who specialized in this kind of information exploitation was so small that their ideas were bound to cross-pollinate the government and the corporate world. Looking back, he figured that the scientists at the labs, the ones who had contributed to his system, eventually sold their ideas to the government.

Stewart was correct.

Monitor110 earned some favorable media attention as one example of a new, innovative approach to managing information. The financial trade press was abuzz. But inside the intelligence community people knew that Stewart's creation had the same core that the Livermore lab had sold to Homeland Security to build ADVISE. The BAG was at the heart of Monitor110. The government's bad idea had made its way to Wall Street.

They knew about it within the National Security Agency, where technicians referred to "ADVISE/Monitor110," as if it were the same system. The agency had discarded the BAG when it failed to produce much more than hair balls. That helped spur the move to in-memory databases.

Recycled ideas. Recycled baggage. Again, the surveillance narrative had reached new heights of absurd complexity. A failed technology to track down terrorists, which had been ditched by the NSA. Then it was repackaged and sold to the Homeland Security Department, whose core mission was to protect the country against terrorists. Then it leaked out into the private sector, where it was adopted by Wall Street moneymen. But the technology died there too, overwhelmed by the proliferation of noisy data on the Internet, particularly junk spam messages about companies and stocks that ended up clogging Monitor110's output. Years later one would have to wonder if it would have been smart enough to detect the pending meltdown of the global economy, which was set off in part by opaque transactions by the very companies that would have purchased such a system.

Monitor110 wasn't built on the BAG alone. Stewart talked to dozens of technologists, at the labs, in academia, and in the private sector. But to those who knew the BAG's sordid tale, Monitor110 was just another casualty of a long struggle. Stewart was reaching for the same, elusive ring as the NSA and Poindexter.

Monitor110 shut down, and its creator moved on to new pursuits. By the end of 2006 Poindexter had engaged in new ventures too, with Saffron, the associative memory technology making gains in Iraq. He'd eventually pitch it to civilian agencies in government too, including the IRS for tax fraud detection.

Poindexter maintained his close ties with high officials in the administration, particularly those like Fran Townsend, who were on the front lines of the terror war. But he couldn't have predicted that one of his oldest allies, and great fans, was about to take over that war, and to change its course for years to come.

CHAPTER 29

ASCENSION

At the age of sixty-three, with a distinguished Navy career behind him and the rewards of a seven-figure salary ahead, Mike McConnell never expected to find himself in the Oval Office. And yet that's where he spent almost every morning now, as the newly minted director of National Intelligence. In February 2007 the onetime NSA director and retired admiral was sworn in as the president's new spy master, the man George Bush would depend on to bring some professionalism and calm back to the cantankerous intelligence community. Bush was convinced that certain career employees, particularly at the CIA, had tried to sabotage his reelection bid in 2004. Unnamed intelligence officials had leaked accounts of "cooked" intelligence on Iraqi weapons programs and claimed that the White House had relied on dubious reporting to make the case for war. The latter turned out to be true, but the intelligence community was hardly vindicated, since its analysts had relied on those sources in the first place. Porter Goss's leak hunt at the CIA and the firing of Mary McCarthy only deepened the distrust between the president and his spies, and it reinforced the feeling among many career intelligence officials that the Bush administration had politicized intelligence to a dangerous degree.

McConnell was widely seen as a professional and a nonpartisan. But he had been reluctant to return to the fold, having been out of government more than ten years now. The NSA was his last post, and he'd done better than most retired intelligence officers in the private sector. McConnell had twice turned down offers to join the Bush administration—once in July 2006, when director of national intelligence John Negroponte offered him the deputy slot, and then again in September, when McConnell was offered the top job. It was well-known that while the DNI was supposed to be the new chief executive of the spy agencies, the defense secretary still controlled most of the intelligence budget. The statute creating the DNI hadn't vested the office with enough legal leverage to overrule the Pentagon.

Had McConnell decided to return in 2006 he would have had to contend with Donald Rumsfeld, who was presiding over an internecine war with the civilian intelligence agencies. Rumsfeld, long distrustful of the CIA, was setting up a covert human intelligence apparatus that reported through the Defense Department chain of command and not to the agency. The CIA had always run foreign espionage operations, and stories abounded about hard-headed, inexperienced Pentagon spies running amok because they weren't coordinating with CIA station chiefs in foreign capitals. Negroponte had been unable to halt Rumsfeld's advances.

But then, in November 2006, Rumsfeld's star finally burned out. Republicans were dealt a "thumpin'" in the midterm elections, as Bush called it, and Democrats took control of both houses of Congress for the first time in a dozen years. Voters had rebuked the Iraq war, and by extension, Rumsfeld's leadership. He was out. The administration announced it was putting up Robert Gates, an ex–CIA director, to replace him.

On December 23, as McConnell was preparing for the Christmas holiday, his secretary walked into his spacious corner office at Booz Allen Hamilton, about twenty miles outside the capital. "The vice president's on the phone," she said.

"The vice president of what?" McConnell asked.

"The vice president of the United States."

McConnell jumped up and grabbed the phone. "Mr. Vice President! Mike McConnell here."

Dick Cheney got right to the point. "Mike, the president and I want you to consider a nomination to be the next DNI."

Cheney had known McConnell from the first Bush presidency, when then captain McConnell was the intelligence officer for the chairman of the Joint Chiefs of Staff, Colin Powell, and unexpectedly found himself helping to fight a war. When Saddam Hussein amassed forces on Iraq's border with Kuwait, McConnell predicted the invasion almost a day early. But he was an intelligence expert and unfamiliar with ground warfare tactics. He'd never expected to be engaged in combat operations. Nevertheless, McConnell was such a quick study that Powell eventually put him in charge of daily press briefings during Operation Desert Storm. After the war Powell and Cheney, who was the defense secretary, supported McConnell for director of the NSA. It was a three-star position, and McConnell had been promoted only recently to be a one-star admiral. McConnell's patrons ensured that he was bumped up in rank.

McConnell told Cheney he was honored to be considered for the DNI job. But he wanted some time to think about it. He was about to have a big family gathering. Would it be okay to give an answer after Christmas?

"Fine," Cheney said.

When McConnell had polled his friends and his wife the two recent times he was offered an administration job, they'd all had the same advice—*don't* take it. He would have had limited ability to be effective, they said. But this new offer came at an extraordinary moment. McConnell had heard that his longtime friend, retired Air Force general James Clapper, was coming back to the Pentagon as Bob Gates's intelligence chief. Clapper was one of the most seasoned military intelligence officers in the country. He'd run the Defense Intelligence Agency as well as the National-Geospatial Intelligence Agency, a client of Booz Allen that specialized in the production of highly detailed maps and ran a constellation of imagery satellites. McConnell called Clapper, whose nomination hadn't yet been announced. They compared notes. Was this the right time to come back? Could they make a difference, get real work done and put the community back on track? McConnell wondered if he should talk to Gates before he made a decision. "*Absolutely* you need to talk to Gates," Clapper said. "Do you have the number for Cables?"

Cables was a kind of superswitchboard that could connect callers to the defense secretary anywhere in the world. McConnell said he probably had the number somewhere, but Clapper gave it to him so he didn't have to waste any time looking.

McConnell identified himself to the operator as a former NSA director, and said that the administration had offered him the intelligence director's position. "I need to speak to your boss," McConnell said.

Moments later Gates called back from aboard his airplane as he flew out of Baghdad. He already knew that McConnell would be offered the post.

"You're supportive of my nomination?" McConnell asked.

"Yes," Gates replied.

McConnell had a list of goals. He thought that the intelligence culture needed to be reformed for the modern age of asymmetric threats. He wanted to update the key executive order, 12333, to make it clear that the DNI was the new leader of the community and had specific authorities. And McConnell thought that surveillance law needed an overhaul. "If I take the job, will you assist me in getting things done?" he asked. Gates assured McConnell that he would.

That was all he needed to hear. The proverbial stars had aligned. Gates at the Pentagon, ready to help. Clapper coming back. Hayden, a former NSA director and a friend now in charge at the CIA. It was a rare moment to serve, and to put the grown-ups back in charge. McConnell called Steve Hadley, Bush's national security adviser, and accepted the nomination.

Bush made the formal announcement in early January, and McConnell was sworn in six and a half weeks later. The morning of the ceremony, held at the DNI's headquarters on an air base outside downtown Washington, McConnell looked out on a sea of familiar faces. There in the front row was Gates. Hayden sat next to him. Like a lot of intelligence graybeards across Washington on that February morning, they had a reason to smile: One of their own was back in charge.

McConnell spent the first few months on the job getting adjusted to the hours. He was up at four in the morning, usually six days a week, sometimes seven. He held a round of meetings with senior staff, warm-ups for the president's daily intelligence briefing that began around seven or eight o'clock. Bush was unusually demanding. Many of his predecessors had taken their daily briefing from someone lower on the totem pole, leaving the chiefs to focus on the business of actually running their organizations. But Bush liked McConnell with him in the Oval every day, as his emissary and his eyes and ears. McConnell found that in order to focus on the items that had brought him back to government in the first place—the management and reshaping of the intelligence community—he had to work until ten or eleven o'clock each night. But he got up to speed, just as he had during the first Gulf War. McConnell learned to master the dual-hatted nature of the job—president's intelligence chief and CEO of American spy craft.

One day in May 2007, McConnell found himself in the Oval Office once again. It was a packed house, with most of the administration's senior national security leadership present. Bush and Cheney were there, as were Gates, Hadley, Fran Townsend, the NSA director, Keith Alexander, and Treasury Secretary Henry Paulson, among others. The purpose of the meeting was to discuss the growing insurgency in Iraq, which was racking up casualties at an alarming rate. McConnell wanted to get Bush's permission to use a particularly modern weapon on the insurgents, one that he had come to admire and fear.

Information operations, or IO in the parlance of its practitioners, was digital combat, a form of physical and psychological attack. It was something McConnell had become well acquainted with during his four-year tenure at the NSA. He had set up an information warfare unit at the agency to specialize in attacking and manipulating an adversary's computer systems. IO encompassed a range of tactics, including targeted hacking to knock out electrical power stations and command centers; scrambling of vital battlefield communications and coordinates; even the falsification of information in an adversary's own databases. Disinformation, deception, and denial were the tools of this thoroughly modern warfare. Now, more than a decade after he'd helped the NSA perfect the technologies, he wanted to use them in Iraq.

Since the American invasion Iraq was becoming a wireless nation. Cellular phone licenses were among the first contracts issued by the provisional government. McConnell had gone to Iraq the previous month, and he knew that the insurgents had shown remarkable deftness in communicating with disposable mobile phones. They also used the Internet to spread propaganda videos featuring grisly beheadings and footage of roadside bombings. The insurgents' entire campaign to rid Iraq of American forces was supported by an information network. McConnell wanted to penetrate it, and to use it against the insurgency.

McConnell explained the principles of information warfare to the president. There was something called "computer network exploitation." This involved stealing and manipulating an enemy's data, and the NSA traditionally handled that function. Then there were outright "computer network attacks," hacking into a system and disrupting or disabling its ability to function. That also fell to the Defense Department, which commanded a little-publicized task force to conduct what the Pentagon benignly referred to as "global network operations." Taken together these two pillars formed the bulk of offensive operations in cyberspace.

McConnell didn't only explain the tactics of information warfare, he told Bush why they worked. Cyberattacks targeted the devices that were most essential to a nation's survival and prosperity—phones, computers, and data networks—but also systems that ran critical infrastructures over the Internet. Electrical stations, dams, and air traffic control were all vulnerable to electronic attack. The U.S. government and many large corporations knew firsthand what havoc a cyberattack could cause to this interconnected system. Their networks had been penetrated by hackers in the past several years at an alarming rate. Secrets had been stolen. Operations disturbed. Intelligence officials had collected evidence that they believed showed hackers based in China, working on behalf of the People's Liberation Army, had wormed their way into the systems that ran electrical generators and the power grid in the United States. The Iraq insurgency depended on a functioning global information network just as the Americans did. And because the system was vulnerable, so were the insurgents who used it.

Bush was impressed. He gave McConnell the go-ahead to begin an information operation in Iraq, the details of which would remain one of the most closely guarded secrets in the military and intelligence communities. As the plan unfolded in the coming months officials credited it with helping U.S. forces track and kill insurgents by compromising their basic communications tools and, in some instances, turning those tools against them. The information operation was credited as one of the most successful aspects of the "surge" Bush ordered in a last-ditch effort to stave off a civil war.

Bush was impressed by the power of these new tactics, but he was also visibly unnerved by the vulnerabilities that McConnell had just described. If the insurgents were this exposed, what about the United States? These phone systems are vulnerable? the president asked. He pointed to the secure phone that sat on his desk. Someone could hack into *that*?

Bush looked around the room at his trusted advisers. *Well . . . yes,* they appeared to say. McConnell certainly knew that. At the NSA he'd helped develop the techniques for cracking other nations' phones. He turned to the president and said, "If the capability to exploit a communications device exists, we have to assume that our enemies either have it or are trying to develop it."

It was a rude awakening for the commander in chief. Bush, like his predecessors, had never really taken network security seriously because no one had broken through to him as dramatically as McConnell just had. Almost a quarter century had passed since John Poindexter wrote a presidential directive appointing a new official to protect government information, and the system was more vulnerable than ever. McConnell had come into the Oval Office ready to talk about offensive tactics. But suddenly, and quite unexpectedly, he had a rare chance to educate the president about the third and final pillar of information warfare: "computer network defense."

Ever since leaving the NSA in 1996, McConnell had been thinking about how computer attackers, whether nation-states, terrorists, or criminals for hire, could effectively bring down major U.S. infrastructures or corporations. At Booz Allen he had built a cybersecurity practice that paid particular attention to the financial sector. Working with officials from the New York Stock Exchange, McConnell developed a report on network vulnerabilities that might allow hackers to break into major banks and then steal or—worse, he thought—alter data, so that the entire system of trust and assurance upon which the U.S. economy rested would be eviscerated. McConnell delivered the report to the government; officials found it so revealing that they decided to classify it lest it give ambitious hackers any bright ideas.

McConnell could see that the president was ready to hear the worst about how poor America's cyberdefenses really were. He turned to Bush and said, "If the 9/11 perpetrators had focused on a single U.S. bank through cyberattack, and it had been successful, it would have had an order of magnitude greater impact on the U.S. economy than the physical attack."

Bush looked shocked, and he seemed incredulous. He turned to Paulson, the secretary of the treasury and the former chairman and CEO of Goldman Sachs. "Is this true, Hank?" Bush asked. Paulson assured him that it was. In fact, he said, his worst fear at Goldman was that some intruder could manipulate the data of a major financial institution so that no one could be sure it was

accurate. That could utterly destroy trust and confidence upon which the entire U.S. economy depended. (A year and a half later Paulson would preside
over an economic catastrophe that came not at the hands of hackers but of
incautious lenders, borrowers, and bond traders, whose faulty assumptions
about risk and reward nearly caused the financial system to melt down.)

Bush stood up from his chair. "This is our competitive advantage for the
next seventy to a hundred years," he said to the room. "Certainly we have to
do what's necessary to protect it." Bush turned to his intelligence director.
"McConnell, you brought this in here. You've got thirty days to develop a plan.
We'll do another Manhattan Project if we need to."

McConnell had an idea where to start. The Defense Department had managed to secure its internal networks by limiting their connections to the public Internet, down to a mere eighteen gateways, McConnell explained. His old
agency, the NSA, had an "exploit capability" that it used to find malicious
signals emitted by viruses and worms that foreign hackers launched against
computers in the United States. The trick was distinguishing those threatening signals from the harmless information that sped around the globe. The
NSA knew how to find those signals in the noise, he explained. The agency
could start looking for foreign threats to American utilities, electrical stations,
and financial organizations coming through those eighteen gateways used by
the Defense Department and then block them. Cyberanalysts had developed
tools and techniques for warfare that now could be brought to bear for civilian defense. The NSA could work in cooperation with another Defense
Department agency that had statutory authority to protect military networks,
and also with the Homeland Security Department, which was the only department legally allowed to work with U.S. companies and utilities to set up
cyberdefenses. Homeland Security lacked the resident cyberexpertise and
political clout to do the job effectively. The NSA would provide the technical
assistance to the department, McConnell said. As long as the NSA wasn't officially in the lead, and was monitoring attacks coming in from abroad, then
it was operating within its legal limits.

McConnell knew the political dangers and how the headline news of a
bold, new cyberinitiative would play: "NSA spies monitoring U.S. computers
for hackers." The smell test stank already. McConnell believed that despite
Americans' love of spy novels and James Bond movies, they mostly associated

intelligence with duplicity and dirty dealings. And lately they associated it particularly with illegal surveillance. People seemed to think that intelligence was something nice to have in a crisis but not something to sustain, he thought. The Berlin Wall had come down in November 1989, and by the next month Washington was full of talk about a peace dividend. The intelligence budgets were slashed in the 1990s. Staff pruned back. The system had atrophied, McConnell thought. He decided that it was his job to build it back up.

But McConnell also thought that if the administration didn't handle this program delicately, it could backfire. At some point they'd have to face the far more daunting question of how to guard against *domestic* cyberthreats. That would mean rewriting privacy laws and enacting a slew of regulations, and having a public debate that would make the Clipper chip look like an academic discussion. But that was a battle for another day, and maybe another intelligence director.

It took ninety days for McConnell, the White House, and the intelligence community to come up with a plan for the president. Bush signed an executive order giving the NSA the go-ahead to stand guard on the Internet gateways. The plan was eventually dubbed the Comprehensive National Cybersecurity Initiative. Initial estimates pegged the price tag of a full defense system at tens of billions of dollars. A second component called for slashing the number of Internet gateways used by civilian government agencies from more than a thousand down to fifty. From the outset the plan was so ambitious and complex that it was guaranteed to outlast Bush's presidency. It was an unprecedented reach of authority for what McConnell thought was an unprecedented threat. The spy chief truly believed that he had protected the rule of law and the security of the nation. But another fight, one that McConnell had in some ways been preparing for his entire professional life, would finally test the balance between those often competing interests.

McConnell was more familiar than most spies with the Foreign Intelligence Surveillance Act, but he hardly knew the law inside and out. That was because, as director of the NSA, he had rarely used it. Most of the agency's work was directed at foreign targets—non–U.S. persons located overseas. FISA came into play when the government wanted to monitor people inside the country.

The 9/11 attacks had turned that arrangement on its head. McConnell knew from the *New York Times* that his old agency was in new waters. The president's secretive terrorist surveillance program had become a public spectacle, and it had imperiled both the NSA and the administration. As McConnell prepared to return to government, it was his opinion that Bush had not been well served by the framing of the program in its early stages. The more appropriate step, he thought, would have been for administration officials to work with Congress to amend FISA back in 2001, at the same time they were making changes to surveillance rules through the Patriot Act. That sweeping piece of legislation passed with near unanimous agreement in Congress. There was every reason to believe that lawmakers would have been equally accommodating with FISA.

McConnell considered himself a civil libertarian. He grew up in segregated South Carolina, where his father was a union organizer and an outspoken progressive. Black men and women were frequent guests at the McConnells' dinner table, which probably couldn't be said about most of the other families in the neighborhood. And the conversations around that table were filled with the father's advice to the son; how he should be thinking about the world around him, whom he should be emulating. Once, while driving with his dad in Greenville, McConnell looked up at a billboard on the side of the highway: "Impeach Earl Warren," it read.

"Dad, who's Earl Warren?"

"He's the chief justice of the Supreme Court."

"Well, why do they want to impeach him?"

"Because he's for integration."

Throughout the South "wanted" posters of Warren proclaimed him "a dangerous and subversive character" at whose "instigation federal marshals and bayonet-equipped federal troops have been employed to terrorize and intimidate white citizens opposed to his integration decrees." As far as McConnell's father was concerned, the chief justice was probably the kind of man his son should try to be. Courageous. An unapologetic arbiter of the law. As McConnell got older and went off to college, Justice Hugo Black became one of his heroes for his stance on integration, expressed most famously in the unanimous *Brown v. Board of Education* decision. Black was a paradox to McConnell, and an unlikely champion for civil rights. As a young politician in

Alabama, he'd joined the Ku Klux Klan to win votes, and in the Senate he'd participated in filibusters of antilynching bills. But Black eventually disavowed his former affiliations, and on the Court he distinguished himself as a literalist, a strict interpreter of the Constitution and an ardent supporter of the rule of law. That endeared him to McConnell, who prided himself as possessing those same qualities.

McConnell's bedrock values were shaken when, as a young intelligence officer, he had learned that the FBI had secretly tapped the phones of both Warren and Black, under orders from bureau director J. Edgar Hoover. It was a searing experience. McConnell would later tell people that "my community" had spied on two men he admired because of how they thought and what they said. Intelligence was McConnell's trade, but it could be a rotten business. By the time he took over at the NSA, he was well acquainted with the agency's own dark days, as was the nation. For thirty years NSA analysts had received daily copies of international telegrams sent to and from the United States. The covert program, known as Operation Shamrock, was believed to have collected 150,000 messages per month at its peak. The NSA had access to almost all the international telegrams of Americans. In scenes reminiscent of the days after 9/11, representatives from the Army Signals Security Agency, the NSA's predecessor, approached telegraph companies in August 1945 asking for access to their traffic and their facilities. The companies' lawyers advised that such interceptions would be illegal in peacetime, but executives agreed to participate after they received the personal assurances of the attorney general, and later the president, that their participation was in the highest interest of national security, and that the companies would be protected from lawsuits should the secret ever get out. The government told the executives that the program was only monitoring foreign targets, but Americans' communications were routinely swept up and disseminated throughout the intelligence community. Some Americans' names ended up on "watch lists" of political undesirables. The watching didn't stop until 1975, when Shamrock was exposed in a wave of hearings on intelligence abuses, the same hearings that led to the passage of FISA.

McConnell was schooled in these scandals, as were all intelligence officers of his generation. The mistakes of the past formed a kind of baseline for how to conduct operations. Targeting Americans for political purposes was forbidden. When officers said that the intelligence community "didn't spy on Americans," that's usually what they meant. Targeting Americans because they might be terrorists, however, was never out of bounds. FISA had been created to allow such surveillance and to keep it under the rule of law. But after 9/11 the law failed, both as a check on unlimited executive power and as a tool that the government could use to successfully monitor threats. McConnell thought that FISA had to be fixed, as part of a fundamental overhaul of the intelligence community. He outlined his vision in an essay for *Foreign Affairs* magazine. Channeling his former colleague John Poindexter, McConnell declared that the agencies should jettison archaic techniques and laws. The walls that had separated foreign and domestic intelligence were coming down, and now was the time to finish the job. "Sticking rigidly to these historical distinctions would be a serious impediment to protecting U.S. national security," McConnell wrote. He called for more investment in cutting-edge technologies "to access and process vast amounts of digital data to find terrorist-related information." He praised efforts being run by the outfits now under his command that took over TIA. And he took on the unresolved debate over when, and how, to spy on Americans, casting it as an integral part of the intelligence community's evolution. "Another challenge is determining how and when it is appropriate to conduct surveillance of a group of Americans who are, say, influenced by al-Qaeda's jihadist philosophy. On one level, they are U.S. citizens engaging in free speech and associating freely with one another. On another, they could be plotting terrorist attacks that could kill hundreds of people. . . . The intelligence community has an obligation to better identify and counter threats to Americans while still safeguarding their privacy."

As McConnell saw it, amending FISA would be the first and perhaps most important step. The law had been tweaked in the past. But Congress had never undertaken a fundamental revision to bring the law in line with twenty-first-century technology. McConnell wanted a crack at that. But while he was preparing for his confirmation hearings, the administration did an about-face on warrantless surveillance, one that seemed to render the debate over amending FISA moot.

On January 10, 2007, a judge on the secretive FISA Court issued orders that essentially blessed much of what the administration had already been doing under its own authority. Without revealing any technical details of the arrangement, Attorney General Alberto Gonzales wrote to the Judiciary Committee a week later and said that the administration had submitted the program to court review. It was now operating under the supervision and authority of a judge.

Gonzales asserted that as early as the spring of 2005, well before the *New York Times* blew the NSA's cover, the administration had been looking for some way to bring its secret operation before the court and still maintain "the speed and agility necessary to protect the nation from Al Qaeda." Now, Gonzales said, they'd found their solution. Gonzales never mentioned whether the Democrats' recent takeover of Congress might have motivated the administration to move with particular haste, so as to avoid an onslaught of oversight hearings and investigations.

The judge's orders, Gonzales wrote, were "innovative" and "complex." It had taken "considerable time and work" for the administration to come up with an approach that would meet its needs and still pass judicial muster. The White House press secretary acknowledged that the NSA program "pretty much continues." And a senior Justice Department official told reporters that neither the "objectives" nor the "capabilities" of the program had changed because of the judge's orders. Problem solved.

Not quite. Five months later, in May, those innovative orders came up for a planned review, but this time with another judge from the eleven-member panel. And unlike the first judge, who had given the administration the latitude it wanted, this one rejected a significant part of the arrangement that had been struck in January. Specifically, he told the administration that whenever it was monitoring communications passing through a piece of equipment in the United States, regardless of *who* was being targeted, FISA applied. Bush officials were shocked.

The judge had homed in on one of the clearest examples of how outdated the law had become. When FISA was written it didn't envision the global telecom system of 2007, in which much of the world's phone call, e-mail, and other telecom traffic moved over equipment based in the United States. A phone call or an e-mail from Pakistan to Turkey probably wound its way through New York. America was the world's communications hub. That meant the NSA could monitor foreign communications without ever leaving home.

The administration thought it had every right to grab those calls and e-mails without a warrant, as it had been doing under the terrorist surveillance program. And officials had strong arguments in their favor. Some FISA experts, including those who had served in Democratic administrations, had said for years that the capture of purely foreign communications like this didn't require a warrant. But now a judge had found otherwise. And when he issued his new orders, the intelligence community was cut off from what it considered one of its most dependable and useful streams of intelligence.

McConnell went to the Hill. In classified briefings during June and July, he explained the judge's ruling to members of Congress. Sometimes in small meetings, and at least once to a packed house of more than three hundred members, McConnell said that foreign-to-foreign collection in the United States had been stopped. The intelligence harvest had plummeted. To explain how this had happened, McConnell would lay out a map of the world overlaid with red lines representing the "pipes" that moved phone and Internet traffic. They all converged on the United States, forming a thick red mass on both coasts. The country looked like a heart, with arteries trailing off into thin capillaries that fed the globe.

The terrorism early-warning system depended on access to those lines. There was no longer a question in McConnell's mind that FISA had to be fixed immediately. "We're in extremis," he told lawmakers.

The judge had issued a thirty-day stay on his ruling, which bought the administration some time to mount a public campaign. On May 21, McConnell published an op-ed in the *Washington Post*. Without revealing the classified order, he laid out the basic problem: "In a significant number of cases, our intelligence agencies must obtain a court order to monitor the communications of foreigners suspected of terrorist activity who are physically located in other countries."

Had McConnell publicly announced that the intelligence community could no longer monitor a huge portion of international communications, terrorists might have tried to exploit that gap. The debate over fixing FISA never questioned that assumption. But changing the law was never about the narrow question of foreign-to-foreign communications. It was about the balance of power, which, as far as many lawmakers were concerned, the Bush administration had abused. They weren't about to be pressured into a hasty rewrite of the law in the face of dire warnings from the administration. They'd heard this kind of doomsaying before. The administration could always be counted on to exaggerate a threat when it wanted to have its way. The FISA debate was going to move, but slowly.

While the administration cajoled members of Congress, warning that they'd better pass a new law before terrorists struck again, American soldiers fell into the intelligence gap. On May 12, Sunni insurgents attacked an Army unit in central Iraq and captured three men. The NSA set out to locate them by homing in on the insurgents' phone calls. Analysts thought they'd found the signals, but they had a problem: Lawyers determined that since some of those communications appeared to pass through telecom equipment based in the United States, the government needed a warrant to intercept them.

This was McConnell's nightmare. It took three days for intelligence officials and Justice Department lawyers to come to some agreement on what the law allowed them to do. They debated the meaning of key parts of the statute and argued over whether the NSA had the authority to conduct the kinds of surveillance that its analysts felt would help locate the soldiers. Justice decided that Attorney General Gonzales had to personally approve surveillance of the insurgents before the NSA could move in.

FISA imagined scenarios just like this, cases when a life-and-death decision had to be made immediately and without normal approvals. Under the law, an agency could begin emergency surveillance and obtain a warrant a short time later. But the lawyers bickered over whether the agencies had met the necessary predicates. It was clear that while the law might come equipped with certain fail-safes, they were so complex and confusing that even the government's own lawyers couldn't agree on how to use them.

The body of one soldier turned up floating in the Euphrates River eleven days after he disappeared. The remains of the other two weren't found for more than a year. Back at the CIA a senior official involved in counterterrorism operations received a report about the condition of the first soldier's body. His captors had tortured him. He'd been burned, cut, and made to suffer.

It wasn't widely known within Congress that the new problem with foreign collection had imperiled the search for the soldiers. When it finally did become public, some lawmakers were incensed that the shortcomings of the law might have cost the men their lives. But initially, McConnell failed to mention that the lawyers' protracted deliberations had kept the clock running. The law had its problems. But so did the bureaucracy. Only after the DNI's office was forced by Congress to turn over a timeline of the events did the true nature of the breakdown come to light. But by that time McConnell had already burned his bridges with the lawmakers he needed on his side.

Throughout the summer of 2007 the Bush administration pressured lawmakers to reach a compromise on FISA. There was talk of a rise in the number of Al Qaeda threats. A plot against Congress was even detected. Lawmakers were less moved by the administration's cage rattling than by their own impending summer recess. Democrats were the party in power now, and if they left town without bringing legislation to the floor, they'd expose their weakest flank— national security policy—to withering assault from Republicans. The Democrats were already sensitive to claims that they'd gone soft in the war on terror. If there actually were an attack blamed on gaps in FISA, the Democrats might never recover. Republicans had already been hammering them for months to move on various bills. Now was the time, with the recess only days away.

On July 31, the top Republican in the House gave the Democrats an unsubtle push. Minority Leader John Boehner told Fox News that the FISA Court had handed down a ruling that prohibited the intelligence agencies from "listening in to two terrorists in other parts of the world where the communication could come through the United States." The ruling itself was classified, and some Democrats tried to claim a tactical victory by asserting that Boehner had irresponsibly revealed secret information. "John should remember the old adage: Loose lips very much sink ships," said Rahm Emanuel, the chairman of the House Democratic caucus. But plenty of members of Congress had already known about the administration's legal predicament. The difference now was that the rest of the country knew it too. Democrats had another reason to move quickly.

The next day, McConnell and his staff pulled an all-nighter to get ready for a meeting with the Democratic leadership. The spy chief had three basic requirements for the new law. First, any surveillance of a U.S. person would require a warrant from the FISA Court. (No one in Congress was seriously arguing it should be otherwise.) Second, he wanted to solve the problem with foreign collections in the United States, making clear that the government didn't need a warrant to monitor those communications that merely transited American equipment. These first two items were relatively uncontroversial. McConnell's third demand would be harder to meet.

He wanted guarantees that any companies that had participated in the warrantless surveillance program—and any future surveillance under the new law—would be immune from civil prosecutions. There were already more than three dozen civil lawsuits pending against AT&T and some of the country's biggest telecom providers, brought by journalists, activists, and phone company customers who claimed that the telecoms had violated their privacy rights in a broad campaign of illegal spying. McConnell knew that without the companies' participation in surveillance the intelligence community couldn't do its job. As in the mid-1990s, the spies could find themselves out of the wiretapping business if the companies refused to help them.

On the afternoon of August 2, Silvestre Reyes, the Democratic chairman of the House Intelligence Committee, joined the Senate majority leader, Harry Reid, and other top members of the party in the office of House Speaker Nancy Pelosi. They called McConnell on the phone and gave him their terms on new FISA legislation. They were prepared to allow warrantless surveillance, but it must be restricted to terrorism cases, they said. Also, the lawmakers wanted to set up surveillance guidelines that would determine which kinds of communications between a foreigner and a U.S. person needed a warrant. The Democrats believed they were giving the administration the powers it needed to fight terrorism while preserving some measure of oversight and privacy protections for Americans.

McConnell rejected their ideas. He said he wouldn't preclude warrantless surveillance of spies and other foreign threats that didn't fall into the category of "terrorist." The whole point of rewriting FISA was to make the law more permissive, not more restrictive. McConnell rejected the guidelines too. Those were a nonstarter for the same reasons. That provision also bumped against the very premise of the terrorist surveillance program: If a foreign terrorist were communicating with someone inside the United States that communication was of foreign intelligence value. The government didn't need a warrant to target the foreigner, regardless of whom he was talking to.

The Democrats had two choices—fight McConnell and deadlock or leave town without action. It was unlikely that they could marshal enough support for a counterplan, since the more conservative wing of the party, known as the Blue Dogs, was itching to vote and was inclined to give the administration the latitude McConnell said it needed. Reyes and the party leaders dropped the terrorism-only provision and the demand for new guidelines.

McConnell had never led political negotiations at this level with the nation's top lawmakers squaring off against the administration. But here he was. And he was winning. He told the Democrats he'd call back in half an hour with a fresh version of the bill.

In the movie of McConnell's short life in politics, this was the freeze-frame. The spy chief telling lawmakers he'd get right back to them. The Democrats believing that they'd still get a palatable law. But McConnell was never really suited to the role of high-stakes negotiator. He'd always had trouble sticking to a script, something his press aides learned painfully when he talked off the cuff during speeches. McConnell was never the most articulate speaker. He often truncated his sentences, omitting pivotal words that were necessary to complete the thought. Once he told a group of college students about how the intelligence community had beaten its enemies in the cold war: "We have worked to achieve deep penetration of those who wish us harm."

McConnell's remarks were rarely so cringe inducing. Sometimes his words were just indecipherable, as when he told a newspaper reporter about bringing the surveillance program before the FISA Court. "The FISA court ruled presented the program to them and they said the program is what you say it is and it's appropriate and it's legitimate, it's not an issue and was had approval." Sometimes the listener had to run the words back in his own head just to make sure he comprehended what the man meant. McConnell usually got away with this verbal clumsiness by playing up his homespun South Carolina roots and by reaching into a pocketful of colorful anecdotes about his time in the military. But when one was bargaining with the most powerful people in the Congress, who were already on the defensive, every word counted. Even the slightest misunderstanding could poison the entire negotiation and damage a man's reputation.

Hours passed after McConnell hung up with the Democrats. Tired of waiting for his call, they phoned his office. McConnell's assistant said he was on the phone with the White House. That was true, but it was probably too much information given the stakes. She might have stalled some other way. When McConnell finally spoke to the members he said he'd been on the phone with "the other side." That too was an indelicate turn of phrase, and it put the Democrats on edge.

McConnell told them he'd been in combat in Vietnam, he'd been shot at, but that he'd never felt so much pressure in all his life. Years later McConnell would insist that he meant pressure from *Congress*. But Reyes, Reid, and the other Democrats thought he meant the White House. To them it was clear what was going on here. Mike McConnell, the supposedly freethinking, nonpartisan intelligence professional, was really a lackey for Bush and Cheney. That suspicion was confirmed when the Democrats looked at the new bill McConnell had sent over. It bore almost no resemblance to the compromise they thought they had struck earlier in the day. It seemed obvious that the White House had gotten hold of the legislation and changed it.

This new law would give extraordinary power to the attorney general to authorize warrantless surveillance. He would decide whom to monitor and under what circumstances. Decisions that had been the province of a federal judge for almost three decades would now reside with a man that many Democrats believed had lied to Congress. Lawmakers were still smarting from Gonzales's earlier testimony about the surveillance regime, when he hedged his answers and coyly let on that there was more to the "president's program" than what the president had acknowledged. It was unthinkable for the Democrats to give Gonzales carte blanche to monitor the global telecommunications system. Whatever assurances McConnell gave that U.S. persons would have warrant protections looked laughable in light of this new proposal.

McConnell was perplexed. The Democrats seemed to think that he was going to come back with a bill that didn't reflect the administration's positions. He didn't think that he'd agreed to anything during the phone call. But the Democrats believed that McConnell had given them certain assurances. This document he handed them now was a breach of trust.

Was it possible the entire affair was a big misunderstanding? Given the high stakes, the rapid-fire pace, and McConnell's own propensity for impreci-sion, that was entirely plausible. McConnell certainly felt so.

The negotiations broke down before midnight. The congressional recess drew closer. That night McConnell put out a public statement that offered one small concession. The new law would require that the attorney general *and* the DNI sign off on surveillances. But it wasn't much of an olive branch. Congress must "urgently close the gap" in a law that "does not allow us to be effective," he said. The next day President Bush paid a visit to FBI headquar-ters in downtown Washington. After meeting with counterterrorism and se-curity officials, he spoke briefly to reporters and tightened the screws on his opponents. "We've worked hard and in good faith with the Democrats to find a solution, but we are not going to put our national security at risk," he said. "Time is short." The administration had successfully jammed FISA through the opposition. The Democrats were outmaneuvered once again.

On August 4, about twenty top Democrats huddled in the Speaker's office. This time they discussed how to handle a surveillance bill passed by their Senate colleagues the previous evening, before they left town. Dubbed the Protect America Act, it made legal most of what the administration had been doing for years in the shadows. It was the solution that the White House wanted. The Democratic leaders had no power to oppose it. The House voted decisively in favor of the bill, with the Blue Dog contingent making up a sig-nificant number of the yea votes.

To say that the Protect America Act had "updated" FISA, or had "fixed" the law, implied that it was a minor modification. But Congress had given the government unprecedented modern surveillance powers. The intelligence agencies would be able to obtain blanket authorizations—not warrants—to monitor whole groups of people, potentially even whole countries. Rather than review those surveillances on a case-by-case basis, the court would sim-ply confirm that the administration had a reasonable basis to believe that the targets were of foreign intelligence value, and that the surveillance wasn't intended to target Americans. The new law didn't allow warrantless surveil-lance of Americans inside the United States, but that hardly mattered if one were trying to gauge just how much it differed from its predecessor. Thou-sands, potentially hundreds of thousands, of Americans' communications would be swept up as the NSA monitored the global telecom system. The best assurance those people had that their information wouldn't be misused now came from the government agents conducting the surveillance. It was up to them to decide whether the phone call or the e-mail had any "nexus to terrorism." McConnell believed that those agents were good people, honest people. And certainly most of them were. But they were the Watchers. Who was watching them?

The Democrats never forgave McConnell. They'd forever see him as a double dealer. A day after the House passed the bill, Bush signed it into law. Democrats consoled themselves with the knowledge that the war was not finished. The lawmakers inserted a six-month sunset clause, which meant that the Democrats could regroup and come back with a new strategy. However, a little-noticed part of the legislation stated that all surveillances authorized by the attorney general and the DNI were good for *one year*. The law might expire in six months, but the watching would remain in effect, potentially for the rest of the Bush administration.

McConnell might have flubbed his lines, but he'd played his part, to the surprise of some colleagues in the administration. At the FBI and the White House some senior officials viewed him as a terrible choice for FISA point man. Based on their conversations, and their review of his speeches and op-eds, he seemed not to appreciate the difference between foreign and domestic surveillance. They also thought that his critique of FISA was imprecise and incautious. Those who really knew the law backward and forward were unnerved when the White House had put McConnell out there in such a politically charged atmosphere. The administration had done it in part because McConnell was seen as a nonpartisan professional. But he'd handled this delicate task without the tact and aplomb it required. When the Protect America Act came up for renegotiation in six months, who knew whether the Democrats would be so pliant?

Still, even his detractors had to acknowledge that McConnell had gotten the job done. The new law gave the administration exactly what it wanted, and from McConnell's perspective, exactly what the intelligence community needed to keep the country safe. He was convinced that it would also protect Americans' privacy and their civil liberties. The rule of law had finally been restored. His principles were assured.

McConnell was a firm believer in the internal culture of the intelligence community, the overlapping layers of regulations and protocols that kept employees honest. That system had failed in the past, he knew. But more often, it seemed to work. People knew right from wrong.

Perhaps McConnell's biggest victory was forcing Congress to admit something he'd been saying for years: Technology was not an unalloyed good. The nation's enemies had turned it into a weapon. He knew that. John Poindexter knew that. All the Watchers knew, and so did the administration. Now the Congress did too.

McConnell's community had been given an extraordinary power. To decide whom to watch and to record, whose information to process and to store away in secret. And then, maybe one day, they might decide whom to hunt. With that power came an awesome responsibility: to ensure that the system wasn't turned against those it had been set up to serve. This was the responsibility to protect. For the intelligence community, it had always been a balancing act. But never before had the scales been so tilted in its favor.

In the coming months McConnell would be judged again. And for all his perceived deceits, for all the missteps and missed opportunities, he would win. But this time he'd have a surprising ally—a young, liberal senator from Illinois with more ambition than the halls of Congress could hold.

CHAPTER 30

RENEGADE

Senator Barack Obama faced an easy vote. It was February 12, 2008, and his chamber was about to take up the hotly debated question of whether telecom companies that assisted the NSA in warrantless surveillance should be exempt from civil lawsuits. Obama was firmly opposed to any grants of legal immunity. On that score he had sided with a vocal and increasingly influential base of political supporters known as the "Netroots." They were an online community of sorts, a federation of technology-savvy activists and bloggers that had grown up in opposition to the Iraq war. They regarded the NSA program as the epitome of the Bush administration's excesses in the war on terror and had astutely calculated that the administration would use claims of state secrets to stymie lawsuits against the government. Suing the companies instead offered some hope of legal accountability for the NSA's spying.

The Netroots reflected the heart of Obama's presidential campaign, which was organized over the Internet and relied upon the collective muscle of millions of individual supporters and their donations. The Netroots had moved their support to Obama after their favored candidate, Senator John Edwards, dropped out of the presidential race in January 2008. At the time, Obama had faced only one substantial piece of national security legislation—the Protect America Act, which he'd voted against back in August.

As the law's sunset date approached, telecom immunity had become a roadblock to further negotiations. Democrats understood that the civil lawsuits might be their only chance to pry more information about the NSA's surveillance program from the administration, which had steadfastly resisted lawmakers' attempts to obtain Justice Department documents supporting the program's legal rationale. The two sides were locked in a classic Washington pissing contest.

Unlike during the previous summer, Democratic lawmakers in the House were ready to make a stand now. They would let the Protect America Act expire rather than enshrine immunity protection in any new law. They hedged their bets, figuring that the administration would either compromise or sweat them out, in which case they'd hope that a Democrat won election in November. That future president might be more forthcoming with intelligence secrets. Obama sided with his fellow party members, but then he upped the ante. He promised to filibuster any bill that included retroactive immunity for telecom companies. The Netroots, joined by prominent liberal activist groups like MoveOn.org, had rejoiced at these barricade heroics. Obama's uncompromising opposition to immunity lifted him in their esteem, and it burnished his anti-Bush bona fides among the liberal base of the Democratic Party that Obama had to win if he hoped to occupy the White House.

When the Senate waded into the controversy that Tuesday morning in February, Obama's vote was a given. Before lawmakers took up the final bill to replace the Protect America Act, they voted on whether immunity should be a part of it. Obama voted to remove the protections for telecom companies. That put him at odds with the majority of his colleagues, who voted in favor of the provision. The stage was set for a dramatic finish in the House as senators moved on to the full bill.

On that vote, Obama's opposition was also a given. The changes that this new bill proposed for FISA were extraordinary. Just like the Protect America Act, it dramatically expanded the government's surveillance authorities, allowing the intelligence agencies to obtain blanket warrants to monitor entire groups of suspected foreign terrorists and other people whom the government deemed a threat to national security. Americans' phone calls and e-mails undoubtedly would be caught up in the electronic dragnet. Meanwhile, the administration assured skeptics that procedures were in place to protect Americans' identities and to keep anyone involved in "incidental collection" from being unjustly targeted. None of the official talking points had changed.

Voting on the bill opened. But when Obama's turn came, he didn't cast a vote at all. The presidential candidate had left Capitol Hill and hit the campaign trail. Later in the day his aides issued a statement of resolve, saying Obama was proud to stand with "a grassroots movement of Americans who are refusing to let President Bush put protections for special interests ahead of our security and our liberty."

Why had he changed his mind? That wasn't immediately clear. The most obvious reason was a new Republican TV ad launched in the days leading up to the vote. "The terrorist threat to America never expires," a narrator intoned ominously. The spot was reminiscent of the "daisy" ad of the 1960s, which featured a countdown to a nuclear explosion followed by a mushroom cloud. This new ad was aimed directly at Obama and his rival for the Democratic nomination, Senator Hillary Clinton. It warned that if they and their Democratic colleagues allowed the Protect America Act to expire, it would "open a critical gap in our intelligence capabilities." The language could have come straight out of Mike McConnell's press releases. The party of the president, who had once found FISA so cumbersome, now claimed that the law had "become vital to our national security." Democrats were holding up the works, the ad alleged, "siding with trial lawyers" who wanted to sue telecom companies that faithfully helped the government look for terrorists.

McConnell's push had paid off. Passage of a new surveillance law had once again been directly linked to the prevention of terrorism. The Republicans had their opponents in the corner, as was true the previous summer.

Or so it seemed. The Senate passed the bill, but the House called the administration's bluff. Members adjourned for recess and let the Protect America Act expire. It was a rare display of partisan resolve and political gamesmanship. The Democrats had actually held the line. Lawmakers said they'd get to work on a replacement when they returned to Washington, and they reminded their colleagues that surveillance begun under the law actually lasted for one year. There was no rush to fix FISA.

The immunity debate raged. Republicans accused Democrats of weakness. Democrats countered that their opponents were fearmongering. As the predictable drama played out, Obama appeared unmoved. But inside his campaign the candidate's top intelligence adviser was questioning the wisdom—and the basic fairness—of Obama's opposition to immunity. A few weeks after the Senate vote, he went public with those concerns, and put a crack in the candidate's hitherto unyielding resolve.

John Brennan was a CIA lifer, and he'd spent much of his career on the front lines of the terror war. He first came to the Middle East as a student in 1975. He spent two semesters at American University in Cairo, and four years later he entered the clandestine service. Brennan spoke passable Arabic and, in the late 1990s, became the agency's station chief in Riyadh, Saudi Arabia. On his watch, terrorists bombed the Khobar Towers, an eight-story building that the Air Force used as a dormitory. Nineteen service members died in an attack reminiscent of the suicide bombing in Beirut.

A year and a half after the 9/11 attacks CIA director George Tenet personally assigned Brennan to a new job—heading up a counterterrorism center that "fused" intelligence on terrorist plots with information obtained from other sources, including news reports. The Terrorist Threat Integration Center was to be a hub for information from across government, a model that John Poindexter had envisioned when he first set up communications channels with the intelligence community through the White House. Brennan was a systems thinker and an unflappable manager, which endeared him to Poindexter. The two had discussed total information awareness at the CIA, when Poindexter was coming on board at DARPA. Over the years, they remained in touch, sharing ideas and talking shop. Poindexter admired Brennan's professionalism, his nonpartisan commitment to the cause. Brennan left government in 2005 to head up a boutique contractor that worked almost exclusively for the intelligence community. Although he eventually went to work for Obama, Brennan maintained his personal contacts in the Republican administration. Fran Townsend, for one, had been a trusted friend and colleague, and they remained confidants.

Brennan was first introduced to Obama by Tony Lake, a former national security adviser who was helping run the campaign's foreign policy team. Brennan knew Lake from the Clinton administration, when he'd helped Lake prepare for the Senate confirmation hearings for his nomination to be CIA director. Republicans blocked the nomination, and Bill Clinton eventually withdrew it. But Brennan and Lake had clicked. So when Obama needed an intelligence adviser, Lake had an obvious recommendation.

The young senator had been in office only since 2004, and he had no practical experience with the policy and operational issues that Brennan had been immersed in for a quarter century. Brennan knew how to work for a president, and for politicians. He was Clinton's daily intelligence briefer at the White House, and he'd been chief of staff to Tenet, who had mastered the art of pleasing the CIA's political masters like few other directors in the agency's history.

Brennan was the total package. He had the Washington résumé and expertise in counterterrorism, and he wasn't intimidated by the Oval Office. He was a natural choice to help Obama sort out and shape his intelligence policies. But there was one problem.

On the most important political question in the national security domain, the candidate's and the adviser's views differed. Obama was one of the most dependable immunity opponents in the Congress. But Brennan, who'd been at the CIA during the days of warrantless surveillance, and had been privy to the government's most valued intelligence streams as director of the terrorism fusion center, firmly believed that the telecom companies must be protected. On March 3, just weeks after Obama voted against immunity, Brennan gave a wide-ranging interview with *National Journal* about his views on counterterrorism, the future of the intelligence community, and the controversy over surveillance.

"There is this great debate over whether or not the telecom companies should in fact be given immunity for their agreement to provide support and cooperate with the government after 9/11," Brennan said. "I do believe strongly that they should be granted that immunity, because they were told to do so by the appropriate authorities that were operating in a legal context, and so I think that's important. And I know people are concerned about that, but I do believe that's the right thing to do."

There was no gray area there. Brennan believed "strongly" in a position that his candidate was ready to filibuster in the Senate. The "appropriate authorities were operating in a legal context." Alberto Gonzales had said the same thing. So had Mike McConnell. Brennan didn't just say that immunity was the legally sound policy. Or the most politically expedient. It was the "right thing to do." He came at the question with the mind and the heart of a spy. Brennan was a seasoned, clandestine operator. He knew as well as any of his veteran colleagues that without the telecom companies the intelligence community would be lost on a digital sea. They weren't just a resource. They were partners. They were friends. And you didn't abandon your friends.

Brennan wasn't alone in this view. Many former high-ranking intelligence officials had come out in favor of immunity. But they weren't advising Barack Obama. At times in the interview Brennan channeled the critique that Mc-Connell, Poindexter, and Hayden had made for so many years. The intelligence agencies had to be able to collect terrorist signals quickly, he said. "We shouldn't be held hostage to a complicated, globalized information technology structure that puts up obstacles to that timely collection. I think there are some very, very sensible people on both sides of the partisan divide trying to make this happen. And it's unfortunate that it's become embroiled now in a partisan debate in some quarters."

When asked what advice Brennan had for the next president, he suggested that "they need to spend some time learning, understanding what's out there, inventorying those things, and identifying those key issues or priorities that they have—FISA or something else. They need to make sure they do their homework, and it's not just going to be knee-jerk responses."

Brennan's expansive remarks infuriated the Netroots. The liberal-progressive blog ThinkProgress.org posted a link to the interview accompanied by an unflattering picture of Brennan in which he appeared to be snarling. "Brennan makes it clear that he agrees with the Bush administration," the post read. "Obama needs to seriously dump this dude," one reader commented. Others in the Netroots questioned whether the candidate was exerting enough control over his advisers, particularly after the campaign issued a statement in response to Brennan's interview that put the two men at odds: "Senator Obama welcomes a variety of views, but his position on FISA is clear. He and Brennan differ."

Four months passed. The Democrats' resolve to stand tall against telecom immunity and expansive surveillance authorities had withered. On the afternoon of July 9, the Senate took up a bill already passed in the House. Dubbed the FISA Amendments Act, it aimed to fix the surveillance law once and for all, and like its predecessor, it enshrined most of the powers that the Bush administration had sought. The bill included immunity for telecoms, and it gave the government broad authority to monitor communications outside the traditional search warrant process. Sixty-nine senators voted in favor of the bill. Obama was one of them. President Bush signed it into law the next day.

The Democrats had caved, but that wasn't surprising. There'd never been a realistic chance that they'd revert to the 1978 version of FISA. And no one in the party had offered a radical new rewrite of the law. The FISA Amendments Act offered some cosmetic changes that allowed the Democrats to appear as if they'd wrung real concessions from the administration, but in practical terms it wasn't much different from the Protect America Act. The political calculation was all too obvious. As the Senate took up the legislation, Obama was preparing to accept his fellow Democrats' nomination for president at their convention in Denver. They weren't about to hand Republicans a talking point as they headed into their own convention only days later, particularly since those yearlong surveillances begun under the Protect America Act would start expiring at the same time. The more pressing question was why Obama himself had voted for the law.

He'd been preparing for the moment before it arrived. The day the House passed their version, almost three weeks before the Senate, Obama announced that he would be voting for the bill. He called it "a compromise." But it was hard to see how the administration and congressional Republicans hadn't won almost everything they wanted. Obama said the new bill would assert the FISA Court's role in monitoring surveillance. But the court was authorized only to review the government's "targeting procedures," which intelligence officials and the attorney general would use to decide whom to monitor. The judges weren't technical experts. They had to rely on the government's assurances that these massive new surveillances weren't going to inadvertently sweep in people they shouldn't. The bill also gave immunity to the telecoms, so by any definition it was a major departure from Obama's previous position. It also effectively legalized most of what the Bush administration had been doing in the dark since 9/11.

Obama's vote was his first break with the supporters who provided both the organizing energy and much of the money that drove his campaign. It was also the future president's first major split with his own party. Twenty-eight Democrats voted against the bill. Senator Joe Biden, whom Obama would eventually pick for his running mate, was among them. Obama had once been ranked the Senate's "most liberal" member by *National Journal,* the same non-partisan political magazine that interviewed Brennan. That status was now in question. Obama had shown the party faithful that on matters of national security he was willing to pay a high political price in order to preserve executive power. The candidate seemed to be living up to the moniker used by his Secret Service protection detail: Renegade.

When Obama tried to explain his change of heart he sounded more like a president than a junior senator. "The ability to monitor and track individuals who want to attack the United States is a vital counterterrorism tool, and I'm persuaded that it is necessary to keep the American people safe," he said in a statement issued through a campaign Web site. Obama pointed out that the electronic surveillance orders begun almost a year earlier would expire in the summer. To him that posed an unacceptable risk.

Obama tried to assuage the Netroots, who vented their accusations of betrayal into the blogosphere. The candidate threw them some red meat: "Under this compromise legislation, an important tool in the fight against terrorism will continue, but the President's illegal program of warrantless surveillance will be over." Obama failed to mention that after the Bush administration brought the program before the FISA Court in January 2007, the president's program was technically no longer operating outside the law. Other times he tried to make the law appear stronger than it actually was. Six days before the vote Obama wrote an open letter to those who opposed his decision: "As I've said many times, an independent monitor must watch the watchers to prevent abuses and to protect the civil liberties of the American people. This compromise law assures that the FISA court has that responsibility." But even a cursory read of the bill showed that the court's authority was greatly diminished. Unless Obama's standards for oversight had changed, he was exaggerating the bill's strengths.

But it was what Obama actually said rather than what he wrote that revealed why he'd changed his thinking. In a press conference in Chicago on June 25, Obama said that he'd learned something about the NSA's program, something that seemed distinct from matters of law and political positioning: "All the information I've received is that the underlying program itself actually is important and useful to American security." There was only one source from which he could have received an assessment about whether the program was actually important. Only one person advising his campaign had been around the intelligence community long enough to make such a judgment. Only one had been personally aware of the NSA's surveillance program and had been instrumental in keeping it alive. It was John Brennan. He'd been at the CIA when the agency was in charge of preparing detailed "threat assessments" every forty-five days about the risk of terrorist attacks inside the United States. The Bush administration used these documents, known by insiders as "the scary memos," to justify the continued authorization of warrantless electronic surveillance. Two months after Brennan took over the Terrorist Threat Integration Center, it was put in charge of preparing the memos based on intelligence coming in from across the government.

As the dust settled on Obama's FISA vote, it was clear that Brennan had played a decisive role in shaping the candidate's thinking. Obama had acknowledged that his decision wasn't based solely on the legislative debate. He had been told that the program was "useful." If that was the case, it shouldn't be scrapped. These surveillance powers should be protected in law. Obama had seen that "the ability to monitor and track individuals" was a vital tool. Why would he give it up when he was so close to winning the presidency?

Obama called his vote "a close call for me." But it was deliberate and considered. He had picked up the support of the Netroots when he threatened a filibuster. By switching positions and voting for the law, he burnished his credentials with another constituency, one that any future president would need on his side—the intelligence community.

On September 2, Mike McConnell prepared for an unusual intelligence briefing. Most mornings he sat with the president in the Oval Office. Now he'd join the Democratic presidential nominee in Chicago, to give him his first classified glimpse into the terror war.

Intelligence officials had learned that the first year of a new presidency was an especially vulnerable period. The 1993 World Trade Center and the 9/11 attacks both occurred within eight months of a change in administrations. At the time of the first attack Bill Clinton had been in office only thirty-seven days. To help keep either candidate from being taken by surprise, McConnell's office prepared briefings for Obama and McCain, who was set to accept his party's nomination that week. After the election the winner would begin to receive a copy of the President's Daily Brief, the classified document that was delivered to the commander in chief every morning.

Obama had traveled to Iraq and Afghanistan in July to meet with U.S. military commanders. His staff informed McConnell that the first intelligence session shouldn't focus on the wars. Obama wanted to know about terrorist threats to the United States.

McConnell's office had planned to meet with the nominee for one hour. But the briefing stretched another thirty minutes. Obama was fascinated. McConnell and his team of briefers saw a familiar expression, the same one that came over every man this close to the ultimate office. It was a mix of shock at the range of threats and a kind of wonder when he realized what extraordinary capabilities the president had to defend the country. The weight of responsibility etched itself into Obama's face. "Until this point, I've been worried about losing this election," he told McConnell and his colleagues. "After talking to you guys, I'm now worried about winning."

In his inaugural address Obama aimed his rhetorical sights squarely at the former president. "As for our common defense," he said, "we reject as false the choice between our safety and our ideals." It was a bold flourish meant to put some distance between himself and George Bush, who was seated only a few feet away from the inaugural podium.

Two days later Obama issued three executive orders on some of Bush's most controversial war-on-terror programs—the interrogation and detention of terrorist suspects. Opponents of the Bush doctrine would declare that with the stroke of a pen Obama had swept away lawless and shameful policies and returned the rule of law as the guiding principle of national security. Certainly the new commander in chief wanted to appear as if he were charting a new course by ordering an end to harsh interrogation techniques, including the notorious waterboarding, and declaring that the infamous island prison at Guantánamo Bay, Cuba, would be shuttered within a year. But a careful reading of the president's orders revealed far less distance between him and Bush than many wanted to see.

It was true that Obama limited the menu of interrogation techniques to those found only in the *Army Field Manual*, a document that some Bush administration intelligence officials—including Mike Hayden—found overly restrictive. "Violence to life and person," "torture," and "humiliating and degrading treatment" were prohibited. And the CIA was ordered to get out of the secret prisons business and close any remaining black sites.

But Obama also set up a special task force whose mission was to determine whether the interrogation techniques in the *Army Field Manual* gave the intelligence agencies "an appropriate means of acquiring intelligence necessary to protect the nation." In other words, if the manual was too conservative, as some felt, what harsher techniques should be used? Later, Obama's nominee to head the CIA, Leon Panetta, said that if he felt it was necessary to use stronger techniques on a terrorist suspect, he would not hesitate to seek the president's approval.

In August, the White House announced that it was setting up a new multi-agency team dedicated exclusively to the interrogation of so-called high-value terrorists, those who might possess critical intelligence about pending attacks. The FBI would take the lead, a clear indication that the administration favored using the noncoercive interrogation techniques practiced by the bureau over the brutal tactics that the CIA had employed. The team would be restricted to the *Army Field Manual* for now, though Obama's advisers said they should also develop a "scientific research program" to study new techniques and review existing ones.

The interrogation unit would be specially trained and stand ready to deploy anywhere in the world on a moment's notice. But that wasn't its most extraordinary characteristic. While the FBI director would lead the group, it would ultimately report to the National Security Council. Not since the days of Ronald Reagan had the NSC staff so directly taken on the management of a sensitive intelligence operation. Obama was going to keep terrorist interrogation in place, and he was going to keep it close to him.

Obama's order to close Guantánamo Bay also wasn't an emphatic rejection of Bush. It was politically audacious to order the prison shut down without a plan for dealing with the more than two hundred people still held there. But only a few months after he signed the order, Obama faced a revolt by members of his own party, who joined Republicans in Congress in strongly opposing any release of detainees into the United States. Lawmakers unanimously denied any funding for the prison closure until the White House came up with a plan for disposing of the prisoners.

The administration also found that some of the detainees' cases posed extraordinary legal challenges. They couldn't be let go, but they also couldn't be tried in U.S. courts, because some of the evidence against them was gathered through extreme techniques that the Obama administration said amounted to torture. The administration acknowledged that some detainees would have to be tried by military commissions, whose standards of due process differed from those of criminal courts. Bush officials had also opted to use military commissions rather than criminal courts, believing they'd offer a better chance to obtain convictions.

Obama had tried to distance himself from Bush in the first forty-eight hours of his presidency, but by the time his first hundred days were through, the president had become accustomed to a new critique, expressed most regretfully by the leftist base of his party: Real change was an illusion. The new president looked more like the old one every day.

On one cornerstone terrorism policy, however, Obama remained conspicuously silent. There were no executive orders issued on electronic surveillance. No speeches about shutting down the NSA programs or revisiting the policy of telecom immunity that he had come around to supporting. Despite continuing protests from the Netroots, the president showed no inclination to dismantle a set of tools that his predecessor had regarded as the "crown jewel" of America's counterterrorism arsenal.

Only weeks after Obama took office, he faced his first test on the NSA surveillance, which had run off the rails in a fashion that many critics of the "FISA fix" had predicted. During a periodic review of surveillance activities officials discovered that the agency had inadvertently collected the phone calls and e-mails of Americans. This was the very "incidental" collection that some had feared. In the course of monitoring supposedly foreign communications, the NSA had trouble distinguishing which phone numbers and e-mail addresses actually belonged to people in the United States. As a result the agency ended up directly targeting Americans without individual warrants—a basic violation of the new law.

This was not a onetime accident. The "overcollection," as intelligence officials called it, was systemic, and a direct result of the difficulty of knowing for sure where a target was actually located on the globe. Members of Congress were only alerted to the overcollection after it had occurred. And that revealed another troubling aspect of the surveillance regime. The NSA hadn't been trying to hide what happened. Rather, officials apparently discovered the violation only after they checked their surveillance logs. The Watchers had been watching the wrong people and didn't know it.

During his campaign Obama had said that he voted for the dramatic changes to FISA because someone needed to "watch the watchers." But it was unclear who was doing that job. The president had said that that duty fell to the FISA Court. But its members only learned of the infractions when they were told by the Justice Department, following a required review of the logs conducted once every six months. This was the new definition of oversight— a twice yearly checkup and a bill of infractions delivered after the fact.

The review began in the closing days of the Bush administration and carried over into Obama's first term. When officials became aware of the problem, the president issued no public remarks. He wrote no executive orders. Instead, his attorney general ensured that new, undisclosed safeguards were put in place. Then he appeared before the FISA Court, where he asked for and obtained a renewal of the program.

Things became clearer after that. Who was watching the Watchers? They were watching themselves.

EPILOGUE

John Poindexter is a man with few regrets. One might reasonably assume that, having been put through the political wringer twice, he has emerged a hardened cynic. And yet his grueling public ordeals have only made him a sunnier optimist. Perhaps that's because now, as he sails into the twilight of his life, Poindexter doesn't have to look very hard to see the evidence of his handiwork, and the beginnings of a legacy.

This isn't wishful thinking on his part. I have no doubt that his vision of a total information awareness society was not only prescient but accurately reflects where we have arrived as a nation. John Poindexter envisioned a world. Mike Hayden made it a reality. Mike McConnell enshrined it in law. And Barack Obama inherited it. In broad strokes, that's how we got where we are now.

When the news of the NSA's warrantless surveillance program first broke in December 2005, Poindexter was pleased to see that Hayden had been following his advice. He'd recognized that in order to find signals in the noise one had to collect information from far and wide. But Poindexter was deeply disappointed that the NSA had not pursued his ideas for privacy protection. Indeed, subsequent reporting revealed that the agency had rejected a new data-analysis system that had such protection built in because it was too expensive and too technically demanding. Apparently, adding a layer of protection technology increased the complexity of the software and made it less flexible. Poindexter knew it would take leaps of innovation to make a privacy appliance work, which is why he envisioned such work as part of a grand "Manhattan Project" for the information age. One can say Poindexter is wrong about some things, but technical engineering isn't one of them.

And there, I think, lies the national tragedy in the personal story of John Poindexter. If our leaders were truly committed to preventing acts of terrorism, and at the same time really wanted to protect individual privacy, then they should have kept Poindexter right where he was, as the lead visionary and chief proponent of a radical new way of thinking about how to secure people's lives and their rights. They should have closely scrutinized his work, kept it limited to research, and exploited his unparalleled technical expertise and his willingness to court controversy without regard for his political reputation. Our government should have used John Poindexter, if for no other reason than that he was willing to be used. Had that happened, I believe we might have avoided the scenario we're presented with today: a rising surveillance state and the near certainty that, in the wake of another major attack, the debate over how to properly balance the competing interests of security and liberty will simply become academic. There will be no time for deliberation, and our leaders will show little restraint. History tells us this is so.

We no longer live in a world where we can reasonably expect certain personal information to remain private. And we have *never* lived in a country where the government willingly restrains itself from collecting, analyzing, and disseminating information about our lives, our associations, and our thoughts. The intelligence surveillance laws and regulations of the late 1970s were short-lived. They were created in reaction to unquestionable abuses of power, but they began to prove their technical inadequacy in less than a decade. They have also been obsessed with regulating the collection of information rather than how it is used, which is the more important component of the intelligence system. Our elected officials could have rolled up their sleeves and dived into this complicated legal bramble, and we might have been better—and safer—for it. Instead, they have created laws that tilt the balance of power back to where it has usually been in the realm of national security—toward the executive branch, and to the president in particular. We have seen the excesses born of this arrangement. But we have never lived in a time when the government has had such remarkable technological ability to watch its own citizens.

Our government officials know that, and they have put us all on notice. One speech by a seasoned career intelligence official reaffirmed this point for me in a way that few public remarks ever have. In November 2007 Donald Kerr, then the deputy director of national intelligence, spoke about how the spy community was operating in the information age. Kerr had spent much of his career in the technical field and was one of the top CIA officials who met with Poindexter about the total information awareness program in 2003. I found his remarks revealing for two reasons: First, what he said, and second, the fact that so few people noticed.

"Nowadays, when so much correlated data is collected and available—and I'm just talking about profiles on MySpace, Facebook, YouTube here—the set of identifiable features has grown beyond where most of us can comprehend." Traditionally, those "identifiable features" included the fragments of data that were unique to one person—a name, a date of birth, a Social Security number. Now we had to add profile pages, social networks, and personal blogs to the mix. "In our interconnected and wireless world," Kerr said, "anonymity—or the appearance of anonymity—is quickly becoming a thing of the past."

All the information needed to positively identify a person had been made public. "Protecting anonymity isn't a fight that can be won. Anyone that's typed in their name on Google understands that," Kerr declared. That was an astounding admission. Not because Kerr was the first person to say it, but because he was the number two spy in the United States. The ability to positively identify an individual is one of the most important and powerful tools available to an intelligence agency that is in the business of tracking people. And now that tool was available to anyone with an Internet connection. A major shift had occurred. Kerr knew that. "I think people here, at least people close to my age, recognize that those two generations younger than we are have a very different idea of what is essential privacy, what they would wish to protect about their lives and affairs. And so, it's not for us to inflict one size fits all."

Kerr's remarks still stand as the most frank public assessment by the government of where we are in our surveillance state. The meaning of privacy has changed and anonymity no longer exists. The nation should come to terms with that fact. As Kerr made clear, the intelligence community already has.

There's another candid assessment from deep inside the intelligence community that gives us an idea of how far the Watchers have come—and how far they have to go. In September 2006, the five-year anniversary of the 9/11 attacks, the Office of the Director of National Intelligence launched one more program aimed at Poindexter's ultimate goal—a fully integrated, self-teaching "system of systems" for detecting signals of terrorist planning. Quietly, officials spread the word about a plan to lash the old TIA programs into a new model. They called it Tangram, after an old Chinese puzzle that arranges seven geometric pieces into hundreds of distinct figures. The same set of shapes—five triangles, a square, and a parallelogram—can be made to look like a dog, a bird, a steamboat, even a woman pouring tea. It was a fitting metaphor for Poindexter's own narrative: breaking himself into pieces only to reemerge in new forms.

But Tangram was hardly a triumph. A document soliciting technical proposals for the system stated that intelligence agencies hadn't been able to move beyond "guilt by association" as the best indicator of whether someone was, or wasn't, a terrorist. That was an arresting fact. For all the money spent, the hours consumed, for all the programs run in secret and at extraordinary political and social cost, the government was not much better at detecting bad guys than they were on 9/11.

"To date, the predominant approaches have used a guilt-by-association model to derive suspicion scores," the Tangram document stated. "In the cases where we have knowledge of a seed entity in an unknown group, we have been very successful at detecting the entire group. However, in the absence of a known seed entity, how do we score a person if nothing is known about their associates? In such an instance, guilt-by-association fails."

The group running Tangram was the successor to the NSA outfit that inherited Poindexter's programs. This was where cutting-edge terrorism research was being conducted, and even these bright minds had come up short. Hunting terrorists in data was still a clumsy business, built on suspicion. The warnings of Erik Kleinsmith's Able Danger analyst echoed in the Tangram document: "Do you have any idea how many people on the planet would go to jail just because they *knew* somebody bad?"

We cannot truly protect the nation this way. The Watchers know that, which is why they've devoted so much energy to the considerable technical challenge that Poindexter first posed in 2002. But just because it's hard to identify terrorists with data doesn't mean that the government will stop trying. As Kerr's remarks made abundantly clear, the government has no shortage of access to information about people. Our current surveillance laws are engineered to allow the intelligence community to consume huge amounts of data, in the hopes that some of it will prove useful. Again we see that the Watchers have become very good at collecting dots but not at connecting them. When we come to terms with this we can begin to think about what function we want our intelligence agencies to serve in the twenty-first century. Now is the time to have this debate—not after the next assault on the United States. If we can't have an honest discussion and form sensible policy in a time of relative stability, with the last major attack more than eight years behind us, then we will end up making momentous decisions in a moment of panic, just as we did after September 11. In that case, we will all suffer the consequences.

Where are the Watchers now? Of the five principal characters in this story—John Poindexter, Erik Kleinsmith, Jeff Jonas, Mike Hayden, and Mike McConnell—not one has abandoned his life's work. None of them is currently serving in government, but they still exert enormous influence through their personal connections, their business relationships, and the sheer force of their ideas. Each still embodies that dynamic mix of guardian and spy. They have come down on different ends of a political spectrum and enjoy different levels of prominence; but they are still Watchers to the core.

McConnell returned to Booz Allen in early 2009, to the same job and the same corner office. He continues to focus much of his public efforts on cybersecurity, and he still speaks publicly—and off-the-cuff. As of this writing, he has no plans to retire.

Hayden also left government in early 2009, following a last-ditch public relations campaign to stay on as CIA director. In the weeks preceding Obama's inauguration, newspaper stories citing unnamed "senior intelligence officials" warned that the new president would have his hands full with the economic crisis, and so he might want to consider keeping some steady leadership in the intelligence community. Hayden even appeared on the NPR news quiz show *Wait, Wait . . . Don't Tell Me!* and said he'd be happy to stay at his post.

In January 2009, just a few days before Obama took office, Hayden, McConnell, and their Bush administration colleagues won an important victory on the legality of warrantless surveillance. A special appeals court, the Foreign Intelligence Court of Review, publicly announced its decision in a challenge to the Protect America Act, the temporary surveillance law that was enacted in 2007. The government had issued a surveillance order under the PAA to an unidentified telecommunications company, which refused to comply on the grounds that the broad electronic monitoring the government wanted would violate its customers' privacy. It was a clear, and perhaps rare, demonstration of a company's power to push back against the government. Federal officials appealed to the court of review, asking the judges to force the company to comply. The court had met only once in its thirty-year history. That time, it sided with the government and in favor of broader surveillance authorities. This time, it did the same. While not endorsing what the court called "broad-based, indiscriminate executive power," the judges nevertheless ruled that the executive branch is exempt from the Fourth Amendment's warrant requirements in certain circumstances. If surveillance involves national security and the collection of foreign intelligence, then the government need not name the specific places, or people, it wishes to monitor. The court ruled that the bucket-style orders allowed by the Protect America Act—and which were also contained in the law that replaced it—were constitutional. Hayden had always argued this was so, at times questioning whether his detractors had even grasped the meaning of the Fourth Amendment. Shortly after the court's ruling was announced, a reporter asked Hayden what he thought. "My reaction?" he answered. "Duh!"

After leaving the CIA Hayden joined a new consulting firm founded by former Homeland Security secretary Michael Chertoff. Hayden was a vocal critic of Obama's decision to restrict CIA interrogators to the techniques described in the *Army Field Manual,* and he rebuked the president for releasing Justice Department memos that formed the legal foundation of the interrogation program.

Kleinsmith continues to work as an analyst trainer for Lockheed Martin. He is writing a book about intelligence, and he speaks publicly about his experience on the Able Danger program. Like a lot of former intelligence officials, Kleinsmith has seen that the private sector is usually more willing to embrace risky new ideas. He feels that he's making more progress transforming intelligence and educating a new workforce than he ever was as a military officer.

Jonas is now a senior scientist with IBM, where he's working on new concepts for understanding data. He lives in Las Vegas. Though he has become publicly aligned with civil libertarians and privacy activists, he retains professional and personal ties to officials in the intelligence community. A few years ago Jonas threw a cocktail party at a Washington-area hotel to thank his associates in both spheres for their support over the years. People who battled one another for a living seemed drawn together by Jonas's exuberant quirkiness, which was on display as he stood on a chair and gave a rambling but heartfelt toast to his guests.

Poindexter is a source of philosophical gravity in the world of the Watchers. His ideas have had a more far-reaching effect than his technology, but he still devotes much of his energy to Saffron, the firm where he sits on the board of directors. He believes that its "associative memory" technology could revolutionize intelligence analysis, and he continues to pitch the idea to high-level officials in government. A few years ago an identity thief obtained Poindexter's Social Security number, filed a tax return in his name, and obtained his personal stimulus check. Poindexter wrote a letter to a top IRS official arguing that the agency should use Saffron to spot anomalies in the tax system that could expose criminal activity. He also thought that a strong privacy appliance would have protected his personal information. While he still sees counterterrorism as the most obvious application for his ideas, Poindexter has broadened his vision and now thinks a TIA system could reduce online crime, assist genetic researchers looking for cures to complex diseases, and maybe even do something about rush-hour traffic.

That dream has attracted followers in other countries. The government of Singapore hired Poindexter as a special consultant to a project based on TIA called Risk Assessment and Horizon Scanning. Officials in the tiny island nation, known for its curious blend of democracy and authoritarianism, first met Poindexter in 2003, when the deadly SARS virus sweeping through Asia took Singaporean officials by surprise. They intend to scan the horizon for signals of the next crisis, and Poindexter has helped them, making a number of trips to Singapore in recent years.

He looks back fondly on his second career in government, but he retains a bitter humor about the experience. Before he left DARPA, Poindexter's colleagues signed and framed a copy of the Information Awareness Office logo. It now hangs on the wall of his family room, along with his other prized memorabilia—photos of him and Reagan, and a painting of USS *England,* the cruiser he commanded in the midseventies. But in the workshop in his basement, where he kept that primitive laptop computer during his White House days, Poindexter has hung a second version of the now infamous logo. This one replaces the open eye on the pyramid with a closed eye, and the globe with a yellow smiley face. In place of the Latin *Scientia est potentia,* it reads "*Ignorantia est beatitis*"—Ignorance is bliss.

Poindexter continues to keep close ties to current and former national security officials. In late 2007, Steve Hadley invited all the living former national security advisers to a private dinner at Blair House, across the street from the White House. It was an extraordinary gathering. Poindexter reminisced with Colin Powell, Condoleezza Rice, Henry Kissinger, and Tony Lake, among others. Everyone in that room, Republican and Democrat, had had their brush with scandal or a moment in time they might prefer to forget. But that night they were a club, and in some way, I suppose, a family. Poindexter may well go down in infamy. But in that tiny circle of presidential advisers, he will always hold a position of esteem.

In the highest reaches of the intelligence community, and particularly among the career class of the national security bureaucracy, Poindexter is still revered as a wise man. Those who've known him well enough to form an opinion generally size him up this way: "He's one of the most brilliant people I've ever met, but he has a tin ear for politics." They say that with a tinge of admiration. Poindexter is one of the few people on the national stage willing to charge headlong into controversy. He courts disaster at every step and yet remains undeterred. He says what he thinks. He does what he thinks is right. These are rare qualities in Washington.

Many times over the course of our interviews, Poindexter told me that despite what people say, he does understand politics; he just chooses not to play it. The fact that he recognizes politics is a game and yet believes that he is somehow exempt from participation tells me that he does have that tin ear. Poindexter is many things. He's a brilliant man. He's an honest man, despite his deceptions in the Iran-Contra affair, for which I believe he has more than paid his debts. And he is a wise man. But he is not, and never has been, bigger than "the system."

Several years ago, not long after I first met Poindexter, I sent him a note to ask if it was accurate to write that he "spends his retirement enjoying his sailboat and thinking of new ways to improve the craft of intelligence." I wanted to write words to that effect in a story. He replied yes, that was true, but he was also "trying to change the world." It was a shocking moment of candor, and I nearly blushed because it seemed so naive. Had someone of his stature, of his hardened experience, really said something so grandiose? The professional skeptic in me dismissed it as an attempt to burnish his own image. But the more I got to know Poindexter, I realized that this was one of the most honest and personal things he'd ever told me. I still think that.

ACKNOWLEDGMENTS

This book would not have been written without the unceasing devotion of two people, whom I am proud and grateful to call friends.

There is my agent and advocate, Tina Bennett. Throughout this journey she has been my guide, my clear-eyed adviser, and my partner. On top of all that, she was as excited as I was about every step along the way. She reassures me with her judgment and enlightens me with her counsel. Tina, my self and this book are better because of you.

And there's my editor, Eamon Dolan. I trusted him with every fragile idea, every midnight notion, and every tiny triumph. The future of storytelling is brighter and more assured because of his presence and his incomparable judgment. Eamon, this book is as much a result of your energy as mine. We started this trip as writer and editor. As blissful as the journey has been, I am happier that we ended it as friends.

I tip my hat as well to Tina and Eamon's able colleagues, Svetlana Katz and Nicole Hughes. Each shepherded this book—and me—through the subtle mechanics of writing and publication. People had told me this was an intimidating process. They obviously didn't have the benefit of these women's guidance. Thanks also to Rachel Burd, who's elegant copyediting improved the manuscript.

I am also indebted to another pair of editors who have overseen my work at two magazines. There's my mentor, Anne Laurent, who first allowed me to write narrative nonfiction. Years ago, she grabbed me by the collar and demanded that I start telling stories on the pages of her magazine, *Government Executive*. She will find her fingerprints on every page of this book, and on great pieces of my life. I also thank my editor at *National Journal*, Patrick Pexton, who gave me the encouragement, the space, and the often unseen support that allowed me to flesh out the essential pieces of this book. He was a tireless supporter of my work, and often its fiercest advocate.

I am fortunate to have two best friends, both arbiters of taste and judgment, who influenced this book in distinct ways. Dave Singleton talked me through each stage of the writing as only a fellow writer can. And Christopher Kerns challenged all of my assumptions and made me a sharper, better thinker.

Katherine Mangu-Ward and Garrett Graff read my manuscript closely, and they offered crucial insights that changed and improved the story. They are also dear friends and luminaries in the next generation of American journalism.

Noah Shachtman and Patrick Radden Keefe provided professional support and friendship. Heidi Hill was invaluable in the early stages of writing my book proposal. I also thank Tim Naftali, an energetic and insightful sharer of bylines and a keen adviser on publishing, and Pam Simmons, who gave me my first break.

My career was fostered and accelerated by a core of men and women, each of whom I've been happy to call boss: Anne Jordan, Elder Witt, Tom Shoop, Tim Clark, Charlie Green, John Fox Sullivan, and David Bradley. Journalism is stronger because of their efforts, which often defy the odds.

Certain friends and colleagues in particular have enriched my life and this book. Alexis Simendinger was an undying source of good humor in the workplace, and equally of trenchant insight. Kirk Victor's perseverance uplifted me on numerous occasions. I'm also indebted to a few close friends and writers who have influenced my work in ways that took years for me to realize: Matt Crenshaw, James Buescher, Mary Dalton, and Kristen Eppley and Jenny Harrison Bunn, the two most constant friends I've ever known.

I offer insufficient thanks to the people who brought me here: my father, Ed Harris, and my mother, Carolyn Harris. Whoever I am, whatever I have done, none of it was possible without you. This is a debt I cannot repay. I can only live by your example.

And finally, there is Joe de Feo, my partner in life and my light. You listened to me talk for two years about other people's lives, but you reminded me that ours was the most important. You are the sharpest mind, the best writer, and the most loyal man I have ever known. You are my watcher.

NOTES

First and foremost, this book is a story. A true story. I have written journalism for the past decade, but I wanted to depart from the conventional style of writing used in magazines and newspapers and create a new narrative here. The reader will discern that stylistically this book has more in common with a novel than it does with reportage.

And yet, that is precisely what informs this book—my years of reporting and writing about intelligence, security, and technology for several magazines. It would have been impossible to write with the authority and insight that a narrative demands had I not come to it with this rich background and the tools of a journalist. While it took me a year to write this book, I spent about eight years researching and reporting it.

Everything the reader finds in these pages is attributable to a person or group of people, and was gleaned from interviews, firsthand reporting, official transcripts, government reports, studies, news articles, books, and other documents. Broadly speaking the sources can be divided into two categories. First, there are the hundreds, perhaps more than a thousand, interviews I have conducted over the years with government officials (at the lowest to the highest levels), corporate executives, lawmakers, congressional staff, experts, academics, technologists, and writers. It would be practically unfeasible, and not terribly informative, to list everyone I've ever talked to about the subjects detailed in this book. And yet those interviews form the basis of my knowledge on those subjects. Additionally, I have likely read tens of thousands of pages of materials over the years, from textbooks to trade press, government audits to confidential documents. They too shaped my understanding and this story.

The second category is narrower but still voluminous. These are the interviews with people identified in this book and with those who worked in the agencies, industries, and organizations in the story. Many of them agreed to be quoted on the record, and in those cases I have listed in these endnotes which people were the source of particular passages and chapters. Many of these people sat down with me for multiple interviews, each of which usually lasted from an hour and a half to three hours. I recorded most of them and took detailed notes. I had also interviewed many of these people before, either about the topics in the book or other matters. I interviewed them again specifically for this project so that they could elaborate, and so that I had the freshest recollections possible. Also, I often went back to the sources to verify the accuracy of a particular quote as well as my summary of what they said and did.

In some cases people spoke with me on the condition that I not use their name or identify them by the place they work. It's always regrettable to have to quote sources on background, or anonymously, but it is a fact of the intelligence beat that many of the most informed and influential people often can't speak openly without fear of reprisal, embarrassment, or even prosecution. I have respected their wishes, verified their statements to the best of my ability, and in these notes I have aimed to give the reader a sense of who some of these people are and how they know what they do.

I have also cited key documents in these endnotes, many of which are publicly available. I kept these references limited to those works that bear directly on the words in the story or that help amplify them.

PROLOGUE

Erik Kleinsmith's account of his work on Able Danger, as well as his destruction of data and analysis derived from the program, comes from a series of interviews I conducted with him in 2005 and 2008. Kleinsmith also testified before the Senate Judiciary Committee on September 21, 2005, and then before a joint hearing of two House Armed Services subcommittees on February 15, 2006. His account is also detailed in the Defense Department inspector general's report on Able Danger, "Alleged Misconduct by Senior DoD Officials Concerning the Able Danger Program and Lieutenant Colonel Anthony A. Shaffer, U.S. Army Reserve," case number H05L97905217, dated September 18, 2006. This report was another valuable resource in reconstructing the events of Able Danger.

9 *the IDC's main floor, which had been designed by a Hollywood visual effects artist:* The designer, Bran Ferren, is a renowned three-time Academy Award winner, former Walt Disney "Imagineer," and founder of the idea lab Applied Minds. He has also served on the National Security Agency Advisory Board and the Army Science Board, and was an adviser to the Senate Intelligence Committee. Descriptions of the IDC were provided by Kleinsmith and former employees I interviewed.

9 *Kleinsmith and his team had uncovered a potential spy network in the United States:* The work on Chinese industrial espionage is detailed in Chapter 8 and comes from interviews with Kleinsmith, former IDC employees, former deputy defense secretary John Hamre, and the Defense Department inspector general's report on Able Danger.

11 *Few outside Kleinsmith's chain of command knew what he had discovered about terrorists in America, or what secrets he and his analysts had stored in their data banks:* The DoD inspector general's report makes clear that Able Danger was known only to a small number of officials. The commission set up to investigate the 2001 terrorist attacks was made aware of Able Danger in the closing days of its work but did not choose to include the program in the final report.

CHAPTER 1: FIRST STRIKE

Accounts of life at the Marine base, and the details of the suicide bombing on the Battalion Landing Team headquarters, come principally from two sources: first, interviews conducted with Marines who served in Beirut (Alan Opra, Bob Jordan, Joe Golebiowski, and especially Glen Dolphin); second, the "Report of the DoD Commission on Beirut International Airport Terrorist Act," published on December 20, 1983. It contains a richly detailed map of the Marine compound and description of the BLT, as well as numerous eyewitness interviews. Other valuable information came from interviews with John Lehman, then the secretary of the navy, and Philip Dur, who was the director of political-military affairs for the Middle East on the National Security Council staff.

15 *He turned, and he thought for a moment, "What's that truck doing inside the perimeter?":* The unnamed guard's account is contained in the DoD commission report.

16 *Alan Soiffert, a twenty-five-year-old staff sergeant from Nashua, New Hampshire, had taken a sniper round in the chest as he patrolled the airport perimeter in his Jeep:* The account of Soiffert's death came from an interview with Bob Jordan. It is also chronicled in a *Time* magazine article, "In the Crossfire," which was published on October 24, 1983, one day after the bombing. It must have been written and filed earlier, because it makes no mention of the suicide attack.

19 *The entire structure rose into the air:* The vivid details of the explosion and the BLT's destruction come from eyewitness statements contained in the DoD commission report. Forensic explosives experts also examined the blast site, and the report contains their findings.

20 *The ring of the secure phone at his home in suburban Maryland summoned Admiral John Poindexter from slumber:* Poindexter's account of the morning of the bombing, and what he did and thought afterward, come from interviews conducted in 2008. These occurred in his home. He showed me the space in his basement where he used to keep his office.

20 *The Situation Room would raise McFarlane on a secure phone, and then he'd have to trot across the dark links to Reagan's cottage, wake him, and impart the dreadful news:* Poindexter recalled that the White House reached McFarlane this way, and the account of his meeting with Reagan is detailed in Robert Timberg's epic book, *The Nightingale's Song* (New York: Simon & Schuster, 1995). I am indebted to this masterful work, and its author, for extraordinary guidance.

21 *McFarlane assumed the political aspects of the job, advising the president and working with Congress, a task that Poindexter was happy to avoid:* This and other reflections by Poindexter about his work on the National Security Council staff, which appear throughout this book, came from interviews in 2004 and 2008. The interviews usually covered events in chronological order, but it was common for Poindexter to jump back in time to a previous event that shed light on the current discussion.

21 *He liked the staff, and they respected him:* This much was clear from interviews with Poindexter's former colleagues, including Phil Dur. Timberg has the same assessment in *The Nightingale's Song.*

24 *Since May, U.S. intelligence agencies had received more than one hundred warnings of car bombs in Lebanon":* DoD commission report.

24 *FBI forensic investigators discovered that the bombers had laden their explosives with ordinary pressurized gas bottles, which magnified the force of the blast:* Ibid.

24 *The National Security Agency . . . snatched a message from the Iranian Ministry of Information and Security to the Iranian ambassador in Syria:* The details of this intelligence failure came out in the course of a lawsuit brought against the government of Iran by family members of some Marines who died in the suicide attack, and also by survivors. In September 2007 U.S. District Court judge Royce Lamberth decided the case in favor of the plaintiffs and ordered Iran to pay more than $2.6 billion.

25 *Hussein Musawi, the head of an Islamic terrorist group called Amal:* For more on Musawi, see Robin Wright's *Sacred Rage: The Wrath of Militant Islam* (New York: Simon & Schuster, 1985). Also see Robert Baer's *See No Evil: The True Story of a Ground Soldier in the CIA's War on Terrorism* (New York: Crown, 2002).

CHAPTER 2: KNOWLEDGE IS POWER

The account of Poindexter's early days at sea come from a 2008 interview, as well as *The Nightingale's Song* (Robert Timberg, New York: Simon & Schuster, 1995). Decades later Poindexter used the analogy of antisubmarine warfare to describe his theories about detecting warning signals of a terrorist plot. I thought it was instructive to use this period of his life to illustrate that concept in vivid fashion. The application of the word "goblin" to terrorists is entirely my own invention, and is meant to draw attention to both the phantom nature of the threat and the artful science Poindexter and others have applied against it.

In this chapter, accounts of how various National Security Council staff working groups functioned are derived mainly from the following sources: interviews with Poindexter; Tim Naftali's *Blindspot: The Secret History of American Counterterrorism* (New York: Basic Books, 2005); and presidential orders and directives published by the National Security Archive and the Federation of American Scientists, both in Washington, D.C., at www.gwu.edu/~nsarchiv/nsa/publications/presidentusa/presidential.html, and www.fas.org/irp/offdocs/nsdd/index.html.

Unless otherwise noted, all statements, thoughts, and actions attributed to Poindexter come from interviews.

28 *You've got all sorts of noises down there in that jungle:* Thach's description of life under the sea appeared in *Time* magazine on April 7, 1958, under the headline "Antisubmarine Boss."

29 *Oliver North . . . walked into Poindexter's tiny West Wing office carrying a stack of photographs snapped by orbiting satellites:* Interview with Poindexter. Details of the satellite photographs also came from interviews conducted in 2008 with John Lehman and Charlie Allen when the latter was serving as the top intelligence official at the Homeland Security Department.

29 *Defense Secretary Caspar Weinberger scuttled the U.S. raid moments before the planes were set to launch:* This is a matter of extraordinary historical significance, and controversy, and it deserves more attention than I can provide here. But briefly, it is known that Weinberger called off the U.S. raid inasmuch as he never gave a final order to launch U.S. aircraft. What is still open to question is why he did that, and precisely what Weinberger knew of the raid before it began. In my reporting I relied especially on four excellent books to get a firm answer: *The Nightingale's Song;* David Martin and John Walcott's often cited *Best Laid Plans: The Inside Story of America's War Against Terrorism* (New York: HarperCollins, 1988); Naftali's *Blindspot: The Secret History of American Counterterrorism;* and my *National Journal* colleague George

Wilson's adventurous account of life aboard a U.S. aircraft carrier, *Supercarrier* (New York: Macmillan, 1986).

I also spoke with Poindexter extensively about the aborted raid. I conclude that Weinberger knew that a joint raid was planned with the French and that he knew President Reagan wanted to move ahead with it. Former NSC staff officials have told me and other journalists that Weinberger was present for a meeting in which Reagan made clear he wanted to launch a retaliatory strike if the intelligence community could determine who was responsible for the Beirut bombing. Based on my interviews with officials, principally Poindexter, Charlie Allen, and later Frances Townsend, I have no doubt that the intelligence community believed with as close to certainty as possible in the trade that the culprits resided at the Sheikh Abdullah barracks.

The subsequent revelations in the civil trial against the government of Iran bolster that conclusion. In his memoir Weinberger said that he only learned about the raid when his French counterpart called him the morning of the attack to ask whether U.S. Navy jets would be taking part. Weinberger claimed that this was the first he'd heard of any raid. But Weinberger offers no evidence to counter the assertions made by several former Reagan administration officials—in the books I cite here and in other venues—that he knew about the raid and was present at meetings when the president said he wanted to strike. It is also inconceivable to me, despite the disorganization that marked the Reagan White House in 1983, that the secretary of defense and one of the president's closest aides would not know about such a significant operation.

It is my opinion, shared by a former NSC staff official who asked to remain anonymous but who provided independent corroboration of what I learned from interviews and research, that Weinberger intervened to stop the raid because he feared broader U.S. military engagement in the Middle East. While that was an understandable concern—and not a small one—I fail to see what authority Weinberger could have to countermand the expressed wishes of the president.

In his memoir Reagan said that he called off the attack at the last minute, after changing his mind. As Naftali observes, "If he did, then he told only Weinberger and left McFarlane and Poindexter in the dark." Naftali also interviewed Poindexter, who said that the president looked surprised when McFarlane informed him that the defense secretary "had canceled the air strike." Poindexter told me the same thing in an interview. If Weinberger and Reagan came to some new agreement about the raid in private, which is possible, then both men took the details to their graves.

30 *North replied that his CIA contact on terrorism, Charlie Allen, had just brought them to his attention:* Interview with Poindexter, confirmed by Charlie Allen.

31 *Poindexter called up his friend CIA director Bill Casey. The two had developed an honest rapport:* The fateful relationship of Poindexter and Casey nearly merits a book of its own. Both men can rightly be called architects of the Iran-Contra affair, and they exerted tremendous influence on the foreign policy of the Reagan administration. Their legacies are intertwined. Casey, who died in 1987, is one of the oddest and most mysterious directors of central intelligence I've ever encountered. His portrait is perhaps best captured in Bob Woodward's riveting account of the CIA in the 1980s, *Veil* (New York: Simon & Schuster, 1987). In an interview, Poindexter told me the story of how he and Casey first came to be on close terms, and it's worth retelling here because it illuminates the characters of both men.

The early part of their relationship was cool and distant. After Poindexter became the deputy national security adviser, he let it be known within the White House that he thought Casey should resign. He said that the CIA was doing a terrible job managing a covert program to aid Contra rebels fighting the socialist government of Nicaragua. A CIA document, known as the "Freedom Fighter's Manual," had leaked to the press; it used cartoon illustrations and simple language to teach average Nicaraguans how to disrupt their government through sabotage and organized violence or by passively combating nationalized industries. (One panel showed a smiling man with dark hair and a mustache, his bare feet propped up on an ottoman, holding a glass of champagne while calling in sick to work.)

Casey found out that Poindexter had spoken poorly of his leadership, and one afternoon he called the admiral in his White House office and requested a private audience. Under direct questioning from Casey, Poindexter repeated what he'd said. He told Casey that the manual was an embarrassment to the administration. He also said that Casey appeared ill, and he noted that the director had been missing a lot of meetings lately.

Casey wasn't Poindexter's boss, but he had every right to chew him up one side and down the other for what he'd said. Instead Casey confided to Poindexter that he had cancer and that when he was away it was because he'd gone to New York to receive treatment. Poindexter never again called for Casey to step aside. "In the future," Casey told him, "if you think I'm not doing something right, just give me a call."

"Yes, sir, I'll do that," Poindexter replied.

32 *Bush led a top-to-bottom review of the government's haphazard counterterrorism and intelligence efforts:* The review, titled "Public Report of the Vice President's Task Force on Combating Terrorism," was published in February 1986. The document contains a helpful chronology of "significant 1985 terrorist events involving U.S. citizens," which gives a good sense of how the Reagan administration viewed the burgeoning antiterrorism campaign.

34 *North had felt overwhelmed when he arrived at the White House:* See Timberg's *The Nightingale's Song,* as well as North's memoir, *Under Fire: An American Story,* cowritten with William Novak (New York: HarperCollins, 1991).

34 *Poindexter knew that North exaggerated his own influence on the NSC staff:* Poindexter's recollections of North come from interviews conducted in 2004 and 2008.

CHAPTER 3: AND HE SHALL PURIFY

Without question, the best and most compelling account of the *Achille Lauro* affair that I encountered was written by Michael Bohn, a former director of the Situation Room and a retired naval intelligence officer. *The* Achille Lauro *Hijacking: Lessons in the Politics and the Prejudice of Terrorism* (Dulles, Va.: Brassey's, 2004) seamlessly weaves Bohn's personal experience working at the White House during the crisis with historical documents, contemporaneous journalism, and more than a dozen interviews with participants, including John Poindexter, Jim Stark, and Nicholas Veliotes. His sources are almost all public, and they provided an invaluable source of research material as I reconstructed the narrative from a new point of view.

In addition to Bohn's work I relied significantly on the following: "The Voyage of the *Achille Lauro*" by William Smith in *Time* magazine, October 21, 1985; the detailed spot reporting of the *New York Times,* which covered the story from multiple cities and continents (see especially a lengthy article penned by E. J. Dionne and Joseph Berger from October 13, 1985, "Italy Said to Free 2 P.L.O. Aides; U.S. Issues Warrant for One; Hostages Tell of 'Death List'; Account of Ordeal"; contemporaneous broadcast news transcripts; and David Martin and John Walcott's *Best Laid Plans: The Inside Story of America's War Against Terrorism* (New York: HarperCollins, 1988). I also conducted detailed interviews about the *Achille Lauro* episode on two occasions in 2008 with Poindexter. Unless otherwise noted, all statements, thoughts, and actions attributed to him come from those discussions.

40 *Abu Abbas, the founder of the PLF:* Abbas was captured by U.S. forces in Iraq in 2003. He later died in U.S. custody the following year. According to a Pentagon spokesman at the time, Abbas died of natural causes.

42 *"He's lying," Poindexter told his colleagues flatly:* Interview with John Poindexter. See also Bob Woodward's *Veil* (New York: Simon & Schuster, 1987), in which the author writes about Mubarak's communications having been intercepted by U.S. intelligence. Poindexter did not acknowledge how the government came to know that Mubarak was lying.

43 *At Poindexter's instruction, North had cultivated a relationship with the military attaché at the Israeli embassy in Washington, General Uri Simhoni:* Interview with Poindexter. Also see Michael Ledeen's *Perilous Statecraft: An Insider's Account of the Iran-Contra Affair* (New York: Charles Scribner's Sons, 1988).

44 *"Just confirm to me that you are not acting on your own":* Interview with Uri Simhoni in *The Reagan Presidency: An Oral History of the Era,* by Deborah Hart Strober and Gerald S. Strober, published by Brassey's of Dulles, Va., in 2003, which is an updated edition of the authors' *Reagan: The Man and His Presidency* (New York: Houghton Mifflin, 1998).

45 *"Let me ask him," McFarlane replied:* McFarlane's interaction with the president is also recounted by Robert Timberg, in *The Nightingale's Song* (New York: Simon & Schuster, 1995).

46 *Eventually, Weinberger reached Reagan aboard Air Force One using a public radio frequency:* See "Reagan Knew Phone Hookup Wasn't Private," Associated Press, and "Hostages and Hijackers; U.S. Plans Were Made on Open Line," by Bill Keller for the *New York Times,* both from October 15, 1985.

46 *As the pilots approached they could make out the shape of a 737 against the starry sky:* The accounts of the midair interception were chronicled by Bohn, Martin, and Walcott, based in large part on contemporaneous news reports. Martin and Walcott also interviewed participants in the crisis, and they obtained transcripts of the air-to-air dialogue between the U.S. and Egyptian pilots through the Freedom of Information Act.

48 *North called a friend who knew the prime minister's mistress and tracked them down at his residence in Rome:* The friend was Michael Ledeen, author of *Perilous Statecraft.* Poindexter confirmed Ledeen's role, and Simhoni spoke of it as well, in the oral history compiled by Strober and Strober.

49 *"Thank you, Mr. President. But you should really salute the Navy":* Interview with Poindexter. Also see Timberg's re-creation of the scene in *Nightingale's Song.*

CHAPTER 4: UNODIR

Unless otherwise noted, all statements, thoughts, and actions attributed to Poindexter in this chapter come from interviews conducted in 2004 and 2008, as well as in numerous electronic messages we exchanged in the intervening years. To my knowledge Poindexter has not given detailed interviews about his role in the Iran-Contra affair to any journalist.

Much of the narrative of Iran-Contra comes from official investigations and histories. For a thorough and concise account of the enormous volume of information on the operations, and of the days and months preceding their exposure, see "Iran-Contra: The Final Report," by independent counsel Lawrence Walsh. Bob Woodward's *Shadow: Five Presidents and the Legacy of Watergate* (New York: Simon & Schuster, 1999), provides a narrative account based substantially on the point of view of former secretary of state George Shultz. And the "Report of the Congressional Committees Investigating the Iran-Contra Affair," with its "minority report," provides much historical information and, equally as important, political context. The National Security Archive's *The Iran-Contra Scandal: The Declassified History* (New York: The New Press, 1993) is an unmatched collection of original documents from the era, including the second finding on the Iran arms initiative written by Poindexter.

50 *Reagan had admonished his NSC staff to "keep the Contras alive, body and soul":* See Walsh.

52 *In the corridors of the State Department and the Pentagon, there were agitated complaints and whispers about a rogue NSC staff that had "gone operational":* This is conveyed in the aforementioned histories, and it was reiterated during interviews I conducted with former NSC staff officials who served in the Clinton and then the Bush administrations, all of whom were working in the long wake of Iran-Contra.

52 *Poindexter wrote a lengthy national security directive, which Reagan signed in September 1984, that established a high-level committee to set security policies for sensitive government computer networks:* The directive is number 145, titled "National Policy on Telecommunications and Automated Information Systems Security," www.fas.org/irp/offdocs/nsdd145.htm.

54 *"I think we ought to keep trying," Reagan said, after the others had stopped talking. "I just couldn't live with myself if we didn't take all possible action to get them back":* Some accounts of this meeting have Reagan saying, "The American people will never forgive me." Woodward recounts it this way in *Shadow,* based on notes taken by Shultz's executive assistant, Charles Hill. Poindexter, however, recalls that the president said, "I just couldn't live with myself." I cannot explain the discrepancy, and although the distinction might appear trivial, since both accounts make it clear that Reagan was personally committed to action regardless of the political or legal consequences, I have concluded that the second version is more accurate. Poindexter vividly recalled the scene, imparting such details as what Reagan was wearing and how he sat on the ottoman. This meeting clearly made an impression on him. I also think that Poindexter knew Reagan's mind as well as any of his aides at this time. It is also clear to me from other sources— most notably the president's own diary entries and his public statements—that he held himself responsible for the fate of the hostages.

55 *Poindexter had no intention of notifying Congress; indeed, he took an expansive reading of the law's requirement that Congress be apprised of all findings in a "timely manner":* The National Security Act requires that the president notify the intelligence committees of any covert operations in a timely manner, and the lack of specificity in that deadline has been a source of contention for decades. I mention this here because on many occasions Poindexter emphasized to me that he used a literal reading of this requirement to his advantage. The law does not say what "timely" means, so, in the absence of any firm definition, Poindexter felt that it was generally the president's prerogative to decide when a covert intelligence operation could, and should, be revealed to Congress.

The law gives the president broad discretion to delay notification until after the operation has commenced, so Poindexter's reading might have been legally defensible. But politically, it was dangerous. He knew as well as anyone that the committees despised learning of covert operations after the fact. In particular, operations conducted in Latin America had been the subject of intense debate on Capitol Hill, and when the administration failed to keep Congress fully and currently informed, it threatened to erode the tenuous trust that intelligence committee members had built with CIA director Bill Casey. In April 1984 the Senate Intelligence Committee discovered that the CIA had been planting mines in the harbors of Nicaragua. Democrats and Republicans considered this an act of war, and they were furious that Casey hadn't brought the operation to their attention; it turned out that he buried the news in a piece of lengthy testimony that he delivered to the committee more than a month earlier. The "notification," such that it was, had gone unnoticed.

By the time Poindexter took over as national security adviser he was well aware that Congress had inserted itself into the administration's national security policy in large measure because members felt that they hadn't been told all the facts. By not notifying them of the Iran initiative he was playing with fire.

55 *Poindexter knew the president saw things much more simply, as a straight exchange of missiles for influence:* This may be one of the most misunderstood points of the entire Iran-Contra affair. For as much as the administration tried to portray the Iran operation as more than a simple arms-for-hostages swap, the president always saw it that way. It's clear from my interviews with Poindexter, as well as Reagan's inability to articulate the reasons for the initiative after it was exposed, that the president always saw the plan as a simple quid pro quo. To me, the fact that Poindexter also knew this and yet tried to articulate a broader rationale in the second finding reveals two important truths: First, he believed that the American public was up to the task of understanding a complex, multifaceted policy. And second, he believed that the president would never be forgiven if it turned out that his ostensibly elaborate plan was actually very simple. In both these assumptions, Poindexter erred. Iran-Contra was so convoluted that not even its participants discerned all the moving parts. And as it turned out, while Reagan's legacy was certainly tarnished by the scandal of a cover-up, his basically good intentions to bring Americans home shone through, and perhaps helped save his presidency.

I once asked Poindexter, If you could do anything over again from the Iran-Contra days, what would it be? He thought a moment and said, "I'd have come up with a public relations strategy, because we always knew that if we were exposed, we'd have a hard time explaining to people what we'd been doing." I think that Poindexter thought too much. He probably takes that criticism as a point of pride. "Nobody is obliged to be ignorant," he has told me on several occasions. But Poindexter often puts unrealistic demands on people, and sets impossible expectations. The fact is, he is vastly smarter than most, and he has lived most of his life being rewarded for that intelligence. But during Iran-Contra, and years later, it betrayed him.

57 *"You can meet with anyone in our government at any time," Poindexter promised the relatives.... "He's a classy guy," the daughter of one hostage told a reporter:* Joan Mower, "Families of Hostages in Lebanon Visit White House, Embassies, Capitol Hill," Associated Press, January 21, 1986.

58 *They were lies. Or, in the most charitable light, deliberately misleading partial truths:* See Walsh's Iran-Contra report. Walsh called these claims, as well as "virtually identical" statements in a letter sent September 12, 1985, to Rep. Michael Barnes, the chairman of the House Foreign Affairs Subcommittee on Western Hemisphere Affairs, "false denials of contra-aid activities." Walsh writes, "In addition to written representations, McFarlane on September 5, 1985, met with leaders of the Senate Select Committee on Intelligence and assured them no laws had been broken and no NSC staff member had aided the contras or solicited funds on their behalf. On

September 10, 1985, he made similar assurances in a meeting with Hamilton and other House Intelligence Committee members; the Hamilton meeting was followed up with written questions and answers, in which McFarlane again misrepresented the facts. In these responses, he stated that North had not helped facilitate the movement of supplies to the contras and that no one on the NSC staff had an official or unofficial relationship to fund-raising for the contras." Walsh also notes that "McFarlane later admitted that his responses to Congress were 'too categorical' and they were at the least, overstated. He claimed, however, that he did not lie." On March 11, 1988, McFarlane pleaded guilty to four misdemeanor counts of withholding information from Congress. He was sentenced to two years' probation, $20,000 in fines, and 200 hours community service. Reagan pardoned him on December 24, 1992.

59 *Poindexter expressed his satisfaction to North in an electronic mail message: "Bravo Zulu," the naval signal for "well done":* See *The Iran-Contra Scandal: The Declassified History* for communications between North and Poindexter. In an interview Poindexter emphasized, regretfully, that he hadn't meant to seem to praise North for successfully lying to members of Congress. He didn't believe that he'd done so. Rather, Poindexter thought North had performed well by not revealing the operation while still answering the committee's questions.

59 *The sole survivor, an American named Eugene Hasenfus, told his Sandinista captors that he worked for the CIA:* See Walsh's Iran-Contra report.

60 *Administration officials told Congress that Hasenfus did not work for the CIA, which was true. He worked for North:* Ibid.

60 *in due course discovered that their Iranian contacts were utter charlatans:* After McFarlane and company had played out the charade with their alleged intermediaries, it was clear that Ghorbanifar could not make good on his promises because he was in no position to assist the Americans with gaining the hostages' release. Walsh also notes that Ghorbanifar was unfavorably regarded in the intelligence community well before he became the NSC staff's "first channel" among Iran, the United States, and Israel. "Ghorbanifar was . . . well known to the American intelligence community as a prevaricator. The CIA had concluded, after past interaction with Ghorbanifar, that he could not be trusted to act in anyone's interest but his own. So strong were the CIA's views on Ghorbanifar that the Agency issued a 'burn notice' in July 1984, effectively recommending that no U.S. agency have any dealings with him."

61 *Look on the bright side, North encouraged:* See Walsh's Iran-Contra report.

61 *"Oh shit," McFarlane thought:* Ibid.

61 *George Shultz, the secretary of state, was apoplectic:* For a recounting of the tense meeting in which Poindexter pushed back at Shultz, see Woodward's *Shadow*.

63 *But as the mock journalists volleyed questions at the president, he forgot his lines:* interview with Poindexter. Also see Larry Speakes's memoir, cowritten with Robert Pack, *Speaking Out: Inside the Reagan White House* (New York: Charles Scribner's Sons, 1988), and Edmund Morris's *Dutch: A Memoir of Ronald Reagan* (New York: Random House, 1999).

64 *"Oh, shit," Meese said:* See Woodward's *Shadow*. Walsh's independent counsel report also chronicles how Meese and his colleagues exposed the link between the Iran and Contra operations, but it omits the former attorney general's expletive.

65 *With the click of a button, he deleted them:* Interviews with Poindexter in 2004 and 2008. Also see Walsh's Iran-Contra report.

65 *Reagan took his pen and across the top of the article scrawled a note of praise: "Great—RR":* Poindexter kept the original copy with Reagan's note; he showed it to me and gave me a copy.

66 *Poindexter fixed his eyes on the twenty-five-year-old jury foreman:* David Johnston of the *New York Times* provided the most vivid accounts of the trial that I found. His rendering of the day of the verdict ran on April 7, 1990, under the headline "Poindexter Is Found Guilty of All 5 Criminal Charges for Iran-Contra Cover-Up."

67 *"an overwhelming set of facts":* Another Johnston piece, "Foreman of the Jury in Poindexter's Trial Discusses the Case," ran on April 9, 1990.

CHAPTER 5: A CONSTANT TENSION

71 *There was a time when everyone was linked to a lug nut, and the agents of the FBI liked it that way:* My reporting on the evolution of telecommunications and surveillance technology,

beginning in the mid-1980s, involved interviews over the years with dozens of law enforcement officials, technology experts, telecom executives, and lawyers. But I make special note here of a few who were instrumental in helping me to understand the issues involved in the subject of this chapter, the Communications Assistance for Law Enforcement Act: James Kallstrom, who ran wiretapping operations for the FBI in its New York field office; Jerry Berman, an attorney who helped craft the Foreign Intelligence Surveillance Act and CALEA and who founded the Center for Democracy and Technology; Beryl Howell, who worked for Senator Patrick Leahy on the CALEA legislation; and Al Gidari, a lawyer who represented wireless telecom carriers. Interviews with all these experts took place in 2008. I'm especially grateful to Berman, who hosted me at his home for an afternoon and provided contacts to more sources of expertise and history.

71 *Agents had insinuated themselves into the inner workings of their targets by surreptitiously snatching their own words off copper phone lines:* Kallstrom provided valuable, firsthand accounts of the relationship between FBI agents and the telecom companies. He also gave me vivid descriptions of the telephone switching stations.

71 *"Go up on RR326":* Kallstrom's words.

72 *The FBI's friends in the phone company put the bureau on notice:* Kallstrom recalled that this was a period of tremendous anxiety within the bureau and especially in the New York field office.

73 *"If we don't do something, we'll be out of the wiretapping business":* Interview with Kallstrom. These were his words to officials in Washington.

75 *Beginning in August 1994, senior law enforcement officials sat down for meetings in Washington with a coalition:* Interviews with Berman and Howell, as well as others involved in the negotiations who asked not to be named here.

76 *He held up a glass jar full of rocks and asked the room, "How many of you would say this jar is full?":* Interview with David Johnson, attorney and telecommunications expert, in 2008.

78 *Freeh made the political call: Let's take what we can get here:* Interview with Kallstrom.

78 *He thought it looked like the Cadillac of wiretaps:* Interview with Gidari. He also provided firsthand accounts of the tense meetings between federal officials and telecom employees.

CHAPTER 6: THE GENOA PROJECT

Unless otherwise noted, statements, thoughts, and actions attributed to John Poindexter in this chapter came from interviews conducted mostly in 2008, as well as from electronic message exchanges.

81 *He had occasion to thank George H. W. Bush personally for not pardoning him: "I'm glad I did it on my own":* This account of the White House encounter with Bush and Reagan comes from Robert Timberg, *The Nightingale's Song* (New York: Simon & Schuster, 1995).

82 *"The buck stops here with me," he intoned:* See the "Final Report of the Independent Counsel for Iran/Contra Matters," by Lawrence Walsh. This is perhaps Poindexter's most memorable line.

82 *He smoked throughout the proceedings, lighting the bowl with a silver Zippo that was mailed to him by the owner of the company, an ardent political supporter:* The lighter was a gift from Harriett Wick, who in addition to having the perfect name for the head of a lighter manufacturer was also the daughter of the Zippo's inventor. Poindexter told me that during the Iran-Contra hearings Wick sent him a rare, solid-gold lighter that the company had manufactured to celebrate its fiftieth anniversary. She had apparently seen him smoking a pipe on television and offered the token as a show of support; it was engraved with his initials. Poindexter was still an active-duty military officer and unable to accept such an expensive gift—his lawyers had the lighter appraised at nine hundred dollars. He sent the Zippo back to Mrs. Wick with his thanks and regrets. She replied with a silver lighter valued at about ninety dollars, below the threshold of acceptable gifts to military officers. Poindexter kept this lighter and used it for years.

84 *One afternoon, Poindexter headed over to the DARPA offices to meet with Brian Sharkey, a taciturn ex–submarine hunter:* Sharkey spoke to me about his history with Poindexter and their work together in 2004.

86 *In 1992, State's inspector general chided Clarke:* See "Arms-Export Reports Further Strain U.S.-Israeli Ties," by Thomas Friedman in the *New York Times*, March 15, 1992. Also see "Israel Arms Sales Illegal, U.S. Finds," by David Hoffman and R. Jeffrey Smith in the *Washington Post*, March 14, 1992.

87 *Clarke's first test on terrorism came quickly:* See Richard Clarke's memoir, *Against All Enemies: Inside America's War on Terror* (New York: Free Press, 2004).

90 *Officials also found three attaché cases containing liquid, fans, vents, and batteries in a Tokyo subway station:* For a detailed chronology of the cult's activities, see "Global Proliferation of Weapons of Mass Destruction: A Case Study on the Aum Shinrikyo" by the U.S. Senate Government Affairs Permanent Subcommittee on Investigations, from October 31, 1995, www.fas.org/irp/congress/1995_rpt/aum/index.html.

91 *Clarke would have understood as well as anyone how intelligence often was abused and misused by human analysts:* As a seasoned security official, Clarke would have had many occasions to witness the political uses of intelligence. Perhaps the most famous instance occurred in the aftermath of the 9/11 attacks. In Clarke's memoir, he describes at length his opinion that the Bush administration stretched the facts and cherry-picked intelligence in order to find a connection between Al Qaeda and the Iraqi government, one that he believed didn't exist.

92 *But upon first glance, she thought he could have been an English professor as easily as a former national security adviser:* Interview with Mary McCarthy in 2008.

92 *Poindexter briefly gave McCarthy the rundown on the Genoa program:* Interviews with McCarthy and Poindexter.

92 *McCarthy had published articles connecting this systemic problem to high-profile intelligence failures:* McCarthy's writings are some of the most prescient essays on the future threat of terrorism to the United States that I've read. They are frequently cited by intelligence historians in academic and professional journals. See McCarthy's papers "The National Warning System: Striving for an Elusive Goal," published in the *Defense Intelligence Journal* in 1994, as well as "The Mission to Warn: Disaster Looms," published in that journal's fall 1998 edition.

93 *The team built another staging center near the DARPA building, hiring a Hollywood set designer and former head of Disney Imagineering to give the place a futuristic quality:* Interview with Poindexter. Other officials who visited the center and saw the Genoa demos also recalled its location and its interior.

CHAPTER 7: THE NEXT GENERATION

95 *When Curt Weldon picked up the phone to call George Tenet, the director of the CIA, he wasn't expecting much:* See the transcript of two of Weldon's long speeches on the floor of the House of Representatives, in which he recounts much of the narrative about Dragomir Karic and the Information Dominance Center. The first was on May 21, 2002, at www.fas.org/irp/congress/2002_cr/h052102.html. The second was on June 27, 2005, at www.fas.org/irp/congress/2005_cr/s062705.html. I also wrote about the Karic case and quoted from Weldon's remarks in a story for *National Journal*, "Intelligence Designs," published December 3, 2005. I interviewed Weldon about these matters in his office in 2005. Then, in 2006 I interviewed him again and shadowed him around Washington for a day, as part of a profile I wrote for *National Journal* titled "The Troublemaker," published on September 29, 2006.

97 *Weldon once walked out on a closed-door briefing by CIA officials:* See "Missile-Threat Report 'Politicized,' GOP says," by Rowan Scarborough and Bill Gertz in the *Washington Times*, January 30, 1996.

98 *When Erik Kleinsmith got the request from Weldon's office to draw up a profile on the enigmatic Karic, he didn't expect it to be an onerous task:* Kleinsmith's account of the work on the Karic program come from interviews conducted in 2005 and 2008. All descriptions of his early work at the Information Dominance Center and any statements, thoughts, and actions attributed to him also come from those interviews.

103 *The IDC was the next generation of intelligence, Weldon thought:* Weldon's fixation on intelligence is well known. For a good encapsulation of his thinking, which usually runs contrary to the norm, see his book *Countdown to Terror: The Top-Secret Information That Could*

Prevent the Next Terrorist Attack on America . . . and How the CIA Has Ignored It (Washington, D.C.: Regnery Publishing, 2005).

103 *Over at the Pentagon, word was getting around about the IDC's exploits:* It was clear from interviews with Weldon and Kleinsmith that this was the case. Other interviews, especially with John Hamre, then the deputy secretary of defense, confirmed this. The IDC was an up-and-coming outfit.

CHAPTER 8: THE CHINA EXPERIMENT

104 *The Defense Department had been aware for some time that hostile intelligence services were running agents against U.S. government facilities and military contractors:* See the Defense Department inspector general's report on the Able Danger program, "Alleged Misconduct by Senior DoD Officials Concerning the Able Danger Program and Lieutenant Colonel Anthony A. Shaffer, U.S. Army Reserve," case number H05L97905217, dated September 18, 2006. It states: "In February 1999 Dr. John Hamre, former Deputy Secretary of Defense, proposed a 'threat mapping model' for industrial security. Dr. Hamre testified the proposal was a reaction to 'an active espionage operation by a hostile intelligence force.'"

I also interviewed Hamre about the Able Danger program, and about the Information Dominance Center and its work on industrial espionage, in 2005. We also exchanged a few follow-ups by e-mail.

104 *a special congressional committee had revealed that since at least the late 1970s, Chinese spies had stolen design information about advanced thermonuclear warheads from the U.S. national laboratories:* This document, "U.S. National Security and Military/Commercial Concerns with the People's Republic of China," is better known as the Cox Report, after its chairman and chief proponent, Christopher Cox, who was then a Republican congressman from California. The report was classified, but a redacted version was released publicly in May 1999, at www.house .gov/coxreport/. The report prompted renewed attention to the problem of industrial espionage, but it was not without its critics. Some accused the panel of overstating both the threat of Chinese espionage and the capability of the weapons for which designs were allegedly stolen. The report was also inextricably linked to questions of Chinese political influence on Democratic campaigns and President Bill Clinton. Nevertheless, I mention the report here because it laid bare publicly what senior officials in the Pentagon already knew: Chinese intelligence operations against the U.S. industrial base were in full swing. It is worth noting that less than a decade later intelligence officials would allege publicly that Chinese agents were stealing proprietary information again, but this time over the Internet, by hacking into the computers of U.S. government officials and business executives.

105 *Not long after, he reported his impressions back to Weldon: "It's amazing what they're doing down there":* Interview with Weldon. Hamre also confirmed that he shared his thoughts with the congressman.

106 *Hamre wanted to know whether he should invest in these cutting-edge tools for the new Joint Counterintelligence Assessment Group, or JCAG:* Interview with Hamre. Also see the Defense Department inspector general's report on Able Danger.

106 *Kleinsmith saw a perfect opportunity to impress the Pentagon brass:* All the details about the IDC's work on the China experiment came from interviews with Kleinsmith in 2005 and 2008. In 2005, I also interviewed a former employee of the IDC who worked for Kleinsmith but asked not to be named. The inspector general's report also provides corroborating information about these accounts. Interviews with Hamre and a former congressional official also added important details about the reaction senior officials had to the IDC's work.

110 *The FBI had set up a covert spying operation against the Black Panthers:* In the course of my reporting I spoke with a former member of this FBI team who confirmed its mission and requested anonymity.

112 *That's how the Army's lawyers saw it, and they conveyed that concern to the Pentagon's senior leadership:* The Defense Department inspector general's report documents this chain of reporting.

113 *Hamre wanted to come up to the Hill and talk to the staffers personally:* This account comes from a 2008 interview with Tim Sample, who eventually became the staff director of the House

Intelligence Committee under Porter Goss. Sample worked for the CIA as an imagery analyst before coming to the Hill.

113　*The committee staff also wondered why the IDC was on this job in the first place:* Interview with Sample.

CHAPTER 9: ABLE DANGER

Unless otherwise noted, accounts of the IDC's work on Able Danger come primarily from interviews with Kleinsmith and a former IDC employee who worked with him and asked not to be identified. Where other sources amplify certain passages, I note them.

115　*A pair of officers showed up unannounced, a Navy commander and a Marine captain:* This encounter is also documented in the Defense Department inspector general's report on Able Danger, "Alleged Misconduct by Senior DoD Officials Concerning the Able Danger Program and Lieutenant Colonel Anthony A. Shaffer, U.S. Army Reserve," case number H05L97905217, dated September 18, 2006.

116　*When it came to Al Qaeda, Special Operations most wanted one thing: Boots on the ground to go after the terrorists:* The report of the National Commission on Terrorist Attacks Upon the United States, better known as the 9/11 Commission, contains an authoritative history of Special Operations' efforts against Al Qaeda during this time. See *The 9/11 Commission Report: Final Report of the National Commission on Terrorist Attacks Upon the United States* (New York: W.W. Norton, 2004).

116　*The military hadn't seen anything comparable since the bombings in Beirut fifteen years earlier:* While this is demonstrably true, I also note here that in the course of reporting over the years I interviewed a survivor of the bombing at the embassy in Kenya, Ambassador Prudence Bushnell. She provided vivid memories of the event, which helped underscore both the ferocity of the explosion and the extent of the damage.

116　*In October 1999, the chairman of the Joint Chiefs had directed Special Operations to map out Al Qaeda and all its support mechanisms, including its linchpin members:* The 9/11 Commission's report contains no mention of Able Danger, although its staff did interview officials who were involved in the program. The Defense Department inspector general's report established that Able Danger began pursuant to the chairman of the Joint Chiefs' orders to target Al Qaeda.

117　*Special Operations had ideas about how to hit Al Qaeda:* This account is contained in the 9/11 Commission's report.

117　*The agency had reestablished contacts more recently, and they were paying some dividends:* The CIA's lack of human intelligence–gathering capabilities in Afghanistan and other key counties is well documented. But the 9/11 Commission's report also provides a well-sourced account of this problem. The report also documents the CIA's plans for striking at Al Qaeda.

118　*Special Operations begged to differ:* The turf war that erupted between Special Operations and the CIA is documented in the 9/11 Commission's report. Kleinsmith and the former IDC employee also told me that by the time Special Operations reached out to their team, officers were fed up with the CIA's approach to dealing with Al Qaeda and were prepared to try a new approach.

120　*They ran the usual sources—public information on the Internet, as well as the Joint Worldwide Intelligence Communications System:* Interview with Kleinsmith. Also, in a separate discussion, a former intelligence employee who worked at the IDC but was not involved in the Able Danger program confirmed that the center had access to the joint communications system.

123　*Less than a month later, the staff of the House Intelligence Committee learned that Special Operations had tapped the IDC for data analysis:* Interview with Tim Sample, who eventually became the staff director of the House Intelligence Committee under Porter Goss.

123　*In the winter of 2000, with the IDC several weeks into its Able Danger work, no one in the senior ranks of the Army or the Pentagon realized that Kleinsmith's team was once again pulling in thousands of names of U.S. persons:* The chronological record contained in the Defense Department inspector general's report confirms this. Again, Kleinsmith was aware that legal concerns about the IDC's work persisted, but they hadn't yet impeded his work on Able Danger.

124　*Rear Admiral Michael Lohr, the legal counsel to the chairman of the Joint Chiefs of Staff, got involved:* See the Defense Department inspector general's report. It also contains excerpts from Lohr's memo.

124 *Weeks before Lohr wrote his memo, Philpot briefed General Peter Schoomaker, the Special Operations commander:* Ibid.

127 *At the time, the NSA was using Parentage to trace attacks on computer networks back to a discrete Internet address:* See notes on research into "high confidence systems" on the Web site of the National Coordination Office for Networking and Information Technology Research and Development, at www.nitrd.gov/pubs/bluebooks/2000/hcs.html.

CHAPTER 10: "YOU GUYS WILL GO TO JAIL"

Unless otherwise noted, accounts of the IDC's work on Able Danger come primarily from interviews with Kleinsmith and the former IDC employee who worked with him but asked not to be identified. Where other sources amplify certain passages, I note them.

129 *Colonel Tony Gentry, the top lawyer for the Intelligence and Security Command, had paid Kleinsmith a visit:* Interviews with Kleinsmith in 2005 and 2008. The Defense Department inspector general also found that Kleinsmith was advised that he was facing a ninety-day deadline and would have to destroy information ("Alleged Misconduct by Senior DoD Officials Concerning the Able Danger Program and Lieutenant Colonel Anthony A. Shaffer, U.S. Army Reserve," case number H05L97905217, dated September 18, 2006). Kleinsmith also testified before the Senate Judiciary Committee on September 21, 2005, about his meeting with Gentry.

132 *The analysis would move to a private facility, an intelligence operations center owned and operated by Raytheon in Garland, Texas:* Interviews with Kleinsmith and the former IDC employee. Also see Defense Department inspector general report. Also discussed in interview with Curt Weldon in 2005.

133 *Back in the White House, Dick Clarke and the other career NSC staffers had been working furiously, and now they were in panic mode:* See Dick Clarke's memoir, *Against All Enemies: Inside America's War on Terror* (New York: Free Press, 2004), and the 9/11 Commission's report.

133 *What is it that fits? she asked herself. What is it that matters?:* Interview with McCarthy.

133 *In June 2001, the intelligence community issued a warning that a major Al Qaeda attack would occur within the next several weeks:* For a concise account of the frenzied months preceding the 9/11 attacks, see PBS's *Frontline: The Man Who Knew,* a profile of former FBI special agent John O'Neill. He was one of the few at the bureau to give early warnings of the Al Qaeda threat. O'Neill died at the World Trade Center on September 11, 2001.

134 *Clarke held a meeting in his office during which CIA officials briefed domestic law enforcement agencies about the possibility of an attack in America:* Ibid.

134 *McCarthy, as part of the professional staff, agreed to stay on board temporarily. But as she prepared to head back to the CIA, she worked up a memo for the new national security adviser, Condoleezza Rice:* Interview with McCarthy.

134 *McCarthy asked Poindexter whether he had any advice for Rice, one adviser to another:* Interviews with McCarthy and Poindexter.

135 *The Pentagon chiefs had assured themselves that the IDC's methods were unsound. Their reports to Able Danger certainly weren't actionable:* In my interview with Hamre he made clear that he and others felt that the methods and results of the IDC couldn't be trusted entirely. This work had always been experimental. Pentagon officials gave a similar assessment years later in public when the Able Danger program was first exposed.

CHAPTER 11: ECHO

All statements, thoughts, and actions attributed to John Poindexter in this chapter come from interviews conducted in 2004 and 2008 unless otherwise noted.

142 *Across Washington millions of workers and tourists retreated via the only mode of transportation still functioning dependably—their feet:* The accounts of life in Washington that day are drawn from voluminous newspaper and television reports on the events of that day as well as on my own discussions with friends and colleagues.

142 *Agents screamed at the crowd to run, take off your shoes if you have to, but run, as fast as you can:* This account was chronicled in various newspaper articles, but it was also relayed to me by

a White House staffer days after the attacks; she had to take off her shoes and run from the building.

143 *Mary McCarthy would not forgive herself, then and years later, for not finding the right signal in that ceaseless chatter that crossed her desk in the summer of 2001:* Interview with McCarthy. I add that this is a sentiment shared by many of the government officials who were working on Al Qaeda before the 9/11 attacks. They will be forever haunted by the memories of what they believed they failed to do.

CHAPTER 12: A NEW MANHATTAN PROJECT

All statements, thoughts, and actions attributed to John Poindexter in this chapter come from interviews conducted with him in 2004 and 2008 unless otherwise noted.

As in the previous chapter, accounts of the events of the days immediately following the attacks were chronicled in many newspaper articles and television broadcasts.

144 *"That's funny," Brian Sharkey told his old friend when he rang. "I was just thinking about calling you":* Interviews with Poindexter. I also spoke with Sharkey in 2004 about his recollections of that day.

145 *Sharkey had introduced the phrase two years earlier in Denver during a speech at the annual DARPATech conference:* A copy of his remarks is available at www.darpa.mil/darpatech99/ Presentations/Scripts/ISO/ISO_TIA_Sharkey_Script.txt.

149 *He just wasn't prepared to come back, and Poindexter didn't want to force him:* Interview with Poindexter.

150 *Poindexter found himself sitting in Tether's office, suit-clad, a PowerPoint briefing on his laptop, ready to explain TIA:* Poindexter provided me with the original TIA briefing he gave to Tether. All the passages cited here come directly from the briefing. Others I interviewed—notably a number of leading civil liberties activists—saw a later version of this briefing and still recalled many of the slides verbatim, without being prompted by me.

153 *Poindexter told Tether that he would build "privacy-protection" technologies into TIA's design:* The question of when Poindexter envisioned a privacy component to TIA has been a subject of some controversy. Did he imagine this as part of the system from the outset or was this component added later to appease privacy advocates? I conclude that it was the former. The early briefings clearly show that Poindexter envisioned some role for privacy, and this is fleshed out in subsequent briefing slides that he wrote not much later. My interviews with his staff, and with some of his most vocal critics, corroborate this. Also, some of the early research contracts awarded by the Information Awareness Office, before the TIA program became publicly well-known, contemplate this privacy research.

CHAPTER 13: THE BAG

155 *Mike Wertheimer was looking forward to some quiet time with his wife:* Mike Wertheimer told me about the 2001 Columbus Day weekend, as well as the meeting in the NSA's conference room, during a conversation we had in Chicago on September 6, 2007, at a conference called "Analytic Transformation," sponsored by the Office of the Director of National Intelligence, where he was employed. At this time, the NSA's warrantless surveillance program had already been disclosed and acknowledged by President George Bush. Also, on May 18, 2006, Michael Hayden, the director of the NSA at the time the program was conceived, testified about the meeting before the Senate Select Committee on Intelligence. The matter came up in response to questioning during Hayden's confirmation hearing to become the next director of the Central Intelligence Agency.

Wertheimer recalled the story about his family and his father during our conversation. He also spoke about it later that evening when he gave a speech to the conference attendees. A transcript of the speech is available on the Web site of the Office of the Director of National Intelligence.

I also interviewed Wertheimer for a profile in *National Journal*, "The Liberator," published on September 22, 2007.

157 *Hayden explained to his employees that four days earlier the president had granted the agency new authorities that allowed the NSA to greatly expand its surveillance net:* See Hayden's May 2006 testimony.

157 *The agency could now target the communications of anyone reasonably suspected of being a terrorist, or those associated with them, without a warrant:* Bush acknowledged this much after the *New York Times* revealed the warrantless surveillance program in December 2005.

157 *But now the analysts could listen in and determine if the conversation, or the parties involved, had any "nexus to terrorism":* In interviews with two very senior Bush administration officials I was told that "nexus to terrorism" became the key phrase used for deciding when to monitor the content of communications.

My reporting on how the surveillance program actually worked, in terms of how analysts probed communications and made decisions about whom to monitor, involved interviews with government officials—at mid and senior levels—as well as private-sector individuals. No one would agree to be quoted by name in describing the mechanics of the system. Where possible and necessary, I will illuminate key insights into the program with mention of specific sources.

159 *"We're going to do exactly what he said," Hayden told his staff, referring to Bush. "Not one photon or one electron more":* Hayden made this statement in his May 2006 confirmation hearing.

159 *To Wertheimer, it seemed like the right thing to do:* Conversation with Wertheimer in Chicago.

159 *"I will play in fair territory. But there will be chalk dust on my cleats":* This became a favorite phrase of Hayden's, and was cited by lawmakers and journalists. Speaking at the Duquesne University commencement ceremony on May 4, 2007, Hayden repeated the phrase and noted that he'd used it in the past.

159 *On the morning of 9/11, Hayden had been working for two hours already when news reached him that a plane had struck the North Tower:* Hayden recalled his experience on the morning of the attacks before a joint inquiry of the House and Senate Intelligence committees. His statement for the record was delivered on October 17, 2002. Also see James Bamford's *Body of Secrets: Anatomy of the Ultra-Secret National Security Agency* (New York: Anchor, 2002) and *The Shadow Factory: The Ultra-Secret NSA from 9/11 to the Eavesdropping on America* (New York: Doubleday, 2008).

160 *The image popularized in Hollywood productions like* Enemy of the State, *which premiered the year before Hayden took over, had made the agency seem stronger and more independent than it really was:* Over the years intelligence officials have repeatedly pointed to this film as an example of how Hollywood distorted their capabilities—at least before the 9/11 attacks. Some of them said they only wished the NSA had been as sophisticated as it was portrayed on-screen.

161 *Immediately after the attacks he ordered the agency to "go up on," or monitor, a set of hot targets, foreign entities that the agency believed were connected to terrorism:* This account is based on an interview with two NSA officials in 2005. They were not authorized to be quoted by name.

161 *Hayden broadened the reach of his signals-gathering agency in those first days after 9/11:* The interview with the NSA officials made clear this had occurred. And subsequently, five inspectors general who reviewed the NSA's surveillance program corroborated the account. The unclassified version of their "Report on the President's Surveillance Program" was released on July 10, 2009. They wrote, "In the days immediately after September 11, 2001, the NSA used its existing authorities to gather intelligence information in response to the terrorist attacks." Those existing authorities, the inspectors general noted, were the Foreign Intelligence Surveillance Act and Executive order 12333.

161 *They handed over leads about potential targets inside the country to the FBI:* See the aforementioned inspectors general report. Also see the *New York Times*'s report of January 17, 2006, "Spy Agency Data After Sept. 11 Led F.B.I. to Dead Ends," by Lowell Bergman, Eric Lichtblau, Scott Shane, and Don Van Natta, Jr. Hayden also remarked on the flow of information to the FBI in remarks at the National Press Club, on January 23, 2006. He said, "Now, as another part of our adjustment, we also turned on the spigot of NSA reporting to FBI in, frankly, an unprecedented way."

162 *As Hayden saw it, all these hot communications constituted* foreign *intelligence:* Hayden explained this logic in detail during his remarks noted above at the National Press Club. For more explanations on how the Bush administration believed that the NSA's surveillance program comported with laws and the president's constitutional authorities, see the Justice

Department's white paper titled "Legal Authorities Supporting the Activities of the National Security Agency Described by the President," dated January 19, 2006.

164 *After the briefing wrapped up, Pelosi thought about what Hayden had said:* A redacted version of a letter Pelosi wrote to Hayden, which was later released publicly, states in part, "During your appearance before the committee, you indicated that you had been operating since the September 11 attacks with an expansive view of your authorities with respect to the conduct of electronic surveillance." The letter indicated that NSA was "forwarding" information to the FBI. As the *Washington Post*'s Dafna Linzer reported on January 4, 2006, "Two sources familiar with the NSA program said Pelosi was directly referring to information collected without a warrant on U.S. citizens or residents."

164 *Not long after the attacks, George Tenet made the rounds to the various intelligence agency chiefs, and he asked Hayden a question: "Is there anything more you can do?" "Not within my current authorities," Hayden replied:* Hayden recounted this story at his May 2006 confirmation hearing, and he also reminded the senators that he had "briefed the committee in closed session" about it. The inspectors general report on NSA's surveillance program reiterates this account. They write, "When Director of Central Intelligence Tenet, on behalf of the White House, asked NSA Director Hayden whether the NSA could do more against terrorism, Hayden replied that nothing more could be done within existing authorities."

164 *Hayden had in mind a far more aggressive role for his agency, and one that mirrored the plan Poindexter was hatching at precisely the same time. Hayden wanted to build an early-warning system for terrorist attacks:* Again, see Hayden's 2006 testimony, his National Press Club speech, and the report of the inspectors general.

164 *Well before the attacks, Hayden understood his agency was still collecting intelligence with a cold war mind-set:* A frank assessment of NSA's challenges and priorities at the dawn of the twenty-first century is contained in a once classified report that the agency prepared in December 2000 for the incoming Bush administration. Titled "Transition 2001," it warned officials that they "must understand that today's and tomorrow's mission will demand a powerful, permanent presence on a global telecommunications network that will host the 'protected' communications of Americans as well as targeted communications of adversaries." This report, as well as other documents that shed light on internal NSA thinking, is on the Web site of the National Security Archive, at www.gwu.edu/~nsarchiv/NSAEBB/NSAEBB24/index.htm.

For another useful source of insight into the NSA's mind-set before the 9/11 attacks, see Hayden's testimony before the House Intelligence Committee delivered April 12, 2000. Hayden said, "NSA is not authorized to collect all electronic communications. NSA is authorized to collect information only for foreign intelligence purposes and to provide it only to authorized government recipients." The subject of the hearings centered on allegations that the NSA had engaged in industrial espionage, providing intelligence on European corporations to their American competitors. Hayden reminded lawmakers that the rules governing surveillance grew out of the abuses of an earlier generation, and that the agency had surely learned its lesson. His testimony gives a thorough account of how Hayden thought FISA and Executive order 12333 governed his agency's actions.

164 *So, he tasked a team of senior managers, including Wertheimer and another NSA lifer named Maureen Baginski, to reshape signals intelligence for the digital age:* The *New Yorker*'s Elsa Walsh recounts this mission in her profile of Baginski, "Learning to Spy," published on November 8, 2004.

165 *Hayden explained that any effective system for spotting terrorists before they struck had to meet three criteria:* Hayden recounted this meeting in his 2006 confirmation hearing.

166 *They would also need access to a source that the NSA had not been collecting systematically in the past: e-mail:* Two former administration officials said in interviews that the NSA hadn't systemically collected e-mails, and that after the 9/11 attacks, agency officials realized this had been a mistake.

166 *Wertheimer had led an exercise to find out whether Russian mobsters were supplying weapons of mass destruction to Iran:* See Walsh's *New Yorker* piece.

166 *As Hayden set up the new surveillance program, it was increasingly clear to NSA officials that e-mail, not phone calls, would constitute the bulk of their collection:* A former senior intelligence official, who had direct knowledge of the NSA's capabilities and was read into the surveillance

program, emphasized that the agency was more interested in e-mails than in any other kind of communication.

167 *Hayden had come up with a plan, and Bush personally felt it was a good idea:* Bush emphasized his support for the program on numerous occasions, and he personally intervened with the *New York Times* to keep the newspaper from writing about it. See the president's remarks during a press conference on March 20, 2006, in which he said that "after September the eleventh, I spoke to a variety of folks on the front line of protecting us, and I said, Is there anything more we could be doing, given the current laws? And General Mike Hayden of the NSA said there is." Bush said that Hayden described the surveillance program as "hot pursuit" and that Hayden "designed a program that will enable us to listen from a known al Qaeda, or suspected al Qaeda person and/or affiliate."

167 *On September 25, Yoo sent a memo to a senior official in the Justice Department:* See "Memorandum for David S. Kris, Associate Deputy Attorney General" regarding "Constitutionality of Amending Foreign Intelligence Surveillance Act to Change the 'Purpose' Standard for Searches." A copy of the memo is on the Justice Department's Web site.

168 *But then Yoo offered an unsolicited assessment:* A Justice Department official told me that Yoo was never asked to offer an opinion regarding the modification of FISA, and that Kris was surprised to read an expansive analysis of the president's surveillance authorities.

170 *"I can't not do this," Hayden told himself:* In Hayden's 2006 confirmation hearing, Senator Kit Bond asked, "Did you believe that your primary responsibility as director of NSA was to execute a program that your NSA lawyers, the Justice Department lawyers, and White House officials all told you it [*sic*] was legal and that you were ordered to carry it out by the president of the United States?" Hayden replied, "Sir, when I had to make this personal decision in early October, 2001—and it was a personal decision—the math was pretty straightforward. I could not not do this."

171 *Stellar Wind:* This code name was first reported by Michael Isikoff in *Newsweek* on December 22, 2008, in his article "The Fed Who Blew the Whistle." I asked a former senior administration official if this was the code name for NSA activities, including those that became the center of major internal controversy in 2004. The former official confirmed that Stellar Wind was the code name. It's worth mentioning an amusing anecdote here, because it sheds light on the often fragmentary process of reporting about the intelligence program. In late 2007, while reporting a story about the NSA's surveillance activities before the 9/11 attacks, I interviewed a former White House official who referred to the warrantless surveillance program but actually had trouble recalling its name. This official couldn't remember if it was called "star something" or "whirlwind." I know from interviewing a former high-ranking intelligence official who advised the president on a regular basis that the NSA activities were often just referred to as "the president's program."

171 *They called it the Big Ass Graph:* The term "big ass graph" is known to those with deep technical knowledge of surveillance, and who are also close to the agencies and companies with expertise in that realm. Poindexter, for one, knows the term, and that it refers to a program developed by a computer scientist mentioned in a later chapter. The source for the use of "big ass graph" and "the BAG" as a synonym for the NSA's surveillance program is a private-sector official with technical expertise and direct knowledge of the program.

CHAPTER 14: ALL HANDS ON DECK

All statements, thoughts, and actions attributed to John Poindexter in this chapter come from interviews unless otherwise noted.

Details of all Information Awareness Office programs came from interviews with former office staff, including Doug Dyer and the late Tom Armour. When the IAO was still active its Web site was also a richly detailed repository of information about the programs. Many of those documents have been removed from their official pages, but they continue to reside on Web sites hosted by archivists, historians, and activists.

172 *Bob Popp had always wanted to work for DARPA, but the right job had yet to come along:* I first met Popp in 2002, when he was working for John Poindexter at DARPA. I conducted interviews

with him again in 2008. All statements, thoughts, and actions attributed to him here come from those interviews unless otherwise noted.

In his e-mail Poindexter explained that he had read Popp's proposal.

174 *McCarthy was incredulous. "No, John! You're going to do this? No." "Yes, I am," Poindexter replied resolutely":* Interviews with Poindexter and Mary McCarthy. Her thoughts on TIA and Poindexter's role also come from an interview.

176 *In one chart, Poindexter had used "profiling" to describe a method of screening particular individuals for terrorist characteristics:* Interview with Popp.

180 *Lukasik assembled a group of academics:* I interviewed Steve Lukasik about his work on red teams in 2008. Lukasik generously supplied access to documents chronicling the team's work. Poindexter also described the concept and the team's work in multiple interviews, as did Popp.

CHAPTER 15: CALL TO ARMS

All statements, thoughts, and actions attributed to John Poindexter in this chapter come from interviews unless otherwise noted.

Poindexter described his meeting with Rumsfeld in detail, and on several occasions in interviews spoke about their history working together in the Pentagon. After the program attracted significant controversy in November 2002, Rumsfeld publicly acknowledged that he had met with Poindexter about Total Information Awareness. But, as detailed in subsequent chapters, he played down his knowledge of the program.

187 *It was the Information Dominance Center, former home of Erik Kleinsmith and the Able Danger team:* Poindexter's selection of the IDC as a home base for his network is documented in the IAO literature. I also discussed the selection of the site with Popp in interviews.

188 *Poindexter drew an impressive crowd for his first TIA briefing:* Details of the meeting at the CIA come from interviews with Poindexter and an interview with Alan Wade in 2008.

190 *Fran Townsend seemed like she would know for sure:* I interviewed Townsend in 2009 about her consultations with Poindexter. All statements, thoughts, and actions attributed to her in this chapter come from the interview and some follow-up questions via e-mail.

193 *Perhaps no one understood that better than Mike McConnell. As a former director of the National Security Agency:* Poindexter and McConnell provided accounts of their meeting in separate interviews conducted in 2008 and 2009, respectively. They corroborated each other's account, although McConnell was quick to emphasize that he was concerned Poindexter would end up creating dossiers of innocent people. Poindexter, in our interview, focused more on McConnell's offer to pave a path with influential members of Congress, which McConnell confirmed he was willing to do, provided that he could give assurances Poindexter's research was limited to foreign intelligence.

195 *Under a contract Poindexter awarded later that year, worth more than $8 million, Booz was tapped to help bring a prototype TIA system to life:* A list of the contracts awarded by the Information Awareness Office is maintained by the Electronic Privacy Information Center. It is available at http://epic.org/privacy/profiling/tia/contractors_table.html.

195 *Bob Popp sat at his desk, thinking about a sandwich:* Popp told me the story of how he designed the logo during an interview. Poindexter concurred that the logo was Popp's inspiration and that he thought highly of it.

197 *The TIA network attracted new members every month:* A brochure written to promote the network and detail its work lists the number of members that joined on a month-by-month basis. It was prepared after TIA was officially shut down and Poindexter had left government. The document is unclassified but it is not, to the best of my knowledge, publicly available. I obtained it from a private-sector source who was not employed by DARPA.

197 *At the beginning of his research experiments Poindexter drew a bright line in the kinds of data he would use:* Interviews with Poindexter and Popp. McConnell confirmed that Poindexter told him the research would be divided into two paths. This is also spelled out in DARPA's "Report to Congress Regarding the Terrorism Information Awareness Program" dated May 20, 2003.

CHAPTER 16: FEED THE BAG

200 *Dr. J. C. Smart started his technical career at the Lawrence Livermore National Laboratory:* Smart's detailed biography is publicly available. Poindexter confirmed that he is the inventor of the BAG. Also, an internal document about a Homeland Security Department data-mining program, mentioned in a subsequent chapter, lists Smart as the creator of the BAG and details how it was used in the intelligence community.

  A number of other technical experts who were familiar with the BAG and the concept of graphic analysis provided valuable sources of background information for this chapter. In addition, a private-sector source who declined to be named, but who has direct knowledge of the NSA surveillance program, provided detailed information and documentation about how the technology was used in multiple interviews.

201 *James Payne, the head of Qwest Communications' federal government business unit, accompanied the company's chief executive to a business meeting with Hayden at his Fort Meade headquarters:* Payne testified about this meeting to federal agents investigating Nacchio. Sections of the transcript of the interview are contained in the case documents for *USA v. Nacchio.* See particularly "Exhibit 1 to Mr. Nacchio's Reply to SEC. 5 Submission," which contains "FBI Form '302' Regarding November 14, 2005, Interview of James F. X. Payne."

202 *The CEO, Joe Nacchio, wanted a piece of a new NSA contract called Groundbreaker:* This is detailed in Payne's interview with federal authorities and in Nacchio's case documents.

202 *Payne had made plenty of drop-in calls like this before to discuss potential business with large, important clients:* See Payne's interview with federal authorities.

202 *he was an old hand in the close-knit club of federal telecom contractors and agency executives:* I covered the government telecommunications market as a technology reporter for *Government Executive* magazine, beginning in 2001. In that capacity, I met Payne and other executives with various companies.

202 *The company had allocated portions of its telecom network for the agency's exclusive use:* As I detail in my article "NSA Sought Data Before 9/11," Qwest worked for the agency beginning at least in 1999. Internet number registration files showed that Qwest allocated a portion of its network that year to the Maryland Procurement Office, the NSA's contracting unit. In March 2001, Payne sent an e-mail to colleagues noting that Qwest was already a "provider" of telecom services to the NSA through existing contracts.

202 *The agency was going after digital spies, not terrorists:* This information came from an interview with a former White House official, who at the time was involved in network defense and other intelligence programs. This official told me in early 2001 that the NSA proposal to Qwest was "Can you build a private version of Echelon and tell us what you see?" Echelon is a name used within the intelligence community to refer to a signals-gathering-and-dissemination network operated by the NSA and its official counterparts in Australia, Canada, New Zealand, and the United Kingdom.

203 *Government officials had also begun to fear a "digital Pearl Harbor":* One of the most prominent officials warning about such a catastrophe after 9/11 was Dick Clarke, who became the Bush administration's "cyberczar."

203 *It promised faster, more powerful data flows, and it caught the attention of senior U.S. military officials:* This interest is documented in Nacchio's trial documents. Also see "NSA Sought Data Before 9/11." It was common knowledge among reporters covering technology in government that Qwest was making inroads with the defense and intelligence communities because of its high-speed network.

203 *In late 1997 a three-star general met with Nacchio at his Denver office and later told one of Nacchio's associates that he wanted to use the company's network "for government purposes":* See Nacchio's trial documents.

204 *Hayden's proposal struck Nacchio, Payne, and Qwest's lawyers as potentially illegal:* Ibid.

204 *In the weeks after the attacks the NSA asked telecom executives for access to their customer records as well as direct, physical access to their data:* This is based on my reporting of the request. See "More than Meets the Ear," in *National Journal* on March 18, 2006, and "Tinker, Tailor, Miner, Spy" in *Slate.* See also "NSA Has Massive Database of Americans' Phone Calls," by Leslie Cauley, published in *USA Today* on May 11, 2006.

204 *If analysts started with a list of phone numbers, they could find all the other numbers called from*

those phones, and so establish the close circle of people in the targets' daily lives: Recall that this is what the Parentage tool that Erik Kleinsmith used during Able Danger was designed to do. The NSA was using that tool before 9/11 to trace the locations of cyberhacks—the same kind of intelligence it wanted Qwest to help provide before the terrorist attacks.

205 *Agency officials rebutted by questioning the company's patriotism. They let it be known that Qwest's competitors were already on board:* See my previous reporting in *Slate* and *National Journal,* as well as *USA Today*'s article.

205 *Lawyers for telecom and Internet companies were working overtime to comply with the government requests:* A number of said lawyers agreed to describe their work complying with these requests on the condition that they not be identified by name. They also didn't disclose the names of their clients.

206 *The Treasury team, dubbed Operation Green Quest, was specifically interested in a money-moving system called* hawala: Interview with Marcy Forman, head of Green Quest, in 2002. See my story "Disrupt and Dismantle," published in *Government Executive* magazine in February 2002.

206 *The FBI unit, called the Financial Review Group, set out to discover the financial linkages that tied the nineteen hijackers to one another and to their sources:* See "Disrupt and Dismantle."

207 *FBI agents also dove into credit and debit card histories housed at First Data in Colorado:* See Ron Suskind's *The One Percent Doctrine: Deep Inside America's Pursuit of Its Enemies Since 9/11* (New York: Simon & Schuster, 2006). I also interviewed a former Justice Department official who worked in an FBI command center immediately after the 9/11 attacks, helping to track financial information.

207 *A unit at the Customs Bureau in Northern Virginia also joined the fray:* See "Disrupt and Dismantle."

208 *But financial data was also poured into the BAG and overlapped with phone and e-mail communications in an effort to dig deeper into terrorists' social networks:* Interviews with private-sector source who had direct knowledge of the BAG and the NSA's surveillance activities.

208 *It plugged into an array of data sources, including those at AT&T, one of the oldest and most important telecom providers:* The most well-known source for this information is a former AT&T employee named Mark Klein, who went public with a set of documents that he said showed a secret facility meant to siphon off customer data at an AT&T site in San Francisco.

Separately, a former senior administration official confirmed to me that the company was supplying the NSA with massive amounts of communication data. In the words of this official, the agency was making a "mirror" of AT&T's databases.

Also see Leslie Cauley's article in *USA Today*, "NSA Has Massive Database of Americans' Phone Calls," May 11, 2006. Citing sources with direct knowledge of the arrangement, Cauley wrote that "the National Security Agency has been secretly collecting the phone call records of tens of millions of Americans, using data provided by AT&T" and other companies. At the time, AT&T responded to the *USA Today* story with a written statement: "We do not comment on matters of national security, except to say that we only assist law enforcement and government agencies charged with protecting national security in strict accordance with the law."

Also see James Bamford's *The Shadow Factory: The Ultra-Secret NSA from 9/11 to the Eavesdropping on America* (New York: Doubleday, 2008), in which he offers a technical description of how information from AT&T's networks was provided to the NSA.

208 *What to do with it—how to make sense of it—that's what mattered most:* This is a general problem in all kinds of analysis of massive amounts of data, regardless of the agency. But the NSA's problems in particular were conveyed to me by sources with knowledge of its work and were also highlighted in the 2009 report by five inspectors general, who concluded that the NSA program was of limited use. See "Report on the President's Surveillance Program," released on July 10, 2009.

CHAPTER 17: SHIPS PASSING IN THE NIGHT

210 *Poindexter secured a meeting with Bill Black, Hayden's number two and a career NSA employee:* Poindexter provided me with calendar entries as well as e-mails from NSA employees confirming his meetings with Black and Michael Hayden.

211 *There he learned that a large percentage of phone calls, no matter which carrier generated them, passed through AT&T circuits:* Interview with Poindexter in 2008.

211 *Poindexter told Black that he wanted the NSA on his network:* Ibid. Documentation obtained independently of Poindexter and his staff confirms that the NSA joined the network and eventually added more nodes than any other agency. This information is contained in an unclassified description of the Total Information Awareness network.

211 *Instead of just monitoring individual targets, the terrorist hunters began to look for patterns:* See "More than Meets the Ear," my article in *National Journal,* March 18, 2006. This account is based on interviews with government and private-sector officials about the NSA's surveillance activities.

212 *Rather than leading them to sleeper agents, the NSA's intelligence usually led them to the doorstep of an innocent American, or a Pizza Hut:* "Spy Agency Data After Sept. 11 Led F.B.I. to Dead Ends," by Lowell Bergman, Eric Lichtblau, Scott Shane, and Don Van Natta, Jr., *New York Times,* January 17, 2006.

212 *"I don't need this," the official said. "I just need you to tell me whose ass to put a Hellfire missile on":* Interview with said CIA official, who asked not to be named. This individual had direct responsibility for the agency's counterterrorism program.

212 *Poindexter knew that had long been the agency's problem:* Interview with Poindexter. Even though he wasn't read into the agency's terrorist surveillance program, it was no secret that the NSA had been grappling with this problem for some time.

212 *Exactly seven weeks later, on March 25, Poindexter went back to the fort and sat down with Mike Hayden:* Calendar entries and e-mails provided by Poindexter.

CHAPTER 18: FULL STEAM AHEAD

214 *Once the first node was installed on the TIA network, in early 2002, Poindexter set out an ambitious schedule to enlarge his laboratory and build a working TIA prototype:* The "Report to Congress Regarding the Terrorism Information Awareness Program," among other unclassified program documents and descriptions from the Information Awareness Office, charts the progression of the technology experiments. Additionally, a brochure I obtained from a source outside of Poindexter's office lists a chronology and gives the wind-based code name of every experiment as well as a description of what it entailed. Poindexter and Popp were able to amplify this information with other details during interviews.

214 *Paul Polski, an old Navy Academy classmate, called Poindexter for help on an ambitious project to screen millions of airline passengers against terrorist watch lists and intelligence databases:* Interview with Poindexter. I also interviewed Polski about his career in 2003.

216 *The FBI hired ChoicePoint, a data-aggregation firm based outside Atlanta, to give agents access to billions of records on nearly every person inside the United States:* Under the Freedom of Information Act I obtained contract documents that detail the arrangement between the bureau and ChoicePoint. See my story in *National Journal,* "The Private Spy Among Us," published on November 5, 2005.

216 *The TIA researchers nicknamed the database Ali Baba, after the Arabian folk character who opens a cave full of hidden treasure with the magic words "open sesame":* Interviews with Poindexter and Popp.

216 *Simulated intelligence was also used to create ever more complicated synthetic worlds for testing the red team's attack templates:* Ibid.

217 *NSA analysts did remove the experimental data crunching, linking, and extracting tools from the TIA network and quietly put them into service as part of the agency's warrantless surveillance regime:* Interview with private-sector source who had direct knowledge of the NSA's terrorist surveillance program. Poindexter and Popp said they were unaware of what any agency did with the tools once they were removed from the network. They said they had no knowledge of those tools being used for the NSA's secret program.

219 *The Highlands Forum was created in 1994:* For a vivid history of the Highlands Forum, complete with descriptions of the Carmel locale, see Brian Friel's article "Start Your Engines," published in *Government Executive* magazine in May 15, 2006. Also see the transcript of an April 5, 2001, interview with O'Neill on the Highlands Forum process held at the Center for Information

Policy Research at Harvard University, http://pirp.harvard.edu/pubs_pdf/o%27neill/o%27neill
-i01-3.pdf.

220 *But O'Neill had paired him up with an outsider, a thirty-eight-year-old computer software
designer from Las Vegas named Jeff Jonas:* Unless otherwise noted all statements, thoughts, and
actions attributed to Jonas, as well as the details of his career, come from an interview I
conducted with him in 2008.

220 *When it came time for Jonas to speak, Poindexter thought he might be a comedian:* Interview
with Poindexter.

225 *Poindexter knew technology better than he did gambling, and in NORA, he saw potential:* Ibid.

225 *Jonas stepped into Poindexter's office at DARPA headquarters:* I interviewed Jonas, Poindexter,
and Popp about this meeting.

227 *DARPA was considering whether to convene a study group to look at the balancing act of privacy
and security, from a technical perspective:* I interviewed three participants about this meeting—
Poindexter, Fran Townsend, and Marc Rotenberg, the president and executive director of the
Electronic Privacy Information Center. The final paper, titled "Security with Privacy," was
published on December 13, 2002, at http://epic.org/privacy/profiling/tia/isat_study.pdf.

CHAPTER 19: THE UNRAVELING

230 *They all asked the same question: "Did you see the following?":* Interview with Popp in 2008.

230 *John Markoff had first reported about TIA less than a week earlier:* "Pentagon Plans a Computer
System That Would Peek at Personal Data of Americans," *New York Times*, November 2, 2002.

230 *The* Washington Post *followed with a story:* "U.S. Hopes to Check Computers Globally,"
November 12, 2002.

231 *Popp's first reaction was not to worry:* Interview with Popp. He also described the reaction
within Poindexter's office.

231 *Privacy activists could scarcely believe their luck. Was Poindexter really so politically tone-deaf?:*
Interview with Barry Steinhardt of the American Civil Liberties Union in 2008.

231 *The* Washington Post *editorial board observed:* "Total Information Awareness," November 16, 2002.

232 *As Poindexter sat before fifty or so curious, skeptical, and undoubtedly confused members of
Congress and their staffs, he hoped his guiding principles would keep him afloat:* Accounts of
the briefing came from Poindexter and Popp. The staffer who confronted Poindexter confirmed
the account.

233 *The secretary of defense ordered Poindexter gagged:* At the time Poindexter denied all requests
for interviews, including mine. He later told me that he was ordered by Rumsfeld's office not to
speak publicly.

233 *"If we need a big brother, John Poindexter is the last guy on the list that I would choose":* Senator
Charles Schumer on ABC's *This Week with George Stephanopoulos*, November 24, 2002.

234 *a columnist for the independent* San Francisco Weekly *turned the tables on the supersnoop:*
"Calling All Yahoos: Worried About What John Poindexter's Up to as Federal Information Czar?
Call His Home Number and Ask," by Matt Smith, November 27, 2002.

234 *"I don't know much about it," Rumsfeld said:* See Defense Department transcript, "Secretary
Rumsfeld Media Availability En Route to Chile," November 18, 2002, at www.defenselink.mil/
transcripts/transcript.aspx?transcriptid=3296.

CHAPTER 20: GOING BLACK

236 *That was the message that John Hamre brought back to his friend Poindexter after a scouting
mission on the Hill:* Interview with Poindexter in 2008. Popp also confirmed that Hamre went
to the Hill to gather information. Hamre's think tank, the Center for Strategic and International
Studies, was also under contract to Poindexter's office, examining models of oversight or legal
protections that might permit agencies to conduct pattern-based searches of data. This was the
policy side of the privacy equation that Poindexter was trying to balance. He'd first approached
the National Academies of Sciences with the job, but when officials there thought the research
was too politically sensitive to take on, Poindexter asked Hamre's group to do it.

237 *"The problem is that he may be the right man":* Bob Levy, a Cato Institute senior fellow, spoke
at a Cato forum on December 12, 2002.

237 *"not only Timothy McVeigh," who bombed the Murrah Federal Building in Oklahoma City,*

"but most farmers in Nebraska": Paul Rosenzweig of the Heritage Foundation testified at a hearing about TIA before the House Government Reform Committee Subcommittee on Technology, Information Policy, Intergovernmental Relations and the Census on May 20, 2003. His remarks were covered by Sarah Lesher in "Antiterrorism Measures Under Scrutiny," *The Hill,* June 4, 2003.

237 *The presentation lacked details, Steinhardt thought:* I interviewed Steinhardt about the meeting, his thoughts on TIA, and his appreciation of Poindexter in 2008. I also interviewed Popp about the meeting with Steinhardt and Dempsey.

239 *In those fumbling moments Tether turned to Popp to fill in the gaps. He was mortified:* Interview with Popp.

239 *To forestall a showdown on the Hill, Poindexter wrote a detailed review of TIA and the Information Awareness Office:* This is DARPA's "Report to Congress Regarding the Terrorism Information Awareness Program," at http://w2.eff.org/Privacy/TIA/TIA-report.pdf.

240 *Poindexter, who'd been telling Tether that he wanted to resign since the spring, now said he would leave by the end of August:* Interview with Poindexter.

241 *rumors started circulating among the press corps that Rumsfeld had fired Poindexter:* These rumors were known to me through the course of my reporting on Poindexter and his resignation.

241 *"I'm going to turn SAIC loose," Poindexter told Tether:* Interview with Poindexter.

241 *"You've got a $20 million contract on the line," Popp said:* Interview with Popp.

241 *He called his friend Bob Beyster:* Poindexter and Popp separately provided details about SAIC's intervention on their office's behalf.

242 *This time they used descriptions of TIA and the Information Awareness Office that Poindexter and Popp had written themselves:* I obtained a copy of this presentation from a source who asked to remain anonymous.

242 *At Poindexter's request, he came down to Fort Belvoir, to the TIA network hub:* Interviews with Poindexter and Popp.

243 *NSA was a logical place for TIA to go:* I first reported the move of the TIA programs to the NSA in *National Journal.* See "TIA Lives On," published on February 23, 2006. I note here that neither Poindexter nor Popp was a source of this information. Later, Popp publicly confirmed that the move had occurred in an interview with PBS's *Frontline:* "Spying on the Home Front," May 15, 2007.

Before he died, I also interviewed Tom Armour, the program manager for Poindexter's Genoa II program, about the unit that eventually took over the work of the Information Awareness Office. He said that Advanced Research and Development Activity pursued technologies that would be useful for analyzing large amounts of phone and e-mail traffic. "That's, in fact, what the interest is," he said. Armour told me that when TIA was still being publicly funded its program managers and researchers had "good coordination" with their counterparts at ARDA and discussed their projects on a regular basis. Armour declined to speak with me about the transition of the former Information Awareness Office programs to ARDA, and he was not a source for that information.

244 *Popp drew up a simple list:* Interview with Popp.

245 *Hayden sat down with the Democratic and Republican heads of the House and Senate Intelligence committees:* On May 16, 2006, the Office of the Director of National Intelligence declassified a list of all the briefings the administration had given members of Congress about the terrorist surveillance program.

245 *Harman thought that the PowerPoint presentation she saw was pretty thin stuff:* On September 20, 2006, Harman said during a House Intelligence Committee markup of a surveillance bill, "There has also been a stunning dearth of oversight over the President's NSA program in this committee. Months ago, I asked that Committee members meet with the NSA Inspector General, Members of the FISA Court, the Department of Justice, the FBI, and the CIA to learn whether the program has helped stop any terrorist attacks. The Majority denied each of those requests. I have asked for a copy of the President's Authorization for the Program and for other core documents. The Administration has refused to produce them. In June, I asked you, Mr. Chairman, to write a letter with me to the NSA Inspector General asking to review his seven reports on the program. You did not send that letter. A two-hour PowerPoint presentation from an NSA official, or an occasional briefing by the NSA Director, does not constitute sustained,

serious oversight. None of these briefings has been on-the-record, on the purported theory that we could not find a single cleared stenographer, even though thousands of Executive Branch officials have been briefed into this program! The American people deserve better."

246 *Later that day, he penned a letter to Cheney:* A copy of Rockefeller's letter was released after the NSA surveillance program was publicly exposed, at www.talkingpointsmemo.com/docs/rock -cheney1.html.

246 *Before he headed home for good, Poindexter stopped in at the Pentagon, to say good-bye to Rumsfeld:* Interview with Poindexter.

CHAPTER 21: BASKETBALL

251 *Brian Sharkey sent an e-mail to firms working with his company:* I obtained a copy of this e-mail from a private-sector source that is independent of Sharkey's firm. This individual asked not to be identified.

251 *One of Sharkey's colleagues sent a follow-up message to Hicks employees:* Ibid.

251 *Appropriators spelled out in the classified annex which elements would continue to receive funding:* I verified the continuation of the specific programs with individuals who have direct knowledge of what's contained in the classified annex and who asked not to be identified. Additionally, I obtained an official document that describes which programs continued and how they progressed from a source who asked not to be identified. See also my story "TIA Lives On" in *National Journal*, February 23, 2006.

252 *Now known as the Research Development and Experimental Collaboration, or more simply, "the RDEC":* The aforementioned official document also describes the RDEC in detail. I interviewed former government officials and private-sector sources all knowledgeable of the RDEC and its work. These people asked not to be identified. I also spoke for background purposes with a Homeland Security Department intelligence official who confirmed the RDEC's existence and its purpose. See my story "Signals and Noise" in *National Journal*, published on June 19, 2006.

252 *But he regretted that the privacy research had been tossed into the dustbin:* Interviews with Poindexter. He has emphasized on numerous occasions his disappointment that the privacy research was discontinued. I have found no evidence that he could have ensured that it was. The move of the programs from DARPA to the NSA's research unit was handled primarily in Congress, and by that time Poindexter was persona non grata there. Popp also had no real power to force the NSA group to take up the privacy research. He could only try to persuade them. Ultimately, it was the call of the officials working there, who were under the purview of Mike Hayden.

253 *"When I walked away from that program," he would recall years later, "I wanted nothing to do with it ever again":* Mike Wertheimer told me this during our conversation at the "Analytic Transformation" intelligence conference in Chicago (cited also in chapter 13) on September 6, 2007, which was sponsored by the Office of the Director of National Intelligence, where he was employed.

It's worth noting here that Wertheimer's judgment is not unique. Indeed, many surveillance experts, scholars, and lawyers told me that the Bush administration was justified in taking extraordinary steps in the immediate aftermath of the 9/11 attack to prevent another act of terrorism. In that exigent breach, these people said, violations of FISA could be forgiven. (Speaking on background, even an attorney with the American Civil Liberties Union expressed this view to me and said he could have accepted a program of warrantless surveillance for six months to a year after the attacks.)

But, in these experts' opinions, in the absence of another attack or a clear and present threat to the United States, the administration should have rescinded the extraordinary authorities or sought changes to the law that would give the NSA the powers it needed to collect intelligence on terrorists. The fact that Wertheimer, a career NSA official, shared this view, and that he was in a position to know the severity of the terrorist threat in the months and years after 9/11, helped inform one of my core conclusions: The Bush administration squandered an opportunity to craft some middle ground, one that would have given the NSA the powers it legitimately needed in a manner that the public could accept.

253 *One senior CIA official who was privy to the security agency's reporting routinely saw American*

citizens and other U.S. persons directly named in its reports: Interview with said official, who asked not to be identified, in 2008.

253 *Popp tried one last time to revive the privacy research:* Interview with Popp in 2008.

CHAPTER 22: RESURRECTION

254 *Poindexter hadn't been far from Townsend's mind:* Interview with Fran Townsend.

254 *Poindexter said that he'd like to get together:* Interviews with Townsend and John Poindexter.

255 *Syracuse University had invited him:* I was also invited to speak on this panel, and it was on this occasion that I first met Poindexter. He sought me out and apologized for not agreeing to my previous interview requests. Not long after this meeting, I began the series of interviews that eventually culminated in this book. All the dialogue and descriptions contained in the passage about the Syracuse episode come from my first-person reporting. I also interviewed the student identified here, Sam Alcoff, and spoke more with Poindexter about his reactions to what Alcoff said.

259 *The participants gathered at Cantigny:* The conference materials for "Counterterrorism Technology and Privacy," held June 24 and 25, 2004, as well as the guest list, are available on the McCormick Foundation's Web site, www.mccormickfoundation.org/publications/counterterror ism.pdf. I spoke with one of the participants on background to better understand the format and how the participants interacted. I also interviewed Poindexter and Steinhardt about the conference.

259 *both men had been informed about the NSA surveillance program:* See Barton Gellman's *Angler: The Cheney Vice Presidency* (New York: Penguin Press, 2008).

260 *Looking back, Steinhardt still felt that killing TIA—at least in one form—counted as a win:* Interview with Steinhardt.

261 *the attendees drew up a lengthy set of principles:* This report is also publicly available. It is titled "Counterterrorism Technology and Privacy" and was published by the McCormick Tribune Foundation as part of the Cantigny Conference Series. A copy is available at the McCormick Foundation's Web site, www.rrmtf.org/publications/counterterrorism.pdf.

261 *It wasn't warrantless "wiretapping" that had senior lawyers at Justice on edge. Rather, it was the layer of surveillance that often preceded it:* A former senior administration official told me that it was the collection and mining of metadata, provided by telecommunications companies, that prompted Justice Department officials to object to the NSA surveillance.

The legal rationale for this objection, and the apparent acceptance of targeted warrantless surveillance, has never been fully explained. It is possible officials believed that because the government predicated targeted surveillance on some "reasonable belief" that the participants involved in a phone call or e-mail had a nexus to terrorism, they then had the authority to collect intelligence. In the case of mining metadata, however, there could be no reasonable basis for suspicion, because, by design, the surveillance involves a massive, arguably indiscriminate, sweep of mostly innocuous communications. Put another way, it's a lot less "reasonable" to go fishing for bad guys without a known suspect than it is to try and find them through more discrete, targeted surveillance, particularly when there's some reason to believe that a party to the communication is connected with terrorists.

In any case, the former administration official confirmed that it was this massive surveillance that prompted the extraordinary showdown between Justice officials and the White House. This account is supported by reporting in *Newsweek,* specifically Daniel Klaidman's article "Now We Know What the Battle Was About," published on December 13, 2008. Attorney General Alberto Gonzales had also hinted in testimony before the Senate Judiciary Committee on February 7, 2006, that the objections raised by Justice's lawyers involved some other activity than targeted warrantless surveillance, which at that point President Bush had acknowledged publicly as the "terrorist surveillance program." Gonzales again appeared before the panel on July 24, 2007, to answer questions about the NSA's surveillance. In each of his appearances, Gonzales seemed to indicate that there was no opposition to that program within the administration. But when it became clear that there was, in fact, tremendous concern about it, some lawmakers accused Gonzales of lying. Not long after his testimony Justice Department officials spoke to reporters anonymously and said that the program in question that had caused such consternation involved data mining. They didn't go into specifics. See "Former U.S. Official: Gonzales 'Splitting

Hairs' in Testimony," published on CNN's Web site on July 30, 2007. Also see "Gonzales Denies Improper Pressure on Ashcroft," by David Johnston and Scott Shane, *New York Times*, July 24, 2007.

For an in-depth account of the standoff between Justice and the White House, see Gellman's *Angler*. Also see an adaptation of the book published in the *Washington Post*, September 14, 2008, titled "Conflict Over Spying Led White House to Brink."

Also see the memoir of Jack Goldsmith, the former head of the Office of Legal Counsel, *The Terror Presidency: Law and Judgment Inside the Bush Administration* (New York: W. W. Norton & Co., 2007).

262 *Brenner and Potenza . . . had assured Hayden he could rely on those presidential authorities that Ashcroft was supposed to review. But the White House had forbidden the NSA men to see the underlying analysis, prepared by Yoo:* See Gellman.

262 *he'd spent the past few years telling congressional officials, in his limited briefings, that the NSA's lawyers had signed off on the program:* Hayden emphasized this in numerous public statements about the surveillance program. One of his most detailed accounts was presented at the National Press Club, in an address to reporters on January 23, 2006.

CHAPTER 23: THE BREAKTHROUGH

This account of the NSA's foray into in-memory databases comes from the following sources. First, a private-sector individual with direct knowledge of the NSA's surveillance efforts and the technology underpinning them, who requested anonymity when speaking about intelligence programs. This individual spoke with me at length in 2008 about these efforts and pointed me toward a number of publicly available sources that amplified the account. These included press releases from companies that had sold the NSA the computers and servers necessary to build the in-memory system. This individual also supplied me with an internal e-mail from an NSA employee describing some of these efforts.

I was able to independently verify with a number of other sources that the NSA was exploring in-memory databases. These included former intelligence officials and experts on the technology who verified that my characterizations in this chapter—which are meant to make the technology understandable to lay readers—are an accurate reflection of how these systems work. I also conducted a background interview with a researcher who had done work on in-memory databases for the NSA and who requested anonymity.

In this chapter I use the phrase "logic layer" to describe a kind of vocabulary that told a computer what the cacophony of phone records and e-mails, words and numbers running through its brain actually meant, and more important, what they meant in relation to one another. The meaning of logic layer deserves a bit more explanation here. Computer engineers use the word "ontology" for a complete set of terms, definitions, and often explanations of how objects relate to one another. (Ontology is a branch of philosophy that deals with the nature of being.) When engineers speak of a logic layer they mean the application of an ontology to a computer system. So, while the terms "ontology" and "logic layer" are not interchangeable, they are linked to each other. I use the latter term in this chapter, which is all about putting the ontology to use.

267 *Back in the late 1990s officials had started to worry about whether the power would run out:* See "NSA Risking Electrical Overload," by Siobhan Gorman, *Baltimore Sun*, August 6, 2006.

267 *In 2001 a group of database builders in Washington State decided to test the speed of a disk-based database and one built entirely in memory:* The company in question is called McObject, and research papers detailing these experiments are available on its Web site, mcobject.com.

CHAPTER 24: EXPOSED

271 *Not long after Townsend moved into her new West Wing office, an NSA employee came to see her:* Interview with Fran Townsend in 2009. Unless otherwise noted all statements, thoughts, and actions attributed to Townsend in this section come from the interview.

271 *Before a meeting in the Oval Office, which was also attended by Mike Hayden, Comey asked Townsend, who was still a deputy, if she had ever heard of the code name Stellar Wind:* Barton Gellman recounts this exchange in *Angler: The Cheney Vice Presidency* (New York: Penguin

Press, 2008), but he does not use the code name Stellar Wind. I insert it here because I have confirmed with a former administration official that this was the name.

272 *But Alexander also had a contentious relationship with Mike Hayden:* Former officials who have known and worked with both men described this conflict. They described both men as having different views about how the NSA should work with other intelligence officials. Alexander was more open to sharing, they said.

274 *Curt Weldon had been hearing things:* In interviews conducted in 2005 and 2006, Weldon described for me the process by which he became aware of the Able Danger program, as well as what he believes was a cover-up by the administration.

274 *In October 2003, some staffers flew to Bagram, Afghanistan, where Shaffer was stationed, and they interviewed him:* The Defense Department inspector general's report on Able Danger documents this meeting ("Alleged Misconduct by Senior DoD Officials Concerning the Able Danger Program and Lieutenant Colonel Anthony A. Shaffer, U.S. Army Reserve," case number H05L97905217, dated September 18, 2006). The 9/11 Commission has also verified that it occurred.

276 *Hadley had taken a look at the chart, and he seemed impressed. "I have to show this to the big man," he said, meaning Bush:* The Defense Department inspector general also cites this exchange, which Weldon writes about in his book, *Countdown to Terror: The Top-Secret Information That Could Prevent the Next Terrorist Attack on America . . . and How the CIA Has Ignored It* (Washington, D.C.: Regnery Publishing, 2005).

277 *The story was far more complex, and more disheartening, than the one Weldon was telling. Erik Kleinsmith sure thought so:* Interviews with Kleinsmith in 2005 and 2008. He also felt that plenty of others, not just Weldon, were trying to distort the Able Danger story or hadn't understood it. Kleinsmith felt that the program was not about finding and preventing the next attack so much as finding "actionable intelligence" and using new forms of analysis. The distinction might seem minor to some, but to Kleinsmith it was important.

277 *"I myself do not remember seeing either a picture or his name on any charts":* Kleinsmith testified before the Senate Judiciary Committee on September 21, 2005.

279 *Weldon later dismissed Kleinsmith as a know-nothing:* In a phone conversation in December 2005, Weldon told me that Kleinsmith didn't know much about the Able Danger program and insisted that he was a marginal player in the operation.

CHAPTER 25: REASONABLE BELIEFS

282 *the former director of the NSA, now the second most senior spy in government, joined President Bush in an Oval Office meeting with Bill Keller, the* Times's *executive editor:* Keller described the meeting in detail to PBS's *Frontline,* in interviews for its documentary *News War,* which aired February 13, 2007. The producers interviewed Keller on three occasions in 2006.

New York magazine also recounted the Oval Office meeting, from an interview with Keller, in an article published on September 11, 2006, called "The United States of America vs. Bill Keller."

283 *On January 23, 2006, he addressed a crowd of journalists and a few activists at the National Press Club:* I was present for that address. The accounts of Hayden's demeanor and his facial tic are mine. The latter is something I have observed on the numerous occasions I've been in Hayden's presence while covering him.

288 *A USA Today poll taken not long after the* Times *story appeared:* The results of the poll were published on May 14, 2006. In response to the question "Based on what you have heard or read about this program to collect phone records, would you say you approve or disapprove of this government program," 51 percent of respondents said they disapproved, 43 percent said they approved, and 6 percent said they had no opinion. Of those who approved, 69 percent agreed that they felt that way because "investigating terrorism is the more important goal, even if it violates some Americans' civil liberties." Those who opposed the program were asked, "Do you think there would ever be circumstances in which it would be right for the government to create a database of telephone records, or would it not be right for the government to do this under any circumstances?" Sixty percent answered, No, it wouldn't be right under any circumstances. But 34 percent of those who opposed the program said, Yes, there are circumstances under which it would be right.

The *USA Today* poll, cosponsored by Gallup, had a margin of error of plus or minus 4 percentage points. It also differed from a poll released three days earlier by ABC News and the *Washington Post*, which found that 63 percent of respondents said the program was an acceptable means of investigating terrorism. In covering its own poll *USA Today* noted, "The findings may differ because questions in the two polls were worded differently." The ABC-*Post* poll asked, "It's been reported that the National Security Agency has been collecting the phone call records of tens of millions of Americans. It then analyzes calling patterns in an effort to identify possible terrorism suspects, without listening to or recording the conversations. Would you consider this an acceptable or unacceptable way for the federal government to investigate terrorism?" The *USA Today*–Gallup poll included more respondents and, as the paper noted, "was taken after Americans had a day or two to hear and think about the program."

In my personal experience, which is hardly scientific, people are genuinely divided over the question. Clearly it depends on how the question is asked, but I think it's a fair characterization to say that reasonable people have different views on whether it's appropriate for the NSA to collect and analyze the communications of Americans for the purposes of detecting terrorism. However, I doubt they would support such covert intelligence-gathering if the purpose was to identify political opponents—which would be illegal—or even common criminals.

CHAPTER 26: BETRAYAL

293 *"Do you have any contact with journalists?" one interrogator asked a thirty-year intelligence officer working at the agency:* This account comes from a discussion in 2006 with said intelligence officer, who asked not to be quoted.

294 *Amid the internal probes Goss imposed new, tighter restrictions on the books, articles, and opinion pieces published by former employees who were still working for the agency under contract:* I wrote about this new policy for *National Journal* in "Silencing the Squeaky Wheels," published on April 27, 2006.

294 *Careerists at the agency thought that Goss had been sent to clean house and to whip them into shape:* I base this view on my own background conversations with career officers at the CIA, including some who worked for Goss and approved of his mission.

294 *the* Post *revealed a global network of CIA-run prisons in foreign countries:* See Dana Priest's "CIA Holds Terror Suspects in Secret Prisons," *Washington Post*, published on November 2, 2005.

294 *Senior operations officials . . . were devastated. . . . The* Post *story also put on ice a plan to open a new, more sophisticated prison that the agency had built from the ground up in a friendly country:* Interview with a former senior operations official with direct responsibility for the terrorist detention and interrogation program, who asked not to be identified.

295 *What McCarthy learned in the course of her investigation made her a target:* This assessment, with which I concur based on my own reporting, is expressed in R. Jeffrey Smith's *Washington Post* article "Fired Officer Believed CIA Lied to Congress," published on May 14, 2006. McCarthy's dismissal was covered by most of the major news organizations as well. In our interviews, McCarthy did not speak about her views on what anyone at the CIA had told Congress about its detention and interrogation programs.

296 *McCarthy told Poindexter she was not the source of that prisons story:* The account of Poindexter and McCarthy's meeting comes from an interview with McCarthy and an electronic exchange with Poindexter in 2006, shortly after McCarthy was dismissed from the CIA.

297 *Some of her friends thought that Goss was looking to scare the spy workforce:* In background conversations, some of McCarthy's friends and former associates told me this. These individuals didn't want to be quoted but shared their opinions after McCarthy was dismissed from the agency. Also see Smith's piece, in which people who are reported to know McCarthy share their views.

298 *He once threw a cocktail party for his new friends at the Ritz-Carlton, not far from the Pentagon, and entertained them with a professional "mentalist," who performed card tricks and sleights of hand:* I attended this party on May 6, 2008.

298 *During the lunch break he found himself standing in line for a sandwich next to a guy he'd never met, but who'd also grown up in the Bay Area:* Interview with Jim Harper in 2008.

299 *Harper suggested that they write a paper together:* Interviews with Harper and Jeff Jonas in 2008.

299 *In December 2005, he spoke before a meeting of the Homeland Security Department's Data*

Privacy and Integrity Advisory Committee: A transcript of the proceedings is available at the Homeland Security Department's Web site. The meeting took place on December 6, 2005, in a ballroom at the J. W. Marriott Hotel in Washington, D.C. www.dhs.gov/xoig/assets/mgmtrpts/privacy_advcom_12-2005_mins_am.pdf.

300 *Poindexter read the paper and found it both flawed and misguided:* Interview with Poindexter.

301 *The paper was only ten pages long, but it was a watershed:* The paper, "Effective Counterterrorism and the Limited Role of Predictive Data Mining," was published by the Cato Institute on December 11, 2006, at www.cato.org/pub_display.php?pub_id=6784.

301 *Jonas's admiration for Poindexter never dimmed:* Interview with Jonas in 2008.

CHAPTER 27: BOJINKA II

302 *"probably the most sustained period of severe threat since the end of the Second World War":* British home secretary John Reid's comments were reported by the *Guardian* in "Anti-terror Critics Just Don't Get It, Says Reid," published on August 10, 2006.

302 *Agents kept close watch on Ali:* The British government presented the narrative of their investigation at Ali's trial. Other excellent sources of UK reporting include BBC News, which published a helpful and detailed summary called "Airlines Plot: The Allegations" on its Web site during the trial in 2008. The Canadian Broadcasting Corporation also provided detailed coverage of the plot and the trial. In particular, see the article "Montreal, Toronto Flights Targeted in Alleged British Bomb Plot" that it published on April 3, 2008, on its Web site. Also see the analysis of *Times* (London) reporters Sean O'Neill and Michael Evans, "How the Plan Was Put Together: Little Did Ahmed Ali and His Cohorts Know That They Were Under Round-the-Clock Surveillance While Plotting Their Attacks," published on September 9, 2008.

303 *Undercover officers observed Ali as he paid cash for a £138,000 flat:* See "Terror Mastermind Abdulla Ahmed Ali Guilty of Bombing Plot," by Nico Hines, *Times* (London), September 8, 2008.

303 *Back in Washington, senior intelligence and security officials had been watching developments across the pond since late June:* In 2009, I interviewed Fran Townsend and Michael Jackson, the former deputy homeland security secretary, about the planes bombing plot. I conducted multiple interviews with Jackson on the subject.

Jackson told me that throughout late June and all of July it wasn't clear that the suspects were targeting airliners. "There was some concern" of that, Jackson said, but he noted that given past bombings in the UK, authorities had reason to suspect the individuals under surveillance might target the ground transportation system, or build a car bomb.

306 *Keith Alexander, the NSA director, had been giving daily briefings at the White House that summer:* Interview with Townsend.

306 *Townsend thought the intelligence advanced the government's understanding of the plot:* Ibid.

307 *Jackson sketched out the first notions of a passenger-profiling system:* Interview with Jackson in 2008.

308 *Jackson and others could see this was potentially as big a plot as the United States had faced since 9/11:* Ibid.

308 *Precisely what prompted the Brits to make their move on August 10 would remain a subject of speculation:* Jackson declined to say whether the surveillance of Ali checking flight timetables was the signal that told investigators that this was an aviation-centered attack. But there were "clear and multiple reinforcing data streams" that indicated this, he said. Jackson informed Kip Hawley, the director of the Transportation Security Agency, of a threat to airliners two days before the surveillance at the Internet café occurred. The record as expressed in news reports and in evidence at trial shows that Ali's visit to the café signaled to investigators that the plot had progressed into a definite targeting stage.

310 *After the British tipped off the Americans, the NSA was able to intercept e-mails that Ali sent to an apparent terrorist minder in Pakistan, an Al Qaeda operative named Rashid Rauf:* See my piece "E-mails Help Convict Would-Be Bombers," published in *National Journal's* blog Tech Daily Dose, on September 9, 2009.

312 *Ali, who denied the breadth of the plot at his trial, nevertheless admitted that he at least planned to set off a bomb in Heathrow Airport:* On September 8, 2008, Ali and two other men were found guilty of conspiracy to murder. One man was found not guilty, and the jury failed to reach a

verdict on four others. For a concise wrap-up of the verdicts, see Hines's London *Times* article, noted above.

312 *U.S. law enforcement officers arrested seven men in Florida on the dubious charge that they were plotting to blow up the Sears Tower:* The first trial in the case ended in December 2007 with the acquittal of one defendant, Lyglenson Lemorin. The jury deadlocked on the other six defendants, Narseal Batiste, Patrick Abraham, Stanley Grant Phanor, Rotschild Augustine, Burson Augustin, and Naudimar Herrera. After a second trial in 2008, the jury also failed to reach verdicts. Finally, in May 2009, Herrera was acquitted; Augustine, Phanor, and Augustin were convicted on two counts of providing material support to a terrorist organization; Abraham was convicted on three charges; and Batiste was convicted on four charges. He was the only defendant to be convicted of all the charges that made up the government's indictment. For a complete synopsis of the case, see "Five Convicted in Plot to Blow Up Sears Tower," by Damien Cave and Carmen Gentile in *New York Times*, May 12, 2009.

CHAPTER 28: INHERIT THE WINDS

316 *a team that had formed to run Homeland Security's ADVISE program and build a working prototype huddled at the Johns Hopkins Applied Physics Laboratory:* The detailed notes and minutes of this meeting were provided to me by a private-sector source who asked not to be identified. I had been aware of the ADVISE program for some time in the course of my reporting on intelligence and homeland security. Also see the Homeland Security Department inspector general's report on the program, "ADVISE Could Support Intelligence Analysis More Effectively," released July 2, 2007. OIG-07-56. www.dhs.gov/xoig/assets/mgmtrpts/OIG_07-56_Jun07.pdf.

316 *Steve Dennis, a technology official from Homeland Security, offered up the history of the program:* This narrative is contained in the aforementioned document from the private-sector source.

316 *KSP stood for Knowledge System Prototype, a major initiative under way at the signals agency:* The KSP was described to me by the private-sector source as well as in an e-mail from an NSA employee. For more descriptions of the KSP, see the Defense Department's "Joint Transformation Roadmap," published on January 21, 2004. This publicly available document was prepared by the U.S. Joint Forces Command for the director of the Office of Force Transformation at the Pentagon. www.ndu.edu/library/docs/jt-transf-roadmap2004.pdf. "Force transformation" was the top policy initiative of Donald Rumsfeld when he was secretary of defense.

317 *Known as the Threat and Vulnerability Information System, it included a "threat mapper":* A description of the system is contained in the testimony of Charles McQueary, the undersecretary for science and technology at the Homeland Security Department, before the Senate Appropriations Subcommittee on Homeland Security on March 2, 2004.

317 *Toward the end of the discussion someone noted that Poindexter's old TIA network was testing components for the ADVISE system:* The reference in the notes of the September 2005 meeting on the ADVISE program is to the RDEC.

317 *Poindexter had trouble keeping up with all the ersatz programs that rode his wake:* Interview with Poindexter.

318 *Jeff Stewart sensed that this new whirlwind of corporate information was something to be embraced:* I interviewed Stewart in 2008 about Monitor110, his concept, and his work forming the start-up. It received some attention in the financial press as well. See "Monitor 110 Brings Blog Intelligence to Wall Street," by Richard Koman in *Silicon Valley Watcher*, September 21, 2006. A helpful chronology was also written by Roger Ehrenberg, an investor in Monitor110, on his blog Information Arbitrage. Called "Monitor110: A Post Mortem," it was posted on July 18, 2008, and contained background on how Ehrenberg met Stewart and what they hoped the technology would be able to do.

320 *inside the intelligence community people knew that Stewart's creation had the same core that the Livermore lab had sold to Homeland Security to build ADVISE. The BAG was at the heart of Monitor110:* This is based on an interview with the private-sector source, as well as the internal NSA e-mail, which specifically discussed ADVISE and Monitor110.

CHAPTER 29: ASCENSION

Unless otherwise noted statements, thoughts, and actions attributed in this chapter to Mike McConnell come from interviews I conducted with him in 2009. I also covered McConnell throughout his tenure as director of National Intelligence, from February 2007 to January 2009. See "The Return of the Grown-Ups," published in *National Journal* on January 13, 2007; "The Boys Are Back in Town" in the April 2007 issue of the U.S. Naval Institute's journal *Proceedings*; and "Clearing Barriers," *Government Executive* magazine, May 7, 2007.

322 *the rewards of a seven-figure salary ahead:* The *Wall Street Journal* reported that in 2007 McConnell was earning $2 million a year. See Siobhan Gorman's "McConnell to Return to Booz Allen," January 27, 2009.

322 *Bush was convinced that certain career employees, particularly at the CIA, had tried to sabotage his reelection bid in 2004:* This was conveyed to me by a former administration official, who spoke on condition of anonymity.

322 *McConnell was widely seen as a professional and a nonpartisan:* I wrote about McConnell's return to government for *National Journal, Proceedings,* and *Government Executive*. See above.

323 *Rumsfeld, long distrustful of the CIA, was setting up a covert human intelligence apparatus that reported through the Defense Department chain of command:* Intelligence experts presumed that after Rumsfeld left office his successor, Bob Gates, would curtail these activities. See my article "Rolling Back Pentagon Spies," *National Journal,* March 9, 2007.

325 *McConnell spent the first few months on the job getting adjusted to the hours:* McConnell described his daily routine in a speech at the Excellence in Government conference in Washington on April 4, 2007; http://odni.gov/speeches/20070404_speech.pdf. This was his first major public address, and he chose to lead off by telling the audience how grueling his new hours were. McConnell often cited the physical and time demands of the job when he spoke publicly. Transcripts of all McConnell's major speeches are available at the Web site of the Office of the Director of National Intelligence.

325 *Bush liked McConnell with him in the Oval every day, as his emissary and his eyes and ears:* Bush made no secret of his desire to keep his intelligence directors close. It was well known to journalists covering the White House and the intelligence community that McConnell was in the Oval Office almost every day, personally delivering the president's intelligence briefing.

326 *McConnell wanted to get Bush's permission to use a particularly modern weapon on the insurgents, one that he had come to admire and fear:* Interview with McConnell in 2009 and two former senior administration officials in 2008; both former officials were in the Oval Office during the meeting. They asked not to be identified.

    Lawrence Wright of *The New Yorker* also wrote about this meeting in his profile of McConnell, "The Spymaster," published on January 21, 2008.

326 *McConnell explained the principles of information warfare to the president:* Interview with McConnell and aforementioned former administration officials.

327 *Intelligence officials had collected evidence that they believed showed hackers based in China, working on behalf of the People's Liberation Army, had wormed their way into the systems that ran electrical generators and the power grid:* I wrote about this in a piece for *National Journal* titled "China's Cyber Militia," published on May 31, 2008. Sources for these and other allegations about Chinese cyber activities include Joel Brenner, who was then the government's head of counterintelligence; Tim Bennett, the former president of a trade group called the Cyber Security Industry Alliance; and a network forensics expert who works for intelligence and law enforcement agencies and asked not to be identified. A CIA official, Tom Donohue, had said publicly that cyberhackers had seized the computer systems of utility companies outside the United States and had demanded a ransom. And in a speech at the White House on May 29, 2009, President Barack Obama acknowledged, "We know that cyber intruders have probed our electrical grid and that in other countries cyber attacks have plunged entire cities into darkness." This was the first time that a U.S. president had admitted that the nation's electrical grid had been penetrated over the network.

327 *Bush was impressed. He gave McConnell the go-ahead to begin an information operation in Iraq:* Interview with McConnell and one of the previously mentioned former senior administration officials present at the Oval Office meeting.

327 *The information operation was credited as one of the most successful aspects of the "surge":* The aforementioned administration official confirmed that this operation was used during the surge. McConnell didn't address that point.

327 *he was also visibly unnerved by the vulnerabilities that McConnell had just described:* Interviews with previously mentioned former officials; also, see Wright's account in *The New Yorker*.

328 *He turned to the president and said, "If the capability to exploit a communications device exists, we have to assume that our enemies either have it or are trying to develop it":* Interview with one of the previously mentioned former administration officials. McConnell didn't recall the exact quote but didn't dispute this account.

328 *officials found it so revealing that they decided to classify it:* McConnell to Wright, *The New Yorker*.

328 *He turned to Bush and said, "If the 9/11 perpetrators had focused on a single U.S. bank through cyberattack, and it had been successful, it would have had an order of magnitude greater impact on the U.S. economy":* This is the quote as it appears in Wright's piece. McConnell agreed it was accurate, as did the two former administration officials who were also in the room.

328 *"Is this true, Hank?" Bush asked:* Interview with McConnell and the two officials. Brenner, the counterintelligence chief, also told me in an interview that the exchange among Bush, McConnell, and Henry Paulson was accurate.

329 *"This is our competitive advantage for the next seventy to a hundred years," he said to the room:* Interview with McConnell. The account was confirmed by one of the former administration officials, who was present.

329 *Homeland Security lacked the resident cyberexpertise and political clout to effectively do the job:* This is my assessment, based on my coverage of the department.

329 *McConnell knew the political dangers:* See Wright's profile, *The New Yorker*.

329 *McConnell believed that despite Americans' love of spy novels and James Bond movies, they mostly associated intelligence with duplicity and dirty dealings:* McConnell spoke about this love-hate relationship with spies in a speech at Furman University, his alma mater, on March 28, 2008. At http://odni.gov/speeches/20080328_speech.pdf.

332 *The covert program, known as Operation Shamrock, was believed to have collected 150,000 messages per month at its peak:* See the U.S. Senate's "Final Report of the Select Committee to Study Governmental Operations with Respect to Intelligence Activities," also known as the Church Committee, published April 23, 1976, www.icdc.com/~paulwolf/cointelpro/churchfinal reportIIIj.htm.

333 *McConnell thought that FISA had to be fixed:* It's true that McConnell came into office with reform of FISA on his agenda. But a former senior administration official, speaking on background, told me that the White House had been eyeing him for this job as well, because McConnell would bring the reputation of a professional and the imprimatur of the intelligence community to the debate. McConnell wanted to change the law. But the White House was making a political calculation in allowing him to become the point man for that effort.

333 *He outlined his vision in an essay:* See "Overhauling Intelligence," *Foreign Affairs*, July/ August 2007.

333 *On January 10, 2007, a judge on the secretive FISA Court issued orders that essentially blessed much of what the administration had already been doing under its own authority:* See letter from Alberto Gonzales to Patrick Leahy and Arlen Specter, January 17, 2007, http://graphics8 .nytimes.com/packages/pdf/politics/20060117gonzales_Letter.pdf.

334 *unlike the first judge, who had given the administration the latitude it wanted, this one rejected a significant part of the arrangement that had been struck in January:* Interview with McConnell.

336 *His captors had tortured him. He'd been burned, cut, and made to suffer:* Interview in 2008 with former senior CIA official, who asked not to be identified.

337 *The next day, McConnell and his staff pulled an all-nighter to get ready for a meeting with the Democratic leadership:* The play-by-play of McConnell's negotiations with Democratic lawmakers is detailed concisely in Wright's *New Yorker* piece. Many journalists, including me, covered these negotiations.

339 *"We have worked to achieve deep penetration of those who wish us harm":* See McConnell's commencement address to George Washington University's Columbian College of Arts and Sciences on May 17, 2008, http://odni.gov/speeches/20080517_speech.pdf.

339 *"The FISA court ruled presented the program to them and they said the program is what you say it*

is and it's appropriate and it's legitimate, it's not an issue and was had approval": See the transcript of McConnell's interview with Chris Roberts of the *El Paso Times*, published on August 22, 2007.

340 *McConnell would insist that he meant pressure from* Congress: Interview with McConnell.

342 *At the FBI and the White House some senior officials viewed him as a terrible choice for FISA point man:* These sentiments were conveyed to me by two former senior officials, one each at the White House and the FBI, who asked not to be identified. One of McConnell's former aides also told me that it had been a bad idea, politically, to put him in charge of the FISA reform effort.

CHAPTER 30: RENEGADE

347 *He spent two semesters at American University in Cairo, and four years later he entered the clandestine service:* See Eli Lake's "CIA Vet Aids Obama On Anti-Terrorism," *Washington Times*, March 1, 2009.

348 *Brennan gave a wide-ranging interview:* I conducted the interview for *National Journal*. See "The Counterterror Campaign," March 7, 2008.

350 *Obama announced that he would be voting for the bill:* See the June 29, 2008, post "Barack Obama on FISA" at my.barackobama.com.

351 *Obama had once been ranked the Senate's "most liberal" member:* See *National Journal*'s "2007 Vote Ratings," published January 21, 2008. Sen. Sheldon Whitehouse, a Democrat from Rhode Island, came in second. Joe Biden, then a Democratic senator from Delaware, came in third.

352 *He'd been at the CIA when the agency was in charge of preparing detailed "threat assessments":* See the "Report on the President's Surveillance Program," released on July 10, 2009, in which the inspectors general of five agencies and departments involved in the program explain the writing of threat assessments, which organizations wrote them, and how they were used. Brennan's tenure at the CIA and later at the Terrorist Threat Integration Center is a matter of public record.

352 *On September 2, Mike McConnell prepared for an unusual intelligence briefing:* The account of Obama's first intelligence briefing comes from an interview with McConnell, as well as from another individual with direct knowledge of the briefing. Tom Fingar, the head of analysis at the Office of the Director of National Intelligence, publicly stated that the meeting took place. He spoke at the "Analytic Transformation" conference in Orlando, Florida, on September 4, 2008.

353 *"Until this point, I've been worried about losing this election," he told McConnell and his colleagues. "After talking to you guys, I'm now worried about winning":* Interview with McConnell.

355 *officials discovered that the agency had inadvertently collected the phone calls and e-mails of Americans:* This "overcollection" was first reported by James Risen and Eric Lichtblau of the *New York Times* on April 15, 2009: "Officials Say U.S. Wiretaps Exceeded Law." I also discussed the matter with a congressional official who asked not to be identified.

EPILOGUE

357 *the agency had rejected a new data-analysis system that had such protection built in:* See "NSA Rejected System That Sifted Phone Data Legally," by Siobhan Gorman, *Baltimore Sun*, May 18, 2006.

361 *A special appeals court, the Foreign Intelligence Court of Review, publicly announced its decision in a challenge to the Protect America Act:* The court decided the case on August 22, 2008, and it was publicly released in redacted form on January 15, 2009. Case No. 08-01, *In Re: Directives [Redacted] Pursuant to Section 105B of the Foreign Intelligence Surveillance Act*, is available from the U.S. Courts at www.uscourts.gov/newsroom/2009/FISCR_Opinion.pdf?WT .cg_n=FISCR Opinion_WhatsNew_homepage, and from the Federation of American Scientists at www.fas.org/irp/agency/doj/fisa/fiscr082208.pdf. Importantly, the court also ruled that incidental collections of Americans' communications, of the kind that were later disclosed by Obama officials to have occurred under the amended FISA, were not in themselves illegal. So long as the surveillance itself was lawful and reasonable, such sweeping up of uninvolved parties wasn't a crime.

362 *It was a clear, and perhaps rare, demonstration of a company's power to push back against the government:* Telecom lawyer and FISA expert Michael Sussmann wrote about the decision and companies' important role as a check on government surveillance in a blog post, "Rare FISA Court of Review Decision on Warrantless Surveillance," on January 15, 2009, www.digestiblelaw .com/electronicsurveillance/blogQ.aspx?entry=5295&id=32.

362 *That time, it sided with the government and in favor of broader surveillance authorities:* See *In Re: Sealed Case No. 02-001*, decided November 18, 2002, http://news.findlaw.com/hdocs/docs/ terrorism/fisa111802opn.pdf.

362 *a reporter asked Hayden what he thought:* See "Court Backs U.S. Wiretapping," by Evan Perez, *Wall Street Journal*, January 16, 2009.

INDEX

Abbas, Abu, 40
Able Danger:
    and Al Qaeda, 10, 117, 118–23, 125,
        127, 274–78
    code name of, 117
    comparisons with, 179, 199, 215
    data deleted, 11, 129–32, 278, 280–81
    data mining in, 69, 123–28, 135, 147, 280
    network mapping by, 10, 123
    public airing of, 276–77, 281
    resurrection of, 274–81
    and secrecy, 133, 236, 277–80
accountability, lack of, 258
Achille Lauro, 36–49, 54
    capture of hijackers, 47–49
    hijackers escaping, 42–47
    interception plan, 43–48
    isolate the ship, 37, 39
    locate the ship, 37, 39
    negotiations with hijackers, 40–41
    Sara Lee decision, 45
    success of mission, 48–49, 50, 115, 313
    take the ship, 38
    track the ship, 37–38
    U.S. citizen killed, 41–42, 48
ACLU (American Civil Liberties Union),
        237–38, 259, 260
Addington, David, 169
Advanced Research and Development
        Activity (ARDA), 244, 246–47, 253,
        293
Advanced Systems and Concepts
        Office, 172–74, 175–76

ADVISE (Analysis, Dissemination,
        Visualization, Insight, and Semantic
        Enhancement), 315–17, 320
Afghanistan, British policy in, 312
airline industry:
    ban on liquids in, 308–9, 311–12
    bomb-sensing equipment, 216
    and British terrorist threat, 304, 305,
        306, 307–12
    invisibility, 83
    passenger profiling, 236, 307–8
    stealth aircraft, 83, 106
    and terrorist patterns, 181–82
    and TSA, 216, 304, 305, 307, 309
Alcoff, Sam, 256–57
Alexander, Keith, 135, 187, 272, 306, 326
Ali, Ahmed Abdulla, 302–3, 304, 305,
        308, 310, 312
Ali Baba, 216, 226
Allen, Charlie, 30, 31, 92, 290, 304, 305
Allen, Dick, 22
Al Qaeda, 1–2, 114, 116–23, 334
    Able Danger study of, 10, 117, 118–23,
        125, 127, 274–78
    bomb-building, 305
    and CIA, 117, 118, 165, 212, 294, 310
    financing of, 206–7
    global network of, 10, 120, 123, 125,
        131, 133
    nexus of terrorism, 157–59, 294
    search for, 116, 120–21, 165, 212, 215
    Special Operations mapping of, 116–18
    spread of, 190, 302–3, 310–11, 333, 337

Al Qaeda (*cont.*)
  U.S. presence of, 10–11, 69, 276
  and USS *Cole*, 135
Al Shiraa, 59, 61
Amal, 25, 29, 30
American Civil Liberties Union (ACLU),
  237–38, 259, 260
Anschutz, Philip, 203
antisubmarine warfare, 27–29, 152
Arafat, Yasser, 39, 40
ARDA (Advanced Research and
  Development Activity), 244, 246–47,
  253, 293
Armour, Tom, 179, 292–93
Army, U.S.:
  and *Achille Lauro*, 38
  Army Field Manual, 354, 362
  and IDC, *see* Information
    Dominance Center
  Intelligence and Security Command, 98,
    129–30, 135, 187
  Intelligence Command, 9, 276
  and intelligence gap, 336–37
  Land Information Warfare Activity, 98
  Signals Security Agency, 332
Ashcroft, John, 216, 233, 236, 261–62, 287
AT&T, 75, 208, 211, 338
Atta, Mohamed, 275, 276, 277, 279, 280
Aum Shinrikyo, 89–91

Bacon, Kevin, 125–26
BAG (Big Ass Graph), 199–201
  as ADVISE, 315–17, 320
  creation of, 200–201
  failures of, 264, 320, 321
  financial data in, 208
  and graph theory, 199, 200, 212, 315
  information overload in, 209, 212, 218, 316
  and metadata, 205
  and Monitor110, 320–21
  Stellar Wind as, 171, 211, 264
  and telecom records, 204–5
Baginski, Maureen, 164–65
Baltimore Gas & Electric, 267
Basketball, 251
Becker, Art, 317
Beirut, Lebanon:
  killings and kidnappings in, 31–32

Marine barracks attacked in, 3, 10, 15–20,
    25–26, 32, 116, 185, 190
  see also Lebanon
Berlin Wall, fall of, 330
Beyster, Bob, 241
Biden, Joe, 350–51
bin Laden, Osama, 69, 88–89, 116–19, 133, 224
Black, Bill, 210–11, 212, 243
Black, Hugo L., 331–32
Black Hawk Down (1993), 118
Black Panthers, 110
Blue Dogs, 339, 341
Boehner, John, 337
Bojinka, 305
Booz Allen Hamilton:
  and Clapper, 324
  and cybersecurity to financial sector,
    328, 361
  and McConnell, 93, 194, 259, 328, 361
  and TIA, 194–95
Brennan, John, 188, 347–49, 351, 352
Brenner, Joel, 259, 262
Britain:
  security threat in, 302–12
  as surveillance state, 213–14
Brown v. Board of Education, 331
Buckley, William, 32
Buckley Air Force Base, Colorado, 203
Bush, George H. W., 32, 81, 87
Bush, George W., 134, 322, 325, 341
Bush administration:
  and Able Danger cover-up, 277
  and Congress, 236, 282, 289, 335–36
  and cybersecurity, 327–30
  and executive war powers, 168, 185, 288–89,
    335–36, 344, 352, 358
  and FISA, 337–43, 349–50
  influence in, 194, 195
  intelligence politicized by, 322
  and Iraqi weapons, 294, 322
  and leaks, 293–97
  and NSA, 165, 167, 252–53
  Office of Legal Counsel, 167–69, 261–62
  and Office of National Intelligence, 272–73
  and privacy concerns, 233–35, 236, 261–62,
    334–35
  questions of illegality in, 168, 261–63,
    271–72, 283–84, 286–87, 361–62

and terrorists, 276, 286, 305, 308, 310–12, 353, 355

and *Times* story, 282–83

and warrantless surveillance, 157–59, 167, 169–71, 206–9, 234, 252–53, 261–63, 283–89, 331, 333–35, 344, 352

and wiretapping, 284

CALEA (Communications Assistance for Law Enforcement Act) [1994], 77–80

Cantigny conference, 259–61, 262

Card, Andrew, 262

Carnivore, 192, 254

Casey, William J., 31, 54

Center for Democracy and Technology, 237

Center for National Security Studies, 259

Center for Strategic and International Studies, 236

Cheney, Dick:

as defense secretary, 86, 324

and information warfare, 326

and McConnell, 323–24, 340

and TIA/NSA, 245, 246, 290, 324

as vice president, 169

Cherry Vanilla World, 217

Chertoff, Michael:

and airport security procedures, 308

and British security threat, 303–4, 305, 306, 308–9

and Cantigny conference, 259

and Homeland Security, 259, 299, 303

private counseling firm of, 362

China:

hackers in, 327

missile sales to, 86

spy network of, 9, 104–9, 112–14, 115, 236

ChoicePoint, 216, 281

CIA (Central Intelligence Agency):

and Al Qaeda, 117, 118, 165, 212, 294, 310

analytic shortcomings of, 92, 95, 97–98, 100, 102, 119

and bin Laden, 118–19

and British terrorist threat, 311, 312

changing after 9/11, 151

communications hotline, 31

counterterrorist center, 92, 117, 134, 352

emergency measures in, 34

and foreign espionage, 323

and interagency rivalry, 24, 30, 86–87, 150, 323

invalid data from, 291

and Iran-Contra, 50, 55, 60, 61

and Karic, 102

laws governing deployment of, 33

leaks from, 293–97, 322

nonproliferation center, 179

prisons and interrogations run by, 294–95, 354

as risk averse, 148

terrorism as low priority for, 88, 147

and terrorist funding, 207

and TIA, 186, 188–90

U.S. persons targeted by, 286

Clancy, Tom, *Clear and Present Danger,* 81

Clapper, James, 93, 324

Clark, Bill, 21

Clarke, Richard, 86–89, 91, 93, 133–34, 193

Clinton, Hillary Rodham, 112, 346

Clinton administration, 87, 295, 347–48

and Balkans, 96–97, 101

and FISA warrants, 190–91

and privacy laws, 112, 192

and wiretapping, 75, 77

Clipper chip, 75, 79, 330

Coast Guard, U.S., 134, 190, 191

Cohen, William S., 112

Comey, James, 261, 262, 271

Commodore, 221

Comprehensive National Cybersecurity Initiative, 330

Congress, U.S.:

and Able Danger, 274–77

antiterrorism laws in, 32

Blue Dogs in, 339, 341

and Bush administration, 236, 282, 289, 335–36

and electronic surveillance, 74–80, 170, 288–89, 290–92, 356

and FISA, 53, 74, 159, 162, 163, 169, 288, 331, 333–35, 336–43

and Gang of Eight, 245–46, 261

and Iran-Contra, 13, 50–53, 55, 57–60, 63, 65–67, 81, 82–83, 185

and NSA, 163–64, 245–46

overlapping executive powers, 53, 163–64, 169–70, 185, 288

Congress, U.S.: (*cont.*)
  political enemies in, 149
  and privacy of U.S. persons, 194, 261–63,
    291–92
  Protect America Act, 341, 342, 344–46
  and terrorist detention, 354–55
  and TIA, 231–33, 236, 239–42,
    244–48, 260
  USA PATRIOT Act, 168, 331
Counterterrorism Security Group (CSG),
  87–88
"Counterterrorism Technology and Privacy"
  (McCormick discussion), 259–61
Craxi, Bettino, 38–39, 41, 48
Crisis Management Center, 22, 23–24,
  45, 87
Crisis Pre-Planning Group (CPPG), 33–34,
  37, 87
Cruise, Tom, 126
Customs Bureau, U.S., 207

DARPA (Defense Advanced Research
  Projects Agency):
  Evidence Extraction and Link
    Discovery, 179
  and Genoa, 93–94, 145, 146
  Information Awareness Office (IAO), 195,
    240, 243
  Information Systems Office, 83–84
  and Spinnaker, 83–84, 85
  and TIA, 145–46, 150, 153, 174–78, 195,
    240, 243
Defense Department:
  and Able Danger, 279
  and black budget, 247–48
  and information warfare, 327, 329
  intelligence budget controlled by, 323
  and interagency rivalry, 323
  and privacy law, 110–14, 124, 129–30
  and situational awareness, 172
  Systems Analysis Division, 23
  and TIA, 234, 239, 240, 247
  see also Pentagon, U.S.
Defense Intelligence Agency (DIA), 31, 93,
  274–75, 290, 324
Delta Airlines, 307–8
Dempsey, Jim, 237, 259
Dennis, Steve, 316, 317

Director of National Intelligence (DNI),
  272–74, 293, 322–25, 341, 360
Disruptive Technology Office, 293
Dolphin, Glenn, 15–20
Downing Assessment Task Force, 93

Eagle, 251
Economist, 240
Edwards, Don, 77
Edwards, John, 344
Egypt, and *Achille Lauro,* 40, 42, 43, 48
Electronic Communications Privacy Act
  (ECPA) [1986], 204
Emanuel, Rahm, 337
encryption technology, 73–74, 75
Enemy of the State (film), 160
EPIC (Electronic Privacy Information
  Center), 228
Executive order 12333 (twelve triple three),
  161–62, 163, 185, 325

FAA (Federal Aviation Administration),
  134, 144, 216
FBI (Federal Bureau of Investigation):
  bureaucracy of, 31, 276
  and ChoicePoint, 216
  data not shared by, 24, 150, 279
  and domestic spying, 110, 162, 192, 254,
    286, 304
  emergency measures in, 34
  false accusations by, 312–13
  Financial Review Group, 206–8
  and FISA, 342
  and Karic, 101–2
  and NSA, 272, 291
  terrorism as low priority for, 88, 147,
    275–76
  and terrorist interrogation, 354
  and terrorist threat, 134
  and TIA, 186, 191
  wild-goose chases of, 133, 212, 291
  and wiretapping, 53, 71–73, 74, 76–79, 332
FCC (Federal Communications
  Commission), 77, 79
Feinstein, Dianne, 289
Financial Crimes Enforcement Network
  (FinCEN), 179, 207
First Data, Colorado, 207

FISA (Foreign Intelligence Surveillance Act) [1978], 330–36
  changing language in, 167–68
  and Congress, 53, 74, 159, 162, 163, 169, 288, 331, 333–35, 336–43
  and emergency surveillance, 336–37
  and Executive order 12333, 161–62, 163
  and foreign/domestic wall, 191, 330, 333, 334–35, 342
  and immunity from civil suits, 338, 349
  McConnell's attempts to update, 331, 333–36, 337–43, 357
  passage of, 53, 74, 288
  and Protect America Act, 341, 342, 344–46, 350, 362
  and September 11 attacks, 331, 333
  sunset clause in, 342, 344
  and warrantless surveillance, 158–59, 169–70, 263, 287, 288, 338, 340, 345, 355–56
  warrants under, 163, 170, 190–91, 205, 263, 287, 338
  and wiretapping, 74, 79, 169, 191
FISA Amendments Act, 349–50, 355, 356
Fitzgerald, F. Scott, 254
Flint, Lara, 259
Foreign Affairs magazine, 333
Foreign Intelligence Court of Review, 361–62
Fourth Amendment, 168, 286–87, 362
Freedom of Information Act, 233
Freeh, Louis J., 74, 78
FutureMAP (Futures Markets Applied to Prediction), 239–41, 244, 246

Gang of Eight, 245–46, 261
Gates, Robert, 323, 324–25, 326
"Geneva," 317–18
Genoa:
  and Aum Shinrikyo, 89–91
  building support for, 92, 93–94, 133, 188, 272
  bureaucratic reluctance to use, 142–43, 143, 145
  purposes of, 89, 91, 146, 199
  Spinnaker as, 85
Genoa II, 179–80
Gentry, Tony, 129–30
Ghorbanifar, Manucher, 60
Gibbons, James, 130–31

Gidari, Al, 78, 79
Giuliani, Rudy, 257
Goldman Sachs, 328–29
Goldsmith, Jack, 261
Gonzales, Alberto:
  as attorney general, 283
  and Congress, 288–89
  and executive powers, 288–89
  and global telecommunications, 340, 348
  and illegal domestic spying, 262, 287
  and immunity from civil suits, 348
  as president's lawyer, 262
  and U.S. soldiers in Iraq, 336
  and warrantless surveillance, 288–89, 291, 334, 340
Goss, Porter, 245, 290, 293–97, 322
GRiD Compass (computer), 21–23
Groundbreaker, 202
Guantánamo Bay, Cuba, 215, 218, 353–55
Gulf War (1991), 187, 323–24

Hadley, Stephen, 276, 283, 326, 364
Hall, Wilma, 86, 88
Hamilton, Lee, 58
Hamre, John:
  and Cantigny conference, 259
  and Center for Strategic and International Studies, 236
  and Chinese spy network, 104–6
  and data-mining tools, 105–6, 108
  and IDC, 105–6, 112, 113, 114
  and TIA, 236, 238
Harman, Jane, 245
Harper, Jim, 298–301
Hart, Gary, 173
Hasenfus, Eugene, 60
hawala (money moving), 206–7
Hawley, Kip, 304–5, 308, 309
Hayden, Michael:
  Air Force career, 273
  and BAG, 171
  as CIA director, 297, 361
  and defense of government secrets, 202–4, 283–88
  and early-warning system for terrorism, 164–67, 218, 264, 286
  and FISA, 158–59, 163, 169, 170

Hayden, Michael: (*cont.*)
    and foreign/domestic intelligence wall,
        162–64, 362
    and National Intelligence Office, 272–74,
        290–92
    and NSA, 156–67
    on prisoner interrogation, 354
    and public relations, 160–61
    and Qwest, 202–4
    and September 11 attacks, 137, 159–60,
        161–62
    and technology upgrades, 164–65,
        271, 349
    and TIA, 212–13, 243–46
    and *Times*, 282–83
    and warrantless surveillance, 157–59, 166,
        169–71, 201–2, 262, 283–88, 357,
        361–62
Heath, James, 99, 135
Heritage Foundation, 298–99
Hezbollah, 190
Hicks & Associates, 148, 251
Highlands Forum, Carmel Valley,
    California, 219–20
Holloway, James, 184
Homeland Security, Department of:
    and ADVISE, 315–17, 320
    and Allen, 290, 304
    and British terrorist threat, 303–4, 305, 307,
        309–10, 311
    and Chertoff, 259, 299, 303
    and cyberdefense, 329
    and data-mining projects, 240
    Data Privacy and Integrity Advisory
        Committee, 299–300
    information sources of, 317
    mission areas of, 317
Hoover, J. Edgar, 332
Human Identification at a Distance, 179
Hurricane Katrina, 311
Hussein, Saddam, 323

IBM, 75, 362–63
Immigration and Naturalization Service (INS),
    122, 134, 317
Information Awareness Office (IAO):
    and DARPA, 195, 240, 243
    logo for, 195–97, 231, 233, 240, 260, 363–64

media attacks on, 231
mission of, 6
and privacy study, 227
and TIA, 174–76, 196, 227, 231,
    233, 239, 243
Information Dominance Center (IDC), 103,
    236, 272, 280
    and Able Danger, *see* Able Danger
    and Al Qaeda, 120–21, 275
    and Army Intelligence Command, 9, 187
    and China, 105–6, 108–9, 112, 113, 115
    and Karic, 98–100, 102
    and link charts, 275–76
    and privacy law, 109–14, 123–24, 130–32
    renewal of clearance, 134–35
    and TIA, 187, 210
    and U.S. Central Command, 135
    and USS *Cole*, 135
Information Systems Office, 83–84
Inouye, Daniel, 242
Institute for Defense Analysis, 228
intelligence:
    black budget for, 247–48
    budget cutbacks in, 105, 330
    central control of, 34
    covert forces in the field, 34
    dark arts of, 97, 294–95, 332–33
    and Executive order 12333, 161–62, 163,
        185, 325
    failures of, 92, 185, 264–67, 356, 358, 360
    FISA, 53, 74, 79, 158–59, 163, 342–43
    flow between governments, 43–44,
        303, 310
    foreign/domestic wall of, 88, 162–64,
        191–92, 197–98, 247, 330, 333, 334–35,
        342, 362
    and Gang of Eight, 245–46, 261
    information overload in, 145, 147, 205,
        208–9, 218, 264–65, 316, 355–56
    information retrieval in, 265–70
    and information warfare, 219–20, 326–29
    and interagency cooperation, 304
    and interagency rivalry, 24–25, 30, 31,
        86–87, 150, 189, 323
    master database for, 99
    metadata in, 205, 218, 284
    and minimization, 163, 253
    and mission creep, 260

misuse of, 5, 118, 159, 283, 294, 312–13, 322, 332

from open sources, 10–11, 106, 107, 111, 120, 122–23, 208

outdated tradecraft of, 99, 147–48, 164

politicization of, 322

private industry mining of, 281

recommended actions, 33

restrictions on gathering, storage, and use of, 11, 33, 110–14, 291–92

signals, 164–65

systemic overcollection of, 355–56

and technology, 84–85, 88, 99, 103, 105–6, 135, 164–65, 178, 200, 300–301, 311, 315, 315–18, 326–29, 343, 349, 358

on U.S. persons, 11, 122, 123, 124, 129–32, 193–94, 212, 216, 247, 277, 284–89, 291–92, 315, 332, 333

warrantless surveillance, 170, 290–92, 330, 333–35, 341, 348, 352, 355–56

watching the watchers, 356, 361

Intelligence and Security Command, 98, 129–30, 135, 187

Internet:

and cybersecurity, 327–30, 361

e-mail records, 166–67, 170, 192, 205, 312

financial news on, 318–19

first, 83

free space of, 76, 123

hackers on, 327

intelligence drawn from, 10–11, 106, 107, 111, 120, 123–24, 208

junk spam/noise of, 320

link charts from, 127, 130

open sources on, 100, 120

and privacy, 76, 77, 167, 192, 204, 359

propaganda spread via, 326

protection from government control, 76, 79, 192

and Qwest, 203–4

IOWA center, 200

Iran:

and Iraq, 51

Ministry of Information and Security, 25

regime change in, 56

and Russian mobsters, 166

U.S. arms embargo, 52, 61

U.S. hostages in, 38, 54–55, 56, 57, 59–61, 62, 65

Iran-Contra affair, 50–67

and CIA, 50, 55, 60, 61

commission report on, 169–70

and Congress, 13, 50–53, 55, 57–60, 63, 65–67, 81, 82–83, 185

and Israel, 51, 52

and North, 50–53, 57, 59–61, 64, 65–66, 238

and Poindexter, 6, 13, 50–53, 55–67, 81–83, 92, 149, 185, 234, 238, 364

and Reagan, 6, 13, 50–52, 54–56, 58, 59, 61–63, 64–65, 81, 82–83, 234

and trial, 66–67, 81, 238

and UNODIR, 54, 56, 63

and U.S. hostages, 54–55, 56, 57, 59–61, 62, 65

Iraq:

British policy in, 312

information warfare in, 326–29

insurgents in, 326, 327

intelligence gap in, 336–37

and Iran, 51

Kuwait invaded by, 323–24

opponents of war in, 323, 344

rules of engagement in, 185

rumors of weapons in, 294, 322

Saffron in, 281

U.S. invasion of, 280–81, 283

U.S. technology in, 321

IRS (Internal Revenue Service), 321, 363

Israel:

and *Achille Lauro,* 37, 44

and Iran-Contra, 51, 52

and missile sales, 86

Palestine vs., 16, 17

U.S. policies about, 86–87

Israeli Defense Force (IDF), 16

Italy, and *Achille Lauro,* 38–39, 48

Jackson, Michael (Homeland Security), 303–5, 307–9

Japan, Aum Shinrikyo attacks in, 89–91

JCAG (Joint Counterintelligence Assessment Group), 106

Johns Hopkins, Applied Physics Laboratory, 316

Johnson, David, 76–77

Joint Worldwide Intelligence Communications System, 120, 187

Jonas, Jeff, 220–26, 297–301, 361
background of, 220–21
and data privacy, 298
and debtor matching, 222–23
and Highlands Forum, 220
and IBM, 362–63
and Las Vegas casinos, 223–24
and NORA, 223–24, 225–26, 251, 297–98

JSOC (Joint Special Operations Command), and *Achille Lauro*, 38, 40, 45, 47–48

Justice Department:
and ChoicePoint, 281
and intercepted e-mails, 312
and legality of procedures, 272, 284, 307
and warrantless surveillance, 345, 356
and wiretapping, 74, 78

Karic, Dragomir, 96–97, 98–102

Keller, Bill, 282–83

Kennedy, Joseph P., 318

Kenya, U.S. embassy attacked in, 10, 116, 190

Kerr, Donald, 188–90, 249, 358–59, 360

Khobar Towers, Saudi Arabia, bombing of, 93–94, 347

Khomeini, Ayatollah Ruhollah, 17

Kissinger, Henry A., 53, 364

Kleinsmith, Erik:
and Able Danger, 10, 11, 118–28, 129–32, 135, 147, 187, 274, 277–80, 360, 362
and China, 105–9, 113
data deleted by, 9, 11, 129–32, 278–79
influence of, 361
as intelligence analysis instructor, 280–81
and Karic, 98–100
and Lockheed Martin, 135, 362
and privacy law, 109–11
and September 11 attacks, 143, 278
and Special Operations, 115–16

Klinghoffer, Leon, 41–42, 48

"Knowledge is power," 197, 231, 364

Krongard, A. B. "Buzzy," 188

Kuwait, Iraqi invasion of, 323–24

Lake, Tony, 86, 87, 347, 364

Lambert, Geoffrey, 132

Land Information Warfare Activity, 98

Las Vegas, casinos in, 223–24

Lawrence Livermore National Laboratory:
and ADVISE, 315, 316, 320
IOWA center in, 200
and Monitor110, 319, 320
on technology and national security, 200

Leahy, Patrick J., 77, 228, 288–89

Lebanon:
British policy in, 312
civil war in, 16
Sheikh Abdullah barracks in, 29–31
Syrian occupation of, 17, 18
terrorist signals ignored in, 24–25
U.S. embassy bombed in, 29–30, 290
U.S. government reaction to suicide bombing in, 20–26
U.S. hostages in, 32, 59, 61
U.S. Marines attacked in, 3, 10, 15–20, 25, 32, 116, 185, 190

Lehman, John, 258

Leopold, Reuven, 83, 84, 85

Libya, and Palestinian terrorists, 57

Lockheed Martin, 135, 362

logic layer, 268–69

Lohr, Michael, 124

Lukasik, Steve, 180, 181

McCain, John, 353

McCarthy, Mary:
and CIA, 91–92, 93, 134, 295–97, 322
and Genoa, 92, 93
and NSC, 91, 93, 133, 134
and Office of Intelligence Programs, 91
and Poindexter, 91–93, 134, 174–75, 193, 296
and terrorist chatter, 133, 143, 175
and TIA, 174–75

McConnell, Mike, 322–36
at Booz Allen, 93, 194, 259, 328, 361
at Cantigny conference, 75
and Clipper chip, 75
and cybersecurity, 327–30, 361
and dark side of intelligence, 332–33
as director of national intelligence, 249, 322–25, 341
and FISA, 331, 333–36, 337–43, 357
and immunity from civil suits, 348–50

and information warfare, 326–29
  as NSA director, 74, 324
  Obama briefing by, 352–53
  and TIA, 193–95
McCormick Tribune Foundation, 258–59
  "Counterterrorism Technology and Privacy,"
    259–61
McFarlane, Robert "Bud":
  and *Achille Lauro,* 44–45
  and Beirut suicide bombing, 20, 25–26
  and Iran-Contra, 51, 55, 57, 58, 59–61, 66
  and Poindexter, 21
  resignation of, 50
McNamara, Robert S., 23, 83
McVeigh, Timothy, 237
Madrid, train bombings in, 312
Manhattan Project, 150, 357
Manningham-Buller, Dame Eliza, 311
Marines, U.S.:
  attacked in Beirut, 3, 10, 15–20, 25–26, 32,
    116, 185, 190
  pulled out of Lebanon, 30
  rules of engagement, 17, 24
  terrorist threats against, 25
Markoff, John, 230
Martin, Kate, 259
Mayfield, Brandon, 312
Meese, Edwin III, 63–64, 65, 66
Microsoft, 75
Miers, Harriet, 283
Milošević, Slobodan, 96, 100–101, 102–3
Mogadishu, Somalia, 118
Monitor110, 319–21
Moreau, Art, 42–43, 44, 45
Moussaoui, Zacarias, 206–7
MoveOn.org, 345
Mubarak, Hosni, 42, 43, 44
Mueller, Robert, 262, 290, 291, 304
Musawi, Hussein, 25
Myers-Briggs Type Indicator, 125

Nacchio, Joe, 202–5
National Association of Securities Dealers
    (NASD), 179
National-Geospatial Intelligence Agency, 324
National Intelligence Office:
  and Hayden, 272–74, 290–92
  and McConnell, 249, 322–25, 341

and Negroponte, 273–74, 290, 293,
    304, 322, 323
and 9/11 Commission, 272
and Tangram, 360
National Journal, 292, 351
National Press Club, 283–84
National Security Agency (NSA):
  and ADVISE, 316, 320
  after 9/11, 156, 157–67
  and BAG, 171, 199–201, 316
  and British terrorist threat, 306, 310, 312
  and Clipper chip, 75, 79, 330
  and cybersecurity, 329, 330
  data shared by, 161, 291–92
  defense of government secrets, 202–4, 284
  and digital revolution, 79–80, 156–57
  and domestic spying, 73–75, 110, 113, 119,
    284
  and early-warning system for terrorists,
    164–67, 201
  failed technology of, 306, 317
  and FBI, 272, 291
  financial intelligence in, 207–8
  and FISA, 158–59, 163, 169
  and foreign/domestic intelligence wall,
    162–64, 192, 198, 356
  and geo-location, 212
  global monitoring system of, 158–59
  information retrieval for, 265–70
  and information warfare, 327, 328, 329
  "in-memory" databases, 267–70
  lack of specificity in, 212, 264, 266, 356
  mandate of, 161–63, 170, 208
  Operation Shamrock, 332
  and privacy protection, 163, 167, 204,
    286–87, 334, 357
  public image of, 160–61
  and Qwest, 201–5
  reputation of, 213
  and September 11 attacks, 159–60, 161–62,
    276
  and Tangram, 360
  and TIA, 186, 210–13, 217–18, 238,
    243–45, 252–53, 261, 292–93
  and warrantless surveillance, 157–59,
    169–71, 205–9, 211, 245, 252–53, 259,
    261–63, 282–89, 290–92, 310, 331,
    334–35, 342, 344–45, 355–56, 357

National Security Council (NSC):
  and *Achille Lauro,* 37, 43–45
  bureaucracy of, 21, 25
  communications hotline, 31
  Counterterrorism Security Group
    (CSG), 87–88
  Crisis Management Center, 22,
    23–24, 45, 87
  Crisis Pre-Planning Group (CPPG), 33–34,
    37, 87
  and interagency rivalry, 25
  and Iran-Contra, 50–67
  and Lebanon suicide bombing, 24–25, 32
  Office of Intelligence Programs, 91–93
  powers of, 33
  Situation Room, 22, 88
  Special Situation Group, 32
  Terrorist Incident Working Group, 37
  and terrorist interrogations, 354
National Weather Service, 268
Navy, U.S.:
  and *Achille Lauro,* 37–38, 45–49
  cutbacks in, 83
  Task Force Alpha, 27–29
Negroponte, John:
  and airline security, 304
  and congressional hearings, 290–92
  as DNI, 273–74, 290, 293, 304, 322, 323
Netroots, 344–45, 349, 351, 352, 355
New York Stock Exchange, 328
New York Times:
  on pre-9/11 failures, 150
  on TIA, 230–31, 254
  on warrantless surveillance, 282–83,
    289, 334
  on worthless intelligence data, 291
Nicaragua:
  Contra rebels in, 50–53, 57, 60
  NSC operations in, 57
9/11 Commission, 215, 272, 274–77
NORA (Non-Obvious Relationship
  Awareness), 223–24, 225–26, 251, 297–98
Noreaster, 238
Northern Ireland, insurgency in, 313
North, Oliver:
  and *Achille Lauro,* 37, 43–44, 45, 48
  and Iran-Contra, 50–53, 57, 59–61, 64,
    65–66, 238

  personal traits of, 34–35
  and satellite photographs, 29, 30
  and terrorism preplanning, 34, 87

Obama, Barack, 344–56, 357, 361
  and change as illusion, 355
  election campaign of, 345–46, 350,
    351, 356
  on executive powers, 351, 352
  on immunity from civil suits, 344–47, 348,
    349–52, 355
  inaugural address of, 353
  intelligence briefings of, 352–53
  split with the party, 350–51, 354
  on terrorist detention and interrogation,
    353–55, 362
  and warrantless surveillance, 355–56
  and war on terror, 353–56
O'Neill, Dick, 219–20
Operation Desert Storm, 187, 323–24
Operation Green Quest, 206–7
Operation Shamrock, 332

Pakistan:
  Al Qaeda in, 302–3, 310–11, 312
  extremists in, 117
Palestine:
  Israel vs., 16, 17
  and Libya, 57
Palestinian Liberation Front (PLF), 39, 40, 41
Pan Am Flight 103 bombing, 57, 216
Panetta, Leon, 354
Parentage (visualization program), 127, 130
Paulson, Henry, 326, 328–29
Paxton, Bill, 126
Payne, James, 201–2, 204
Pelosi, Nancy, 163, 164, 170, 245, 338
Pentagon, U.S.:
  and Able Danger, 123, 130, 135, 275–77,
    279–80, 281
  Advanced Systems and Concepts Office,
    172–76
  bureaucracy of, 25, 276
  and Chinese spies, 104–6, 109
  Criminal Investigation Task Force, 215
  emergency measures in, 34
  futurist projects of, 83
  global network operations of, 327

and interagency rivalry, 25, 86–87
and privacy law, 112, 123, 130
restrictions on Marines by, 24
September 11 attack on, 140, 144, 155, 204
and TIA, 231
Perry, William, 242–43
Phillips, Jonathon, 179
Philpot, Scott:
    and Able Danger, 118–21, 124, 126, 132,
        274, 277
    and Al Qaeda, 118–21, 274
    and destroyed data, 132
    and IDC, 120–21
Pickering, Thomas, 101, 102
PLF (Palestinian Liberation Front), 39, 40, 41
Poindexter, John:
    and *Achille Lauro,* 36–40, 42–49, 50
    author's contacts with, 6
    and Beirut suicide bombing, 20–24
    career of, 21, 27
    on changing the world, 365
    credibility of, 192–93
    current status of, 363–65
    gag order on, 233, 237
    and Iran-Contra, 6, 13, 50–53, 55–67, 81–83,
        92, 149, 185, 234, 238, 364
    legacy of, 218–19, 292, 293, 313, 315,
        317–18, 347, 357–58, 361, 363
    and loyalty, 296
    as national security adviser, 50–67
    privacy concerns of, 137, 252, 357, 363
    and privacy conference, 258–61
    privacy invaded, 234, 363
    public respect for, 364
    and retirement, 240–41, 246
    and September 11 attacks, 139–43
    and Syracuse debate, 255–57
    and technology, 21–23, 52, 85, 146, 177, 281,
        300, 321, 328, 343, 349
    and TIA, *see* TIA
Poindexter, Linda, 67
Poindexter, Mark, 140–41
Poindexter, Tom, 140
Polski, Paul, 215–16
Popp, Bob:
    and Advanced Systems and Concepts Office,
        172–74, 175–76
    and ARDA, 246–47, 253

and Congress, 244–45
and homeland security, 173–74
and IAO logo, 195–97
and NORA, 225–26
and privacy, 253
and TIA, 175–77, 195–97, 217, 230–31, 232,
    237, 238, 239, 241, 243, 244–45
Potenza, Vito, 259, 262
Powell, Colin L., 194, 323–24, 364
Preisser, Eileen, 275, 277, 278
President's Daily Brief, 353
Privacilla, 298–301
privacy law, 358
    and cybersecurity, 330
    DOD 5240.1-R, 110–14, 124, 129–30
    Electronic Communications Privacy
        Act, 204
    and executive war powers, 333, 352
    foreign/domestic intelligence wall in, 88,
        162–64, 191–92, 197–98, 247, 330, 333,
        334–35, 342, 356, 362
    and IDC, 109–14, 123–24, 130–32
    and the Internet, 76, 77, 167, 192, 204, 359
    and NSA surveillance, 290, 334
    and Protect America Act, 341, 342, 344–46,
        362
    see also FISA
Protect America Act, 341, 342, 344–46,
    350, 362

Qwest Communications, 201–5

RAM (random access memory), 266–70
    and in-memory databases, 267–70
    and logic layer, 268–69
Rauf, Rashid, 310, 312
Raytheon, 132, 134
Reagan, Ronald, 225, 292
    and *Achille Lauro,* 44–45, 46, 48–49
    in a fog, 56, 62–63, 65, 82, 83
    and Iran-Contra, 6, 50–52, 54–56, 58, 59,
        61–63, 64–65, 81, 82–83, 234
    and kidnappings in Lebanon, 32
    Medal of Freedom for, 81–82
    and NSA, 161, 163
Reagan administration:
    and Beirut suicide bombing, 20–26
    and Iran-Contra, 13

Reagan administration: (*cont.*)
　and national security, 23–24, 52, 169
　recruitment for, 20–21
　and Sheikh Abdullah barracks, 29–31
　and war against terrorism, 32, 354
Reid, Harry, 338, 340
Reid, John, 302
Reno, Janet, 190
Research Development and Experimental
　Collaboration (RDEC), 252
Reyes, Silvestre, 338, 339, 340
Rice, Condoleezza, 112, 134, 254, 364
Risk Assessment and Horizon Scanning,
　363
Roberts, Julia, 126
Roberts, Pat, 245
Rockefeller, John, 245–46, 290–91
Rosa, Gerardo de, 41
Rosen, Jeffrey, 255–56
Rotenberg, Marc, 227–29, 230, 233, 234, 299
Rudman, Warren, 173
Rumsfeld, Donald H.:
　and CIA, 323
　and FutureMAP, 241, 246
　gag order from, 233
　and Poindexter, 184–86, 233, 234–35,
　　241, 246
　political enemies of, 236, 323
　and war in Iraq, 185, 323
Russia, submarines ("goblins") of, 27–29
Ryan, Meg, 126

Saffron, 281, 321, 363
Safire, William, 230–31, 234, 259
SAIC, 210, 241, 243
St. Lawrence River, spy network on, 108–9
San Francisco Weekly, 234
SARS virus, 363
Schoomaker, Peter, 124
Schumer, Charles, 233, 234
Schwarzenegger, Arnold, 126
Science Applications International
　Corporation, 148–49
Sears Tower plot, 312–13
Senator, Ted, 179
September 11 attacks, 135
　advance warnings of, 2, 25, 155, 160,
　　275–76, 278–79, 281

　aftereffects of, 137, 142–43, 144, 151,
　　155–57, 179, 186, 189, 199–200, 204–5,
　　258, 281, 299, 331, 333, 347
　and Al Qaeda, 102
　anniversary of, 359–60
　and aviation security, 307–8
　and change in administration, 352–53
　and Hayden, 137, 159–60, 161–62
　and Moussaoui, 206–7
　9/11 Commission report, 215, 272, 274–77
　pattern analysis of, 146–48
　and Poindexter, 139–43
　and war on terror, 3
Shaffer, Tony, 274–75, 276, 277–78
Sharkey, Brian:
　and DARPA, 84–85, 89
　and Spinnaker, 85, 86
　and Syntek, 85
　and TIA, 144–46, 148–49, 153,
　　241–43, 251
Sharqi, 252
Shultz, George P., 61–62, 64
Signals Security Agency, 332
Silberman, Lawrence, 168–69
Simhoni, Uri, 43, 44, 45
Singapore, government of, 363
Six Degrees of Kevin Bacon, 125–26
Smart, J. C., 200, 315, 316
Soiffert, Alan, 16
Southern Pacific Railroad, 203
Speakes, Larry, 62–63
Special Forces, and Al Qaeda, 10
Special Operations Command:
　and Al Qaeda, 114, 116–18, 125,
　　133, 275, 76
　and bin Laden, 116–19
　hunting terrorists, 9, 114, 115–18,
　　123–26, 130, 276
　and privacy law, 130–31, 134–35
Specter, Arlen, 277, 278–79, 288
Spinnaker, 83–84, 85, 86
Stark, Jim, 43
Star Trek (films), 100
State Department, U.S.:
　access restricted by, 25
　bureaucracy of, 31
　communications hotline, 31
　conference on global threats, 290

emergency measures in, 34
foreign/domestic terrorism, 88
and interagency rivalry, 25, 30, 86–87, 323
Steinhardt, Barry, 237–38, 259–61
Stellar Wind, 171, 211, 264, 271
Stethem, Robert, 36
Stevens, Ted, 242
Stewart, Jeff, 318–21
Stiner, Carl, 38, 39–40, 45, 47–48
Strategic Command, U.S., 203
surveillance:
    and BAG, 171
    in Britain, 313–14
    and Bush, *see* Bush administration
    court use of evidence, 310, 312
    electronic, 73–80, 119, 127, 170, 237, 254,
        288–89, 290–92, 310, 351, 355, 356
    of e-mails, 166–67, 170, 192, 205, 312
    emergency, 336–37
    and FISA, *see* FISA
    inaccuracy of, 298, 306
    legality of, 168, 262–63, 271–72, 283–84,
        286–87, 361–62
    and national security, 282–83
    and Obama administration, 355–56
    and privacy law, 110–14, 129–30, 204, 333,
        362
    and Protect America Act, 341, 342, 344–46,
        350, 362
    targeted, vs. metadata, 261
    and telecom companies, *see*
        telecommunications
    uncontrolled, 4–5, 238, 253, 256,
        355–56, 358
    and USA PATRIOT Act, 168, 205, 233, 331
    warrantless, 3–4, 157–59, 167, 169–71,
        205–9, 234, 252–53, 261–63, 282–89,
        310, 331, 333–35, 338, 340, 344, 349,
        352, 355–56, 361–62
    and wiretaps, 53, 71–73, 75–80, 127, 192,
        204, 261, 284, 332
surveillance state, rise of, 4
Syntek, 83, 85, 140, 149
Syracuse University, 255–57, 259

Talbott, Strobe, 97
Tandy Corporation, 220
Tangram, 360

Tanzania, U.S. embassy attacked in, 10,
    116, 190
Task Force Alpha, 27–29
Taylor, Elizabeth, 185
telecommunications:
    CALEA, 77–80
    call detail records of, 165–66, 201–2,
        204–5, 218
    cellphones, 72–73, 78
    Clipper chip, 75, 79, 330
    debates on, 75–76
    digital, 72
    and digital spies, 202
    and encryption technology, 73–74
    global monitoring of, 158–59, 208, 340
    immunity from civil suits, 338, 344–47,
        348–50, 355
    intelligence capability in, 201–5, 348–49
    and Internet control, 158, 192
    metadata from, 205, 218, 284
    and privacy laws, 204, 205, 362
    proposed legislation on, 74, 158
    U.S. as hub of, 334–35
    and warrantless surveillance, 157–59, 166,
        170, 204–9, 261–63, 284, 334–35,
        341–42
    wiretapping, 53, 71–74, 76–80, 127, 192,
        204, 261, 284, 332
Tenet, George J.:
    and Brennan, 347
    as CIA director, 95, 151, 347, 348
    and congressional briefing, 245, 246
    and Hayden, 164, 245, 246
    and Karic, 96, 97
    and September 11 attacks, 151, 164, 347
    and weapons in Iraq, 294
    and Weldon, 95, 96, 97
Terrorism Tuesday, 306–7
terrorists:
    Al Qaeda, *see* Al Qaeda
    and BAG, 199–201
    bomb-building, 309
    British cell of, 302–14
    connections among, 123, 126, 147, 151,
        157–59, 162, 166–67, 201, 208, 212,
        303, 305, 306–7, 317, 338–39, 360
    detention and interrogations of, 215, 218,
        294–95, 353–55, 362

terrorists: (*cont.*)
  early-warning system for, 164–67, 201, 218,
    264, 286, 315, 335
  funding streams of, 179, 206–8
  geo-location of, 212
  guilt by association, 127, 360
  information on Internet about, 10–11
  and information warfare, 219–20, 326–29
  Libya as state sponsor of, 57
  metadata on, 205, 218
  "nexus of terrorism," 157–59, 294
  pattern analysis of, 146–48, 180–212, 280,
    299–300, 306
  and public fears, 255
  red team on, 180–83
  signals of, 2, 24–25, 164, 177–78, 180–82
  suicide bombing by, 3, 10, 116
  transnational, 84
  on U.S. soil, 146–48, 280
  warrantless surveillance of, 157–59, 166,
    205–9, 286, 291, 331, 333–34, 338, 346,
    348, 355
  and wealth gap, 313
Terrorist Threat Integration Center, 347
Tether, Tony:
  and DARPA, 176, 195, 239
  and TIA, 145, 146, 148, 150–54, 187,
    195, 240, 241
Thach, John, 28
Thach Weave, 28
Thatcher, Margaret, 38
ThinkProgress.org, 349
Threat and Vulnerability Information
    System, 317
TIA (total information awareness):
  assured transition to, 195
  automated translation in, 146, 180
  basic concept of, 152, 165
  and Basketball, 251
  black budget of, 247–48, 260–61
  campaign to build support for, 186–90,
    210–13, 239, 241–43
  collective reasoning process in, 145
  and Congress, 231–33, 236, 239–42,
    244–48, 260
  and DARPA, 145–46, 150, 153, 174–78, 195,
    240, 243
  and Eagle, 251

  entity databases of, 217
  facial recognition techology, 146, 179, 180
  false positives in, 237, 301
  feasibility of, 237, 281, 297, 299–301
  and foreign/domestic wall, 191–92,
    197–98, 247
  and Genoa II, 180
  goal of, 177–78
  and IAO, 174–76, 196, 227, 231,
    233, 239, 243
  immutable audit trail in, 190, 244
  and information overload, 218
  nonterrorist baselines produced by, 215
  and NORA, 225–26, 297–98
  and NSA, 186, 210–13, 217–18, 238,
    243–45, 252–53, 261, 292–93
  policy debate on, 152, 153
  PowerPoint briefing on, 150–54
  preliminary thinking on, 144–46
  privacy protection in, 153, 180, 189,
    192, 227–29, 237, 238, 244–45,
    252, 290
  prototype of, 186–88, 194–95, 214–17,
    251–52
  public attacks on, 230–31, 233–35,
    236–38, 254, 258, 301
  rank-ordered list of targets for, 214–15
  recruitment for, 178–80, 183
  red teams of, 180–83, 197, 217,
    238, 270
  research thrusts of, 179–80
  selective revelation in, 153, 189, 191,
    192, 244
  speed of work, 215
  termination as such, 251, 260, 292
  Times article about, 230–31, 254
  transition to other programs, 246–47, 261,
    292–93, 333, 360
TIA Network, 187, 189, 197, 211, 214
  and ADVISE, 317
  entity databases of, 217
  and RDEC, 252
  rules of membership in, 217
Time, 28
Topsail, 251
Townsend, Fran:
  and Brennan, 347
  and Coast Guard, 190, 191

and influence, 297
and Iraq, 326
and terrorism brief, 254–55, 271, 304,
    306–7, 310, 321
and TIA, 190–93, 194, 227, 254
Transportation Security Administration
    (TSA), 216, 304, 305, 307, 309
Treasury Department:
  Financial Crimes Enforcement
    Network, 179, 207
  on terrorist financing, 206–8
TWA Flight 847, 36, 54

United Kingdom:
  security threats in, 302–12
  as surveillance state, 313–14
UNIVAC, 200
UNODIR, 54, 56, 63
USA PATRIOT Act, 168, 205, 233, 331
USA Today, 288
U.S. Central Command, 135
U.S. Naval Institute, 258
U.S. persons:
  ChoicePoint data collected on,
    216, 281
  communication with foreign parties,
    169, 170
  definition of, 285–86
  and FISA, 338, 340–42
  intelligence on, 11, 122, 123, 124,
    129–32, 193–94, 212, 247, 277,
    291–92, 315, 332, 333
  and privacy law, 110–14, 124, 130,
    338, 340, 358
  and September 11 attacks, 162
  targeting for political purposes,
    332–33
  warrantless surveillance on, 233–35, 237,
    253, 284–89, 291–92, 338, 341,
    344–45, 349, 355–56
U.S. Strategic Command, 203
U.S. Telephone Association, 75
USS *Cole,* 135, 190
USS *Holder,* 27–29
USS *Iwo Jima,* 39–40

Vanilla World, 217, 226
Veliotes, Nicholas, 40, 41, 42

Wade, Alan, 188–90
Wall Street:
  and cybersecurity, 328–29, 361
  and FutureMAP, 239–41, 244, 246
  intelligence gathering on, 318–21
war:
  antisubmarine, 27–29, 152
  executive powers in, 168, 185, 288–89, 333,
    335–36, 344, 352, 353, 358, 362
  information warfare, 219–20, 326–29
  proportionality of, 170
  rules of engagement, 185
  science of, 23
  and technology, 200
War Games (film), 52
Warner, John, 185
war on terror:
  CIA leaks about, 293–97
  misuse of intelligence in, 294, 322
  and Obama administration, 353–56
  preemption vs. retaliation in, 32, 34
  and Reagan administration, 32, 354
  secret, 32
  and September 11 attacks, 3
  use of fear in, 311–12
  use of intelligence in, 3, 186, 233–35, 283–89
  and Watchers, 4
  see also Bush administration
Warren, Earl, 331, 332
Washington, Denzel, 126
Washington Post, 230, 294, 296, 335
Washington Post smell test, 113, 124, 244,
    281, 329
Watchers:
  goal of, 3
  scope of their net, 3–4
  and security vs. liberty, 4
  and war on terror, 4
  watching, 356, 361
  what they are, 2–3
Watergate, 53, 169, 185
Weinberger, Caspar:
  and *Achille Lauro,* 45–46
  plans canceled by, 29–30, 45
Weldon, Curt:
  and Able Danger, 274–77, 279
  and China, 105
  and former Yugoslavia, 95–98, 100–103

Wertheimer, Mike:
    and e-mail searches, 166
    and executive war powers,
        159, 166, 253
    and privacy laws, 159
    and September 11 attacks, 155–56
    and signals intelligence, 164–65
    and warrantless searches, 252–53
West Berlin, disco bombed in, 57
Western Union, 207

West German government, and
    Achille Lauro, 40
World Trade Center:
    1993 truck bomb in, 87–88, 352
    September 11, 2001, attacks on,
        140–43, 144, 155, 159–60,
        204, 352
Wyden, Ron, 240, 291–92

Yoo, John, 167–69, 262

ABOUT THE AUTHOR

Shane Harris is a staff correspondent for *National Journal,* where he writes about intelligence, counter-terrorism, and security. He has written for other national publications including the *Washington Post, Slate,* the *Bulletin of the Atomic Scientists,* the U.S. Naval Institute's *Proceedings,* and *Government Executive* magazine, where he was a writer and technology editor. He has also provided analysis for CNN, National Public Radio, the BBC, and the Discovery Channel. Shane lives in Washington, D.C. This is his first book. For more information, visit www.shaneharris.net.